THE MILITARY
AIRFIELDS OF BRITAIN
East Anglia
Norfolk and Suffolk

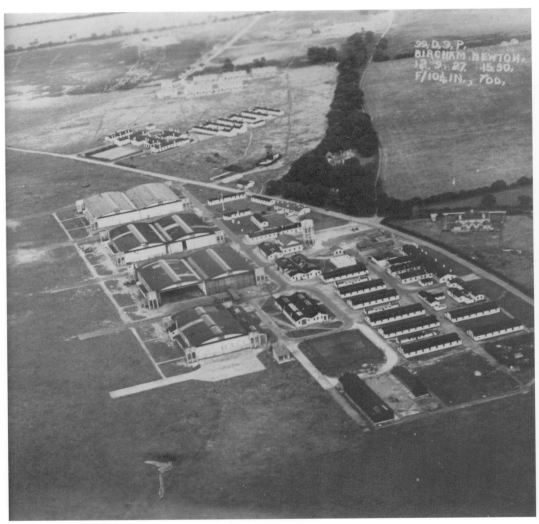

Bircham Newton was one of the few significant airfields in Norfolk during the 1920s, being home to a variety of bomber units.

THE MILITARY AIRFIELDS OF BRITAIN

East Anglia

Norfolk and Suffolk

KEN DELVE

CROWOOD

First published in 2005 by
The Crowood Press Ltd
Ramsbury, Marlborough
Wiltshire SN8 2HR

www.crowood.com

British Library Cataloguing-in-Publication Data
A catalogue record for this book is available from the British Library.

ISBN 1 86126 728 2

Acknowledgements
My thanks for help with compiling this series of books goes to the staff of the Air Historic Branch,
London for their usual patience, co-operation and knowledge; to the staff of the Fleet Air Arm Museum,
Yeovilton; Ray Towler, Barry Abraham and other members of the Airfield Research Group,
Geoff Gardiner for the Watton pictures, Ray Sturtivant for invaluable help with World War One and for
World War One Landing Ground plans, Huby Fairhead for his encyclopaedic knowledge of aviation in this
area and access to his detailed research, for permission to use the World War One Landing Ground plans
from their Air Britain book; also, Aldon Ferguson for advice and a variety of material, and a large number of
individuals who are involved in preserving and presenting particular airfields or who have a general interest
in aviation history and have been happy to share their research. Finally, to two long-established friends and
fellow enthusiasts, Peter Green and Andy Thomas for their help with photographs and advice.

Typeset by Textype, Cambridge

Printed and bound in Great Britain by Biddles Ltd, Kings Lynn, Norfolk

Contents

The impressive memorial at Snetterton Heath with its B-17 atop stainless-steel 'contrails'; most of the ex American bases in East Anglia have memorials.

Series Introduction

This series of books examines Britain's military airfields region by region, covering military aviation from World War One to the present day. There have been two main periods of airfield construction – World War One, when a large number of landing grounds and aerodromes were built for either defensive purposes or training, the majority of offensive operations taking place from airfields in France, and World War Two, when some parts of England housed hundreds of airfields, many of which were 'taking the war to the enemy' on a daily basis. The highpoint of airfields in terms of numbers came in the latter months of 1944, when Britain housed some 1,000 airfields and over 30,000 aircraft, plus a significant number of small or temporary landing strips.

This series is not a detailed history of every airfield but rather a 'user-friendly' reference, which, for each airfield, comprises an outline history along with maps, plans, photographs and data tables containing information such as location, units and memorials. Commercial publishing realities mean that even the entries for major airfields have had to be restricted in size and all airfields and landing strips that had no recorded military usage have been excluded.

Note on Sources

It is a well-established misunderstanding that military records are precise, comprehensive and accurate; sadly this is far from the truth and the problems inherent in first locating and then checking documents are not for the faint-hearted researcher. In addressing the history of airfields in the UK, the researcher has a variety of primary sources to consult; for the RAF the most in-depth, at least potentially, is the F540 Operational Record Book (ORB), a series of records now classified in the AIR 28 series by the National Archives at Kew, London. There are, however, two problems with this document: firstly, only RAF Stations, i.e. independent locations with a station headquarters, were required to compile and submit this monthly record, and that parameter removed many of the wartime airfields and landing grounds; secondly, the quality of record is very variable. The researcher is invariably frustrated by the way in which such records were kept; the compiling officer was following Air Ministry guidelines, but these took no account of the desires and interests of future historians! An airfield could, for example, have gone from a grass surface to a concrete runway with no mention at all in its ORB, and when you consider more minor building works the chances of a mention are even slimmer. Movements in and out of units may or may not be recorded – even if mention is made there is no guarantee that the date given is accurate. This might sound strange, however it has to be remembered that these monthly ORBs were not compiled on a daily basis but were invariably put together in retrospect – at best days after the end of the recorded month but perhaps weeks later.

I spent much of my RAF career compiling ORBs at squadron and station level – as a secondary duty that had to be fitted around my primary aircrew task – and the problems of pulling together information in retrospect, especially from units or individuals that were either too busy or disinterested was a major struggle. The net result was a submission that would get past the signatory (squadron or station commander) and satisfy both the higher command that saw it and the final recipients at Air Ministry/MoD. Because such records were sent via higher commands there was also an element of politics in their content, as few commanders would submit a 'warts and all' record that might ruffle feathers further up the chain. However, even with these constraints and problems, the ORB remains the core historical document at all levels of the RAF organization. To put any appreciable level of detail into the overall research of an airfield requires reference to the ORBs of the based units, those for the flying units being particularly helpful – but with the same set of difficulties outlined above. Squadron ORBs are contained in the AIR 27 series. Other unit records, flying and ground, can also be consulted and, indeed, for some airfields, especially major training units, the unit record is essentially the station record.

The SD161 'location on units' record is an excellent source for unit listings at a particular location for a given month. There is one major drawback, in that it is compiled from other inputs that may not, in themselves, be accurate or up to date; for example, the SD161 might list the presence of a particular squadron or other unit in its monthly entry for an airfield but, in fact, the move of that unit, whilst planned and authorized, might not have taken place or might have occurred at a slightly different time. It is a similar picture with the Secret Organizational Memoranda (SOM) files: these documents were the authorization for units to form, move, change command-allegiance, change name, disband, and so on, and as such they can prove very useful – as long as they are used with care. A planned and authorized action might subsequently be modified or cancelled and the researcher might not have picked up the amendment. An example of this, in respect to airfields, is the authorization under SOM 79/40 (dated 30 January 1940) for 'the requisitioning of land at Bysshe Court, Surrey as a RLG for Redhill, the site is 2½ miles West of Lingfield'. Two months later, however, SOM 194/40 (dated 11 March) stated 'Redhill is to use Penshurst as an RLG and the site at Bysshe Court is not required'.

For Royal Navy/Fleet Air Arm units the official record system is the Ship's Log, which applies to shore sites as well as floating vessels, and these documents can be even more frustrating, as they vary from diary format, often excellent and including photographs, to minimal factual statements that are of little use.

The USAAF units also submitted regular official reports and, as one airfield usually only housed a single Group, the records of that Group can provide some useful details, although they are primarily concerned with operations and not infrastructure.

It would, of course, be impossible to refer to every one of these sources when compiling a series of books such as the Crowood 'Military Airfields in Britain' series and the author freely acknowledges his debt to other researchers who have ploughed this field and produced excellent reference works. A great many of these secondary sources (a term that is no insult to these authors) have been used during the compilation of the Crowood series and a selection of the major ones is given below:

Halley, James J, *The Squadrons of the Royal Air Force and Commonwealth* (Air Britain)

Jefford, C G, *RAF Squadrons* (Airlife)

Sturtivant, Ray; Hamlin, John; Halley, James J, *RAF Flying Training and Support Units* (Air Britain)

Lake, Alan, *Flying Units of the RAF* (Airlife)

Sturtivant, Ray; Page, Gordon, *Royal Navy Aircraft, Serials and Units* (Air Britain)

Airfield Review, Airfield Research Group magazine (see below)

Freeman, Roger, *The Mighty Eighth* (Arms and Armour Press) – the impressive series of books by Roger on the 8th Air Force

Plus the author's own published works such as, *The Source Book of the RAF* (Airlife)

All good historians will confess that everything that appears in print contains errors; some of these are

errors repeated from primary or secondary sources, some are typological (1942 and 1943 are a mere keystroke apart) and some are simply omissions where the author has not been able to fill in the gap or has completely missed a document. All of these errors will be found in this series – I would welcome feedback so that any future updates can be more accurate and complete.

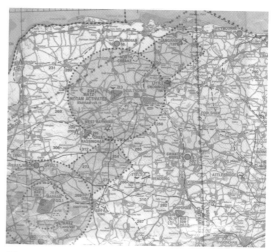

The current range of maps produced by the Civil Aviation Authority for use by General Aviation pilots are an excellent source of information for airfield researchers.

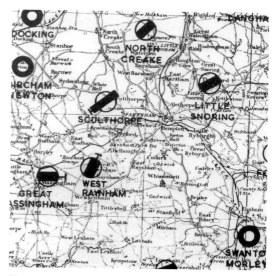

The 1950s airfield survey also included location maps, the main runways being shown but, unlike the 1940s version, with no indication of the shape of the airfield.

Photographs and Plans

Photographs and plans are an essential element of the research and presentation of airfield history and this series attempts to bring together one of the most comprehensive pictorial records yet published. For some airfields there is a plethora of plans, whilst for others the search for a period layout draws a blank. It is a great shame that virtually all of the civilian contractors involved in airfield construction did not maintain, or have subsequently disposed of, their records of this work. Official plans (Air Ministry Drawings) exist for various periods, particularly fine sets being available for late-1944 and the mid-1950s, but in both cases the surviving documents have, in typical military fashion, been amended to the latest issue; for example, airfields no longer in use in December 1944 have been removed from that volume. With the exception of the Air Ministry overall-layout drawings, most plans cover only the main infrastructure of the airfield itself – runways,

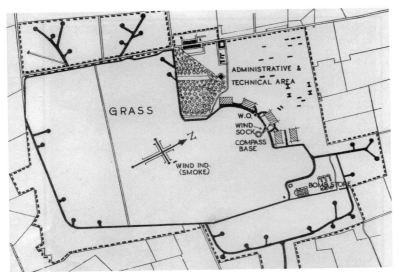

Plan of Marham in 1944; the airfield still has grass surfaces; the arc of C-type hangars is the most distinctive feature.

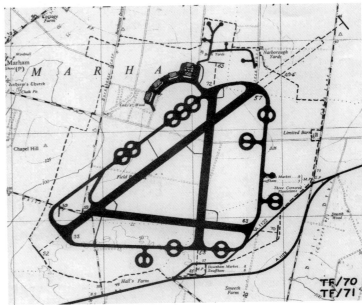

Marham after its mid 1940s rebuild with three hard runways and spectacle dispersals.

Detailed airfield plan showing individual buildings and, in the inset plan, associated off-airfield sites. These official plans exist for about 50% of the airfields listed used during World War Two. NB. All plans used in this book are Crown Copyright via the Air Historical Branch unless otherwise stated.

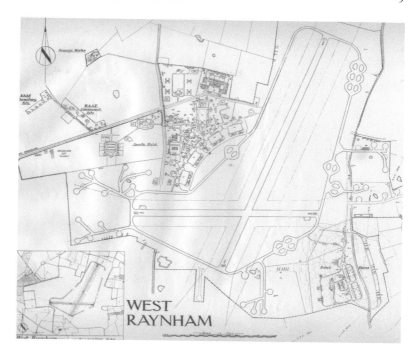

WEST RAYNHAM

peri-track, dispersal and hangars, ignoring the off-airfield sites, such as accommodation and technical. Most of the airfield plans used in this volume are **Crown Copyright via Air Historical Branch** unless otherwise stated. The majority of World War One airfield plans are courtesy of Ray Sturtivant.

Photographs are perhaps an even thornier issue and the quality and number of images varies hugely from airfield to airfield, with training bases being the most poorly represented. The RAF's security-conscious attitude meant that cameras were a real no-no at airfields and, other than occasional official or press sessions and the odd illicit snap, there are massive gaps in the photo coverage. The situation at the USAAF bases was somewhat better, for both official and unofficial photographs; what makes this even easier from the researcher's point of view is the ease of access to this material at the National Archives building in Maryland.

Wartime air-to-ground images are hard to find and, although it seems likely that every airfield in the UK was photographed on numerous occasions during the war, unearthing these images is never easy. The Luftwaffe produced excellent target folders, including aerial photos, of many British airfields and this source of material is superb when you can find it.

A number of photographic surveys of the UK have been flown over the past sixty years; indeed, according to some sources, the 7th Photographic Group

Luftwaffe target map of Marham late 1940; the Luftwaffe series is excellent but can be hard to locate for some UK airfields.

flew a vertical survey of much of Britain during the war and this material would prove invaluable should it be easy to access, which sadly is not the case. Post-

Oblique of Narborough –
the largest aerodrome in
England during World
War One. (Narborough
History Society).

Aerial photograph of Bury St Edmunds (Rougham) with overlay of runways, taxiways and dispersals.

1945, airfields have been popular targets for reconnaissance squadrons to practice both vertical and oblique pinpoint-photography and thousands of negatives would have been exposed – but not necessarily printed or preserved. Keele University is the present home for tens of thousands of air-to-ground photos from World War Two onwards and almost every airfield in Britain is likely to be amongst the collection – if you can locate the individual site. There are three main 'national' collections of aviation images in the UK; the Imperial War Museum and the RAF Museum, both in London, and the Fleet Air Arm Museum at Yeovilton. For the researcher/author this is a somewhat mixed blessing as, whilst the material can usually be studied by prior arrangement, it is often prohibitively expensive to acquire copies for publication. The majority of illustrations used in this series are from private collections and plans/diagrams are from official sources.

The Adam and Eve was the local pub near Coltishall used by 255 Squadron; all squadrons had their favourite watering holes – the author would be interested in this type of information.

Airfield or Aerodrome?

For the sake of ease I have used the term airfield throughout this series, but have freely mixed it with aerodrome and other terms; the purist will rightly say that this is not technically correct and it is true that, at various times, the RAF (and other Services) had definitions they used for specific types of 'air installation'.

The same problem of nomenclature occurs with individual elements of the airfield; for example, taxiway or perimeter track, runway or landing strip? Different sources will provide different definitions and, indeed, the definitions change with the period in question. It is not the purpose of this series of books to get bogged down in the debate on terminology.

Pubs

For every airfield there is the question of drinking! All RAF aircrew and ground crew had their favourite pubs, and usually they went to different ones; likewise, different squadrons might adopt their own pub or pubs. Whilst regular drinking took place in the messes and the NAAFI, a trip down to the 'local' was an essential part of squadron life, with frequent reference to the 'boys' climbing into the Boss's car and tearing off to the pub. You only have to read any autobiography from a wartime-RAF chap to find reference to these forays – often with humorous results. The Americans were even keener on making use of local pubs and every airfield will have had one or more favourite watering holes. Although reference is made to pubs in some of the entries in this series, we have not included complete lists, as this information

is not available. I would like to have included details of wartime pubs in these records but that level of research relies on people with local knowledge and interest – if you know of any pubs that fit this description then let me know and I will update the file!

Messes and Headquarters

Pre-war RAF stations included excellent living accommodation; indeed, one of the great advantages of an expansion-period officers' mess, for example, was that they all followed the same pattern and it was easy therefore to stagger from bar to accommodation wing without getting lost, no matter which airfield you were at! However, with the threat of air attack and with many airfields having little or no accommodation, the military adopted the course of

It was standard practice to requisition nearby large houses for accommodation or HQ purposes; the impressive mansion at Blickling Hall was taken over for use by RAF Oulton.

'acquiring' a suitable local establishment, which in many cases meant a stately home or, at least, very large house. This type of building was taken over by HQ staff and also for use as officers' messes, with the frequent addition of a hutted 'village' in the grounds. As with pubs, this information is not always readily to hand, other than for major HQ-units, and I would like to hear from local researchers who can add details of houses taken over in this way. Perhaps the best known in the UK is the Petwood Hotel at Woodhall Spa, Lincolnshire, which was used as a mess by the officers of 617 Squadron, and which hosts numerous RAF reunions and is a great place to spend a weekend.

Visiting Airfields

The majority of airfield sites are *out of bounds*, either because they are still active military installations or, more commonly, they are in private hands for agricultural or industrial use. While touring the countryside looking for airfields you will come across many variations on the 'KEEP OUT' sign, some couched in pleasant, but firm, tones and others somewhat more vehement in their opinion of any who would dare tread from the public paths. It is worth noting that footpaths exist over many of these airfields and so reference to a good OS map (which is an essential part of any pack-up for the airfield tourer) will keep you on the straight and narrow. Sadly, the footpaths were not laid out with visiting airfield structures in mind and all too often all that is glimpsed is a building, often partly hidden by vegetation, often at some distance from the marked path. You can always try contacting the landowner to seek permission to enter the airfield site and this is certainly worth a try for a pre-planned visit – although finding contact details for landowners can be tricky. As with all outdoor activities you need to have the right clothing and equipment – stout, waterproof footwear (that is not allergic to mud) is an essential if you plan to walk the ground rather then observe from the side of the road. When it comes to photography, a long lens (up to 300mm) is always worth having, as you may not be able to get close to some structures.

A good military maxim is that 'time spent on reconnaissance is seldom wasted' and this equally applies to the research time you spend before taking to the field – study the maps and diagrams in this book, in conjunction with the OS Landranger map, and you will (hopefully) have a much more productive visit. These books are, of course, equally useful for the 'armchair visitor' and provide a wealth of information for those interested in a particular area or type of airfield.

Memorials

I have always been a 'people person' when it comes to aviation history and, to that end, I find the question of memorials fascinating, as these are a means of providing a visible link with, and recognition of, those who were involved with operations from the airfields. Any student of memorials will soon realize the variations that exist in this recognition – and it should be pointed out that the majority of airfields do not have a memorial. The regional variation is enormous and in large part reflects the type of organization operating in a region; for example, the USAAF bases are generally well-represented with

An aerial tour is a great way to look at wartime airfields; some like Sculthorpe are virtually intact as they were in use to recent times, but even where the airfield has all but vanished on the ground there is invariably some vestige to be seen from the air.

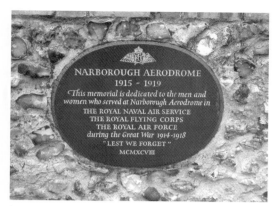

It is rare to find a memorial to World War One; this plaque for Narborough Aerodrome is on the wall of the village church.

The control tower at Lavenham is still in excellent condition; throughout the region towers range from knocked down or derelict to intact and restored, with some of the latter in use as houses and some as memorial museums.

A number of village sign-posts incorporate aviation heritage; the Chedburgh sign includes a Lancaster – although from the historical perspective a Stirling would have been a better choice of aircraft.

memorials, often comprising impressive stones complete with inscriptions, and in many cases twin white flag-poles from which to fly the Stars and Stripes and the Union Jack. This is in large part due to the strength of post-war Associations amongst the American Groups and the creation of Anglo-American friendship groups. Likewise, the RCAF units, especially those of No.6 (RCAF) Group in Yorkshire, are well represented with memorials. Of the RAF operational commands only Bomber Command has an appreciable number of memorials at their former airfields, whilst for others, including Fighter Command, the situation is very variable, with some of the London/Kent Battle of Britain airfields having memorials – the one at Croydon is one of the finest in the UK – but with others having nothing. Taking the country as a whole, there have been two major 'memorial building' phases, the early 1980s and the early 1990s; however, over the last couple of years there has been another burst of activity, although not on the scale of the previous ones. It would be great if every airfield was provided with a memorial that recognized the role it and its personnel played in World War Two, and it is this conflict that memorials commemorate, but this laudable aim is unlikely ever to be achieved, although there are still groups and organizations working towards the creation of such memorials. When looking for memorials it is not always a case of looking in the obvious places, such as the airfield site, as in many cases they are located in the nearby village, either on the village green or in the churchyard (or indeed the church itself). The entries in this airfield series give location details for memorials where appropriate and this will save many an hour of sometimes fruitless searching (been there!); however, I do not claim that I have listed them all or even that they are all where I say they are – so feel free to update our information!

Talking of churches, it is always worth a look in the local church and churchyard – which may not always be the one nearest to the airfield or the village with the same name as the airfield – for additional memorials, such as Books of Remembrance, and for grave stones. Many parish churchyards in the UK include Commonwealth War Grave Commission grave markers, although these do not always relate to the local airfield but might simply be the grave of a local person who had died whilst in military service. Don't, however, simply look for the CWGC markers, as many graveyards will contain other RAF (and even RFC) stones. Not all graves are in the War Graves plot and not all have the standard stone. I did not visit all local graveyards during this survey and so this information has been omitted – but I would be delighted if researchers were able to piece together these details for their airfields.

Non-Airfield Sites

Airfields are only part of the military aviation story and a variety of other locations played roles in the overall picture, from HQ units to training establishments and storage units. However, despite the importance of such sites, they have been omitted from this series except for passing reference where appropriate in an airfield entry. This has been done for reasons of space, as to include all the 'other' sites would have added a significant number of pages – and cost.

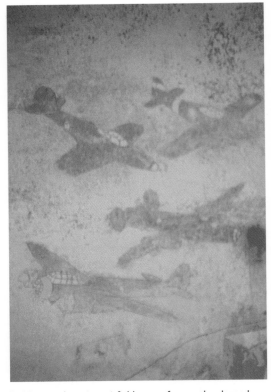

Buildings at American airfields were frequently adorned with murals, some of which still survive – such as these at Seething near Norwich.

Airfield Recording

As part of the on-going research into military airfields there is a vital role for local historians and enthusiasts – by becoming 'local experts' they can help fill in the detail. It is the detail, such as grave records, local pubs, present condition of the airfield and its associated structures, preserved material (museums and local collections) and photographs, that helps provide a more complete picture of the airfield and those who were once based there.

The example form provides a standard record-sheet and in conjunction with the Aviation History Centre we are encouraging individuals to become 'local representatives', in order that the detail can be added for every airfield in the UK. This is not, of course, a permit to go marching over fields claiming right of access! The normal procedures have to be followed, but a local representative can take the time to get to know the airfield and its surrounding area, talking to landowners for access and finding out such lost information as the pubs used by various units. This is a people task – asking questions and chasing up little bits of information with which to build the overall picture.

The Aviation History Centre has agreed to provide basic information as a starting point for anyone wishing to become a local representative and they have also pointed out that you do not actually need to be local – it may be that you have a particular interest in an operational Group, squadron or local area and would like to pursue that interest. Individuals are also not restricted to taking on a single airfield but what *is* required is a responsible attitude when dealing with the landowners, an interest in finding out accurate information and a desire to share that information.

Airfield Research Group

It is worth considering joining the Airfield Research Group: this organization consists of individuals with an interest in research into and, to some extent, preservation of airfields in the UK. They publish an excellent magazine (free to members) and the quality of research is superb. For further details contact: Hon. Secretary, Raymond Towler, 33A Earls Street, Thetford, Norfolk IP24 2AB.

AIRFIELD RECORD			
Airfield name		County	
Lat/Long		OS Map	
Nearest town/village		OS Grid	
AIRFIELD SURVEY			
Control Tower			
Hangars			
Runways			
Perimeter Track			
Dispersals			
Technical Buildings			
Admin Buildings			
Domestic Buildings			
Land Ownership			
Public Access			
ASSOCIATED SITES			
Memorial			
Church (graves?)			
Pubs			
House (mess or HQ)			
Museum			
Other Information			
Date of Record			
Recorded By			

NOTES:
1. Permission must be acquired before entering areas that are not public access.
2. Mark positions of buildings, memorials, etc on airfield plan/map.
3. A photo record should also be made.

Aviation History Centre: navman678@hotmail.com; or via Crowood Press

Introduction – East Anglia

The counties of Norfolk and Suffolk will forever be associated with the United States 8th Army Air Force (AAF), as a large part of the strength of this organization was based within the two counties. However, this part of East Anglia has a far longer and more diverse connection with military aviation than that represented by the three years (1942–5) in which the 'Mighty Eighth' was present.

The region has always been part of the defence of Britain, a role for which the earliest traces are the forts built, almost 2,000 years ago, as part of the so-called 'Saxon Shore' defences in the latter part of the Roman period. This need to defend the part of England's coast that faces the continent of Europe has remained the rationale for a military presence in Norfolk and Suffolk, although many of the medieval castles that are dotted throughout the area owe more to a desire to keep the local population under control rather to than a need to repel foreign invaders. The 'wooden walls' of the Royal Navy were for centuries the island's main defence, and as a seafaring region East Anglia played its part in providing men and ships. It was perhaps fitting therefore that one of the earliest military aviation locations was one associated with ships, but in this case 'ships of the air' – airships.

World War One

East Anglia has had a long association with military aviation, being one of the first regions of England to have a network of military airfields. In World War One this was in large measure due to two requirements: support of naval operations and patrolling the English Channel; and the need to counter German bombing, firstly by Zeppelins and later by aircraft. In the early years of World War One the Admiralty held responsibility for the defence of the Realm, which included defence against air attack, and Royal Naval Air Stations such as that at Great Yarmouth were responsible for combating enemy airships and aircraft.

On the night of 19–20 January 1915 two German airships (LZ3 and LZ4) attacked targets in Norfolk; the bombs that fell on Kings Lynn killed four people and caused £7,740 worth of damage – not a great number of casualties and only a small amount of damage, but a severe shock to a nation that had previously been beyond the range of European wars. The series of airship raids on East Anglia in 1915 and 1916 proved how ineffectual the air defences were, and when London was bombed the crisis led to a major expansion of Home Defence effort and the

Narborough was the major training station in East Anglia, although the majority of small airfields and landing grounds were involved with Home Defence. (Narborough History Society)

transfer of responsibility to the Royal Flying Corps.

This decision led to the development of numerous Night Landing Grounds from which the Home Defence aircraft could attempt to combat the attackers. These landing grounds were invariably little more than a field and usually of little more than 50–60 acres. They were given little in the way of facilities, although some did sprout collections of huts to supplement or replace tents. As they were primarily intended for night-time use they were usually provided with a set of paraffin lamps with which to mark a landing strip, and also a searchlight that was used to help pilots locate the landing ground. Most of these landing grounds had no based aircraft but were used on an 'as required' basis, often with an aircraft taking off from one site and landing at another.

Both counties housed a number of more substantial aerodromes – Narborough, Bircham Newton, Felixstowe and Great Yarmouth being of particular import. The region, or more particularly Norwich, housed a number of companies involved in aircraft construction, the most noteworthy of which was Boulton and Paul.

The end of the war brought a rapid reduction in the size of the newly formed Royal Air Force, and the vast majority of its airfields returned to the agricultural land from whence they sprang.

Between the Wars

In the inter-war period there was little activity in this region in respect of major military airfields, although a few airfields such as Bircham Newton were significant. There was a good deal of aviation taking place, however, as 'barnstormers', joy riders and private flying clubs made their appearance, sometimes using old landing grounds but just as commonly making use of any large field; these activities are outside the scope of this series and the next major period for the military came in the late 1930s with the creation of a number of fully equipped airfields during the Expansion Period when, at last, Britain realized that an air threat did exist from Germany and that the RAF was ill-equipped in terms of aircraft and bases. The Expansion Period airfields were built to a fairly standard pattern and the surveyors hunted far and wide for suitable sites, in many cases dusting off the files relating to World War One landing grounds. Although standard 'patterns' were used, no two airfields were alike, other than features such as an arc of wonderful brick-built C-type hangars – in many ways the defining mark of this period of airfield. Much of the major effort in this building programme took place further north in Lincolnshire and Yorkshire, as the military planners recognized that with Germany as the main enemy there needed to be airfields, especially bomber airfields, in those counties. East Anglia was not ignored, though, and in the period 1935–40 a number of airfields were constructed either as parent stations or satellites.

World War Two

Thus, by the outbreak of World War Two Norfolk and Suffolk had a number of operational bases for bombers, fighters and coastal aircraft; of the bomber bases the majority were within Nos 2 and 3 Groups. For the former the Bristol Blenheim was the main type while most of the latter had received two squadrons of Vickers Wellingtons. These Wellingtons

Bircham Newton was one of the few airfields in this region in the inter-war period.

By the outbreak of the war the main operational types in the region where the Blenheims of No.2 Group, as those of 82 Squadron at Watton, and the Wellingtons of No.3 Group.

No.3 Group re-equipped with the Stirling and these four-engined heavies became a regular site in this Region; Stirling R9358 of 214 Squadron at Stradishall.

were part of the long-range striking force intended to attack Germany itself, while the light bombers would have the dual task of anti-shipping operations and land operations from forward bases in France. The region also included a number of fighter bases, part of the London cover, within No. 12 Group, as well as Coastal Command airfields and a number of special-ist units, although training and experimental units soon departed for airfields that were further west and so less likely to suffer air attack.

It was the bombers that played the most significant part as far as Norfolk and Suffolk were concerned, with No. 3 Group's Wellington units suffering heavy losses in the early part of the war before Bomber Command switched to a night campaign. The other major operational Group, No. 2, contributed to the night offensive but was more often engaged on day-light attacks on shipping and coastal targets, the Blenheims proving vulnerable to anti-aircraft fire and enemy fighters. The rapid fall of France and the increased threat meant that the RAF was short of air-fields in East Anglia and the region underwent a mas-sive building programme from 1941 to 1943. The offensive trend was reinforced in late 1942 with the development of additional airfields for the growing light bomber force of the re-structured No. 2 Group. Furthermore, the imminent arrival of large numbers of American units meant that airfields were very

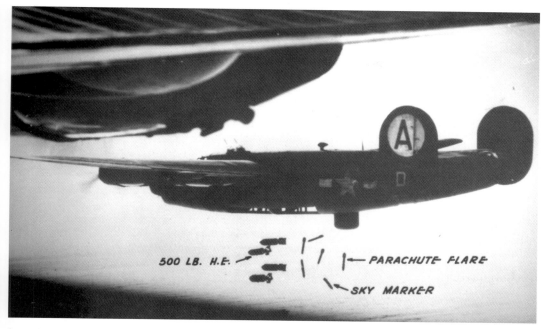

A massive expansion of bombing capacity took place in 1942 and 1943 with the arrival of the 8th Air Force; B-24s of the 44th BG were based at Shipdham. (US National Archives)

Norfolk became home to one of Bomber Command's specialist organisations with the formation of No.100Group in late 1943; Halifax NA695 of 171 Squadron at North Creake April 1945.

much at a premium and massive construction programmes were undertaken. Norfolk became a significant location for the B-24 units of the 8th Air Force, with the areas around Norwich becoming home to the 2nd Air Division. Many of the old airfields now feature impressive memorials to the USAAF crews, who all too often suffered heavy losses in the daylight bombing campaign. The HQ of the Division was at Ketteringham Hall and it had responsibility for thirteen bomber stations, six fighter stations and one combined airfield. Although the 2nd AD retained the Liberator, the other USAAF Groups re-equipped with the B-17 and these, along with the P-47 and P-51 fighters, became common sights in the skies of East Anglia.

USAAF Station Numbers

Norfolk

120	Attlebridge
141	Bodney
355	Coltishall
142	Deopham Green
545	Earsham
133	East Wretham
548	Eccles
554	Fersfield
104	Hardwick
114	Hethel
123	Horsham St Faith
177	Ludham
178	Matlask
176	Narborough
505	Neaton
143	North Pickenham
144	Old Buckenham
108	Old Catton (Camp Thomas)
145	Rackheath
146	Seething
115	Shipdham
138	Snetterton Heath
172	Snettisham
445	Stiffkey
139	Thorpe Abbots
124	Tibenham
376	Watton
118	Wendling
140	Winfarthing

Suffolk

517	Barnham (Little Heath Site)
587	Barnham (Warren Wood Site)
132	Beccles (Ellough)
125	Bungay (Flixton)
468	Bury St Edmunds (Rougham)
151	Butley (Bentwaters)
152	Debach
116	Elveden Hall (Camp Blainey)
134	Eye
153	Framlingham (Parham)
155	Great Ashfield
365	Halesworth (Holton)
135	Hepworth
499	Higham Heath
470	Hitcham
375	Honington
119	Horham
136	Knettishall
137	Lavenham
373	Leiston (Theberton)
369	Martlesham Heath
156	Mendlesham
366	Metfield

126	Rattlesden
157	Raydon
532	Ringshall
555	Shepherd's Grove
361	Snailwell
501	Stowmarket
174	Sudbury (Acton)
382	Sudbury (Constitution Hill)
502	Tostock Park
595	Troston
377	Wattisham

These lists include non-airfield sites that are not covered in the main body of the book but have been included here for the sake of completeness.

Whilst East Anglia in general was very much 'bomber country', this broad statement does not recognize the part played by fighter and coastal units. The Battle of Britain all but passed Norfolk and Suffolk by, although fighter bases such as Coltishall contributed squadrons to the 'Big Wings' operated by No. 12 Group from Duxford. The fighters were also engaged on convoy protection, and as the Luftwaffe switched to night attacks on British cities detachments of night-fighters made their appearance. From 1941 onwards Fighter Command switched much of its attention to the offensive, and fighters flew sweeps over enemy territory as well as providing escort for daylight bombers. In the escort role the USAAF fighter Groups of P-47s and P-51s played a vital role in reducing bomber losses and bases such as Bodney – famous for its P-51 'Blue-nosed Bastards of Bodney' (the 352nd FG) – were in the thick of the fight.

Coastal Command, too, was active, especially from Norfolk, flying anti-shipping missions, including the establishment of one of the highly effective Coastal Strike Wings at Ludham. One other RAF formation is worthy of mention as it was specific to this region. The creation of No. 100 Group in the Bomber Support role saw yet another change to many East Anglian bases, when Norfolk became home to most of the flying units of this secret and highly specialist organization. In realization of the growing importance of Radio Counter Measures (RCM), the Group was formed in November 1943 to bring together the expertise in this field, with two of its main tasks being:

1. To employ airborne and ground RCM equipment to deceive or jam enemy radar systems, radio navigation aids and certain wireless signals.
2. Direct support to night bombing and other operations by attacks on enemy night-fighter aircraft in the air or attacks on ground installations.

By December 1943 the Group had taken control of a number of airfields and its Order of Battle included all four heavy bomber types, these operating in the RCM role, although the ABC Lancasters of 101 Squadron remained attached to No. 1 Group, while the task of offensive action against the German night-fighter force was the task of the Mosquito units. During its operational period with No. 100 Group the Mosquito crews flew 8,000 sorties and claimed 267 enemy aircraft for the loss of sixty-nine of their own number. This highly effective operational Group finally disbanded in December 1945.

Post-1945

The post-war run-down was as rapid as the build-up had been, and although the RAF held onto a great many of the bases as storage facilities, the return of such sites to agriculture was well underway in the 1950s. A period of hectic activity during the Korean War, when many people believed a wider war with communism was possible, was followed by a major reorganization of bases and aircraft as the North Atlantic Treaty Organization (NATO) settled down into its confrontation with the Soviet-led Warsaw Pact and the nuclear umbrella became the main focus of air power and strategy.

East Anglia even played a part in the short-lived ballistic missile capability of the RAF when it housed a number of Thor missile bases. Each of these squadrons had three of the IRBMs (Intermediate Range Ballistic Missiles) and security at the sites, with their American presence as 'owners' of the actual warheads, was tight. This phase was over by 1963 and many of the airfields that had housed the squadrons went into a final decline, although the massive concrete structures of the launch areas proved hard to destroy, and some still exist.

However, East Anglia remained in the front-line of military aviation; post-war euphoria gave way to the heightened tensions of the Berlin Crisis and the Korean War. The stand-off between NATO and the Warsaw Pact saw major developments in the airfield infrastructure in this Region, as this part of Britain

became an important forward-deployment base for units of the United States Air Force (USAF). East Anglia's airfields were a crucial part of the NATO network of airfields throughout the Cold War. In addition to the squadrons permanently based at a number of airfields in Norfolk and Suffolk, dozens more fighter and bomber squadrons were slated for deployment in any period of tension.

In the 1970s and 1980s NATO airfields underwent a 'hardening' process whereby key infrastructure elements were given additional protection to enable them to withstand air attack – the main feature of this was the HAS (Hardened Aircraft Shelter) programme. This type of structure, a steel and concrete shelter capable of holding one or two tactical aircraft, had been in use at NATO's continental bases for some time but it was only the introduction of the Tornado in the early 1980s that brought a concerted programme of HAS building to RAF airfields in the UK.

The 'peace dividend' following the collapse of the Warsaw Pact in the early 1990s has had a major effect

With the Cold War dominating strategy from the 1950s, East Anglia once more became an American 'aircraft carrier'; B-45s of the 47th Bomb Wing on deployment to Sculthorpe.

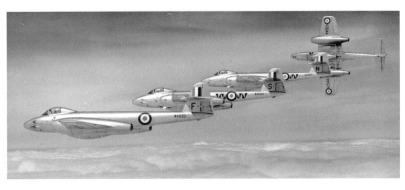

In the post-war period the two counties housed RAF bombers and fighters, with classic types such as the Meteor and Hunter being followed by the Lightning and Phantom; Meteors of 74 Squadron from Horsham St Faith.

The increased threat from long-range Soviet bombers led to a new building programme with airfields being given groups of Hardened Aircraft Shelters; Marham HAS site under build in 1980 for the Tornado.

The 1990s brought a number of airfield closures as part of the 'peace dividend'; some, however, such as Wattisham, were taken over by the Army.

on military installations in the UK, leading to the closure of many airfields, but also the acquisition by the Army of some former RAF property, in part as bases for units moving back to the UK from Germany – the acquisition of Wattisham for the Army Air Corps being a case in point.

Survivors

Norfolk has two current operational military airfields: Marham, home to a large part of the RAF's Tornado force and the RAF's main reconnaissance base; and Coltishall, home to the RAF's Jaguar fleet. It was announced in 2004 that Coltishall was scheduled for closure due to earlier-than-planned withdrawl of the Jaguar, although some still hope that it might become a Eurofighter Typhoon base.

Suffolk is still American country with the sole remaining operational American flying stations in the UK: Mildenhall, a major transport and air-tanker base; and Lakenheath, home to the F-15 Eagle. A number of other airfields are in operational condition but with no based flying units – Honington and Sculthorpe fit into this category.

From a high point of over seventy airfields in 1945 to a mere four; but dozens of others survive to a greater or lesser extent, some still with flying activity, albeit by light aircraft for recreational flying. However, in general terms all too little survives of the majority of these historic locations: a memorial here,

a few decaying Nissen huts there, sometimes a few hangars that are now industrial units, traces of the many miles of concrete surfaces. As the years go by the amount of surviving material reduces, crumbling control towers are knocked down, runways and other surfaces are dug up for road-building hardcore, and Nissen huts succumb to the brambles and trees, and vanish.

Pillboxes were provided for many airfields and these substantial concrete (or brick) structures often survive, sometimes peaking out from an overgrowth of vegetation but sometimes, as here at Marham, somewhat more obvious – despite the toned-down green to make it less visible for passing Royalty!

Snow-covered Nissen huts at Wendling in a wartime shot. The Nissen hut was very much a feature of every airfield, in most cases grouped together at sites in the area around the airfield, with functions from cinema or medical centre to accommodation or workshop.

Operational Period Matrix

Airfield	World War I	World War II	Post-1950*
Aldeburgh	X		
Attlebridge		X	
Bacton	X		
Beccles		X	
Bentwaters		X	X
Bexwell – see Downham Market			
Bircham Newton	X	X	
Bodney		X	
Bungay		X	
Burgh Castle	X		
Butley	X		
Chedburgh		X	
Coltishall		X	X
Cowehithe	X		
Debach		X	
Deopham Green		X	
Docking		X	
Downham Market	X		
Earsham	X		
East Wretham		X	
Eye		X	
Felixstowe	X	X	
Feltwell		X	
Fersfield		X	
Foulsham		X	
Framlingham		X	
Freethorpe		X	
Frettenham		X	
Fritton Lake		X	
Gooderstone		X	
Great Ashfield		X	
Great Massingham	X		
Hadleigh		X	
Halesworth		X	
Hardwick		X	
Harling Road		X	
Hethel		X	
Hickling Road		X	
Hingham		X	
Holt (Bayfield)	X		
Honington		X	X
Horham		X	
Horsham St Faith		X	X
Ipswich		X	
King's Lynn	X		
Knettishall		X	
Lakenheath		X	X
Langham		X	
Lavenham		X	
Leiston		X	
Levington		X	
Little Snoring		X	
Ludham		X	
Marham		X	X
Marsham		X	
Martlesham Heath		X	X
Mattishall		X	
Matlaske		X	
Mendlesham		X	
Metfield		X	
Methwold		X	
Mildenhall		X	X
Mousehold	X		
Narborough	X		
Newmarket Heath		X	
North Creake		X	
North Elmham	X		
North Pickenham		X	
Norwich (Cromer Rd)	X		
Orfordness	X	X	
Old Buckenham		X	
Oulton		X	
Pulham	X		
Rackheath		X	
Rattlesden		X	
Ringstead			
Rougham		X	
Saxthorpe	X		
Sculthorpe		X	X
Sedgeford	X		
Seething		X	
Shepherd's Grove		X	X
Shipdham		X	
Snetterton Heath		X	
Sporle	X		
Stiffkey		X	
Stradishall		X	X
Sudbury		X	
Swannington		X	
Swanton Morley		X	X
Taverham	X		
Thetford (Snarehill)	X		
Thorpe Abbots		X	
Tibenham		X	
Tottenhill		X	
Tuddenham		X	
Wattisham		X	X
Watton		X	X
Wendling		X	
Westley		X	
West Raynham		X	X
West Rudham		X	
Weybourne		X	X
Woodbridge		X	X
Yarmouth	X		

*Post 1950 has been chosen as many airfields were not abandoned until 1946–7, and most sites not actually disposed of until the early 1950s. This refers to airfields operational during the Cold War period of the 1950–1970s.
The table does not include World War One landing grounds that were only re-used as decoy airfields in World War Two.

ATTLEBRIDGE
Station 120

County: Norfolk

UTM/grid: OS Map 133 – TG105148
Lat./Long.: N52°41.30 E001°06.45
Nearest town: Norwich 8 miles to south-east

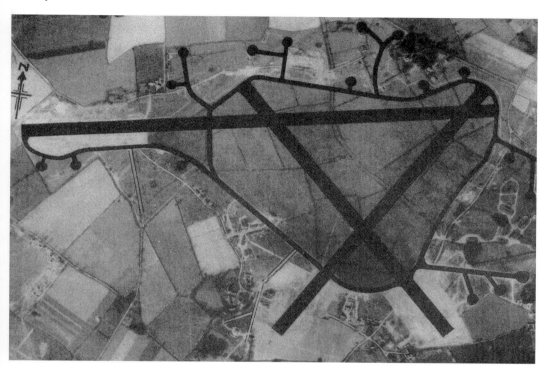

HISTORY

Attlebridge was originally constructed as a satellite for Swanton Morley, within the light-bomber-equipped No.2 Group. Work on the grass airfield commenced in late-1940 and with the initial phase complete the first operational unit, 105 Squadron, moved in with its Blenheims in June 1941, on dispersal from nearby Swanton. However, it was in August that Attlebridge's main operational unit, 88 Squadron, arrived, initially with Blenheim IVs, with which they were soon taking part in the Group's anti-shipping offensive. Part of the squadron was converting to the Boston and, by autumn 1942, this type had replaced the Blenheims, part of a general re-equipment of No.2 Group with new aircraft, the Blenheim having become too vulnerable (losses amongst Blenheims had been horrendous for some months). Conversion and tactical training meant that the squadron was non-operational until early 1942, at which time it re-joined the fray with two main types of mission. The 'bread and butter' operation was the fighter-escorted Circus, but the squadron also undertook a number of

daring low-level daylight attacks. This fine squadron moved out to Oulton in September, the move being motivated by a need to make room for an influx of American squadrons to East Anglia. But first the airfield underwent significant development. In what was to become a typical process for many airfields at this time, construction workers moved in to create a 'standard' Class A airfield with three hard-surface runways linked by a perimeter track around which dispersal points were distributed. The work was carried out by Costain Ltd and was handed over by them in autumn 1942.

The Marauders of the 319th BG arrived in September 1942 in order to train for the forthcoming invasion of North Africa, Operation Torch. However, the airfield was not ideal for their purposes, in part as the infrastructure, especially runways and the surfaces, did not suit the Marauder or its inexperienced crews. It was always intended as a short-term occupation and the 319th had gone by early November. Reconstruction work at Attlebridge continued, including runway extension and additional dispersals and in March 1943 the airfield received its next operational unit. During this period it was still in American hands and used for flying training by the 2nd Bomb Wing and was technically a satellite airfield for Horsham St Faith.

The next operational user, however, was the RAF. The Dutch-manned 320 Squadron had been transferred to No.2 Group and moved from Methwold to their new home – and promptly re-equipped with Mitchells. After a short period of training with the new type, the squadron undertook its first op on 17 August 1943, the target being the rail yards at Calais. The following month the Mitchells departed to Dunsfold and, other than a brief period with 247 Squadron's Typhoons, Attlebridge was once more a building site. Work was needed to bring the airfield to true bomber-status, as it had been allocated to the American strategic bomber forces of VIIIth Bomber Command. Extensions to the three runways meant that a number of local roads had to be closed and extensive areas of farmland brought within the airfield boundary.

March 1944 saw the arrival of the 466th BG and its B-24H, as part of the 96th Combat Bomb Wing within the 2nd Bombardment Division. There was no time to settle in and the Group undertook its first mission on 22 March – the target being Berlin! This was the first of 232 wartime operations by the 466th, the final one taking place on 25 April 1945. For the returning bombers, one of the distinctive landmarks was the tower of Weston Church, just north-east of the airfield. During its operational career from Attlebridge

the Group lost forty-seven aircraft missing in action, plus a further twenty-four listed as 'other operational losses'; over 300 men were killed in action.

With the war over, the Liberators flew home to the USA, most aircraft departing in June. The once busy airfield was transferred to RAF Maintenance Command on 15 July 1945, but there was to be no further requirement for its services, although it was allocated to No.94 MU for use as an ammunition storage-depot. By April 1957, it was listed as 'no longer in the RAF plan'. Disposal finally came in March 1959 and, like many of East Anglia's airfields, it became home to thousands of turkeys, housed in wooden sheds erected on the concrete surfaces of the runways. Large parts of the main site survive, including the control tower (now an office), but there is no public access.

Boston, and crew, of 88 Squadron; the Squadron operated Blenheims and latterly Bostons from Attlebridge.

B-24 of the 466th BG; the Group flew 232 missions from the Norfolk airfield.

AIRFIELD DATA DEC 1944

Command:	US 8th Air Force 2nd BD	Runway surface:	Concrete
Function:	Operational	Hangars:	2 × T.2
Runways:	140 deg 1,400 × 50yd	Dispersals:	50 × Loop
	220 deg 1,400 × 50yd	Personnel:	Officers – 421
	270 deg 2,000 × 50yd		Other Ranks – 2,473

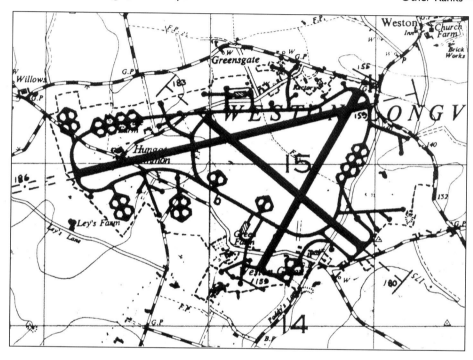

UNITS

HQ Units at Attlebridge

95th BW	12 Dec 1943–Feb 1944

1939–1945

88 Sqn	1 Aug 1941–29 Sep 1942	Blenheim, Boston
105 Sqn	Jun 1941	Blenheim
247 Sqn	7 Aug 1943–13 Aug 1943	Typhoon
320 Sqn	30 Mar 1943–30 Aug 1943	Mitchell
1508 Flt	4 Apr 1943–29 Aug 1943	Oxford

USAAF Units

319th BG	Sep 1942–Nov 1942	B-26
466th BG (96th CBW)		
Identifying letter:		L
Nickname:	The Flying Deck	

Squadrons:	784th BS (Owlish), 785th BS (Eglan), 786th BS (Agram), 787th BS (Behead)
Aircraft:	B-24H, B-24J, B-24L, B-24M
Dates:	7 Mar 1944–6 Jul 1945
Missions:	232
First mission:	22 Mar 1944
Last mission:	25 Apr 1945

MEMORIALS

1. The village sign of Weston Longueville was donated by the veterans of the Bomb Group and its post includes a memorial plaque with the inscription: 'to the 324 men killed in action from the airfield'.

2. Roll of honour and Stars and Stripes in All Saints Church.

BECCLES

County: Suffolk

HISTORY

Beccles was constructed in 1943 for USAAF use and was given the, by then, standard three hard-runways and, as an American 'wartime duration' base, two T.2 hangars. However, surprisingly, no units were allocated and in mid-1944 the airfield was handed to RAF Bomber Command. This, too, proved to be a paper transaction and in August Beccles was given over to Coastal Command's No.16 Group; on 21 August the Mosquitoes of 618 Squadron arrived from Wick. This specialist unit had been training in Scotland since forming with experienced crews the previous year, the intention being that it would employ the *Highball* mine – in effect a variant of the Barnes Wallis bouncing-bomb (mine) used by 617 Squadron to attack the Ruhr dams. With the decision not to employ this weapon against German targets, the squadron was allocated for deployment to the Pacific to use it against the Japanese. Whilst at Beccles and waiting for this move, the crews continued to practise their delivery technique, using a target marked on the runway. They eventually departed, aboard two escort carriers, at the end of

October; for the record, they never did go into action with *Highball*, which remained a promising weapon that never saw service.

The airfield was used for short-term forward-deployment by RAF and FAA aircraft on anti-shipping strikes; such deployments might last a couple of days, as with the Swordfish of 819 Squadron on 13–14 September, for which they had been joined by Albacores of 119 Squadron. The Barracudas of 827 Squadron stayed slightly longer – from 11–28 October – with the same anti-shipping strike role. One notable FAA detachment was that by 810 Squadron's Barracudas, for a few weeks in April–May 1945. This unit was attached to Coastal Command and, with its ASV XI-equipped aircraft, was tasked with hunting for midget submarines in the Schelde area, one sinking being claimed on 13 April.

Such operational detachments came and went but, with the departure of the Mosquito unit, the primary role of Beccles turned to operational support, the most notable being the unsung role of air-sea rescue. The Warwick Is of 280 Squadron arrived from nearby

AIRFIELD DATA DEC 1944

Command:	RAF Coastal Command	Runway surface:	Concrete
Function:	Operational	Hangars:	2 × T.2
Runways:	099 deg 2,000 × 50yd	Dispersals:	50 × Loop
	172 deg 1,400 × 50yd	Personnel:	Officers – 118 (3 WAAF)
	226 deg 1,400 × 50yd		Other Ranks – 2,576 (24 WAAF)

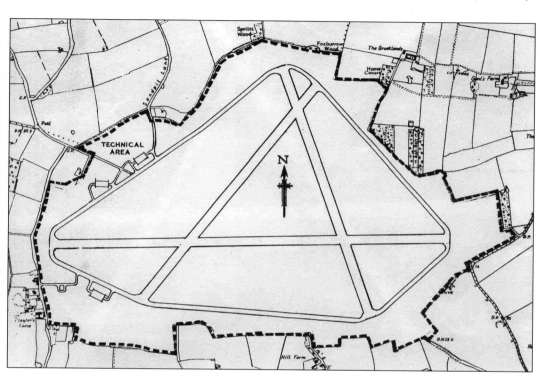

Langham on 30 October and, whilst maintaining detachments at Langham, St Eval and Thorney Island, they remained at Beccles until November 1945. This unit operated Warwicks in conventional and airborne-lifeboat fit and flew hundreds of sea searches over the North Sea. Early the following year they were joined by a detachment from a second ASR unit, the Walrus amphibians of 278 Squadron operating from this Suffolk airfield from February to October 1945, with Sea Otters being added to unit strength from May. The latter's sister-unit, 279 Squadron, arrived at Beccles in September 1945, but this was more of a post-war moving of units prior to disbandment rather than an operational requirement.

Some records show a brief appearance in May 1945 by 288 Squadron, an anti-aircraft co-operation unit, and in the immediate post-war period there were a number of other temporary appearances, but usually of no more than a day or so. By the end of 1945 all but one of the flying units had departed, as Beccles was slated for closure. The Aircrew Holding Unit closed in November and, although there is some debate as to when 279 Squadron left (it had been running a detachment at Pegu since September), the airfield was, to all intents and purposes, closed at the end of 1945.

Beccles (EGSM) is now an active General Aviation airfield operated by Rain Air Ltd with a single concrete/grass runway built on part of the old airfield site – the overall pattern of the wartime airfield is still evident and pilots are warned that 'all other hard surfaces are not available to aircraft'. The current parking area is situated on one of the old dispersal areas.

Beccles housed a number of air-sea rescue units, with the specialist Lancaster equipped with the airborne lifeboat serving with 279 Squadron.

UNITS

1939–1945

Squadron	Dates	Aircraft
278 Sqn	24 Feb 1945–14 Oct 1945	Walrus, Sea Otter
279 Sqn	3 Sep 1945–Dec 1945	Sea Otter, Lancaster
280 Sqn	30 Oct 1944–3 Nov 1945	Warwick
618 Sqn	21 Aug 1944–30 Oct 1944	Mosquito
810 Sqn FAA	8 Apr 1945–3 Jun 1945	Barracuda
827 Sqn FAA	11–28 Oct 1944	Barracuda

BENTWATERS

County: Suffolk

UTM/grid: OS Map 156 – TM350530
Lat./Long.: N52°07.30 E001°26.15
Nearest town: Woodbridge 4.5 miles to south-west

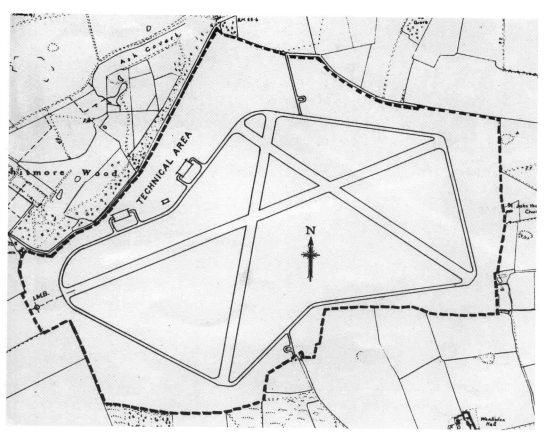

History

In an area already containing a number of major airfields – Debach, Framlingham, Leiston, Martlesham Heath and the emergency runway at Woodbridge were all less than 10 miles away – another major station was under construction in 1943 on the flat coastal region of south-east Suffolk. Work had started in 1942 on a site originally named for the nearby village of Butley but, as Bentwaters, the airfield opened on 17 April 1944 and was intended for USAAF use, having been constructed to the standard mid-war pattern of runways and infrastructure. Although immediately placed under Care and Maintenance, the runways attracted a number of unscheduled visitors, the first of which was a B-17 of the 96th BG – which was promptly damaged by the

obstructions on the runway. With no operational interest being expressed by the Americans, the RAF acquired the airfield and it was allocated to the North Weald Sector of Fighter Command's No.11 Group.

The first operational unit to arrive was 129 Squadron with its Mustang IIIs on 11 December 1944 and, by the end of the month, a further five Mustang units had moved in, making Bentwaters a very busy airfield – and one that was short of facilities. Located on the east coast, Bentwaters was an ideal airfield from which to launch fighter escorts and this became the prime mission of the station's fighters, the first mission taking place on 23 December when four squadrons provided Mustang escort to a force of Lancasters attacking the German city of Trier. These

AIRFIELD DATA DEC 1944

Command:	RAF Fighter Command (ADGB)	Runway surface:	Concrete
Function:	Operational	Hangars:	2 × T.2
Runways:	018 deg 1,400 × 50yd	Dispersals:	50 × Grid
	254 deg 2,000 × 50yd	Personnel:	Officers – 421
	315 deg 1,400 × 50yd		Other Ranks – 2,473

The RAF used Bentwaters for fighter operations from late 1944, Mustangs and Spitfires being operating from here with a number of squadrons; this Spitfire is used to illustrate the type and is not a Bentwaters machine.

bomber escort missions continued to the end of the war, by which time the Bentwaters units had clocked up thousands of operational hours, most of which had brought no contact with the enemy.

With the end of the war, Fighter Command maintained its training routine, whilst at the same time undergoing massive re-organization into its post-war structure. The location of the airfield ensured that it would survive and, whilst units moved – all the Mustangs had gone by late-summer 1945 – and although Spitfires took over for a while, the next significant development was the arrival in 1946 of jets: the first of three Meteor units, 124 Squadron, taking up residence in April. This first operational-jet phase was, however, short-lived and within months the squadrons had gone and Bentwaters became home to

No.226 Operational Conversion Unit (OCU).

After a three-year stint the OCU departed and the airfield was returned to Care and Maintenance, although it had already been earmarked for future use. With the Korean War at its height and increased tension with Russia, there was a major return of American air-power to Europe – and Bentwaters was to spend the next forty years as a USAF base, during which time it was home to a succession of jet-fighter types. The airfield was transferred to USAF control on 16 March 1951 and, in September, the first elements of the 81st Fighter Interceptor Group (FIG) arrived with their F-86A Sabres. These aircraft of the 91st Fighter Interceptor Squadron (FIS) were the first Sabres in Europe. Three years later the unit was given a new role, a new title and new aircraft, becom-

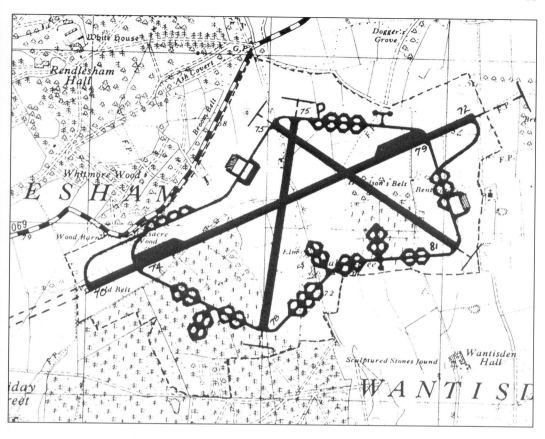

ing the 81st Fighter Bomber Wing (FBW) and receiving F-84F Thunderstreaks. These were subsequently replaced by F-101 Voodoos in December 1958, the unit having become the 81st Tactical Fighter Wing (TFW) in July the same year. Established strength increased when the similarly equipped 92nd Squadron arrived from Manston and both units undertook extensive training and deployments from their Suffolk home. By the time of the 1955 airfield plan, the main runway was 7,900ft long, with a note that it was being extended to 9,000ft with overruns of 1,000ft at each end. Other main facilities listed included:

- Dispersals – fifty loop (70ft diameter), two ORPs of 800ft × 150ft, four aprons and an ASP that together totalled almost two million square feet
- Hangars – two T.2 plus six Butler sheds (80ft 60ft)
- Aviation fuel storage – underground storage for 156,000 gallons in thirteen 12,000-gallon tanks, plus 90,000 gallons in two surface tanks
- Control tower – two-storey with penthouse

Water was supplied from a 380ft-deep borehole and 80,000 gallons were stored on site. Recreational facilities included cinema, clubs, chapel, squash courts and playing fields. An important lodger-unit during this period was the 87th FIS of the 406th FIW, a unit whose F-86Ds were equipped with the Mighty Mouse rocket designed to destroy Russian bomber formations.

In October 1965 the unmistakable roar of the F-4C Phantom was heard, as the first of this type arrived to re-equip the 81st, conversion to type being completed by April 1966. The C-model Phantoms duly gave way to D-models from 1973 but, within five years, these too were being replaced – this time with the single-seat A-10A Thunderbolt. Having become a major NATO jet-base, the airfield underwent a number of enhancement programmes; indeed, there was seldom a year when construction of some sort was not taking place. The three-runway layout had not been used for some time and a single 9,000ft runway (actually 8,947ft by 150ft) oriented 07/25 was maintained as the main operating-surface. The 81st was, in effect, operating from the twin base of Woodbridge

Bentwaters

and Bentwaters; its strength was increased until it had some 120 Thunderbolts, an impressive amount of firepower. As part of the NATO airfield-hardening programme, aircraft shelters had been constructed at both airfields.

The late-1980s saw the arrival of another new type, when the 527th Aggressor Squadron arrived with F-16s in July 1988. For the next five years the twin bases maintained an intensive training-routine but by the early 1990s the draw-down of American forces in Europe was underway and in July 1993 this once thriving complex fell silent. After some debate as to its future, the site was acquired by Bentwaters Parks Ltd and amongst its uses is that of film and TV location. Fortunately, the owners are also keen on the site's heritage and have agreed to the creation of a museum to commemorate the twin airfields of Bentwaters and Woodbridge. The Bentwaters Aviation Society has plans for a museum utilizing part of the former control tower and hardened Wing Operations Centre.

UNITS

1939–1945

64 Sqn	29 Dec 1944–15 Aug 1945	Mustang
65 Sqn	15 May–13 Aug 1945	Mustang
118 Sqn	15 Dec 1944–11 Aug 1945	Spitfire
126 Sqn	30 Dec 1944–5 Sep 1945	Mustang
129 Sqn	11 Dec 1944–26 May 1945	Mustang, Spitfire
165 Sqn	15 Dec 1944–29 May 1945	Spitfire, Mustang
234 Sqn	17 Dec 1944–1 May 1945, 27 Jul–27 Aug 1945, 21 Sep 1945–12 Feb 1946	Mustang, Spitfire

Post-1945

56 Sqn	1 Apr–16 Sep 1946	Meteor
124 Sqn	20 Mar–1 Apr 1946	Meteor
245 Sqn	2–9 Jun 1946	Meteor
226 OCU	10 Oct 1946–26 Aug 1949	Meteor

USAF Units

81st FIG*	6 Sep 1951–1 Jul 1993	F-84, F-101, F-4, A-10, F-16
406th FIW		F-86D

(*subsequently FBW, TFW)

MEMORIALS

1. Planned museum on site.

2. In November 2003 the 81st TFW dedicated a plaque in St Botolph's church, Iken inscribed: 'In appreciation of your kindness and your gracious acceptance of our people in your church, we present this little memento. This is late in concept but heartfelt by all of us from our arrival in 1951 and our final departure in 1993. 81st Fighter Wing.'

3. Brick memorial on airfield inscribed: 'in memory and gratitude to those who served at RAF Bentwaters 1944–1993'.

BIRCHAM NEWTON

County: Norfolk

UTM/grid: OS Map 132 – TF790340
Lat./Long.: N52°52.23 E000°39.15
Nearest town: Fakenham 8 miles to east-south-east

HISTORY

Bircham Newton is one of the most fascinating airfields in Norfolk, with a long history and an interesting mix of buildings, including no less than four main hangar-types. The movement of units in and out of the station was complex, especially during World War Two when many Coastal Command units used Bircham as a main base or for detachments: not all these movements are covered in this brief history, although most do appear in the unit table. This large patch of Norfolk countryside was turned into a flying station in the latter part of World War One, the first occupants being No.3 School of Aerial Fighting and Gunnery, a unit tasked with preparing squadrons for despatch to the Western Front and which arrived from Driffield in May 1918. Whilst this was a vital task, it was Bircham's selection as a 'strategic bomber' base that was of greater significance. As home to the massive Handley Page V/1500 bombers – the first unit, 166 Squadron, having formed at the station in June 1918 – it was at the forefront of air-power

doctrine. These bombers were designed to bomb targets in Germany, including Berlin, but deliveries of the aircraft were slow and, even though a second squadron formed at Bircham, neither was to see operational service before the Armistice was declared in November. In the post-war run-down a number of squadrons made brief appearances here, but usually only as a prelude to disbandment. However, it had been decided to keep the station and for it to remain a bomber base.

In the inter-war period a number of bomber squadrons were formed at Bircham; some stayed in residence for a number of years, whilst others had only brief periods before moving on. The station saw almost every inter-war bomber type use its grass surfaces and, whilst it was primarily a heavy-bomber base, with the likes of the Vimy and the Virginnia, it also housed day-bomber units with the DH9A. One of the more unusual – but local – aircraft was the Sidestrand, a cumbersome bomber produced by

Andover G-EBKW visiting Bircham Newton sometime in the 1920s; at the time this was one of the RAF's main bases in Norfolk.

Boulton & Paul in nearby Norwich. Although established for two bomber-squadrons, the airfield frequently housed additional units but no major construction work was undertaken to reflect this and, during the 1920s and 1930s, the airfield was still dominated by the 1917-pattern hangars.

With the implementation of the RAF's expansion plans, Bircham acquired new hangars, a run of C-types being built, and new 'owners', with the transfer of the airfield to No.16 Group of Coastal Command on 10 August 1936. This opened what was to be Bircham's operational career as a front-line Coastal station. By the end of the month, two units, 206 Squadron and 220 Squadron, both equipped with Avro Ansons, were in residence. Although later famous for its training and support roles, the Anson was, at this time, one of Coastal Command's main operational types and for the next few years the based squadrons undertook training in the various maritime roles, from patrols to anti-submarine attacks. With the opening of air-to-air and air-to-ground training ranges off the coast of North Norfolk, Bircham acquired a lodger unit in the shape of detached Flights from No.1 Anti-Aircraft Co-operation Unit (AACU), whose 'B Flight' operated Westland Wallaces from the airfield during late-summer and autumn 1936. Flights from the AACU made regular appearances at Bircham, primarily for the annual

summer camps (although this could be any time between April and October).

With the outbreak of war, the Anson patrols were stepped up and, on 8 November 1939, an Anson of 206 Squadron was credited with the destruction of a U-boat. The offensive capability of the station increased in August with the arrival of 42 Squadron and its Vickers Vildebeest torpedo bombers, although this was yet another antiquated type that would soon vanish. One of the major tasks for Bircham's units was providing patrols to cover coastal shipping and a number of squadrons operated from here on this task throughout 1940. Mines were a constant threat to shipping and Bircham housed five specially modified Wellingtons, designated DWI, of No.2 GRU, whose task it was to explode magnetic mines. The station's overall capability was increased in November by the formation of 221 Squadron with Wellingtons and Bircham's units remained very active throughout 1941, Blenheims and Wellingtons being the major types in residence. However, the Hudson arrived in late-1941 to replace other types and this soon became the most significant type at Bircham. This aircraft was also used from early 1942 by 279 Squadron, one of the specialist units tasked with Air Sea Rescue, another role for which the airfield became well known. The following year the squadron acquired the Warwick for this task, including some adapted to

AIRFIELD DATA DEC 1944

Command:	RAF Coastal Command	Hangars:	10 × Blister, 3 × C, 3 × Bellman, 3 × Belfast
Function:	Operational Parent	Dispersals:	2 of 'local construction'
Runways:	NE/SW 900yd	Personnel:	Officers – 273 (10 WAAF)
Runway surface:	BRC Netting Track		Other Ranks – 2,712 (544 WAAF)

carry an airborne lifeboat. Initial conversion to type had been carried out by the Warwick Training Unit; this was one of many non-squadron units to operate from Bircham and, in addition to the usual target-towing and support-type work of such flights, Bircham Newton was also home to Meteorological Reconnaissance Flights, which merged to become 512 Squadron in July 1942, although this lasted less than a year and was disbanded to be, in part, replaced by No.1409 Flight. The comings and goings of the numerous flights and squadrons are best understood by studying the units table.

The offensive role of the station brought units in on a temporary basis for specific attacks or for short detachments, either operational or training. The Fleet Air Arm were present from time to time, as indeed they were at most Coastal Command Stations, in this instance with Swordfish of 819 Squadron and Avengers of 855 Squadron; the latter stayed for only a week, whilst the former undertook operational training before deploying to the Continent – eventually returning in early 1945. By late-1944 the airfield had become far quieter as the war entered its final phase and units moved to airfields closer to the scene of action. In the post-war period Bircham's lack of runways – it had remained a grass field throughout – meant that it was not high on the list of airfields with a future. Bircham Newton also has something of a reputation as one of Britain's most haunted airfields and stories of 'encounters' range from a WAAF in the barrack block to the sounds of piston engines and banging of doors.

A number of flying units used the airfield in the late-1940s, as Bircham was 'owned' first by Fighter

Command and then by Transport Command. Finally, in October 1948, Technical Training Command took over and the airfield became home to the Officers' Advanced Training School.

The 1950s site record shows three grass-strips, E–W, N–S, NW–SE: 'the existing grass airfield gives runs of approximately 3,900ft in the directions shown. All approaches are excellent, except that to the North-West.' It went on to say that potential for extending strips would require fairly heavy grading because of ground undulations and gave a maximum strip of 6,000ft. The airfield had semi-buried Avgas storage for 144,000 gallons in twelve 12,000-gallon tanks. Hangar facilities had changed since the 1944 survey and comprised three C-type, two Bellman and one Belfast Truss (150ft × 90ft). As with many East Anglian airfields, the main water-supply came from boreholes, three being operational and supplying a 100,000-gallon storage tank.

The school operated a number of aircraft types and remained in residence until disbanding in 1962, the station closing on 18 December.

A final (short) flurry of flying activity took place in the mid-1960s, when Bircham was used by the West Raynham evaluation unit for the Harrier predecessor, the Kestrel. Although offered for sale in 1964, it was two years later that the Construction Industry Training Board (CITB) acquired the site – and they have remained firmly ensconced ever since. Much of the airfield looks as it ever did and the site is still dominated by the C-type hangars and the neat arrangement of technical, administrative and domestic buildings typical of a fully developed RAF airfield.

DECOY SITES

Q	Burnham Sutton	TF840391
K/Q	Coxford Heath	TF828307

Coxford was provided with dummy aircraft and hangars but had gone out of use by late-1943, becoming a bombing range – it was used by Mosquitoes from Hunsdon to prepare for the attack on Amiens Prison.

Q	Salthouse	TG080425
Q	Sedgeford	TF737363

Blenheims and crews of 235 Squadron at Bircham in October 1940.

Units

Pre-1919

166 Sqn	13 Jun 1918–31 May 1919	FE2b, HP V/1500
167 Sqn	18 Nov 1918–21 May 1919	HP V/1500
274 Sqn	15 Jun 1919–20 Jan 1920	HP V/1500
3 SoAF&G	May 1918–Nov 1918	various
3 FS	29 May 1918–Nov 1918	
5 CS	1 Mar 1919–15 Jun 1919	
6 CS	1 Mar 1919–1 Oct 1919	
7 CS	1 Mar 1919–1 Oct 1919	
8 CS	1 Mar 1919–1 Oct 1919	

1920–1938

7 Sqn	1 Jun 1923–7 Apr 1927	Vimy, Virginia
11 Sqn	16 Sep 1923–31 May 1924	DH9a, Fawn
18 Sqn	7 Jan 1936–7 Sep 1936	Hart, Hind
21 Sqn	3 Dec 1935–25 Jul 1936	Hind
34 Sqn	3 Dec 1935–30 Jul 1936	Hind
35 Sqn	1 Mar 1929–4 Oct 1935	DH9a, Fairey IIIf, Gordon
39 Sqn	12 Jan 1928–29 Dec 1928	DH9a
56 Sqn	30 Dec 1919–22 Jan 1920	SE5a
60 Sqn	1–22 Jan 1920	SE5a
99 Sqn	31 May 1924–5 Jan 1928	Vimy, Aldershot, Hyderabad
101 Sqn	21 Mar 1928–12 Oct 1929	Sidestrand
207 Sqn	1 Feb 1920–29 Sep 1922, 9 Nov 1929–28 Oct 1936	DH9a, Fairey IIIf, Gordon
220 Sqn	17 Aug 1936–21 Aug 1939	Anson
269 Sqn	7–30 Dec 1936	Anson
B Flt 1 AACU	10 Feb 1937–10 May 1937	

1939–1945

42 Sqn	18 Aug 1939–28 Apr 1940	Vildebeest
48 Sqn det	Aug 1939–Jul 1940, 21–23 Feb 1944	Anson, Beaufighter
49 Sqn	10 Feb– 8 Aug 1936	Hind
53 Sqn	Jul 1940–20 Oct 1941, 18 Mar 1943–29 Apr 1943	Blenheim, Hudson, Whitley
59 Sqn det	Jul 1940–Jun 1941	Hudson
119 Sqn	2 Oct 1944–21 Feb 1945, 22 May 1945	Albacore
200 Sqn	25 May–18 Jun 1941	Hudson
206 Sqn	1 Aug 1936–30 May 1941	Anson, Hudson
221 Sqn	21 Nov 1940–29 Sep 1941	Wellington
233 Sqn det	Oct 1939–Aug 1940	Blenheim
235 Sqn	25 Apr 1940–26 May 1940, 24 Jun 1940–4 Jun 1941	Blenheim
248 Sqn	15 Jun 1941–17 Feb 1942	Blenheim, Beaufighter
252 Sqn	21 Nov 1940–1 Dec 1940	Blenheim
254 Sqn	28 Jan 1940–24 Apr 1940	Blenheim
279 Sqn	16 Nov 1941–31 Oct 1944	Hudson
280 Sqn	10 Feb 1942–25 Sep 1943	Anson
320 Sqn	21 Apr 1942–15 Mar 1943	Hudson
407 Sqn	31 Mar 1942–1 Oct 1942	Hudson
415 Sqn	15 Nov 1943–26 Jul 1944	Wellington, Albacore
500 Sqn	30 May 1941–22 Mar 1942	Blenheim, Hudson
521 Sqn	22 Jul 1942–22 Mar 1943	Blenheim, Spitfire, Mosquito, Hudson, Gladiator
524 Sqn	23 Jul 1944–17 Oct 1944	Wellington
598 Sqn	12 Mar 1945–30 Apr 1945	Hurricane, Oxford, Martinet, Beaufighter
695 Sqn	1 Dec 1943–11 Aug 1945	various
819 Sqn FAA	1 Oct 1944–1 Nov 1944, 26 Feb 1945–10 Mar 1945	Swordfish
855 Sqn FAA	7–14 Sep 1944	Avenger
2 GRU	4 Mar 1940–16 May 1940	Wellington
1401 Flt	25 Oct 1941–1 Aug 1942	
1403 Flt	Nov 1940–7 Feb 1942	Blenheim, Hudson
1525 Flt	13 Jul 1942–26 Jun 1945	Oxford
1611 Flt	9 Nov 1942–1 Dec 1943	Henley
1612 Flt	8 Dec 1942–1 Dec 1943	Henley
2 ATC	16 Jun 1943–Jul 1945	
Warwick TF	3 Jul 1943–13 Oct 1943	Warwick, Wellington
ASRTU	13 Oct 1943–20 Oct 1943	Wellington, Warwick, Sea Otter
1626 Flt	30 Nov 1943–1 Dec 1943	Lysander
CCPP	Jun 1944–late-1945	

Post-1945

1510 Flt	22 Nov 1946–15 Sep 1948	Oxford
1555 Flt	19 Mar 1947–31 Aug 1947	Oxford
1559 Flt	9 Mar 1947–9 Aug 1947	Oxford
OATS	25 Oct 1948–1962	

Memorials

1. Commemorative boards located in the CITB Conference Centre.

2. St Mary's churchyard includes a War Graves plot, but there are also a number of pre-1939 RAF graves in the cemetery.

BODNEY
Station 141

County: Norfolk

UTM/grid: OS Map 144 – TL850990
Lat./Long.: N52°33.44 E000°43.7
Nearest town: Watton 4 miles to east

Aerial view of part of the Bodney site, October 2000.

HISTORY

Bodney was built as and remained a grass airfield for its wartime career; however, in that short career it witnessed the tragedies of operations by the Blenheims and Venturas of No.2 Group and the triumphs of the 'Blue-nosed bastards of Bodney', the fighter operations by the distinctive P-51s of the 352nd Fighter Group.

The airfield, located on an area of heathland, was originally established as a satellite field for nearby RAF Watton. In essence, it was little more than a large, roughly circular field, although it was provided with a tarmac perimeter-track and twenty-six hard-standings, mostly in the sparse woodland surrounding the field. Brick structures were kept to a minimum and, in addition to the standard watch-tower, there were assorted Nissen huts, traces of which remain on the site today. As a grass field it first received aircraft from spring 1940, when Watton's Blenheim units

made use of the new 'airfield', and it appears in the records for 21 Squadron and 82 Squadron. The operations by the Blenheim-equipped units of No.2 Group incurred heavy losses but, despite the fact that this aircraft had proved highly vulnerable, there was no replacement in sight and the Group had to persevere. Even over base, aircraft were not safe, as German intruders roamed over southern England; an example being a Blenheim shot down on approach to Bodney on the night of 12–13 February 1941.

Records are not always clear as to which units made temporary use of this grass airfield, but it seems likely that a number of squadrons operating from Watton would also have used Bodney. Amongst the other candidates for 1941 are 105 Squadron, another Blenheim unit, and, more unusually, the Fortress-equipped 90 Squadron. This latter unit was an experimental use by the RAF of the B-17, as the Fortress I,

AIRFIELD DATA DEC 1944

Command:	US 8th AF	Runway surface:	Grass
Function:	Operational	Hangars:	5 × Blister, 2 × T.2
Runways:	NE/SW 1,000yd	Dispersals:	15 × Large asphalt, 12 × Small asphalt
	NW/SE 900yd	Personnel:	Officers – 190
	E/W 900yd		Other Ranks – 1,519

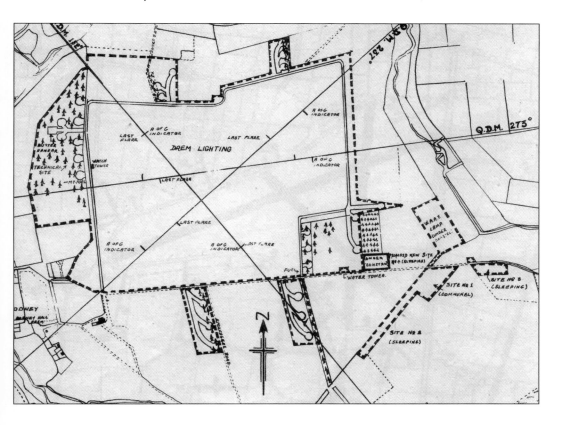

and the squadron formed at Watton on 7 May 1941, commencing operations in July. It was not a successful association and the RAF found little promise in this American bomber; the sight of one operating from the restricted grass-area at Bodney would have been impressive. There is also a suggestion that the Hampdens of 61 Squadron flew from here for a few days in late-March and April 1941.

Having left for the Mediterranean theatre at the end of 1941 – and disbanded there a few months later – 21 Squadron was re-formed at Bodney in March 1942, initially equipped once more with Blenheims and returning to the fray over Europe. However, by this stage the replacement of the Blenheim was

underway, the RAF having selected a variety of American light-bombers; for 21 Squadron the new type was the Lockheed Ventura and the first two aircraft arrived at the end of May. Early enthusiasm soon waned, as the aircraft proved not only troublesome with minor snags, not unusual for a first unit with a new type, but also of inferior performance to that promised. At the end of October the squadron moved with its Venturas to Methwold and Bodney was without an operational unit for the first time since it opened. However, flying continued, as the airfield had been home to a training unit, 17 (Pilot) Advanced Flying Unit, since early 1942. The PAFU was resident at Watton with over 100 Master trainers

Repairing a Blenheim of 21 Squadron after a belly-landing – note the bent props.

and used Bodney as a relief landing ground for almost eighteen months, finally departing in May 1943 to leave the airfield free for its new operational role.

The 8th Air Force arrived in July 1943 and Bodney became Station 141. The 352nd Fighter Group was equipped with P-47 Thunderbolts and, after a few months of acclimatization to its new home and the-atre of operations, flew its first mission on 9 September. This three-squadron unit was part of VIIIth Fighter Command of the USAAF 8th Army Air Force and had been activated in the United States in October 1942, eventually arriving in the UK the following July and moving to Bodney as its first wartime station. The Thunderbolts were engaged in long-range escort and the unit soon estab-lished a fine reputation in the air and on the ground. With limited facilities at Bodney, some use was made of other airfields in the area, although the majority of operational sorties were flown from home base.

The unit converted to the P-51 Mustang in April 1944 and was highly successful with it; this was the type that became associated with the 'blue nose' tag, as the front part of the Mustangs were painted in a vivid blue. This has been preserved into the modern era, with a number of surviving Mustangs wearing the Group's distinctive markings; indeed, at one stage there were more 352nd FG-marked aircraft than any other unit – in part this reflects the ace status acquired by a number of the Group's pilots, including

the top-scoring 8th Air Force P-51 ace, George Preddy. The Mustangs flew escort, sweep and, following the invasion of Europe in June 1944, ground-attack missions, chalking up an impressive tally of victories. Shortly after acquiring the Mustang the Group was awarded a Distinguished Unit Citation for its achievements during an escort mis-sion on 8 May to Brunswick. In December 1944 the Group left Bodney to move to the Continent and, although its was February before all elements had left, for a few months the airfield was virtually abandoned. Then, in mid-April, the roar of the Merlins returned, as the Group came back to Norfolk, flying its final wartime-missions from Bodney. With the end of the war the Mustangs remained at Bodney for some months and it was not until November that the Americans finally returned across the Atlantic and this area of Norfolk heath fell silent for the last time.

After the war, the airfield was returned to its previous owner and reclaimed for agricultural use, although parts of the site have been retained for military (Army) training purposes. Bodney had an intensive war, with the usual selection of highs and lows; a few acres of Norfolk countryside had been turned from agriculture into an airfield and for a few years almost 2,000 people lived and worked in the area. There is now little evidence of its wartime role as an operational airfield, although the remains of the control tower and a few other buildings have survived.

Visit by the all-important NAAFI wagon; a 'tea and wad' were considered essential by RAF ground-crew!

UNITS

1939–1945

21 Sqn det	Sep 1939–Dec 1941	Blenheim
21 Sqn	14 Mar 1942–30 Oct 1942	Blenheim, Ventura
82 Sqn	1 Oct 1940–18 Apr 1941, 3 May 1941–11 Jun 1941	Blenheim
17 (P)AFU	29 Jan 1942–1 May 1943	Master, Anson

USAAF Units

352nd FG (67th FW)

Squadrons:	328th FS, 486th FS, 487th FS
Aircraft:	P-47D, P-51B, P-51C, P-51D, P-51K
Dates:	7 Jul 1943–27 Jan 1945; 14 Apr 1945–3 Nov 1945
Missions:	420
First mission:	9 Sep 1942
Last mission:	3 May 1945 (not from Bodney)

MEMORIALS

Next to main gate of present Army Barracks a memorial stone to 352nd FG, dedicated 9 Jul 1983, inscribed: 'From these fields, American airmen joined their British allies in the cause of freedom.'

The memorial at Bodney, located at the gate of the present military site, to the USAAF units that used the airfield in 1943-1945; there is no memorial to the British use.

BUNGAY (HMS *Europa*) Station 125

County: Suffolk

UTM/grid: OS Map 156 – TM325870
Lat./Long.: N52°25.45 E001°25.15
Nearest town: Beccles 6 miles to east-north-east

The basic airfield layout at Bungay can still be seen from the air, as seen here in May 2002.

HISTORY

By early 1942 the race to create airfields in East Anglia was in full swing and Bungay, located only a few miles from the coast and in the heartland of what was to become 'USAAF territory', was under development as a standard three-runway bomber airfield. Work on the airfield, which was also referred to as Flixton, commenced in 1942, the contractor being Kirk & Kirk Ltd, but like many sites being built during this critical period it was unfinished when its first occupants moved in. It had been allocated to the United States Army Air Force and designated a satellite airfield for Hardwick and because of its nearness to the coast – and thus to occupied Europe – was assigned to a medium-bomber squadron. Hardwick's first resident unit, the 310th BG with its B-25 Mitchells, had taken up residence at their home airfield in December, although only one squadron, the 329th BS, arrived, as the other squadrons had gone direct to North Africa. This was a sojourn of only a few weeks and the squadron left to join the rest of the Group. Its place at Bungay was taken by the 329th BS of the 93rd BG; this Group – the 'Travelling Circus' – having Hardwick as its main base from December 1943; the Squadron operated from Bungay with its B-24Ds to 12 March 1943. This unit specialized in intruder missions probing the German defences, using navigational aids such as Gee to take advantage of bad weather to keep the defenders on alert. However, the squadron rejoined its parent Group at Hardwick in March, to leave Bungay for allocation as a full bomber-station. In common with most airfields allocated to the American bomber force, Bungay had limited facilities, the standard hangar arrangement being two T.2 hangars, as deep servicing was performed at specialist airfields. Additional construction work prepared the airfield

AIRFIELD DATA DEC 1944

Command:	US 8th AF 2nd BD	Runway surface:	Concrete, pitch and wood-chips
Function:	Operational	Hangars:	2 × T.2
Runways:	050 deg 2,000 × 50yd	Dispersals:	50 × Loop
	100 deg 1,400 × 50yd	Personnel:	Officers – 421
	360 deg 1,480 × 50yd		Other Ranks – 2,473

Luftwaffe target photograph of Bungay under construction. (US National Archives)

for its independent role as Station 125 and in November the 'Bungay Buckaroos' – the 446th BG – arrived from America.

This Group had been activated in April 1943 and, under Colonel Jacob J Brogger, the four squadrons of B-24s took up residence, flying their first combat mission on 16 December 1943. The Group operated from Bungay for the rest of the war and chalked up 273 operational missions for the loss of fifty-eight aircraft missing in action. As part of the 2nd Bombardment Division it retained B-24 Liberators throughout, a number of variants being employed. One of its Liberators, 41-29144 Ronnie, survived the war with an impressive tally of 119 missions.

With the war over, Bungay was soon evacuated by the Americans, the bulk of the Group having gone by June 1945. The site was taken over by the Admiralty as HMS *Europa*, effectively a satellite for the nearby HMS *Sparrowhawk* (Halesworth). This was short-lived and the airfield soon reverted to the RAF for use by No.53 Maintenance Unit as a sub-site for their main location at Pulham Market. According to the 1954 survey, the site was allocated to agriculture but certain areas were used by the MU. The report also stated that the main runway, presently 6,000ft and oriented 044/224 degrees, could be extended to 7,500ft but 'would involve the felling of a large number of trees in both the NE and SW approaches, as well as demolishing a house and outbuildings'.

The Maintenance Unit was involved in bomb

'Old Faithful', B-24 of the 446th BG. (US National Archives)

Liberators of the 446th in formation heading towards another target in Germany. (US National Archives)

storage and the airfield was used for this role until 1956, before being finally being sold off in 1962. For many years the runways and perimeter track remained fairly intact, avoiding the normal fate of becoming construction hardcore, but they eventually succumbed in 1984 and little trace now remains of this once impressive bomber base.

However, whilst there might not be much to see at the airfield itself, the Norfolk and Suffolk Aviation Museum (NSAM) is now located close to the former airfield and exhibits many artefacts from the days of the 446th BG, along with an impressive collection of cold-war aircraft.

DECOY SITE

Q	Rumburgh	TM340825

UNITS

1939–1945
USAAF Units
93rd BG

Squadron:	329th BS
Aircraft:	B-24D
Dates:	Dec 1942–12 Mar 1943

310th BG

Squadron:	428th BS
Aircraft:	B-25C
Date:	Nov 1942

446th BG (20th CBW)

Identifying letter:	H
Nickname:	Bungay Buckaroos
Squadrons:	704th BS (Headlock), 705th BS (Accept), 706th BS (Manage), 707th BS (Loosend)
Aircraft:	B-24H, B-24J, B-24L, B-24M

Dates:	Nov 1943–Jul 1945
Missions:	273
First Mission:	16 Dec 1943
Last Mission:	25 Apr 1945

MEMORIALS

1. Plaque in Community Centre dedicated May 1983. Inscription: 'To the people of Bungay. This plaque is dedicated to commemorate our appreciation of your warmth, your friendship, and your hospitality so generously extended to the members of the 446th Bombardment Group USAAF 1943–1945.'

2. Memorial propeller and plaque at Norfolk and Suffolk Air Museum inscribed: 'In memory of all those who gave their lives or served with the 446th Bomb Group (H) at Flixton, Bungay 1943–1945. 20th Combat Wing. 2nd Air Division.'

The Norfolk and Suffolk Aviation Museum includes an excellent history room for Bungay, and a propeller memorial to the Groups that operated from the airfield.

CHEDBURGH

County: Suffolk

UTM/grid: OS Map 155 – TL792565
Lat./Long.: N52°10.53 E000°37.15
Nearest town: Bury St Edmunds 6 miles to north-east

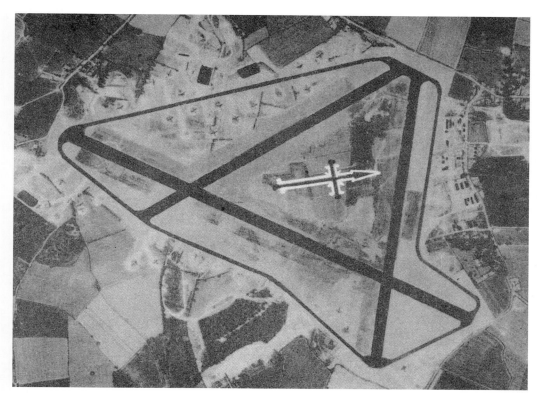

HISTORY

As a Bomber Command satellite, Chedburgh opened on 7 September 1942 as the second such location for the expansion-period airfield of Stradishall and was designed for the new heavy-bombers to the standard pattern of three concrete-runways. The following month, Stirlings of 214 Squadron moved in from Stradishall and this unit was destined to stay in residence for over a year, during which time it operated as part of Main Force on the nightly war against targets in Germany and occupied Europe. Under the policy of using the third Flight of operational squadrons as the nucleus of a new squadron, C Flight of 214 became 620 Squadron in June 1943.

As part of the reorganization of Bomber Command that took effect in spring 1943, Chedburgh became a sub-station for No.31 Base, its parenting base-station being Stradishall, but remained part of No.3 Group, Bomber Command. This arrangement took effect on

26 April 1943 and was unusual in that the two sub-stations housed operational units, whilst the base station housed an HCU. For a period of some months the two operational squadrons operated from Chedburgh, although by mid-1943 the shortcomings of the Stirling had become evident and the decision had been taken to remove the type from Main Force at the earliest opportunity.

By December both operational units had departed: 214 Squadron to Downham Market and 620 Squadron to Leicester East. No.31 Base then took on its assigned role of training Stirling crews for No.3 Group – Chedburgh becoming a major training-base as the home of 1653 Heavy Conversion Unit, with an establishment of 30-plus Stirling Is and IIIs. In the year that the HCU was in place, hundreds of aircrew passed through its hands on the intensive course.

However, December 1944 brought a return to

AIRFIELD DATA DEC 1944

Command:	RAF Bomber Command	Runway surface:	Concrete
Function:	Operational	Hangars:	3 × Glider, 2 × T.1, one × B.1
Runways:	173 deg 1,400 × 50yd	Dispersals:	36 × Heavy Bomber
	231 deg 2,000 × 50yd	Personnel:	Officers – 171 (10 WAAF)
	302 deg 1,400 × 50yd		Other Ranks – 1,692 (231 WAAF)

Stirling BF382 at Chedburgh, October 1942, the same month that the Squadron moved here from Stradishall.

operational flying, as the HCU left for North Luffenham and the Lancasters of 218 Squadron arrived from Methwold. These aircraft flew Main Force missions to the end of the war, the Squadron finally disbanding in August 1945.

Post-war the airfield was fleetingly used by two Polish transport squadrons, 301 and 304 Squadrons, equipped with Warwicks and Wellingtons respectively. Although these were ex-Coastal Command, they were, like many of the multi-engine squadrons, converted to a transport role in the immediate post-war period. In January 1946 the more suitable transport conversion of the Halifax, the C.VIII, joined 301 Squadron, the same type re-equipping the other Polish unit in May. Both squadrons flew transport routes to the end of the year, at which point they were disbanded, bringing to an end a fine wartime record for these two Allied units.

With no further need of this wartime airfield the site was dismantled and sold off in October 1952. Some traces of the airfield remain and a number of buildings, including hangars, are still in use, primarily for light industry.

UNITS

1939–1945

214 Sqn	1 Oct 1942–10 Dec 1943	Stirling
218 Sqn	5 Dec 1944–10 Aug 1945	Stirling, Lancaster
620 Sqn	17 Jun 1943–23 Nov 1943	Stirling
1653 HCU	21 Nov 1943– 27 Nov 1944	Stirling

MEMORIALS

1. Memorial stone dedicated Oct 1992, inscribed: 'Royal Air Force Chedburgh. In Memory and in Honour of the Men and Women of the Royal Air Force, the Dominions and the Polish Air Force who served at RAF Chedburgh 1942–1946 and of those who gave their lives in the Fight for Freedom. To live in the hearts of those who never forget is not to die. Royal Air Force 214, 620 & 218 Squadrons and 1653 Heavy Conversion Unit, Polish Air Force 301 & 304 Squadron.'

2. Roll of honour in the church and the village sign shows a Lancaster.

The memorial on the village green includes a plan of the airfield (on top) and the plaque commemorates all the units to have served here.

COLTISHALL

County: Norfolk

UTM/grid: OS Map 133 – TG270225
Lat./Long.: N52°45.15 E001°21.30
Nearest town: Norwich 8 miles to south

HISTORY

The summer 2004 announcement that Coltishall is scheduled for closure is yet another blow to what little remains of the RAF in East Anglia and its demise will bring to an end the history of one of Norfolk's most significant airfields – an operational fighter base for over sixty years. The airfield has its origins in the late-1930s expansion period with the decision to construct a bomber airfield to the north of Norwich and work commenced in February 1939 for a grass airfield with C-type hangars and permanent buildings. However, with a re-organization of Fighter Command's Sector organization it was decided that the new airfield should be used for fighters and when it opened in June 1940 it was as part of No.12 Group. Aircraft had been using the airfield since the previous November, Blenheims from Watton and Horsham

having dispersed here from time to time.

By the first week of June the Station had two squadrons in residence – Spitfires with 66 Squadron and Hurricanes with 242 Squadron, the latter under the command of Squadron Leader Douglas Bader. Coltishall's fighters had two main roles: providing air defence over East Anglia and providing fighter cover for convoys and coastal shipping. It was the latter that brought the first action and on 10 July Sergeant Robertson of 66 Squadron shot down a Do17, which has also been credited as the first victory of the Battle of Britain. Coltishall's fighters continued to play a part in the air battles of 1940, with a number of squadrons rotating through the airfield. The Sector Operations Room moved off the airfield and, after a short spell in a hut at Catton, it took over Stratton

AIRFIELD DATA DEC 1944

Command:	RAF Fighter Command	Runway surface:	Sommerfeld Track
Function:	Sector Station	Hangars:	5 × C, 6 × Over Blister, 2 × Extra Over Blister
Runways:	096 deg 2,000 × 50yd	Dispersals:	6 × Single-engine, 14 × Twin-engine
	050 deg 1,400 × 50yd	Personnel:	Officers – 137 (9 WAAF)
	150 deg 1,400 × 50yd		Other Ranks – 2,066 (496 WAAF)

Hurricane Z2588 of 242 Squadron with ground-crew watching a vic arriving back at the airfield sometime in late 1940. (Andy Thomas)

Strawless Hall, from where it controlled the battle in this part of East Anglia. Squadrons continued to fly Channel patrols and a number of successes were achieved, but the Luftwaffe seldom appeared over this Sector and the major contribution to the Battle of Britain was to provide squadrons for the Group's Big Wing concept, based at Duxford, aircraft deploying to Duxford as required. By October, Coltishall was home to four squadrons and had been allocated Matlaske for use as a satellite airfield. Squadrons continued to rotate but the most significant change was the arrival of night-fighter detachments, initially Defiants of 151 Squadron but later including Beaufighters and even the impressive, but not very effective, Turbinlite Havoc.

By 1941 Fighter Command had switched to the offensive and Coltishall's squadrons joined in sweeps over France and escorted daylight bombers. The same year saw the arrival of ASR aircraft at Coltishall, a role that the airfield subsequently performed for much of its history, with the initial small complement of aircraft of No.5 ASR Flight expanding in October to become 278 Squadron and taking up residence at Matlaske, but continuing to use Coltishall. The third American Eagle squadron, 133 Squadron, formed at Coltishall in July 1941 but, after an initial two-week work-up period, moved its Hurricanes to Duxford.

A second satellite-airfield opened in November 1941, Ludham being located seven miles east of

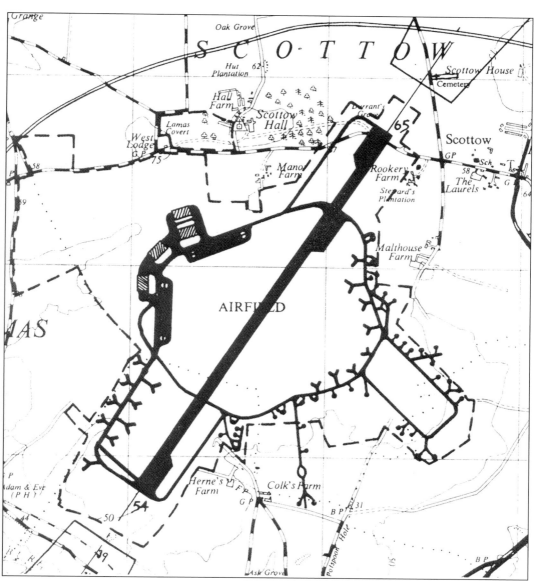

Coltishall. In addition to the ever-rotating based units, Coltishall was used as a forward base by a number of squadrons, these detachments lasting anything from a single day to a few weeks. The airfield and its satellites were well positioned for both offensive and defensive work over the Channel and North Sea, as well as the increasing weight of attacks being made against land targets on the fringes of occupied Europe. Beauforts, Whirlwinds, Bostons and a range of other types appeared at Colt from time to time, as did some of Bomber Command's 'heavies', although for the latter it was usually a case of an emergency landing at the nearest airfield. Fighters, too, forward deployed to Coltishall and, as the Germans launched a new series of night raids against cities, Norwich being attacked a number of times, the role of the night fighters from Coltishall became increasingly important, with 68 Squadron's Beaufighters proving particularly successful – the Squadron had been in residence since early March 1942.

Since 1974 Coltishall has been home to the Jaguar, an association of over 30 years; Jaguars of 41 Squadron have been in residence since 1976.

For a few weeks in late-1942, the 346th Fighter Squadron of the USAAF's 350th Fighter Group was in residence, the Group's main base at Duxford being unable to accommodate them. It was intended that the Group would operate P-39s in the ground-attack role but during its initial training phase it used a mix of Spitfires and P-39s. However, it was re-allocated to the 12th Air Force and the 346th moved out in early January.

The pattern of operations continued through 1943 and into 1944, with bomber escort, sweep and air defence, the latter now having to cope with hit-and-run raids by fighter-bombers such as the Fw190. The night-fighter units had continued to add to their scores and when 68 Squadron finally left the station, for Coleby Grange in February 1944, it was credited with having destroyed seventy enemy aircraft. They were replaced by an equally experienced unit, 25 Squadron. By spring 1944 the bulk of the RAF's attention had turned towards the forthcoming invasion and, whilst much of the air campaign for the past few months had been waged with this in mind, it was now time to concentrate tactical aircraft for the new battle. In many respects Coltishall became something of a backwater, although its squadrons continued to fly a variety of operational missions and its runways were still used for forward deployment. In the closing

months of the war the station's fighters, Spitfires and Mustangs, had two main tasks: providing escort for the Coastal Command Strike Wing from Langham and flying sweeps looking for V-2 rocket sites in Holland.

RAF Coltishall had been an active operational station for six years and in the immediate post-war period it became home to No.133 (Polish) Wing with three squadrons of Mustangs. This was now a Polish station, but it was only a temporary measure pending the decision on the future of the Poles; with the disbandment of the Polish units the station was handed back to the RAF at an emotional parade in February 1947. Coltishall now became a night-fighter station for No.12 Group and, as such, housed two Mosquito units, 23 and 141 squadrons, being joined by 264 Squadron in January 1948 to form a Mosquito Wing of three squadrons. All three moved out temporarily in November 1949 for building work, including runway improvements, to take place but were back in residence by September 1950. The jet era arrived in 1951 and Vampire, Venom and Meteor night fighters duly took their place with the squadrons. Building work again took place in late-1956, a major runway improvement programme being contracted to John Laing and Co.; the squadrons moved to Horsham St Faith and, whilst

Impressive line-up of Lightnings of 74 Squadron.

there, commenced conversion to that peculiarly British aircraft, the Javelin.

A January 1959 survey showed a single, rigid, concrete runway 7,500ft × 150ft with an overrun of 600ft at the north-east end and 800ft at the south-west end. Other installations included:

- Dispersals – Lens (50ft diameter), two Operational Readiness Platforms (750ft × 150ft), two Aircraft Servicing Pans (750ft × 230ft) and four aprons totalling 120,000sq ft
- Hangars – four C-type, all with annexes
- Fuel storage – eighteen underground tanks each holding 12,000 gallons of aviation fuel
- Control tower – a two-storey building of reinforced concrete

The arrival of Javelins at Colt in May 1959 was rapidly followed by the arrival of Hunters, courtesy of 74 Squadron. Of perhaps even greater interest was the appearance of the Lightning, pre-production examples of which arrived to join the Air Fighter Development Squadron, an element of the Central Fighter Establishment. Shortly afterwards it was announced that 74 Squadron would become the RAF's first operational Lightning unit, thus sealing Coltishall's connection with this much-loved aircraft. The squadron left in March 1964 but, within weeks, the Lightning was back when No.226 OCU took up residence from Middleton St George. This training unit remained at Coltishall until September 1974, when its task was taken on by the Lightning Training Flight at Binbrook; it had trained over 800 Lightning pilots.

The departure of this classic British fighter heralded the arrival of an Anglo-French fighter-bomber, the Jaguar. Before moving on to the aircraft with which the airfield has been associated for three decades a word must be said about helicopters and historic aircraft. Coltishall's Search and Rescue role has been performed by a variety of helicopters since mid-1956 and the first detachment of Whirlwinds from 22 Squadron. Detachments from 22, 202 and 275 Squadrons have been present at Coltishall over the years, although in the latter period the task was primarily held by the Wessex HAR.2s of 22 Squadron. The final SAR detachment departed in July 1994. One of the most popular residents of the airfield was the Battle of Britain Memorial Flight, in residence from April 1963 to March 1976.

The first Jaguar unit, 54 Squadron, arrived in August 1974 and for the past thirty years Coltishall has been one of the RAF's main Jaguar bases. Over that period it has housed an average of three squadrons, one of which, 41 Squadron, has specialized in the Tactical Reconnaissance role. Since 1991 the station's aircraft have been almost constantly engaged on active operations and in the last decade the aircraft have been given significant upgrades to increase their operational capability. The arrival of the training units, 16 (R) Squadron from Lossiemouth in July 2000, consolidated all RAF Jaguars at Coltishall.

DECOY SITES

Q	Beeston St Lawrence	TG318227
Q	Suffield	TG242320

Units

1939–1945

Unit	Dates	Aircraft
1 Sqn	8 Apr 1945–14 May 1945	Spitfire
25 Sqn	5 Feb 1944–27 Oct 1944	Mosquito
26 Sqn det	Jan 1945–Apr 1945	Mustang
29 Sqn det	Apr 1941–May 1943	Beaufighter
42 Sqn det	Mar 1941–Jun 1942	Beaufort
64 Sqn	15 Oct 1940–11 Nov 1940, 25 Sep 1943–29 Apr 1944+	Spitfire
66 Sqn	29 May 1940–3 Sep 1940	Spitfire
68 Sqn	8 Mar 1942–5 Feb 1944, 28 Oct 1944–16 Mar 1945	Beaufighter
72 Sqn	20 Oct 1940–29 Nov 1940+	Spitfire
74 Sqn	9 Sep 1940–15 Oct 1940; Post 1945	Spitfire; Hunter, Lightning
80 Sqn	20–29 Sep 1944	Spitfire
93 Sqn det	Dec 1940–Nov 1941	Havoc
118 Sqn	17 Jan 1943–15 Aug 1943	Spitfire
124 Sqn	10 Feb 1945–7 Apr 1945	Spitfire
125 Sqn	18 Oct 1944–24 Apr 1945	Mosquito
133 Sqn	31 Jul 1941–15 Aug 1941	Hurricane
137 Sqn	8–31 Nov 1941	Whirlwind
151 Sqn det	Dec 1940–Apr 1943, Aug 1943–Mar 1944	Defiant, Mosquito
152 Sqn	17 Dec 1941–17 Jan 1942	Spitfire
154 Sqn	12 Mar 1942–5 Apr 1942	Spitfire
195 Sqn	21 Aug 1943–24 Sep 1943	Typhoon
222 Sqn	11 Nov 1940–6 Jun 1941	Spitfire
229 Sqn	1 Jul 1944–25 Sep 1944, 2 Dec 1944–10 Jan 1945	Spitfire
234 Sqn	28 Jan 1944–18 Mar 1944	Spitfire
242 Sqn	18 Jun 1940–26 Oct 1940, 30 Nov 1940–16 Dec 1940	Spitfire
255 Sqn	Jul 1941–2 Mar 1942	Beaufighter
257 Sqn	16 Dec 1940–7 Nov 1941	Hurricane
266 Sqn det	Mar 1942–Aug 1942	Typhoon
274 Sqn	20–29 Sep 1944	Tempest
278 Sqn	21 Apr 1942–21 Apr 1944	Walrus, Lysander
288 Sqn det	Jan 1943–Nov 1944	various
303 Sqn	25 Sep 1944–4 Apr 1945, 16 May 1945–10 Aug 1945	Spitfire, Mustang
307 Sqn det	May 1944–Jan 1945	Mosquito
312 Sqn	11 Jul 1944–27 Aug 1944	Spitfire
315 Sqn	24 Oct 1944–1 Nov 1944,	Spitfire
316 Sqn	28 Apr 1944–4 Jul 1944, 27 Aug 1944–24 Oct 1944, 16 May 1945–10 Aug 1945	Spitfire, Mustang
409 Sqn det	Feb 1943–Mar 1944	Beaufighter
453 Sqn	30 Sep 1944–18 Oct 1944	Spitfire
488 Sqn det	Sep 1942–Aug 1943	Beaufighter
602 Sqn	30 Sep 1944–18 Oct 1944, 19 Apr 1945–15 May 1945	Spitfire
603 Sqn	10 Jan 1945–24 Feb 1945, 5–28 Apr 1945	Spitfire
604 Sqn det	Sep 1940	Beaufighter
611 Sqn	4 Aug 1943–30 Apr 1944	Spitfire
616 Sqn	3–9 Sep 1940	Spitfire
841 Sqn FAA	Dec 1942–Jul 1943	Albacore, Swordfish
2 ADF	18 Mar 1941–23 Jul 1943	
12 Gp TTF	Aug 1941–Oct 1941	
1489 Flt	8 Dec 1941–13 Apr 1943	Lysander, Henley, Master

USAAF Units

Unit	Dates	Aircraft
346th FS	Oct 1942–2 Jan 1943	P-39, Spitfire

Post-1945

Unit	Dates	Aircraft
6 Sqn	15 Nov 1974–date	Jaguar
16 Sqn	Jul 2000–date	Jaguar
22 Sqn det	Jun 1956–18 Jul 1994+	Whirlwind, Wessex
23 Sqn	23 Jan 1947–19 Nov 1949+, 22 Sep 1950–15 Jan 1952, 4 Jul 1952–12 Oct 1956, 28 May 1957–7 Sep 1958, 5 Jun 1959–9 Mar 1963+	Mosquito, Vampire, Venom, Javelin
41 Sqn	1 Oct 1976–date	Jaguar
54 Sqn	15 Aug 1974–date	Jaguar
74 Sqn	8 Jun 1959–2 Mar 1964	Hunter, Lightning
141 Sqn	15 Feb 1947–21 Nov 1949+, 23 Sep 1950–14 Oct 1956, 28 May 1957–1 Feb 1958	Mosquito, Meteor, Venom, Javelin
202 Sqn det	Aug 1964–1982+	Whirlwind, Sea King, Wessex
264 Sqn	13 Jan 1948–19 Nov 1949+, 2 Oct 1950–24 Aug 1951	Mosquito, Meteor
275 Sqn det	Oct 1956–?	Sycamore
306 Sqn	10 Aug 1945–6 Jan 1947+	Mustang
309 Sqn	10 Aug 1945–6 Jan 1947	Mustang
215 Sqn	8 Aug 1945–14 Jan 1947	Spitfire
318 Sqn	19 Aug 1946–12 Dec 1946	Spitfire
809 Sqn FAA	Aug 1952–Jan 1953	Sea Hornet
16 OTU	1 Mar 1946–15 Mar 1947	Mosquito
AFDS	1 Sep 1959–5 Oct 1962	Lightning
LCS	4 Jan 1960–Aug 1961	Lightning
BBMF	1 Apr 1963–1 Mar 1976	Lancaster, Spitfire, Hurricane
226 OCU	20 Apr 1964–Apr 1991	Lightning, Jaguar

DEBACH
Station 152

County: Suffolk

UTM/grid: OS Map 169 – TM240540
Lat./Long.: N52°08.08 E001°16.23
Nearest town: Woodbridge 3 miles to south-east

This May 2002 shot shows that parts of the runways at Debach are still in place and the overall plan of the airfield can still be seen.

HISTORY

The airfield was located close to RAF Woodbridge in Suffolk and was built by American engineers of the 820th EAB (Engineer Aviation Battalion) in 1943–44 to the, by then, standard layout of three intersecting runways, a pair of T.2 hangars and fifty hardstands. As a bomber station, accommodation was provided for 2,500 personnel and the area around the airfield housed a number of domestic and technical sites – clusters of Nissen huts, although nearby Thistledon Hall was also taken over for accommodation.

Debach was one of the last airfields taken over by the Americans and its operational unit, the 493rd BG, arrived at Station 152 in April 1944. Under the command of Colonel Elbert Helton, the B-24 Liberator-equipped Group was known as 'Helton's Hellcats' and flew the first of its 158 missions on 6 June 1944 – D-Day – as part of the 3rd Bombardment Division. This

was the last 8th Air Force Bomber Group to become operational and by the end of the war it had lost forty-one aircraft missing in action. Although the plan had been to remain at Debach for the duration of the war, it became apparent that the concrete and tarmac runway was not going to withstand the wear and tear of almost daily heavy-bomber operations – poor construction technique being blamed, one of very few instances of a construction problem. The Group had re-equipped with B-17s in September 1944 and at the end of the year the aircraft moved to Little Walden, whilst repair work was carried out at Debach. The Fortresses returned in April and the Group flew its final operational sorties from its Suffolk home, the last mission being flown on 20 April. With the war over, Debach was soon abandoned by the Americans, the aircraft flying out in June and July.

AIRFIELD DATA DEC 1944

Command:	US 8th Air Force 3rd BD	Runway surface:	Concrete and tarmac
Function:	Operational	Hangars:	2 × T.2
Runways:	180 deg 2,000 × 50yd	Dispersals:	50 × Spectacle
	250 deg 1,400 × 50yd	Personnel:	Officers – 421
	310 deg 1,400 × 50yd		Other Ranks – 2,473

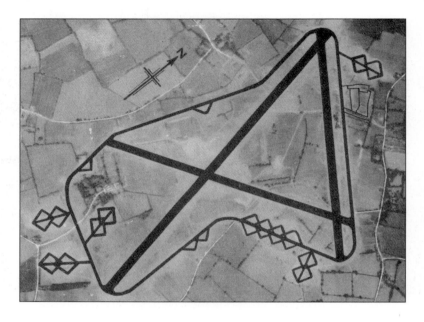

There was no further requirement for the airfield and after brief use to house German POWs and then displaced persons, final closure came in 1948. The site was eventually sold for agricultural use, although a number of buildings were taken over for light-industrial use.

Missions:	158
First Mission:	6 Jun 1944
Last Mission:	20 Apr 1945

MEMORIALS

Village sign has plaque to 493rd BG.

B-17 of the 493rd BG landing at Debach, January 1945. (US National Archives)

UNITS

1939–1945
USAAF Units
493rd BG (93rd CBW)

Identifying letter:	X
Nickname:	Helton's Hellcats
Squadrons:	860th BS (Shunter), 861st BS (Begman), 862nd BS (Compar), 863rd BS (Pilar)
Aircraft:	B-24H, B-24J, B-17G
Operational:	Apr 1944–6 Aug 1945

DEOPHAM GREEN
Station 142

County: Norfolk

UTM/grid: OS Map 144 – TM030990
Lat./Long.: N52°33.08 E000°59.38
Nearest town: Attleborough 2 miles to south

September 2002 overflight of the site of Deopham Green; the runways are virtually gone but the perimeter track defines the airfield.

HISTORY

The airfield at Deopham Green, situated just north of Attleborough, was built by John Laing & Sons to Class A specification for the Americans in 1942–43, although it was not finally occupied until early 1944. A stretch of Norfolk Breckland (a sandy-heath area well suited to airfield construction) was acquired and, with local roads closed or diverted and hedgerows and trees removed, a pattern of concrete-and-tarmac runways, connected by a perimeter track with dispersals for four bomber squadrons was laid out. There was also an extensive bomb-dump on the southern side of the airfield. As the airfield was ready by the middle of 1943, it is surprising that no units were moved in and somewhere in the records there must be a note that explains this situation!

The well-equipped airfield eventually received its first bombers in January 1944, when the B-17Gs of the 452nd Bomb Group arrived from the USA. The Group had been activated in June 1943 and

Deopham was to be its home for the duration of its wartime career. Under the command of Lieutenant Colonel Herbert Wangeman, the Group flew its first mission on 5 February 1944 as part of 3rd Bombardment Division, the target being Brunswick. Colonel Wangeman failed to return from a sortie three days later and the Group went on to have a record number of commanders, although only two were lost in action. Spring 1944 was a period of particularly high losses for this Group and by the end of the war its 250 missions had cost it 110 aircraft missing in action, one of the higher percentage totals. The unit was awarded a Distinguished Unit Citation for its role in the 7 April 1945 attack on Kaltenkirchen.

As at many airfields, an assessment was made in 1944 of its suitability for expansion, especially runway lengthening, but this was 'not recommended' on the grounds that it would involve demolition of a school, a farm and ten cottages. By the end of August

AIRFIELD DATA DEC 1944

Command:	US 8th Air Force 3rd BD	Runway surface:	Concrete and tarmac
Function:	Operational	Hangars:	2 × T.2
Runways:	110 deg 1,400 × 50yd	Dispersals:	9 × Loop, one Frying Pan
	240 deg 2,000 × 50yd	Personnel:	Officers – 421
	350 deg 1,400 × 50yd		Other Ranks – 2,473

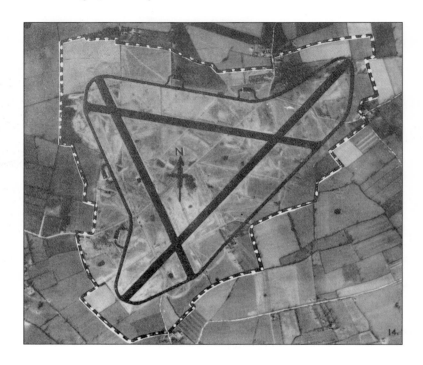

'E-Rat-Icator'; B-17 of the 452nd BG, the only unit to operate from Deopham Green. (US National Archives).

1945 the Americans had departed for home and the station passed to RAF Maintenance Command; this was a short-lived transfer and the airfield was closed on 1 January 1948. Disposal proceedings saw most of the land revert to agriculture and the return of some of the local roads. One of the local roads, linking Deopham Green with Little Ellingham, reopened using part of one of the runways and it is evocative to drive around this site – including standing next to the memorial and staring down the line of runways that once witnessed massed take-offs by Flying Fortresses. In addition to surviving runway and taxi-way surfaces, a number of buildings can still be seen on the site.

The brick pillar memorial sits alongside what would have been the intersection of the runways.

Units

1939–1945

USAAF Units

452nd BG (45th CBW)

Identifying letter:	L
Squadrons:	728th BS (Pinetree), 729th BS (Instinct), 730th BS (Spencer), 731st BS (Acquit)
Aircraft:	B-17G
Dates:	3 Jan 1944–6 Aug 1945
Missions:	250
First mission:	5 Feb 1944
Last mission:	21 Apr 1945

Memorials

1. Brick pillar with engraved map of airfield, located on intersection of old runways, inscribed: 'February 1944–April 1945, Deopham Green, from this airfield 250 missions were flown by the 452nd Bomb Group (H). This memorial commemorates all those who served here. Dedicated 15th May 1992.'

2. St Andrews church Hingham, plaque by war memorial, inscribed: 'Memorial dedicated to the men of the 452nd Bomb Group (H) who sacrificed their lives in World War II that the ideals of democracy might live.'

DOCKING

County: Norfolk

UTM/grid: OS Map 132 – TF786390
Lat./Long.: N52°55.18 E000°39.39
Nearest town: Fakenham 10 miles to south-east

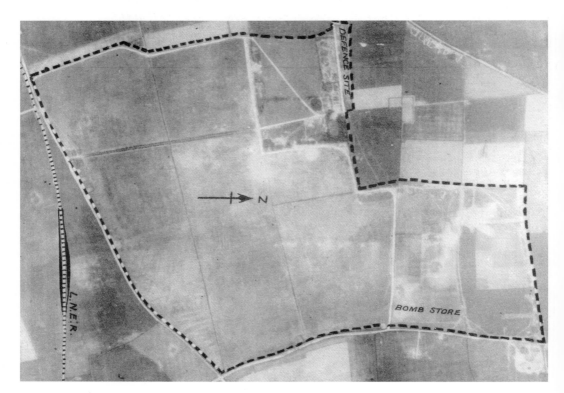

HISTORY

East Anglia is not famed for its Coastal Command locations, but Docking is one of a small number of airfields in Norfolk that played an important role in the maritime war. This grass airfield opened in mid-1940 as a satellite for the busy station at Bircham Newton and was probably first used in June or July by 235 Squadron's Blenheims. However, this early phase in the airfield's use is difficult to pin down and it is likely that a number of Bircham's units made occasional use of Docking. Hudsons, Blenheims and Wellingtons were all seen in this remote part of Norfolk during this period and the airfield infrastructure was gradually developed, eventually growing to comprise eight Blister hangars and assorted technical, administrative and domestic buildings – although the airfield surface remained grass. The primary task of the squadrons was convoy escort, although a number of anti-shipping sorties were also flown. Docking remained active as an offensive airfield throughout

the war, being used by based aircraft, detachments or as a forward-operating location. The operational units list shows a variety of types and roles but the airfield was also home to equally important support units, the most significant of which were those involved with meteorological observation and reports.

No.1401 Meteorological Reconnaissance Flight, based at Bircham Newton, used Docking as a satellite between October 1941 and August 1942; this was the first of a number of units performing the all important, but underrated, meteorological-research task from this airfield. From May 1942 a new aircraft type made a brief appearance, when Bristol Beaufighters of first 235 Squadron and then 254 Squadron each spent a few months in residence. These were used for shipping strikes but soon moved on to new bases as Coastal Command formed Strike Wings.

The Canadians of 407 Squadron brought their

As a Coastal Command station, Docking was home to a number of Wellington operators during the war; this is not a Docking-based aircraft.

Hudsons to Docking in October 1942, tasked with anti-shipping work in the Channel and North Sea, a hazardous task. Wellingtons arrived in January 1943 to supplement, and eventually replace, the Hudsons and conversion training took place while the Hudsons remained operational, before the squadron left for Skitten in February. There is some suggestion that the torpedo Hampdens of the Canadian 415 Squadron used Docking from time to time, whilst operating a forward detachment at Bircham in late-1942. With this coming and going of units, Docking was certainly a busy station and a number of training and support units used the now well-established airfield, an increasing array of temporary buildings springing up to meet the changing requirements. Specialist flights included the Beam/Blind Approach Training Flights and conversion units such as the Warwick Training Flight. The latter arrived as part of the re-equipment of the Command's Air Sea Rescue units and Docking was the first station to receive the new type, although the WTF soon hopped over to Bircham.

No.521 Squadron was one of the specialist units based at Docking; this unit re-formed at Docking in September 1943 and operated a variety of types on the Met task previously performed by No.1401 Flight. Flying aircraft that varied from Gladiators, which remained in use until nearly the end of the war, to Venturas, the squadron acquired the weather information upon which the operational units depended.

Wellingtons had been a frequent sight at Docking for much of the war and 415 Squadron operated the Wellington and the Albacore on detachment from Bircham during the first half of 1944. For a few weeks in July 1944 another specialist unit operated from this Norfolk airfield with the type; 524 Squadron had the task of hunting for E-boats off the coast of Holland – and having located targets, calling in strike aircraft. At the end of July the unit moved to Bircham Newton, bringing to an end the airfield's operational phase, except for limited use in the autumn by the Fleet Air Arm's Avenger-equipped 855 Squadron. However, it is likely that deployed aircraft still flew operational missions from here. The airfield's main task in the latter months of the war was training, albeit on a small scale, and it essentially reverted to its original role of being a satellite for Bircham Newton.

There was no post-war need for the airfield and its run-down was rapid, apparently passing from Coastal Command to No.54 (Training) Group in September 1945. This was little more than an administrative manoeuvre and, although Docking remained on the RAF's books for another decade, it gradually deteriorated until sold off in April 1958.

Airfield Data Dec 1944

Command:	RAF Coastal Command	Runway surface:	Grass
Function:	Operational Satellite	Hangars:	8 × Blister, one × A.1
Runways:	NE–SW 1,730yd	Dispersals:	nil
	E–W 1,400yd	Personnel:	Officers – 62 (2 WAAF)
	N–S 1,100yd		Other Ranks – 819 (90 WAAF)

235 Squadron were based at Docking from May to July 1942 flying Beaufighters.

Decoy Sites

Q	Burnham Sutton	TF840391
	Egmere	TF896386
Q	North Creake	TF896392

Units

1939–1945

53 Sqn	17 Feb 1943–17 Mar 1943	Whitley
143 Sqn	27 Jul 1942–27 Aug 1942	Blenheim
221 Sqn	25 Dec 1941–8 Jan 1942	Wellington
235 Sqn	31 May 1942–16 Jul 1942	Beaufighter
254 Sqn	10 Oct 1942–7 Nov 1942	Beaufighter
304 Sqn	2 Apr 1943–7 Jun 1943	Wellington
407 Sqn	10 Nov 1942–16 Feb 1943	Hudson, Wellington
415 Sqn det	Nov 1943–Jul 1944	Albacore, Wellington

502 Sqn	12 Jan 1942–22 Feb 1942	Whitley
521 Sqn	1 Sep 1943–30 Oct 1944	Gladiator, Hampden, Hudson, Ventura, Hurricane
524 Sqn	1–25 Jul 1944	Wellington
855 Sqn FAA	7–17 Aug 1944, 14 Sep 1944–13 Oct 1944	Avenger
1522 Flt	Oct 1941–16 Apr 1942	Oxford
1525 BATF	Jul 1942–May 1945	Oxford
2 ATC	Jun 1943–?	
Warwick TF	28 Jun 1943–3 Jul 1943	Warwick, Wellington
1401 Flt	25 Aug 1943–1 Sep 1943	Spitfire, Hampden
1693 Flt	31 May 1945–11 Aug 1945	Anson

DOWNHAM MARKET
(Bexwell)

UTM/grid: OS Map 143 – TF630036
Lat./Long.: N52°777736.32 E000/24.22
Nearest town: Downham Market 1 mile to west

County: Norfolk

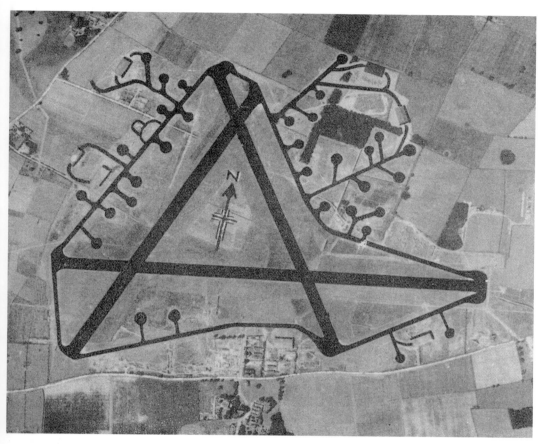

HISTORY

One of East Anglia's numerous bomber airfields, Downham Market started life in 1942 as a satellite for Marham and was soon playing an active part in the nightly bombing offensive over Germany. The airfield is also noteworthy as being a 'double VC' base, a record marked in a memorial in the churchyard opposite the remains of the airfield at Bexwell. Although this is only a small collection of buildings just east of Downham Market, the airfield was locally referred to a Bexwell (this may in part be due to the location at Bexwell of an emergency landing ground during World War One). Marham, some ten miles east, was a busy airfield by late-1941 and was in need of a suitable satellite for the new bomber-types entering

service, primarily the Stirlings with which 218 Squadron had been operating since January. With the decision to transfer Marham to Mosquito ops with No.2 Group, the heavies moved to Downham and it became home base for 218 Squadron from July. During an almost two-year association with the airfield, the Squadron's Stirlings operated as part of Main Force Bomber Command, within No.3 Group, which from late-1942 had become designated as a Stirling Group under Bomber Command's policy of concentrating a single aircraft-type in each operational Group.

The nightly bomber war called for ever increased effort and, despite the shortcomings of the Stirling as

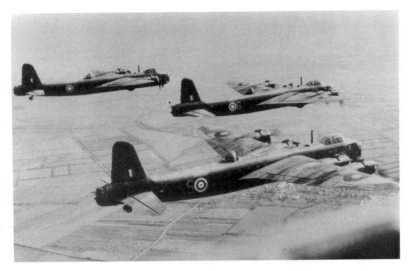

Stirlings operated from Downham Market from July 1942 to Mar 1944.

218 Squadron Stirling; as part of No.3 Group this Squadron spent almost two years operating from Downham.

a bomber, it was decided to form additional units; at Downham a new unit, 623 Squadron, formed around the nucleus of 218 Squadron's 'C Flight' in August 1943 – and flew its first operational mission the day it formed, 10 August. This squadron remained at Downham until December, when it was disbanded due to a shortage of Stirlings, its aircraft being distributed between the Heavy Conversion Units. The operational pace was maintained, however, by the arrival, for a few weeks, of 214 Squadron from Chedburgh, although this unit moved out again in mid-January.

Meanwhile, Downham had gained its first VC. On the night of 12–13 August 1943, Flight Sergeant Louis Aaron was awarded this highest gallantry medal for his heroics in getting his crippled aircraft to North Africa after a raid on Turin. The second VC came a year later, 8 August 1944, and was awarded to Squadron Leader Ian Bazalgette – a Master Bomber with the Pathfinder Force.

A major change came in February 1944, when Downham was transferred to the Pathfinder Force, joining No.8 Group with whom it remained for the rest of the war. This also brought a change of units, the airfield saying a sad farewell to 218 Squadron and the Stirling with the arrival, or rather the formation, of a new unit – 635 Squadron. This unit was formed by two Flights from experienced Pathfinder Lancaster squadrons ('B Flight' from 35 Squadron and 'C Flight' from 97 Squadron) and undertook its first operation

AIRFIELD DATA DEC 1944

Command:	RAF Bomber Command	Runway surface:	Concrete
Function:	Operational	Hangars:	3 × T.2 (Glider), 2 × T.2, one × B.1
Runways:	034 deg 1,400 × 50yd	Dispersals:	36 Frying Pan
	093 deg 1,900 × 50yd	Personnel:	Officers – 193 (8 WAAF)
	337 deg 1,400 × 50yd		Other Ranks – 1,852 (318 WAAF)

on the night of 22–23 March, a night when Main Force sent over 800 aircraft against Frankfurt. The Mosquito-equipped 571 Squadron formed at Downham Market on 7 April 1944, but flew no missions from here, moving instead to Oakington to become part of the Light Night Strike Force (LNSF). However, another Mosquito unit, 608 Squadron, formed on 1 August 1944, equipped with Mosquito XXs, though it also flew the MkXXV and the MkXVI. This Squadron, having disbanded in Italy, re-formed at the Norfolk base within No.8 Group, its task being nuisance bombing rather than path-finding; the increasing use of Mosquitoes of the LNSF for this role placed a massive strain on the German defences.

Downham completed its war with these two operational units, the final sorties being flown in late-April.

Within three months of the end of the war both squadrons had disbanded and Downham was closed to all flying in April 1946. The decision on post-war basing saw no role for the airfield and, whilst it was kept on the military rolls for another decade, it was finally disposed of in 1957. Little remains to be seen from the air, although the practised eye will pick up the overall shape of the airfield and at certain times of the year traces of the airfield surfaces can be seen; however, a number of buildings survive in use by light-commercial operations.

DECOY SITES

Q	South Acre	TF796122
Q	Wormegay	TF653125

UNITS

1939–1945

214 Sqn	10 Dec 1943–16 Jan 1944	Stirling
218 Sqn	7 Jul 1942–7 Mar 1944	Stirling
571 Sqn	7–22 Apr 1944	Mosquito
608 Sqn	1 Aug 1944–28 Aug 1945	Mosquito
623 Sqn	10 Aug 1943–6 Dec 1943	Stirling
635 Sqn	20 Mar 1944–1 Sep 1945	Lancaster

MEMORIALS

VC memorial in churchyard; the inscription is a long one, as it summarizes the two actions for which the awards were made.

EAST WRETHAM
Station 133

County: Norfolk

UTM/grid: OS Map 144 – TL910810
Lat./Long.: N52°28.16 E000°48.34
Nearest town: Thetford 6 miles to south-west

HISTORY

From the start of the war, Bomber Command adopted a policy of creating satellite airfields for its main bases, although this often involved little more than a suitable stretch of grass from which to operate the main bomber-types, such as the Wellington. The main purpose was to reduce the threat from air attack and East Wretham was typical of the sites chosen – an area reasonably close to the parent airfield, in this case Honington, and not requiring too much in the way of development; in other words no major ground works. The grass landing-ground was developed in late-1939/early 1940 and was given minimum facilities before it opened; first use was probably spring 1940, with Honington Wellingtons making brief visits. In September the first resident squadron moved in. No.311 (Czech) Squadron had been using the airfield for its training work-up since forming in July and to April 1942 this unit operated as part of

No. 3 Group, taking part in a wide range of operations with Main Force. At least twice during 1941 the airfield was on the receiving end of Luftwaffe bombs, although on both occasions it was by single aircraft dropping a small number of bombs and little damage was caused. A greater danger came from German night-intruders and in an area with so many airfields the raiders had little trouble finding targets, as airfields put lights on for returning bombers; the Squadron lost at least one aircraft to this cause – a Ju88 shooting down a Wellington on the night of 8–9 April 1941. The Czech Training Unit became No.1429 Flight in January 1942 and this unit's Wellingtons and Oxfords operated from East Wretham until July, when they moved to Woolfox Lodge. The operational squadron had already departed, as the airfield had been allocated to the Americans for use as a fighter field; in part this was

During its RAF operational period of 1940 to mid 1943 East Wretham was associated with the Wellington.

Wellingtons of 311 Squadron, a Czech bomber unit, operated from her from September 1940 to April 1942.

because of the increasing difficulty of maintaining the grass surface for bomber operations. However, before the change could be actioned it was postponed and another Wellington unit moved in – albeit as a temporary measure.

In November the Wellingtons of 115 Squadron arrived from Mildenhall; this squadron had been in the bomber war from 'day one' and had flown numerous ops with a variety of Wellington marks, the Mark III equipping the squadron by the time it arrived at East Wretham. By this time Bomber Command was in the throes of re-equipping with four-engine types and relegating the sturdy Wellington to other roles; in March 1943 the first Lancaster IIs arrived for 115

Squadron and these were soon in action over Germany, the squadron continuing to operate as part of Main Force. To fulfil the conversion task a Lancaster training-flight was formed, but a change in policy removed this type of unit from squadron control and created a new series of Heavy Conversion Units, the one at East Wretham becoming 1678 HCU. The almost constant moving of units in East Anglia at this period saw both Lancaster operators depart in August and the delayed handover to the USAAF take place.

There is some dispute as to the planned use of the airfield; some records mention a plan to create a Class A bomber-station complete with runways and

AIRFIELD DATA DEC 1944

Command:	US 8th AF	Runway surface:	Grass
Function:	Operational	Hangars:	6 × Blister, 2 × Bellman, 1 × Canvas – steel frame
Runways:	NE/SW 1,880yd	Dispersals:	24 × Macadam, 12 × Punched Planking
	NNW/SSE 1,400yd	Personnel:	Officers – 190
	N/S 1,400yd		Other Ranks – 1,709

infrastructure, whilst others suggest it was always destined to remain grass and would thus acquire fighters. The latter proved to be case and the 359th FG, equipped with P-47 Thunderbolts, took up residence in October 1943 under the command of Colonel Avelin P Tacon Jr. The unit had been activated in January and, after a period of training Stateside, had arrived in the UK in October, moving straight to East Wretham. After a period of theatre acclimatization, the Thunderbolts flew their first escort mission on 13 December. They remained operational from this Norfolk field to the end of the war, converting to the P-51 in May 1944. By VE Day they had flown 346 missions, claiming 253 aerial victories for the loss of 106 aircraft missing in action. Their combat record included one Distinguished Unit Citation, for defence of the bombers during the 11th September 1944 attack on Merseburg.

With the end of hostilities, the Group remained at its Norfolk base until November, before saying farewell to the local area and returning to the United States. Having passed back to the RAF, East Wretham was allocated to Fighter Command to become part of No.2 Group, although with no based units. In May 1946 it was transferred to Bomber Command but two months later the paper trail moved it again, this time to Technical Training Command. However, no-one had any real use for the airfield and it passed its final military days as a resettlement camp for the Poles. The bulk of the airfield area was sold in 1954 but parts were retained within an Army training range, now the Stanford Practical Training Area (subsequently STANTA). Part of it is in a bird reserve and can be visited; traces of the airfield include part of the old bomb-dump.

UNITS

1939–1945

115 Sqn	8 Nov 1942–6 Aug 1943	Wellington
311 Sqn	16 Sep 1940–28 Apr 1942	Wellington
1429 Flt	1 Jan 1942–26 Jun 1942	Wellington
1678 HCU	18 May 1943–6 Aug 1943	Lancaster

USAAF Units
359th FG (67th FW)

Squadrons:	368th FS, 369th FS, 370th FS
Aircraft:	P-47D, P-51B, P-51C, P-51D, P-51K
Dates:	Oct 1943–Nov 1945
Missions:	346
First mission:	13 Dec 1943
Last mission:	20 Apr 1945

MEMORIALS

Plaque on village war memorial (by the church) with inscription: 'This plaque commemorates the visit by survivors of the 359th Fighter Group in remembrance of those who served and died in the cause of freedom 3rd August 1985.' The cemetery of St Ethelberts also includes a group of gravestones to Czech personnel, plus two Poles.

The only memorial at East Wretham is a plaque to the 359th FG attached to the base of village's war memorial cross in the churchyard.

EYE
Station 134

County: Suffolk

UTM/grid: OS Map 144 – TM130750
Lat./Long.: N52°20.00 E001°08.00
Nearest town: Stowmarket 11 miles to south-south-west

Like many old airfields Eye now houses an industrial park, although from the air the pattern of runways and perimeter track is still very evident; September 2002.

HISTORY

As the USAAF's requirement for airfields in East Anglia increased with the decision to accelerate the rate of build-up of both bomber and fighter Groups, the need to acquire ever more tracts of suitable land led to the construction, in 1943, of this airfield within the 3rd Bombardment Division area. The airfield at Eye was a joint construction by American military engineers and British contractors and opened in early 1944 with a generally standard bomber-layout for four squadrons. However, the layout was unusual in that a section of spectacle hardstands was constructed to the west of the A140 Ipswich to Norwich road, as it was not practical to divert or close this road. By this stage of the war this was not a major problem but it did require sentries, extra security and closure to road traffic during operations!

Under the command of Colonel Lloyd H Watnee, the 490th Bomb Group had left the USA in early April, the air echelon flying the southern deployment route (via Africa) to the UK. Its B-24s duly arrived at Eye in the latter part of April and began the usual period of training and familiarization before being declared operational. This was short-lived and the Group undertook

its first mission on 31 May; this proved to be the first of some 158 missions, during which the unit lost twenty-two aircraft missing in action – one of the lowest percentage losses within the Division. The 3rd Air Division was designated to re-equip with the B-17 and the 490th duly received Fortresses from summer 1944. The airfield underwent little further development, although, as with most such bases, it was 'Americanized' in terms of the usage of buildings and the appearance of artwork inside buildings; sadly there appears to be little detail for Eye, unlike some of the region's airfields where wall murals survive.

The Group flew its last mission on 20 April and, after a few weeks of partying and training flying, the mass exodus back to the USA began; by late-August Eye was virtually a ghost town. The airfield was handed back to RAF Bomber Command in November 1945 but was essentially just another piece of real estate on the books and no use was made of the site; surprisingly, however, it was not part of the 1950s sell-off and was not disposed of until 1962–63. Parts of the airfield were returned to farmland but large areas were given over to industrial use.

Airfield Data Dec 1944

Command:	US 8th Air Force 3rd BD	Runway surface:	Screeded Finish
Function:	Operational	Hangars:	2 × T.2
Runways:	212 deg 2,000 × 50yd	Dispersals:	50 × Spectacle
	270 deg 1,400 × 50yd	Personnel:	Officers – 421
	328 deg 1,400 × 50yd		Other Ranks – 2,473

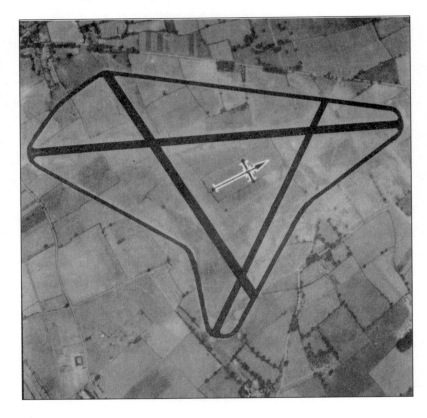

Units

1939–1945
USAAF Units
490th BG (93rd CBW)

Squadrons:	848th BS (Ratchet), 849th BS (Abrade), 850th BS (Baddog), 851st BS (Gotam)
Aircraft:	B-24H, B-24J, B-17G
Dates:	1 May 1944–Aug 1945
Missions:	158
First mission:	31 May 1944
Last mission:	20 Apr 1945

Memorials

Plaques on the wall adjacent to church gate.

The airfield at Eye under construction by US Engineers in June 1943. (US National Archives)

FELIXSTOWE (HMS *Beehive*)

County: Suffolk

UTM/grid: OS Map 169 – TM280330
Lat./Long.: N51°56.42 E001°19.00
Nearest town: Felixstowe

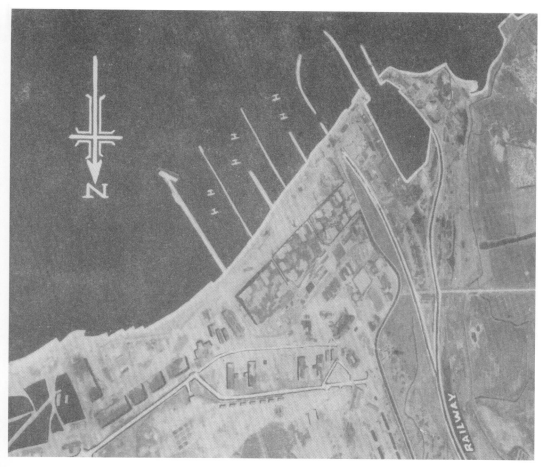

HISTORY

For a maritime county such as Suffolk, it was appropriate that one of its major military 'airfields' should be a seaplane base – and Felixstowe, a site now pretty much forgotten in military terms, was just such a site. Opened on 5 August 1913 as 'Sea Planes, Felixstowe', this Royal Naval Air Station was involved in both operational flying and trials work and it was with the latter that Felixstowe earns its place in British aviation annals. As an operational base its flying boats and seaplanes were involved with escorting shipping and anti-submarine patrols, as well as fighter patrols against German airship raids. From an early stage it was also involved in test and evaluation work with a variety of seaplanes and flying boats; indeed, its CO for much of the war, Commander J C Porte, went on to be closely involved in the development of new aircraft, such as the Porte Super Boat and Felixstowe Fury. In the latter months of the war the Station was incredibly busy, with a large number of Flights operating from its anchorages and slips, although pairs of these were combined in August 1918 to form squadrons. In 1913 the site had consisted of one short wooden-slipway and three sheds; by 1918 it comprised three large hangars, four slipways and a variety

Perth of 209 Squadron on
the slip; the Squadron was
here from May 1935 to
August 1939.

of temporary buildings covering thirty acres, making
it one of the largest and best developed air-stations of
the period.

The station was so well developed that it was an obvious candidate for retention in the post-war period; when
the final operational unit, 230 Squadron, moved to
Calshot in May 1922 the site was suddenly quiet,
although preparations were being made for the arrival of
the Marine and Armament Experimental Unit, which
duly moved in from Isle of Grain. The unit was renamed
the Marine Aircraft Experimental Establishment in
April 1924 and its task of testing all new types of flying
boat and seaplane – for RAF or civil use – was both
essential and fascinating. In common with the other
experimental establishments it also undertook research,
in this case into such topics as hulls, floats, engines and
marine craft. This unit remained the core of
Felixstowe's activities up to the outbreak of World War
Two and the part it played in the RAF's water-borne
activities cannot be overstated. It was not, however, the
only important unit at the station.

The RAF's High Speed Flight was established here
in 1926 and the following year was successful in winning the Schneider Trophy. This feat was repeated in
1929 and in 1931 – the latter, by Flight Lieutenant
Boothman, gave the RAF the trophy outright. There
was, of course, a more serious purpose to the HSF and
its work was of importance in aerodynamics and performance – the winning Supermarine S.6 donated
much to the later Spitfire.

It was during the 1930s that many of the temporary buildings were replaced by more permanent
structures and by 1935 it was home to a permanent
squadron – 209 as well as the MAEE. Aircraft flew
left-hand circuits over Harwich harbour and landing
permission was indicated by a green Aldis signal.

Plan of Felixstowe in 1916, an impressive base with its slipways and landing ground at Landguard Common.

Moorings comprised four RAF buoys and aircraft
were guided to the moorings by seaplane tender.

At the outbreak of World War Two the MAEE
moved to safer havens in the North and the operational squadron deployed to Invergordon, leaving
Felixstowe for new owners. The Navy took back what
they had once owned and the site became HMS
Beehive, although a number of RAF lodger-units
remained, such as No.26 Air Sea Rescue (Marine
Craft) Unit and No.85 MU, whose task it was to
recondition and store flying boats. The Navy didn't
want it for aircraft and instead it was home base for
almost forty motor-torpedo and motor-gun boats,
tasked with convoy protection as well as hunting
down their opposite numbers, the German E-Boats.
As far as aviation was concerned it saw a short period
of use in late-1940 by ex-Dutch Navy Fokker T8-Ws,
but its main use was post-March 1942 as a seaplane
repair/modification centre. This latter work was vital

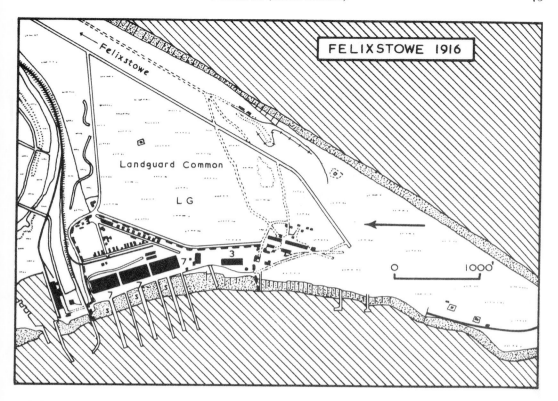

and most RAF types passed through Felixstowe, the MU also having the task of fitting special equipment such as Leigh Lights.

With the end of the war the MAEE returned and, with the RAF once more back in control, the station also took on the task of training flying-boat pilots, as well as becoming home to the Marine Craft Training School. After a brief but hectic period in the immediate post-war years, which included trials on airborne lifeboats, ex-German types and even jet flying-boats such as the Saro SR.A/1, the RAF's interest in flying boats waned and the MAEE was progressively reduced in size and importance.

The 1954 survey stated that 'for normal flying aircraft up to 60,000lb can generally take-off and alight in any direction' but it also detailed two alighting lanes: N/S at 2,000yd and E/W at 2,500yd. Water conditions were given as 'good throughout the year with moderate swell or chop during southerly gales'. Moorings comprised three standard aircraft buoys plus one warping buoy and a storm buoy at Harwich Harbour; in addition there were six Marine Craft moorings, these being used by No.1103 Marine Craft Unit. The large slipway was somewhat restrictive in that 'Solents and Sunderlands can only be beached or launched three hours either side of high tide' and

the fact that 'the apron was in a bad state of repair'. Lifting facilities comprised two gantries and one 50-ton crane. Six hangars of various sizes were available.

In April 1954 Felixstowe had transferred from Fighter Command ownership to No.27 Group of Technical Training Command and the departure of MAEE made room for two RAF Regiment squadrons, 63 and 194. However, two years later, aviation returned with the arrival of 'B Flight' of 22 Squadron, this unit's Whirlwind helicopters performing the SAR role from here until May 1961. The other element of the SAR capability, the Marine Craft Unit, had finally left in 1959. The final few years of the station's history saw it almost solely involved with the RAF Regiment, whose final departure, to Cosford in July 1962, brought to an end the military presence at one of Britain's premier marine stations.

UNITS

Pre-1919

230 Sqn	Aug 1918–7 May 1922	F2a, F3, H12, H16, F5, Fairey IIIb, Fairey IIIc
231 Sqn	Aug 1918–7 Jul 1919	F2a, F3, F5
232 Sqn	Aug 1918–5 Jan 1919	F2a, F3

Blackburn Shark K5607 in service with the MAEE, February 1936. The Marine Aircraft Experimental Unit/Establishment was a very important unit and Felixstowe's place in RAF history was significant because of the work conducted by this unit.

247 Sqn	20 Aug 1918–22 Jan 1919	F2a, F3
259 Sqn	Aug 1918–13 Sep 1919	F2a, F3
261 Sqn	20 Aug 1918–13 Sep 1919	F2a, F3
327 (FB) Flt	May 1918–Aug 1918	F2a
328 (FB) Flt	May 1918–Aug 1918	F2a
329 (FB) Flt	30 May 1918–Aug 1918	F2a
330 (FB) Flt	30 May 1918–Aug 1918	F2a
333 (FB) Flt	31 May 1918–Aug 1918	F2a
334 (FB) Flt	31 May 1918–Aug 1918	F2a
335 (FB) Flt	15 Jun 1918–Aug 1918	F2a
336 (FB) Flt	31 Jul 1918–Aug 1918	F2a
337 (FB) Flt	15 Sep 1918–?	F2a

4 CS	6 Jan 1919–1919	

1920–1939

209 Sqn	1 May 1935–19 Sep 1937,	Southampton,
	17 Dec 1937–27 Aug 1939	Perth, London,
		Singapore,
		Stranraer

210 Sqn	1 Mar 1931–15 Jun 1931	Southampton
MAEU/E	17 Mar 1923–21 Sep 1939	various
FBDF	1 May 1924–1932	various
HSF	1926–Jul 1927,	various
	Apr 1928–18 Sep 1928,	
	Nov 1928–Apr 1929	

Post-1945

22 Sqn	May 1956–29 May 1961	Whirlwind
MAEE	1 Aug 1945–Aug 1954	various

MEMORIALS

Plaque at Town Hall with inscription: 'In commemoration of a long and happy association between Royal Air Force Felixstowe and local townspeople. 1913–1962.'

FELTWELL

County: Norfolk

UTM/grid: OS Map 143 – TL710900
Lat./Long.: N52°28.43 E000°31.00
Nearest town: Brandon 5 miles to south-east

HISTORY

The earliest use of Feltwell was in the latter part of World War One, when a field in the area was used as a temporary base by a number of RAF training units, the most significant of which were No.7 Training Depot Station, Midland Area Flying Instructors' School and finally, the Northern Area Flying Instructors' School. The latter probably remained to early 1920, when it disbanded and the landing ground was abandoned. There appears to be little record of the 'airfield' at this time and there is debate as to what happened to it between 1920 and the early 1930s, when the site was chosen for an expansion-period airfield. Laid out on the edge of Feltwell Fen, the oval of grass was provided with a semi-circle of C-type hangars on its northern edge and the, by then, usual array of administrative and technical buildings, as well as accommodation for almost 2,000 personnel.

RAF Station Feltwell opened on 12 March 1937 under the command of Wing Commander L H Slatter OBE DSC DFC and the following month received its complement of two bomber squadrons within No.3 Group; in fact, only one unit arrived – 214 Squadron from Scampton with its Harrow IIs, the second unit, 37 Squadron, being created from 'B Flight' of 214. The Harrows were, in theory at least, heavy bombers and, despite their antiquated appearance and performance, were amongst the RAF's most modern equipment. Fortunately both squadrons re-equipped with Wellingtons before the start of the war

Harrows lined up outside the hangars shortly after Feltwell opened in 1937. This was very nearly one of the bomber types with which the RAF went to war.

and it was the Wellington with which Feltwell was most associated during its wartime career.

As the sole operational resident by September 1939, the honour of opening Feltwell's operational career fell to 37 Squadron, the Wellingtons going into action on the first day of the war. For the next three years, Feltwell's Wellingtons were part of Bomber Command's night war and, whilst squadrons changed during that period, the routine at the airfield remained constant – including bombers and their crews that failed to return. Inevitably with bombs and fuel being handled there was scope for accidents and few RAF airfields escaped without at least one major incident – Feltwell's occurred on 3 August 1940 when Wellington L7781 blew up.

The airfield was home to the New Zealand Training Flight from early 1940; this was expanded to become an operational unit, as 75 (NZ) Squadron in April, joining 37 Squadron in Main Force and giving Feltwell the standard establishment of two bomber-squadrons. Later in the year, 57 Squadron arrived and 37 Squadron left for Malta – an experienced outfit being sent to an area in need of bomber support. One of very few recorded attacks on the station took place on 27 October, when a hangar caught fire and some other minor damage was caused; at least two similar single-aircraft raids were recorded in 1941.

In July 1941, Feltwell joined the ranks of VC stations when Sergeant J Ward of 75 Squadron

received this highest gallantry award for his actions on the night of 7–8 July. Methwold was acquired as a satellite airfield and, under the Bomber Command re-organization, Feltwell became a Base Station. However, a major change occurred in summer 1942 with the transfer of the aerodrome to No.2 Group, meaning that the Wellingtons had to move out to make way for new medium-bomber units. This was the period when the Group was introducing new aircraft and for Feltwell this meant the Lockheed Ventura; both new units, 487 Squadron RNZAF and 464 Squadron RAAF, spent much of the rest of the year on work-up with this new type, as did 21 Squadron at nearby Methwold. Operational debut came on 6 December with the dramatic and effective low-level attack on the Philips radio works at Eindhoven, Holland. After a series of Circus missions the two units departed in April 1943, as No.3 Group re-acquired the airfield.

Although one operational squadron used Feltwell for much of 1943, the airfield's major role for the rest of the war was a base for training and support units, including a number of specialist organizations. The Radio Countermeasures aircraft of 192 Squadron were here from April to November 1943, supported by No.1473 Flight and the Bomber Development Unit (BDU), but it was the training role performed by No.3 Lancaster Finishing School that dominated 1944. This unit was responsible for Lancaster conver-

AIRFIELD DATA DEC 1944

Command:	RAF Bomber Command	Runway surface:	Grass
Function:	Operational	Hangars:	5 × C
Runways:	E/W 1,800yd	Dispersals:	20 × Pan
	NE/SW 1,400yd	Personnel:	Officers – 126 (9 WAAF)
	NW/SE 1,200yd		Other Ranks – 1,712 (349 WAAF)

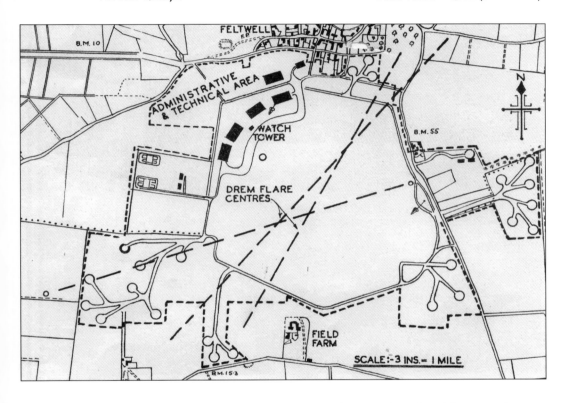

sion of all crews destined for No.3 Group's operational squadrons and in fourteen months at Feltwell it passed out hundreds of aircrew after a short but intensive course on the Lanc. The decision to locate this unit at Feltwell may have had something to do with the fact that it was still a grass airfield, the surface of which was unsuitable for heavily-laden operational four-engine types. With the requirement for new crews much reduced, the LFS disbanded at the end of January 1945. Training continued in the shape of the G-H Flight to train navigators in the use of new long-range navigation equipment; in February the BDU returned and continued its trials work, which included the new Avro Lincoln, as well as air-to-air refuelling.

Whilst units moved around post-war, the airfield was retained, transferring to Flying Training Command in April 1946 and becoming home to No.3 Flying Training School from South Cerney. Instead of bombers the circuit pattern over the fens now buzzed with Tiger Moths, Harvards and Prentices, as student pilots learnt their trade.

The 1954 survey detailed two runways, comprising a Sommerfeld Track strip of 4,200ft oriented 076/256 degrees and a grass strip of 4,500ft oriented 043/223 degrees. A third potential strip was mentioned but to provide this 9,000ft strip would involve 'very heavy grading, severing the B1112 and the demolition of a bungalow, house and bakery'. The airfield had underground storage for 144,000 gallons of aviation fuel (twelve 12,000-gallon tanks) and dispersals comprised sixteen 'round type' (125ft diameter) and a 180,000sq ft apron.

The School closed in April 1958 and the station

A Thor missile site, for 77 Squadron, was constructed on part of the part of the airfield site in the late 1950s; this November 1958 shot shows one of the launch pads.

reverted to Bomber Command for its final 'operational' phase of activity as part of the RAF's strategic missile force. Between September 1958 and August 1963, Feltwell was a major part of the Thor IRBM network, housing the Command Strategic Missile School in addition to being HQ for five Thor squadrons (77, 82, 107, 113 and 220) and home base for the three launchers of 77 Squadron.

Since the departure of the missiles in 1963, the airfield has housed a variety of units, from the Officer Cadet Training Unit that moved in from Jurby to the present occupants from the USAAF – whose activities are kept a secret! Feltwell's primary unit is Space Command's 5th Space Surveillance Squadron and the airfield is parented by Lakenheath.

DECOY SITES

Q	Brandon	TL7886
	Eriswell	TL746797
Q/K	Lakenheath	TL735814
Q	Lakenheath Warren	TL765804
Q	Southery	TL672948
Q/K	Stanford Warren	TL735814

UNITS

Pre-1919

7 TDS	1 Nov 1917–22 Apr 1919	
NA FIS	Jul 1918–Mar 1920	
MA FIS	22 Apr 1919–1919	

1920–1938

| 37 Sqn | 26 Apr 1937–30 Nov 1940 | Harrow, Wellington |

| 214 Sqn | 12 Apr 1937–3 Sep 1939 | Harrow, Wellington |

1939–1945

57 Sqn	20 Nov 1940–5 Jan 1942	Wellington
75 Sqn	4 Apr 1940–15 Aug 1942	Wellington
192 Sqn	5 Apr 1943–25 Nov 1943	Halifax, Mosquito, Wellington
464 Sqn	1 Sep 1942–3 Apr 1943	Ventura
487 Sqn	15 Aug 1942–3 Apr 1943	Ventura
NZ Flt	12 Feb 1940–4 Apr 1940	
BCSMS	3 Jan 1941–30 Nov 1962	
1519 Flt	Dec 1941–3 Jul 1945	Oxford
BDU	6 Apr 1943–13 Sep 1943, 7 Dec 1943–25 Feb 1945	Various
1473 Flt	14 Sep 1943–28 Nov 1943	Anson, Wellington
3 LFS	21 Nov 1943–31 Jan 1945	Lancaster
BCRS	29 Dec 1944–Sep 1946	
G-H TF	29 Dec 1944–5 Jun 1945	Lancaster
1688 Flt	25 Feb 1945–19 Mar 1946	Spitfire, Hurrricane

Post-1945

77 Sqn	1 Sep 1958–10 Jul 1963	Thor SSM
651 Sqn	1 Apr 1947–1 Sep 1957	Auster
3 FTS	Apr 1946–31 May 1958	
1903 Flt	30 Jan 1956–Nov 1956	Auster
1913 Flt	1 Apr 1957–1 Sep 1957, Mar 1957–1 Sep 1957	Auster

FERSFIELD (Winsfarthing) Station 140

County: Suffolk

UTM/grid: OS Map 144 – TM080850
Lat./Long.: N52°25.23 E001°03.15
Nearest town: Norwich 16 miles to north-east

The perimeter track, and traces of the runways, make the site at Fersfield easy to spot from the air, as seen here in June 2003.

HISTORY

Of all the airfields in East Anglia Fersfield is one of the strangest, as it has very little of a history but was home to one of the most fascinating projects of the later war-years. This Suffolk location was constructed as a standard bomber-airfield during 1943 and was destined for a full USAF Bomb Group of four squadrons. The airfield opened in July 1944 as Station 140 and was allocated to the 388th BG, based at nearby Knettishall. Fersfield was a remote location and this was probably the main reason for its selection as a base for the highly secret Project Aphrodite and the reason why the 388th had two airfields.

The only operational use of Fersfield was by the Aphrodite detachment, the Bomb Group having been selected to crew war-weary bombers – B-17s packed with up to 20,000lb of explosive to turn them into flying bombs. With a crew of two the idea was

for the aircraft to be flown to the coast, at which point the crew would bale out and be picked up, whilst the 'bomb', now under radio control from another aircraft, would fly on and be guided in to destroy heavily defended targets. Whilst the idea was sound, the execution left much to be desired and whilst almost twenty such missions were flown, none was a success; by the end of 1944 the project had been abandoned. If the general war situation had not been favourable it is likely that the idea would have been refined and that it could have been made viable. Thus, as an operational airfield for almost a year, Fersfield has the distinction of flying the smallest number of operational missions but also of being one of the most closely guarded secrets of the war.

The airfield was handed to the RAF and was allocated to No.2 Group, by then part of the Tactical Air

AIRFIELD DATA DEC 1944

Command:	US 8th AF	Runway surface:	Concrete
Function:	Not assigned	Hangars:	2 × T.2
Runways:	066 deg 2,000 × 50yd	Dispersals:	50 × Spectacle
	186 deg 1,400 × 50yd	Personnel:	Officers – 421
	304 deg 1,400 × 50yd		Other Ranks – 2,473

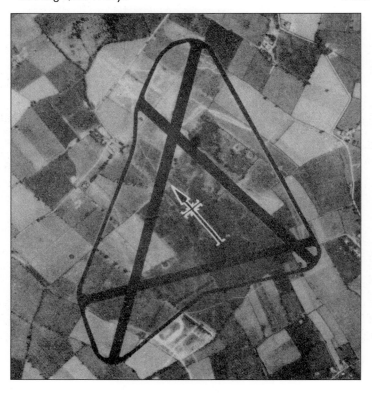

Force, and was primarily used as a reserve base, although a few operations were flown from here by the Group's Support Unit in December. Its secretive location – and nearness to the East coast – made it ideal for one more special task: three Mosquito squadrons staged here before making the dramatic attack on the Gestapo HQ in Copenhagen on 21 March 1945.

In the immediate post-war period the airfield received a number of Mosquito squadrons but at least one of these, 140 Squadron, is recorded as having no aircraft. The main occupants were the Group training and support units, the latter becoming the Group Disbandment Centre in August, tasked with disbanding No.2 Group units. This task was soon over and the site was put up for disposal, rapidly returning to agriculture. Little trace now remains, although the airfield can be discerned from the air and a ground tour reveals crumbling remains of buildings, most of which will soon have vanished.

UNITS

1939–1945

107 Sqn	3–10 Jul 1945	Mosquito
140 Sqn	9–12 Jul 1945,	Mosquito
	19 Sep 1945–10 Nov 1945	
180 Sqn	7–14 Jun 1945	Mosquito
2 Gp TF/SU	Dec 1944–31 Dec 1945	

USAAF Units
388th BG

Squadrons:	Det for Project Aphrodite and Project Batty
Aircraft:	B-17
Dates:	12 Jul 1944–1 Jan 1945

FOULSHAM

County: Norfolk

UTM/grid: OS Map 133 – TG027270
Lat./Long.: N52°48.1 E001/0°.3
Nearest town: East Dereham 8.5 miles to south-west

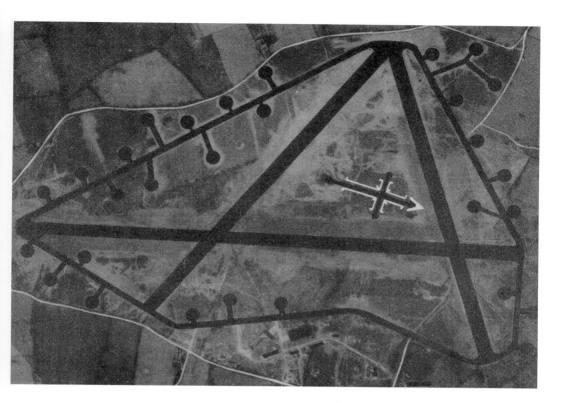

HISTORY

Foulsham is not remembered as one of the 'famous' airfields of East Anglia, but it does hold a place in RAF history as the base for the first RAF operators of the B-25 Mitchell – although the association was not necessarily fortuitous, as both the aircraft and the airfield proved problematical. The site in North Norfolk had been selected in 1940 and work on constructing a bomber airfield commenced the following year, the intention being to allocate it to No.2 Group for use by medium bombers, as it was only a few miles north of Swanton Morley. As only semi-permanent structures were built, including a number of T.2 hangars, the airfield opened in May 1942 but it was decided by the opening-up party that it was not ready to receive operational aircraft. Although there may have been limited use of the landing area it was not until October that Foulsham received its resident units, with the arrival of 98 Squadron and 180

Squadron; both had formed at West Raynham in September to operate one of the new medium-bomber types acquired by No.2 Group. By early 1942 the re-equipment programme was underway, as a variety of American types were entering service to replace the long-serving and long-suffering Blenheims; the B-25 Mitchell duly arrived at Foulsham and the conversion and work-up commenced, the intention being to have the squadrons operational at the earliest opportunity.

Intensive flying was the order of the day and, despite the inevitable serviceability and spares problems of any new type, reasonable progress was made; however, the armament of the Mitchell was somewhat more problematic and various modifications had to be adopted before the type could be considered operationally ready. As the winter of 1942 wore on crews were also frustrated by the condition of

AIRFIELD DATA DEC 1944

Command:	RAF Bomber Command	Runway surface:	Tar and wood-chips
Function:	Operational	Hangars:	9 × T.2, one × B.1
Runways:	190 deg 1,900 × 50yd	Dispersals:	36 × Heavy Bomber
	260 deg 1,400 × 50yd	Personnel:	Officers – 110 (9 WAAF)
	326 deg 1,350 × 50yd		Other Ranks – 2,380 (346 WAAF)

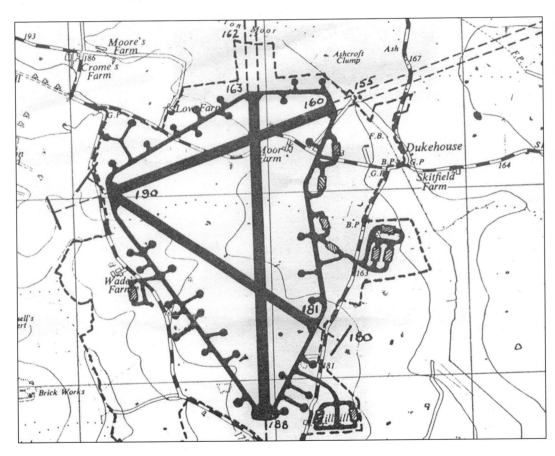

the airfield surface, caused by Foulsham's mud. Although the first missions were flown in January 1943, it was spring before the Mitchells began to play a full part in the bombing of occupied Europe, by which time Foulsham had acquired Attlebridge as a satellite. Almost before their campaign had started, it was brought to an end, at least as far as Foulsham was concerned, with a move to Dunsfold – part of what was to be a major re-organization of units and airfields in preparation for the planned invasion of Europe in 1944. The airfield had fleetingly moved from Bomber Command to Fighter Command in June 1943 but in

September it moved back again and was handed over to No.3 Group. The same month saw the arrival of two Lancaster units, 514 Squadron forming here and eventually flying its first operational missions on 3 November, before departing to Waterbeach three weeks later. The second Lancaster unit, 1678 HCU was established to train crews for the operational squadron and when the latter left so too did the conversion unit. This move was generated by a decision to concentrate Bomber Command's most secretive organization in this corner of Norfolk.

The first of the Radio Counter Measures units to

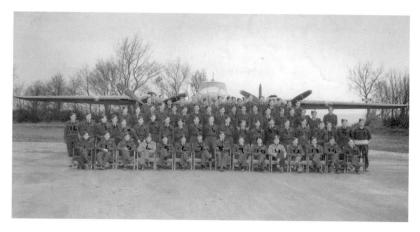

98 Squadron personnel pose with a Mitchell in January 1943; the Squadron operated the type from Foulsham October 1942 to August 1943.

arrive was 192 Squadron from Feltwell in late-November; it was equipped with a variety of aircraft types, most of which sported unusual aerials and equipment for their task of listening to and deceiving the German radio and radar forces. With the formation of No.100 Group, Foulsham joined the new organization in December and retained this Special Duties role to the end of the war. A number of other units connected with this work operated from Foulsham: for example, No.1473 Flight arrived in December on joining the Group and effectively became 'C Flight' of 192 Squadron.

April 1944 saw the arrival of the Special Duty Radar Development Unit, which was almost immediately renamed the Bomber Support Development Unit (BSDU). This was one of a number of unsung trials and development units that played crucial roles in supporting the operational squadrons and developing equipment and tactics. Such was the importance of the RCM units to the bomber war that Foulsham was one of the limited number of airfields to be equipped with the fog-dispersing FIDO system during 1944. The USAAF operated a detachment of the 7th Photographic Group, attached to 192 Squadron, from Foulsham from August 1944 to the end of the following March, but the exact nature of their work, for which they flew special F-5 version of the P-38 Lightning, is uncertain. With the departure of the BSDU in late-1944 the airfield became home to the Australian 462 Squadron, this Halifax-equipped and experienced bomber-unit having been transferred to No.100 Group. Both operational squadrons were fully engaged in the final months of the war providing support to Main Force as well as undertaking a number of special missions. As far as the airfield itself was concerned little had changed, other than that there was less mud, as runways had been consolidated with a tar and wood-chip surface and dispersal areas had been improved. Most buildings were still of a temporary

nature and the most distinctive features were the nine T.2 hangars, a number of which still survive at the site.

With the end of the war Foulsham's temporary nature meant that it had little future; the flying units had gone by autumn 1945 and in November the station was handed to No.40 Group and for a short period was administered by 258 MU. It remained on the books for some while but was finally sold off, returning back to the agricultural land from whence it came. Driving around the lanes you can still glimpse a T.2 hangar, a stretch of runway or faint traces of other structures.

DECOY SITE

Q/K	Fulmodestone	TG009306

UNITS

1939–1945

Unit	Dates	Aircraft
98 Sqn	15 Oct 1942–18 Aug 1943	B-25
180 Sqn	19 Oct 1942–18 Aug 1943	B-25
192 Sqn	25 Nov 1943–22 Aug 1945	Halifax, Wellington, Mosquito
462 Sqn	29 Dec 1944–24 Sep 1945	Halifax
514 Sqn	1 Sep 1943–23 Nov 1943	Lancaster
12 GMS	Apr 1943–Mar 1944	Horsa
1678 HCU	16 Sep 1943–Dec 1943	Lancaster
1473 Flt	12 Dec 1943–1 Feb 1944	
BSDU	17 Apr 1944–23 Dec 1944	Mosquito
7th PRG det	Aug 1944–Mar 1945	F-5

MEMORIALS

1. Plaque in church.

2. Plaques at base of village sign.

FRAMLINGHAM (Parham) Station 153

UTM/grid: OS Map 156 – TM330605
Lat./Long.: N52°11.38 E001°24.30
Nearest town: Framlingham 3 miles to north-west

County: Suffolk

May 2002 aerial shot of Framlingham showing that the airfield is still distinctive from the air.

HISTORY

Although officially known as Framlingham, the airfield was also referred to as Parham, this being the nearest village to the actual site of the airfield; this situation was not unusual and the decision was sometimes based on the location of the nearest railway station – this being the main means of transport for most personnel during this period – or because of possible name confusion with another airfield. It is interesting to note that the Germans also called it Parham; it is given this name on the Luftwaffe target map.

Framlingham was another of the Class A airfields constructed in 1942 for the influx of heavy bombers from the United States and, as such, it was to the American standard with three hard-runways and a perimeter track linking the fifty loop-type dispersal points. Buildings were kept to a minimum and the

largest were the two T.2 hangars, whilst one of the most substantial buildings was the control tower; most other structures were of a more temporary nature and the area on and around the airfield sprouted the usual conglomerations of Nissen huts. When the B-17s of the 95th Bomb Group touched down on this stretch of Suffolk countryside in May 1943, the airfield was still not fully ready; nevertheless, they flew their first operational mission on the 13th of the month. Four weeks later disaster struck the Group when it lost half of its attacking force during a mission to Kiel; this was a heavy blow to the new Group and it was decided to move them to another airfield to rebuild both strength and confidence before they could return to the battle.

On 14 July Colonel Edgar M Wittan brought the 390th Bomb Group to Framlingham and 'Wittan's

AIRFIELD DATA DEC 1944

Command:	US 8th AF 3rd BD	Runway surface:	Concrete, tar and wood-chips
Function:	Operational	Hangars:	2 × T.2
Runways:	173 deg 1,400 × 50yd	Dispersals:	50 × Loop
	234 deg 1,400 × 50yd	Personnel:	Officers – 421
	282 deg 2,000 × 50yd		Other Ranks – 2,473

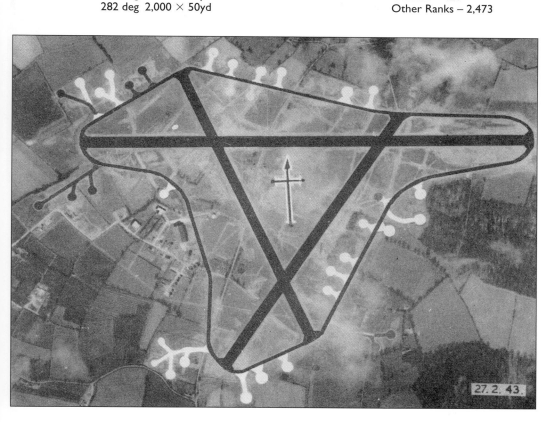

Wallopers' were to remain operational from this airfield to the end of the war. This B-17 unit had been activated in January 1943 and, on arrival in the UK, was allocated to the 4th Bombardment Wing of VIIIth Bomber Command, although the designations soon changed and it became part of the 3rd Bombardment Division. The Group flew its first mission on 12 August and in its wartime career recorded 300 missions for the loss of 144 aircraft missing in action. Almost every bomber airfield had at least one wartime disaster and for Framlingham this came late in December 1944, when a fully laden B-17 crashed on take-off, exploding – with the loss of the crew – and damaging almost every house in the village of Parham. In addition to the all too frequent task of

removing dead or wounded crewmen from aircraft, this type of incident brought the realities of war home to many an airfield. The Group received two Distinguished Unit Citations for its ops from Framlingham: one gained on 17 August 1943 for a Regensburg mission and one on 14 October the same year when the target was Schweinfurt. Also worthy of note is that Hewitt Dunn, one of the 390th's crewmen, was the only man in the 8th Air Force's bomber units to fly 100 missions.

With the end of the war an airfield that once hummed with the activity associated with four squadrons of B-17s, and a local area that had become used to base dances and the presence of American servicemen in pubs and villages, became silent almost

B-17 of the 390th BG being
prepared for another
mission, 20 August 1943.
(US National Archives)

Aircrew prepare maps and target information for a daylight
mission; the 390th BG flew 300 missions from
Framlingham.

overnight when the 390th returned to the United
States in August 1945. The airfield was briefly used
as a repatriation centre for Polish nationals but
most of the site was soon back under agriculture,
although it was not until the early 1960s that leasing
of land became selling of land. Amongst the landowners were some with an interest in the site's aviation
heritage and, in due course, a preservation group was
created, which led to the restoration of the control
tower and the establishment of the 390th Bomb
Group Memorial Museum. Since its opening in May
1981 the museum has expanded its exhibits, including
acquiring a Blister hangar, and is a fine tribute to the
history of one of East Anglia's American bases.

UNITS

1939–1945
USAAF Units
95th BG

Squadrons	334th BS, 335th BS, 336th BS, 412th BS
Aircraft	B-17
Dates	12 May 1943–15 Jun 1943

390th BG (13th CW)

Identifying letter:	J
Nickname:	Wittan's Wallopers
Squadrons:	568th BS (Cavort), 569th BS (Boaster), 570th BS (Anteat), 571st BS (Longshore)
Aircraft:	B-17F, B-17G
Dates:	Jul 1943–Aug 1945
Missions:	300
First mission:	12 Aug 1943
Last mission:	20 Apr 1945

MEMORIALS

1. Plaque on wall of control tower with inscription:
'This memorial honours the men of the 390th Bomb
Group (H) who gave their lives during the period
1943–1945, operating from Station 153, Parham.
Dedicated May 1981.'

2. 390th BG Memorial Museum in the tower and
surrounding buildings.

GREAT ASHFIELD
Station 155

County: Suffolk

UTM/grid: OS Map 155 – TM010665
Lat./Long.: N52°15.15 E000°56.45
Nearest town: Bury St Edmunds 10 miles to west

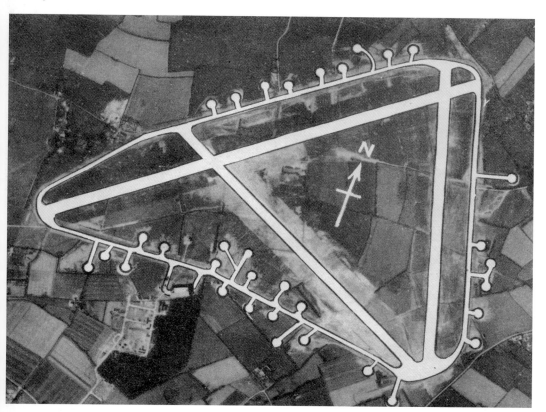

HISTORY

Constructed by John Laing & Son in 1942, Great Ashfield was laid out to standard Class A requirements in terms of runways, except that runway 13/31 was 1,500 yards long rather than the normal 1,400 yards – although there does not seem to have been any particular reason for this. The original plan appears to have been to allocate the airfield to a Heavy Conversion Unit and thirty-three frying-pan dispersals were laid out. However, the decision to assign it to the Americans meant that it was given additional dispersals, up to the standard fifty for a USAAF heavy-bomber base. However, the first aircraft to use the runways were Stirlings of No.1651 Conversion Unit based at Waterbeach, but this was on an opportunity basis pending the arrival of the airfield's designated resident unit.

The B-17s of 'Vans Valiants', the 385th Bomb Group being named after their first CO, Colonel Elliott Vandevanter, arrived at Great Ashfield in late-June 1943 and three weeks later flew their first bombing mission as part of 4th Bombardment Wing. The airfield was transferred to the USAAF in August and the 385th was to be the sole operational unit to use Great Ashfield; by the time they flew their last mission on 20 April 1945 the Group had recorded 296 missions for the loss of 129 aircraft missing in action. This loss rate and the statistics of over 18,000 tons of bombs and nearly 300 enemy aircraft claimed as destroyed were fairly average, but it is important to put such bare numbers into perspective. Great Ashfield was a community of 3,000, whose task it was to carry the war to the enemy on a daily basis and for

AIRFIELD DATA DEC 1944

Command:	US 8th AF 3rd BD	Runway surface:	Concrete and wood-chippings
Function:	Operational	Hangars:	2 × T.2
Runways:	068 deg 2,000 × 50yd	Dispersals:	33 × Frying Pan, 17 × Spectacle
	132 deg 1,500 × 50yd	Personnel:	Officers – 421
	360 deg 1,400 × 50yd		Other Ranks – 2,473

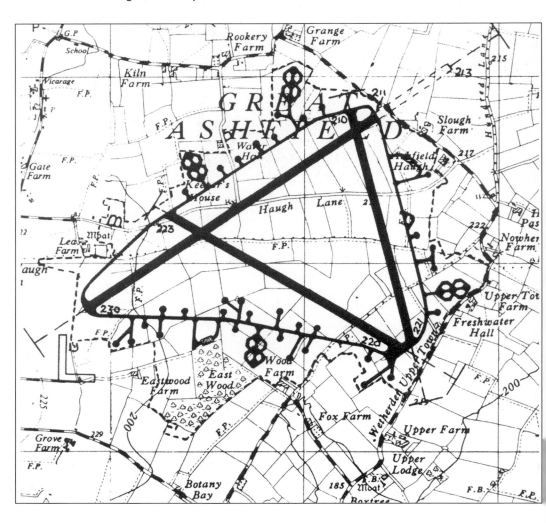

whom there was that strange, almost unreal combina-
tion of everyday life on base and in the local
community mixed with the loss of comrades. During
its operational career the Group received two
Distinguished Unit Citations, for Regensburg on 17
August 1943 and Zwickau on 12 May 1944. Very few
of the USAAF bases in Britain came under enemy

air-attack, so the intruder that bombed Great
Ashfield on the night of 22–23 May 1944 provided
an incident worthy of record – especially as its bombs
hit a hangar and destroyed a B-17.

With the end of the war the 385th quickly abandoned the airfield, the air echelon flying out in late-
June and the entire American presence having ended

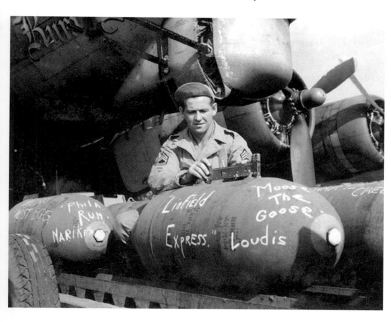

550th BS B-17 of the 385th BG – with messages scrawled on bombs, a tradition that most bomber units upheld.

by early August. The airfield was returned to RAF control and was used by maintenance units for bomb storage until it was closed and sold in 1959–60.

The site has been returned to agricultural use and there is little evidence of its wartime usage other than a few strips of concrete.

Decoy Sites

Q	Gislingham	TM064731
Q	Ixworth	TL948714

Units

1939–1945
USAAF Units
385th BG (4th CBW/93rd CBW)

Identifying letter:	G
Nickname:	Van's Valiants
Squadrons:	548th BS (Summer), 549th BS (Fancyfrock), 550th BS (Alfrek), 551st BS (Boston)
Aircraft:	B-17F, B-17G
Dates:	Jun 1943–Aug 1945
Missions:	296
First mission:	17 Jul 1943
Last mission:	20 Apr 1945

Memorials

1. In village churchyard with inscription: 'In memoriam of the officers and men of the 385th Heavy Bombardment Group US Army Air Force who gave their lives in the air battles over Europe 1943–1944. This plaque is placed here by the comrades of those men as an everlasting tribute to their heroic sacrifice and unselfish devotion to duty.'

2. Roll of Honour in church plus memorial altar.

3. Village sign shows a B-17.

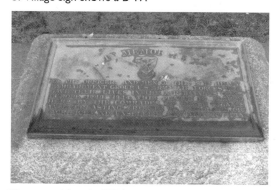

The memorial to the 385th is situated in the village churchyard.

GREAT MASSINGHAM

County: Norfolk

UTM/grid: OS Map 132 – TF805235
Lat./Long.: N52°46.47 E000°40.56
Nearest town: Fakenham 7.5 miles to east-north-east

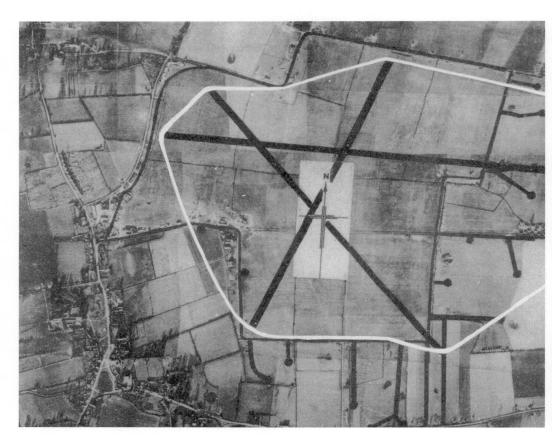

HISTORY

This patch of Norfolk countryside was requisitioned in 1940 to become a satellite airfield for nearby West Raynham and, as such, it was given little in the way of facilities; the area was cleared of hedges and trees, a few ditches were filled and with the erection of a number of temporary buildings – and tents – Great Massingham was ready to receive aircraft of No.2 Group. The airfield opened in July and before the first squadron moved in on a permanent basis, 18 Squadron with its Blenheims from Raynham, it was almost certainly used on a temporary basis, although records for this type of activity are scarce. The Blenheims were operational immediately, as the Squadron had been flying the type since the start of the war. Whilst there was some improvement in

facilities over the ensuing months, including the erection of Blister hangars, Massingham was still a basic airfield when the Squadron departed in April 1941. The new residents, 107 Squadron, operated the same type, although the airfield also witnessed a short period of work-up and evaluation by the Fortress Is (B-17s) of 90 Squadron.

With the Blenheim at the end of its operational life, the light-bomber squadrons of No.2 Group received new aircraft; in the case of 107 Squadron this was the arrival in early 1942 of Boston IIIs, one of the better aircraft acquired by the Group for low-level intruder type work, the first operation being flown on 8 March. The unit was primarily tasked with Circus and Ramrod missions over occupied

90 Squadron flew its B-17 Fortress Is out of Great Massingham for a few weeks in summer 1941.

A number of buildings survive at the site, including hangars and the control tower.

specialized Flights. This was part of a general re-organization of Norfolk's airfields to make room for the squadrons of this specialist Group. No.1692 Bomber Support Training Flight was equipped with Beaufighters and was responsible for training night-intruder crews during short but intensive courses. They were joined in June 1944 by the Mosquitoes of 169 Squadron from Little Snoring and Massingham was very much back in the front line. These intruder Mossies flew from here for the rest of the war. The night-time forays of these specially equipped aircraft took a steady toll on German night-fighters and were an integral party of the strategy designed to reduce bomber losses; indeed the Squadron's motto on its badge was 'hunt and destroy.'

Post-war the flying units soon disbanded and although the Central Fighter Establishment (CFE) spent a year here – and brought a variety of aircraft – they too had gone by December 1946. The airfield was maintained as an RLG for West Raynham but there was really no need for two airfields only a few miles apart; indeed, such closeness was more of a liability and Great Massingham closed its runways as the 1950s opened. The site was sold off in April 1958 and became farmland. A number of wartime structures survive, including the tower and a hangar, and a windsock still flies, as a stretch of the field is used by light aircraft. A public road now follows part of the old perimeter track and makes for an atmospheric drive as you strive for a glimpse of surviving buildings and imagine the Blenheims, Bostons and Mosquitoes that once trundled around this corner of Norfolk.

Europe, the intention being to encourage interception by the Luftwaffe who could then, it was hoped, be destroyed by the escorting fighters! A second Boston unit, the French 342 Squadron, was based at Massingham from July to September but its departure, which had been preceded by that of 107 Squadron, left the airfield with no operational unit – an ideal time for a rebuild. This departure phase also included the mixed equipment of the Bombing and Gunnery Flight, a unit whose main base was West Raynham but who made frequent use of Great Massingham.

Following this major reconstruction work, including three concrete-runways, the longest of which was 2,000 yards, the station re-opened in April 1944 for No.100 Group, the first units being two

AIRFIELD DATA DEC 1944

Command:	RAF Bomber Command	Runway surface:	Concrete
Function:	Operational	Hangars:	4 × T.2, one × B.1
Runways:	040 deg 1,400 × 50yd	Dispersals:	21 × Spectacle, 15 × Pan
	100 deg 2,000 × 50yd	Personnel:	Officers – 97 (6 WAAF)
	150 deg 1,400 × 50yd		Other Ranks – 1,226 (120 WAAF)

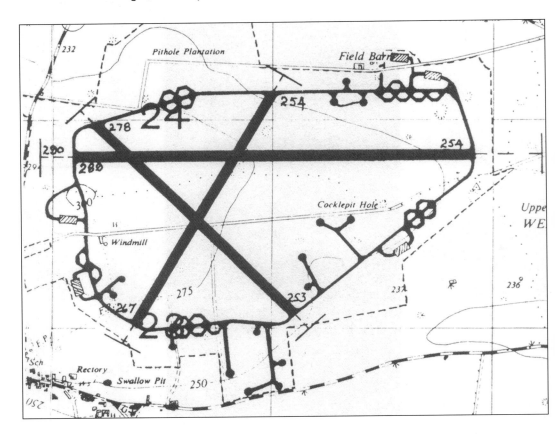

UNITS

1939–1945

18 Sqn	8 Sep 1940–3 Apr 1941	Blenheim
90 Sqn	c.May 1941–Jul 1941	B-17
107 Sqn	11 May 1941–20 Aug 1943	Blenheim
169 Sqn	4 Jun 1944–10 Aug 1945	Mosquito
342 Sqn	19 Jul 1943–6 Sep 1943	Boston
1482 Flt	29 May 1943–17 Sep 1943	Lysander, Blenheim, Defiant
1692 Flt	21 May 1944–16 Jun 1945	Anson, Mosquito
1694 Flt	21 May 1944–30 Jul 1945	Spitfire, Martinet
1692(BS)TU	17 Jun 1944–16 Jun 1945	Mosquito
CFE	Oct 1944–Nov 1945	Mosquito, Spitfire, Tempest

HALESWORTH
Station 365

County: Suffolk

UTM/grid: OS Map 156 – TM400795
Lat./Long.: N52°21.45 W001°32.34
Nearest town: Southwold 7.5 miles to east

Flying over Halesworth in May 2002 it was easy to imagine it as an active wartime airfield.

HISTORY

For an airfield that had less than two years of wartime operations, Halesworth managed to accrue a varied and interesting history – from a famous Fighter Group, through 100 heavy bomber operations, to the vital work of an Air Sea Rescue unit. Located just over five miles from the Suffolk coast, the site was requisitioned in 1942 and work commenced immediately on the construction of a three-runway standard bomber airfield with fifty loop-type hardstands, two T.2 hangars and a variety of temporary buildings. Although designed as a bomber base, its closeness to the east coast made it an obvious choice for fighter operations as, when it opened in 1943, there was a desperate need to increase the combat radius of the escort fighters in an effort to help reduce bomber losses.

Hence, on 8 July 1943, the P-47s of the 56th Fighter Group – 'Zemke's Wolfpack' – touched down, having made the short hop from Horsham St Faith. This was an experienced fighter unit, having flown its first mission in mid-April, and under Colonel Hubert Zemke it

acquired a reputation for tenacity and efficiency, eventually claiming the record for having the most aerial victories of any 8th Air Force fighter unit. The Group spent almost ten months operating from Halesworth and during that time continued to develop fighter escort tactics, as well as pioneering other aggressive methods of destroying German aircraft, such as attacks on airfields. During its time at Halesworth it received one Distinguished Unit Citation, awarded for the period 20 February to 9 March 1944, when the Group claimed ninety-eight enemy aircraft. However, continued expansion of the bomber force meant that a well-equipped – at least in terms of operating surfaces – airfield such as this was 'too good' for fighter ops and so the Thunderbolts moved out in April 1944 to be replaced by heavy bombers.

The 489th Bomb Group had been activated in October 1943 and, post-training and equipped with B-24s, duly made its way over the Atlantic, arriving at Halesworth a few days after the fighters had left.

AIRFIELD DATA DEC 1944

Command:	US 8th AF 2nd BD	Runway surface:	Tar and wood-chips on concrete
Function:	Operational	Hangars:	2 × T.2
Runways:	190 deg 1,400 × 50yd	Dispersals:	50 × Loop
	240 deg 2,000 × 50yd	Personnel:	Officers – 443
	290 deg 1,400 × 50yd		Other Ranks – 2,529

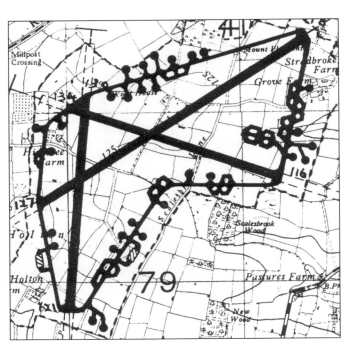

Under the command of Colonel Ezekiel Napier, the unit flew its first mission on 30 May as part of the 95th Combat Bomb Wing within 2nd Bombardment Division; indeed, from May 1944 the 95th BW were headquartered at Halesworth. It was to be a fairly brief operational career and after 106 missions, incurring twenty-nine Liberators missing in action, the 489th was declared non-operational in preparation for a return to the United States and re-assignment to the Pacific Theatre. The Group did not depart as an entity but rather as a number: most aircraft and crews were assigned to other units in the UK and the numberplate was re-established in the US for a B-29 Group. After a few weeks with little activity, other than visitors and diverted aircraft, Station 365 received its final wartime occupants as, once more, Thunderbolts appeared in the circuit. On 16 January the specially modified P-47s of the Air Sea Rescue Squadron arrived from Boxted and, within days, became the 5th Emergency Rescue Squadron. With

an ever-increasing number of Allied aircraft crossing the Channel, the ASR services had been on the increase for some time; this unit had originally been formed the previous May and its P-47s carried large underwing fuel tanks, a belly container with two British 'M type' dinghies for dropping to survivors in the water, and smoke marker under the wings.

The unit acquired a number of OA-10As (Catalinas) equipped for ASR work and, from March, also worked with B-17s modified to carry airborne lifeboats; the first (successful) operational use of the latter took place off Denmark on 31 March.

In February 1945, the 496th Fighter Training Group moved in from Goxhill and stayed until June 1945, equipped with the P-51 Mustang for pilot conversion and operational training, a gunnery and target-towing flight being attached for the latter purpose.

Both American units had gone by June and Halesworth was returned to the Air Ministry for use by Bomber Command; with a surfeit of airfields they

P-47s of the 56th FG operated from Halesworth from July 1943 to April 1944.

Missions:	447 (including from other bases)

489th BG (95th CBW)

Identifying letter:	W
Squadrons:	844th BS (Steerage), 845th BS (Hourglass), 846th BS (Ember), 847th BS (Gallop)
Aircraft:	B-24H/J
Dates:	1 May 1944–Nov 1944
Missions:	106

496th FTG

Squadrons:	555th FS
Aircraft:	P-51
Dates:	15 Feb 1945–Jun 1945

transferred it on 5 August to the Fleet Air Arm, who decided that it would make a suitable training base. For a few brief months in late-1944/early 1945, this Suffolk airfield saw British types in its circuit, as Mosquitoes, Barracudas, Oxfords and others operated with two advanced-flying training units. The first unit to arrive was 798 Squadron from Lee-on-Solent and their main task was to give ex-FAA prisoners of war a refresher flying-course, hence the diverse collection of types operated. This squadron departed in November, being replaced a few days later by 762 Squadron, which, whilst at Halesworth, acquired a Mosquito element.

However, by mid-January this unit departed to Ford and silence descended on Halesworth; after a period of food storage by the Ministry of Food the site was finally disposed of in 1963. Its hard-surfaced runways became home to poultry sheds and, other than the traces of the original operating-surfaces, little now remains at Halesworth.

UNITS

HQ Units at Halesworth

95th BW	5 May 1944–Aug 1944

1939–1945

762 Sqn FAA	3 Dec 1945–15 Jan 1946	Wellington, Oxford, Mosquito
798 Sqn FAA	6 Sep 1945–28 Nov 1945	Barracuda, Firefly, Harvard

USAAF Units

56th FG (65th FW)

Nickname:	The Wolfpack
Squadrons:	61st FS, 62nd FS, 63rd FS
Aircraft:	P-47C, P-47D, P-47M
Dates:	9 Jul 1943–19 Apr 1944

MEMORIALS

1. Marble pillar with inscription: 'Dedicated to all who served here with the 489th Bomb Group (USAAF) especially those who gave their lives in the cause of freedom and human dignity. The 489th Group was stationed at Halesworth airfield from April to November 1944, and flew 106 operational missions in B-24 Liberator heavy bombers. Colonel Ezekiel W Napier, Commander.'

2. Aircraft drop-tank with painted inscription.

3. Four-bladed propeller as cross in churchyard plus plaque with inscription: 'Lieut. Andrew Johnson RFA, attached to RFC, killed at Flanders 30th October 1917, age 20, 21 Squadron.'

One of the memorial stones in the memorial area at Halesworth.

HARDWICK
Station 104

County: Norfolk

UTM/grid: OS Map 134 – TM250900
Lat./Long.: N52°28.12 E001°18.43
Nearest town: Bungay 5.5 miles to east

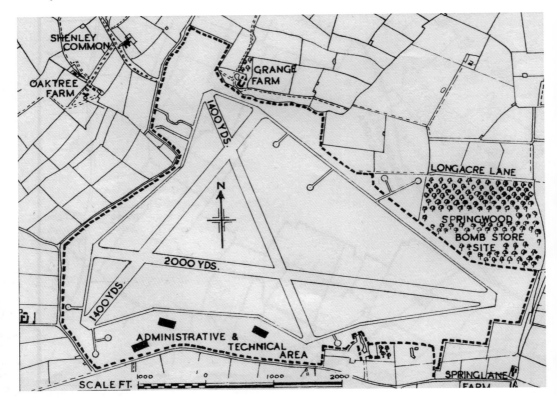

HISTORY

Like other wartime USAAF airfields in East Anglia, Hardwick was originally destined for the RAF and land had been requisitioned in 1941 to the west of Bungay. During late-1941/early 1942, another great swath of Suffolk countryside was transformed from peaceful agriculture to a 'state of the art' military airfield. State of the art at this time meant three runways with, in this case, the main 2,000yd runway running roughly north/south, along with perimeter track, three T.2 hangars and thirty frying-pan dispersals. The bulk of the construction work was carried out by John Laing & Son and before work was complete the decision had been taken to allocate the airfield to the USAAF. Improvements necessary for American heavy-bomber use were carried out, primarily the addition of extra dispersals and increased fuel-storage. Most of the accommodation was of the 'temporary'

style, mostly comprising Nissen huts of various styles, many of which soon sprouted signs showing that the USAAF was 'in town'.

First to arrive was the 310th BG and its B-25s, one squadron of which was located at nearby Bungay; this unit arrived in September 1942 and stayed only two months before moving to the North African theatre, but new residents moved in straight away.

The 329th Bomb Squadron of the 93rd Bomb Group arrived at Hardwick in November 1942 and was soon joined from Alconbury by the rest of the Group; the 93rd – 'The Travelling Circus' – spent the rest of the war operating Liberators out of Hardwick although, unusually for a USAAF Bomb Group, squadrons deployed to other airfields from time to time. By the time it flew its last mission on 25 April 1945 the Group had recorded 396 missions, not all from Hardwick, and

AIRFIELD DATA DEC 1944

Command:	US 8th Air Force 2nd BD	Runway surface:	Concrete and tarmac
Function:	Operational	Hangars:	3 × T.2
Runways:	020 deg 2,000 × 50yd	Dispersals:	50 × Loop
	080 deg 1,400 × 50yd	Personnel:	Officers – 443
	140 deg 1,400 × 50yd		Other Ranks – 2,529

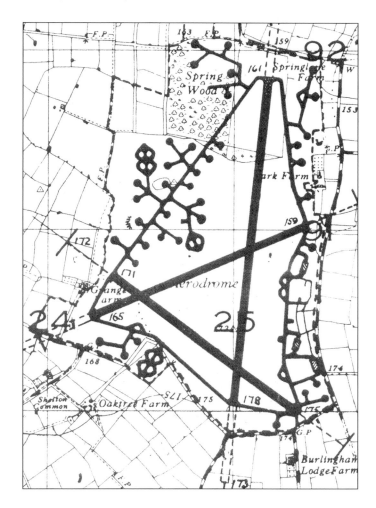

lost 100 aircraft missing in action. In addition to two Distinguished Unit Citations (North Africa December 1942–February 1943 and Ploesti 1 August 1943) it also had two Medal of Honour winners (Lieutenant Colonel Addison E Baker and Major John L Jerstad, both for the Ploesti raid). The Ploesti raid had been flown from North Africa.

Having settled back into the daylight offensive from the UK, the 93rd notched up more missions than any other Bomb Group in the 8th Air Force and also had the first B-24 to complete fifty missions ('Boomerang'). As with all similar airfields this intensive pattern of operations and all that went with them came to an abrupt halt in April 1945. After the parties had ended, the Group focussed on its next main task – going home. The first aircraft had left the

'Katy Bug', a B-24 of the 93rd BG in a posed shot with armourers preparing a bomb-load. (US National Archives)

UK by 24 May and by the middle of June the ground party had boarded the Queen Mary for the 'cruise home' (they had travelled to the UK in the Queen Elizabeth some three years earlier).

After the Americans left, in June 1945, the airfield passed to RAF Bomber Command but they had little need of yet another basic airfield and no use was made of the site.

The airfield remained in the RAF plan and in the 1954 survey was listed as 'inactive' but allocated to 'flying'. All three tarmac-runways were in reasonable condition but many other buildings were in a poor state, the SQH, for example, being listed as 'derelict'. Extension of the main runway (008/188 degrees) to 9,000ft would 'require a minimum of grading, but unclassified roads would be severed at each end. Demolition of four cottages to clear the Northern approach would be essential.'

Hardwick was eventually closed in June 1962 and was put up for disposal.

American aircraft operate from the site once more, as the present owner of part of the airfield has a fine collection of warbirds – including a P-51 – using a grass strip on one side of the old airfield area. A significant number of buildings survive and a number of these have been turned into a museum, alongside which is yet another of the excellent memorial stones that grace many of these ex-USAAF bases.

DECOY SITE

Q   Shotesham   TM266957
Located at Fyland Farm and also known as Hempnall, this site was unusual in that it was manned by USAAF personnel.

UNITS

HQ units at Hardwick
20th BW   7 Nov 1943–13 Jun 1945

1939–1945
USAAF Units
310th BG	Sep 1942–Nov 1942	B-25

93rd BG (20th CBW)
Identifying letter:	B
Nickname:	The Travelling Circus
Squadrons:	328th BS (Oxpug), 329th BS (Furcoat), 330th BS (Maywind), 409th BS (Thrufare)
Aircraft:	B-24D, B-24H, B-24J, B-24L, B-24M
Dates:	6 Dec 1942–19 May 1945
Missions:	396 (including 41 from North Africa)
First mission:	9 Oct 1942 (from Alconbury)
Last mission:	25 Apr 1945

MEMORIALS

Granite memorial with inscription: '93rd Bombardment Group (Heavy) 328th, 329th, 330th and 409th Bombardment Squadrons and attached units, 20th Combat Wing Second Air Division 8th United States Army Air Force. From this airfield and others in England and North Africa, the 93rd Group flew a total of 391 combat missions in support of the Allied war effort during World War II. These missions were flown from 9 October 1942 until 25 April 1945. This monument is dedicated to the memory of those lost in the war and to the survivors who helped achieve ultimate peace and victory. Two Medals of Honour. Two Presidential Unit Citations: North Africa and Ploesti. Battles and Campaigns: American Theater. Antisubmarine ATO. Air Combat – EAME Theater. Air Offensive – Europe. Antisubmarine – ETO. Egypt-Libya. Ploesti. Tunisia. Naples-Foggia. Sicily. Normandy. Northern France. Rhineland. Ardennes-Alsace. Central Europe. Dedicated 25 May 1987.'

Fine memorial stone to the 93rd BG, located alongside a group of surviving wartime buildings.

HETHEL
Station 114

County: Norfolk

UTM/grid: OS Map 144 – TG154006
Lat./Long.: N52°33.40 E001°10.33
Nearest town: Norwich 6 miles to north-east

September 2002 aerial view of Hethel.

HISTORY

Hethel was one of the first-phase of wartime new-build bomber-stations in Norfolk, with land being requisitioned in 1940 and work commencing the following year, the bulk of the construction being carried out by Wimpey. As the airfield was intended for bomber use, it was provided with three hard-runways, plus taxiway and dispersal but, as a wartime expedient-airfield, it was to receive little else in the way of permanent structures. The original plan to accommodate an RAF unit was changed before Hethel opened in 1942 and it was allocated to one of the new American formations – the 12th Army Air Force. This Command formation is seldom referred to in histories of air operations from Britain, as it was a short-lived basing for new American units to position and work-up ready for the forthcoming operation in North Africa.

As Station 114, Hethel welcomed the 320th Bomb Group – but none of its B-26 Marauders arrived, as

the aircraft had flown a southern route direct to North Africa; the Group's ground element moved out of Hethel within weeks of arriving and, with construction work still underway, the airfield was still waiting for its first aircraft. By this time the build-up of USAAF heavy-bomber groups was underway and Station 114 was duly allocated to the 8th Air Force. Infrastructure at the airfield was improved to include the standard heavy Bomb-Group requirements of fifty hardstands, although Hethel was also given three T.2 hangars rather than the usual two.

This part of Norfolk was destined to become Liberator country and, as such, the airfield received the 389th Bomb Group – 'The Sky Scorpions'. Under the command of Colonel Jack W Wood the Group moved in to Hethel in June 1943 and was to remain throughout the war. However, with the operation in North Africa occupying much of the Allies' attention in late-1943, the 389th were temporarily

B-24 of the 389th BG approaching the target area – note the flak puffs in the background; the Group flew over 300 missions from Hethel.

Servicing a B-24 of the 389th; working in the outdoors during a Norfolk winter could prove something of a challenge to the ground-crew but as with moist USAAF bases Hethel had very limited hangar space. (US National Archives)

assigned to that theatre and deployed to bases in North Africa; it was from there that the first operational missions were flown on 9 July. A number of aircraft remained at Hethel and training and familiarization continued, whilst the Americans settled into the local area, both operationally and socially.

It was not until 7 September that the Group mounted its first operational mission from Hethel; by the time it flew its last one on 25 April it had flown 321 missions, 307 of these from Hethel, for the loss of 116 aircraft missing in action. The Group established a reputation for accuracy and, as such, acted as pathfinders for 2nd Bombardment Division for a time in 1944; other than that, the life of the 389th and Hethel followed the normal pattern of an 8th Air Force bomber station – intensive daylight operations,

periods of heavy losses, the frequent sight of damaged aircraft with dead or injured crewmen and the round of on-base and off-base social life: all aspects that are now difficult to picture when you survey the quiet landscape that pervades sixty years after the war.

With the last mission flown and the war in Europe over, the Americans quickly departed, the first aircraft leaving in late-May. Hethel was not destined for immediate closure, as its position in the East of England made it a useful fighter base, and it was duly allocated to No.12 Group of Fighter Command. In early September 1945, the Mustangs of 65 Squadron and 126 Squadron arrived and, whilst the former re-equipped with Spitfires in early 1946 before departing for Spilsby, it was the Mustang that was the commonest sight and sound over Hethel. In March 1946,

AIRFIELD DATA DEC 1944

Command: US 8th AF, 2nd BD

Function: Operational Station
Runways: 240 deg 2,000 × 50yd
300 deg 1,400 × 50yd
350 deg 1,400 × 50yd

Runway surface: Concrete, partly covered with tarmac and wood-chips
Hangars: 3 × T.2
Dispersals: 50 × Loop
Personnel: Officers – 443
Other Ranks – 2,529

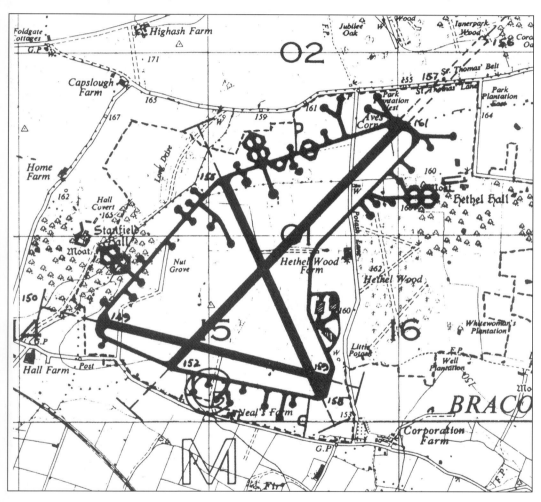

two Polish Mustang squadrons arrived, but this was a temporary measure pending the RAF's decision on what to do with the Polish units. With Russia controlling Poland there were many who did want to, or could not, return to their homeland. By late-1946 both squadrons had disbanded, the decision being taken to absorb a limited number of Polish aircrew into RAF squadrons. All flying at Hethel ceased but the airfield was kept open, although as a Personnel Transit Centre as part of the massive task of de-militarizing Britain – the airfield having been transferred to Technical Training Command. The site was also used as a re-homing centre for displaced persons for a short while.

By the early 1950s the site was under the control of

the Ministry of Agriculture but was still in the RAF plan and, whilst farmed, was available for use. The 1954 survey showed Hethel as inactive and with little potential for extension of the runways: 'the extension of No.1 runway [046/226 degrees] to the North-East would cut an unclassified road and a considerable proportion of Ketteringham Park would be taken up, many trees would have to be felled.' The closing comment was that 'the site is said to be very wet'. However, as far as the RAF was concerned, Hethel was soon declared surplus to requirements and was sold off in the early 1960s.

The old runways can still be noisy but instead of aircraft engines the sound comes from high-performance cars, as the major occupant of Hethel for the past forty years has been Lotus Cars. A number of the old wartime buildings, including hangars (but not always in their original position) are still in use, although new buildings have also been erected. Away from the main airfield site a small clutch of buildings, centred on the old chapel (complete with wall murals), have been restored and are now open as a museum.

UNITS

HQ units based at Hethel

14th BW	9 Jun 1943–1 Jul 1943
2nd BW	14 Sep 1943–12 Jun 1945
20th BW	24 Sep 1943–7 Nov 1943

1939–1945

65 Sqn	6 Sep 1945–11 Feb 1946	Mustang, Spitfire
126 Sqn	5–15 Sep 1945; 5 Oct 1945–10 Mar 1946	Mustang

USAAF Units
320th BG

Squadrons:	441st BS, 442nd BS, 443rd BS, 444th BS
Aircraft:	B-26
Dates:	12 Sep 1942–2 Dec 1942

389th BG (2nd CBW)

Identifying letter:	C
Nickname:	The Sky Scorpions
Squadrons:	564th BS (Complex), 565th BS (Protrap), 566th BS (Boorish), 567th BS (Lounger)
Aircraft:	B-24D, B-24H, B-24J, B-24L, B-24M
Dates:	11 Jun 1943–30 May 1945
Missions:	321 (including 14 from North Africa)
First mission:	9 Jul 1943
Last mission:	25 Apr 1945

Post-1945

303 Sqn	23 Mar 1946–11 Dec 1946	Mustang
316 Sqn	15 Mar 1946–11 Dec 1946	Mustang

MEMORIALS

1. Part of domestic site has been preserved and is now a memorial to the 389th, centred on the old chapel (complete with surviving murals) and with a memorial plaque.

2. In Wymondham churchyard in memory of the Base Protestant Padre, Captain Earl Widen.

3. In June 1946 a memorial plaque was dedicated in Carleton Rode Church, in memory of seventeen members of the 389th Bomb Group who were killed in a mid-air collision over the parish on 21 November 1944. A stained-glass window in the church is also dedicated to the crew members killed in this collision. Carleton Rode is situated about six miles south-west of Hethel off the B1113.

4. Memorial Headstone in Hethel churchyard and the 389th Roll of Honour inside the church.

A number of buildings have recently been restored, including the old chapel, the interior of which still sports a number of wall murals.

HONINGTON
Station 375

County: Suffolk

UTM/grid: OS Map 144 – TL890755
Lat./Long.: N52°20.38 E000°46.29
Nearest town: Bury St Edmunds 7 miles to south-south-west

HISTORY

Although Honington no longer has based flying-squadrons it remains an active RAF airfield as home to the RAF Regiment; however, during its sixty-year history it has been home to a wide range of aircraft types and for many years was a key station in Bomber Command and its successor formation, Strike Command, as well as fulfilling a wartime role with the 8th Air Force.

A sizeable swathe of Suffolk countryside to the south of Thetford was acquired in the early 1930s for an Expansion-Period airfield; the plan was for a major bomber-station and Honington, named after the village to the east of the site, was given the usual arc of C-Type hangars plus the usual cluster of brick-built technical and administrative buildings, although at this stage the flying area itself was simply a large area of grass. The airfield duly opened on 3 May 1937 and was allocated to No.3 Group; two months later the first aircraft arrived when the Wellesleys of 77 Squadron and the Heyfords of 102 Squadron moved in from Finningley. A year later, two Harrow-equipped squadrons turned up (75 Squadron and 215 Squadron) to become the new resident units and, by mid-1939, both had re-equipped with Wellingtons – the type with which Honington was to enter the war.

A further change-round of units brought 9 Squadron to the airfield and it was this unit that was to be most associated with the RAF's wartime operations from this Suffolk base. The Wellingtons were airborne on 'day one' of the war and from then until their departure to Waddington in August 1942 they suffered the highs and lows of Main Force bomber operations. During three years of ops the squadron suffered heavy losses and participated in every major attack made by Bomber Command; when they eventually left Honington they re-equipped with Lancasters and continued to play a major part in bomber operations. They were not the only Wellington unit using Honington, but the others were seldom involved for more than a month or two and it was IX Squadron (the preferred way of presenting the squadron number) that was the major unit.

The Czech-manned 311 Squadron formed at Honington in July 1940 but soon moved to the satellite airfield at East Wretham. As you can see from the list of units, a number of other operational squadrons passed through during this period and the station was

also home to a variety of training Flights. In common with all airfields in this part of England, the location was well known to the Luftwaffe and it did receive a number of small scale and not very effective raids, although on one occasion a number of airmen were killed by bomb blast.

RAF activity was wound down in mid-1942 in preparation for the airfield being handed to the Americans, under whom it became Station 375. For most of the rest of the war Honington acquired the essential, but not very glamorous, role of a technical-support installation – becoming No.1 Strategic Air Depot (SAD). With only limited facilities at front-line airfields, the USAAF adopted a centralized-repair policy and established a number of Air Depots to carry out this work, which included equipment and sub-assemblies as well as airframe repair. This is where battle-damaged and worn-out airframes were taken apart and rebuilt to create 'new' aircraft, which often comprised parts from a variety of aircraft. The scale of the work was such that a sub-site at Troston, north-west of the airfield and linked by taxiway, was created to handle much of the equipment repair and refurbishment. Infrastructure work at Honington including laying an east/west steel-matting runway and additional dispersal points (seventy-five rather than the usual fifty) and building nine Blister hangars to supplement the four C-Type hangars. To save time and effort it was common practice for damaged

Line-up of Wellingtons at Honington in 1938; the Station's Wellingtons were active on Day One of the war.

The airfield's main wartime role was as a Strategic Air Depot responsible for maintenance and repair, primarily of B-17s but other USAAF types as well.

bombers to be instructed to land at Honington rather than at home base. Although No.1 SAD handled a variety of aircraft, the bulk of its work was with the B-17, especially those of the 3rd Bombardment Division. It is hard to express just how important this type of facility was and to convey the nature and scale of the work, except to say that large numbers of

bombers were returned to service thanks to the hard work of the technicians at the Air Depots.

Honington's later war was not entirely peaceful as, in February 1944, it became home to the P-38 Lightnings of the 364th Fighter Group. This unit had been activated in June 1943, embarked from the US in January and, under Lieutenant Colonel Frederick C Grambo, took up resi-

P-51 of the 364th FG under repair; this Fighter Group operated P-38s and then P-51s from Honington between February 1944 and November 1945.

It is not possible to site a cross strip within the existing airfield boundary because of the disposition of hardstandings and bomb stores.' Other infrastructure elements included:

- Dispersals – twenty-two H type (115ft × 50ft), two loos, two caravans and five aprons totalling 201,600sq ft
- Hangars – five C type, one T.2, one Robin and two Blister (unserviceable)
- Aviation Fuel – underground storage for 504,000 gallons in forty-two 12,000 gallon tanks
- Control tower – two-storey brick structure

dence at Honington. The unit flew its first mission as a group on 3 March, by which time its CO had already been lost in action, his place being taken by Colonel Roy Osborn. The Group gave up its Lightnings and re-equipped with P-51Ds in late-July and it was with these that it earned a Distinguished Unit Citation for 'defence of bombers' during the Frankfurt raid of 27 December. By the end of the war the Group had clocked up 342 missions for the loss of 134 aircraft missing in action; they claimed some 450 enemy aircraft, including over 250 aerial victories.

Unlike most other airfields used by the 8th, Honington was not immediately abandoned; the 364th departed in November but the airfield became HQ of VIIIth Fighter Command. The American tenure continued into 1946 and Honington had the distinction of being the last wartime station to be handed back to the RAF (in February), although the last Americans did not depart until March. With its extensive workshops – but limited runway infrastructure – it was a good location for a maintenance facility and was handed to Transport Command for use by No.1 Transport Aircraft Modification Unit (the name changing to Transport Command Major Servicing Unit in July 1946). The major work carried out by this unit was on Dakotas and with the 1948 Berlin Airlift Honington had yet another busy period. The following year the airfield passed to its original owners, Bomber Command, but for a number of years it was used by No.94 Armament Maintenance Unit and the only significant development was the extension and resurfacing of the hard runway ready for its next assignment as a jet-bomber base.

The 1954 survey showed a single tarmac-runway of 9,000ft × 200ft, oriented 081/261 and with minimal overruns at each end (200–300ft). As to further extensions: 'it is possible to extend the runway to the WSW [to 11,000ft] but the work will be fairly heavy.

In 1955 the airfield was once more home to operational squadrons and received a four-squadron Wing of Canberras: the first three squadrons of which arrived in February and the fourth in May. The Honington Wing badge was the outline of a pheasant, each squadron using a different colour, but the distinctive sound of Avon-engined Canberras was only heard for two years, although in that time they took part in the Suez operations, flying from Cyprus.

Even before the Canberras had gone the next bomber type had arrived – the Valiant-equipped 7 Squadron reforming at the Suffolk airfield in November 1956. For the next decade Honington was very much at the cutting edge of Bomber Command and housed a number of V-bombers – Valiants and Victors – some in the nuclear-bombing role and some, with 199 Squadron, in the specialist electronic-warfare role. Whilst the core of the airfield remained unchanged, such as the single, long runway and the C-Type hangars, a great many buildings were modified: some were knocked down and new ones built to meet the particular requirements of the various user units. We seldom talk about bomb stores but these, too, underwent an almost continuous period of change, including greatly enhanced security during the nuclear period.

A change of policy that saw the strategic nuclear-deterrent move from aircraft to submarines brought a run-down of the RAF's V-bomber force and for Honington this meant the departure of units and, from 1965 to 1968, a period under Care and Maintenance.

Whilst the RAF had lost its strategic nuclear-role it had not lost the nuclear role *in toto* and, with the acquisition of the Buccaneer, Honington was brought back to life. No.12 Squadron re-formed at Honington in October 1969, followed a year later by 15 Squadron. The RAF was intending to use the Buccaneer for strike (nuclear) and conventional bombing as well as maritime attack and for a brief period in 1971 the maritime aspect of Honington was boosted by the presence of the Shackletons of 204 Squadron. However, they soon departed and the

Valiant crew of 90 Squadron planning a sortie, August 1960; Honington housed a Valiant Wing in the late 1950s/early 1960s.

future of the airfield was very much a Buccaneer one, with operational squadrons, a Fleet Air Arm presence (809 Squadron) and, of particular importance, the presence of No.237 Operational Conversion Unit, tasked with training of Buccaneer aircrew. In addition to the distinctive Buccaneers the circuit was also graced by Hunters, as the OCU used this type for parts of the syllabus.

For a decade Honington was synonymous with the Buccaneer but, with the changing shape of the RAF, a new type was destined to dominate the airfield's final operational decade. In January 1982 the Tornado Weapons Conversion Unit (TWCU) was established at Honington, joined a few months later by the RAF's first operational Tornado squadron – a return to its World War Two haunt for IX Squadron. As far as the airfield infrastructure was concerned the major difference was the creation of a Hardened Aircraft Shelter (HAS) site and associated buildings. All RAF Tornado aircrew had to pass through the 'tender mercies' of the TWCU after their conversion to type at Cottesmore (TTTE) and before joining their squadrons. With the build-up of the Tornado force the Buccs had to move out, 237 OCU going to Lossiemouth in October 1984. With the major Tornado strength being destined for stationing in Germany, IX Squadron moved overseas in October 1986 and TWCU, later taking the shadow number of 45 (Reserve) Squadron, became the sole flying resident at Honington – until January 1990 when XIII Squadron re-formed here to become a Tornado recce unit.

The swingeing defence cuts of the early 1990s took an axe to the RAF's front-line strength, resulting in the disbandment of squadrons and the closure of airfields. For Honington the next result was the departure of its flying units, TWCU to Lossiemouth and XIII Squadron to Marham. However, the base survived – and indeed to some extent thrived – when it became home to the RAF Regiment.

DECOY SITES

Q	Ixworth	TL948714
	Snarehill	TL806895
Q/K	Thetford	TL896810

UNITS

HQ units at Honington

VIIIth FC	26 Oct 1945–20 Mar 1946
3rd AD	27 Oct 1945–21 Nov 1945
Advanced Mobile Air Depot	

1920–1938

75 Sqn	11 Jul 1938–13 Jul 1939	Harrow
77 Sqn	7 Jul 1937–25 Jul 1938	Audax, Wellesley
102 Sqn	7 Jul 1937–11 Jul 1938	Heyford
215 Sqn	25 Jul 1938–10 Sep 1939,	Harrow
3 Gp PF	Jun 1937 – Oct 1937	Tutor

1939–1945

9 Sqn	15 Jul 1939–7 Aug 1942;	Wellington;

AIRFIELD DATA DEC 1944

Command:	US 8th AF	Runway surface:	Steel matting (280 deg), Grass
Function:	Operational	Hangars:	9 × Blister, 4 × C
Runways:	280 deg 2,000 × 40yd	Dispersals:	75 × Concrete and Cement
	NE/SW 1,400yd	Personnel:	Officers – 190
	SE/NW 1,400yd		Other Ranks – 1,519

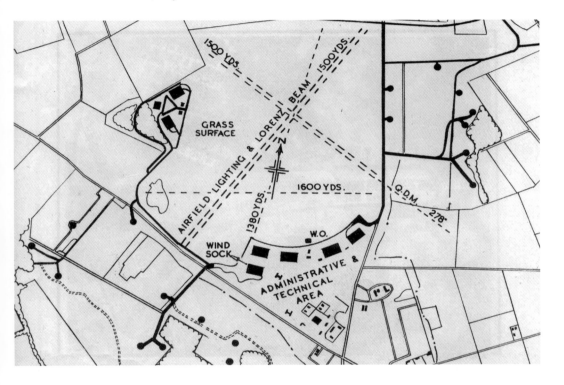

	1 Jun 1982–1 Oct 1986	Tornado	Last mission:	6 May 1945		
103 Sqn	16 Jun 1940– 3 Jul 1940	Wellington	**Post-1945**			
105 Sqn	11 Jun 1940–10 Jul 1940	Blenheim	7 Sqn	1 Nov 1956–26 Jul 1960	Valiant
214 Sqn	5–12 Jan 1942	Wellington	10 Sqn	6 May 1955–15 Jan 1957	Canberra
215 Sqn	8 Apr 1940–18 May 1940	Wellington	12 Sqn	1 Oct 1969–Oct 1980	Buccaneer
311 Sqn	29 Jul 1940–16 Sep 1940	Wellington	13 Sqn	Jan 1990–1994	Tornado
			15 Sqn	15 Feb 1955–15 Apr 1957;	Canberra;
1505 Flt	1 Jan 1941–5 Sep 1942	Wellington		1 Oct 1970–Jan 1971	Buccaneer
1513 Flt	22 Sep 1941–31 Oct 1942	Oxford	44 Sqn	20 Feb 1955–16 Jul 1957	Canberra
1504 Flt	14 Aug 1942–3 Nov 1942	Oxford	51 Sqn	23 Mar 1970–30 Sep 1970	Comet,
					Canberra
USAAF Units			55 Sqn	1 Sep 1960–24 May 1965	Victor
364th FG (67th FW)			57 Sqn	Feb 1955–Nov 1956;	Canberra;
Squadrons:	383rd FS, 384th FS, 385th FS			1 Jan 1959–1 Dec 1965	Victor
Aircraft:	P-38J, P-51D		58 Sqn	23 Mar 1970–30 Sep 1970	Canberra
Dates:	Feb 1944–Nov 1945		90 Sqn	1 Jan 1957–16 Apr 1965	Valiant
Missions:	342		199 Sqn	1 Oct 1957–15 Dec 1959	Valiant,
First mission:	3 Mar 1944				Canberra

Honington became the RAF's first operational Tornado base when IX Squadron reformed with the Tornado GR.1.

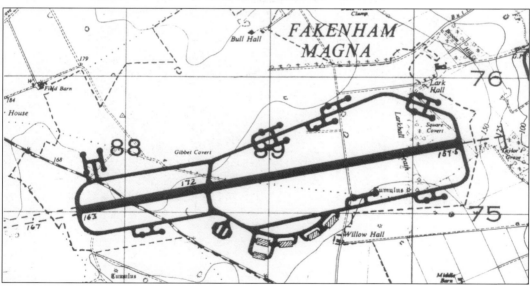

204 Sqn	1 Apr 1972–28 Apr 1972	Shackleton
208 Sqn	1 Jul 1974–1 Jul 1983	Buccaneer, Hunter
543 Sqn	23 Mar 1970–1 Oct 1970	Victor
809 Sqn FAA	14 Mar 1973–6 Aug 1978+	Bucanneer
1 TAMU/TCMSU	1 Apr 1946–31 Mar 1950	
237 OCU	1 Mar 1971–19 Oct 1984	Buccaneer, Hunter
TWCU/45	8 Jan 1982–24 Apr 1987,	Tornado
(R) Sqn	24 Nov 1987–Apr 1992	

MEMORIALS

1. Plaques on wall by guardroom.

2. Memorial by main gate with inscription: 'Eighth Air Force USAAF. In memory of the men of the 1st Strategic Air Depot RAF Honington AAF595 1942–1946. Never forgotten, forever honoured. Dedicated 26 September 1987.'

HORHAM
Station 119

County: Suffolk

UTM/grid: OS Map 156 – TM210730
Lat./Long.: N52°18.38 E001°14.02
Nearest town: Eye 6 miles to west

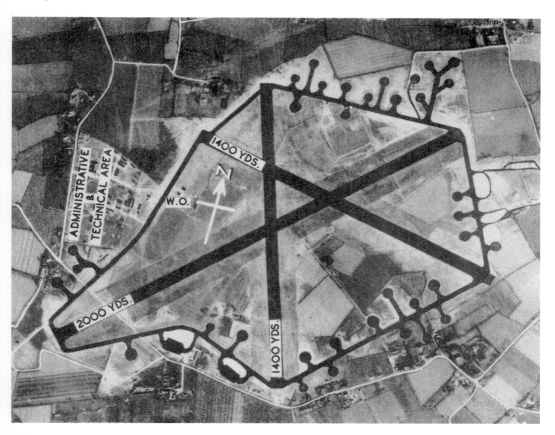

HISTORY

Constructed as part of the clutch of airfields in central Suffolk, Horham was originally destined for RAF occupation and, after land had been acquired in early 1941, construction of a three-runway station started. Like most of the airfields in this region the main runway was roughly SW/NE to cater for the prevailing wind and one road had to be closed to provide enough space for this 2,000-yard strip. Numerous hedgerows were ripped up, trees removed, ditches filled in or covered – and drainage laid. In addition, a series of dispersals was laid around the eastern half of the airfield, the majority of these being frying-pan type set off the perimeter track. However, at an advanced stage in the construction it was decided that Horham would be used by units of the

12th Air Force for their pre-North Africa work-up.

The A-20 Havocs of the 47th Bomb Group arrived in October 1942, amongst the earliest USAAF flying-units to take up residence in East Anglia, and for the next few months they flew training sorties from this brand-new, but in many ways still poorly-equipped, airfield. It was only ever planned as a temporary measure and in January the Group duly moved to North Africa, leaving Horham to await its next residents. The wait was not a long one and in May 1943 another twin-engined type joined the circuit; however, the B-26 Marauders of the 323rd Bomb Group had barely been seen by the locals when the unit upped sticks and moved to Earls Colne in Essex. This was part of the settling down phase of the

AIRFIELD DATA DEC 1944

Command:	US 8th AF, 3rd BD	Runway surface:	Concrete
Function:	Operational Station	Hangars:	2 × T.2
Runways:	074 deg 2,000 × 50yd	Dispersals:	50 × Loop
	190 deg 1,400 × 50yd	Personnel:	Officers – 443
	310 deg 1,400 × 50yd		Other Ranks – 2,529

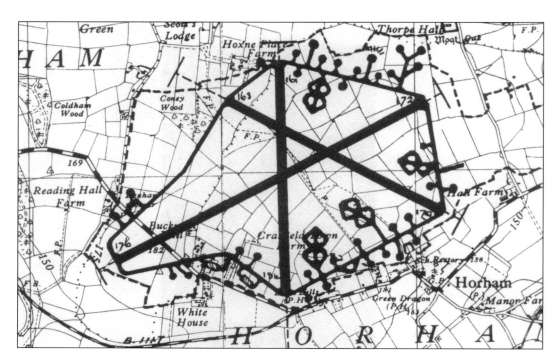

8th Air Force as it sorted out its units and command organization. Within days Horham received the unit that was to spend the remainder of the war operating from its runways. The 95th Bomb Group had been at nearby Framlingham since early May, but that airfield had proved unsatisfactory and the decision was taken to move the B-17 unit to Horham; however, the Group had also suffered a disastrous start to its operational career and the move may have had as much to do with morale as facilities.

The B-17s flew their first mission from Horham in July and over the next two years established a fine reputation, notching up a number of distinctions; for example, it was the only 8th Air Force Bomb Group to receive three Distinguished Unit Citations (Regensburg 17 August 1943, Munster 10 October 1943 and Berlin 4 March 1944) – the latter DUC recognized the fact that it was the first Group to bomb Berlin (for the loss of four aircraft). In its

wartime total of 320 missions, the 95th lost 157 aircraft missing in action but, after its poor start from Framlingham, its Horham period was one where losses were average. The end of the war brought an almost immediate cessation of activity and by August the Americans had gone, having donated the station's Stars and Stripes flag to Stradbrooke church (a village just east of the airfield). From October the RAF was using Horham as a satellite for No.25 and No.263 Maintenance Units, but this activity had ceased by 1948.

The site was retained in the RAF plan to spring 1957, although in the 1954 survey it was listed as inactive and used for agriculture. The hangars, two T.2s and one Blister, were in use by the Ministry of Food, who also occupied most of the other buildings on the technical area; most other buildings on the site were listed as in bad condition, with some of the dispersal buildings having been demolished and

Contrails stream from a high-flying B-17 formation that includes aircraft of the Horham-based 95th Bomb Group. (US National Archives)

others in use for farm stock. The concrete runways were reasonable and, whilst two could be extended, including the North/South runway, to 9,000ft, the work was assessed as complicated and difficult.

The site of Horham was finally disposed of in the early 1960s; a few groups of buildings survive but most of the airfield structure has gone.

UNITS

HQ units at Horham

13th BW	13 Sep 1943–6 Aug 1945

1939–1945
USAAF Units

47th BG	5 Oct 1942–Jan 1943	A-20

322nd BG

Squadrons	453rd BS, 454th BS, 455th BS, 456th BS
Aircraft	B-26
Dates	12 May 1943–14 Jun 1943

95th BG (13th CBW)

Identifying letter:	B
Squadrons:	334th BS (Neglect), 335th BS (Inland), 336th BS (Landberg) and 412th BS (Abush)
Aircraft:	B-17F, B-17G
Dates:	15 Jun 1943–19 Jun 1945
Missions:	320 (including missions flown from other bases)

First mission:	13 May 1943 (from Framlingham)
Last mission:	20 Apr 1945

MEMORIALS

Near village church a stone in shape of aircraft fin with inscription: 'In memory of the men of the 9th Bombardment Group who served at Horham airfield and to those who gave their lives in the cause of freedom, 1943–1945. 334th, 335th, 336th and 412th Bomb Squadrons and supporting units, Headquarters 13th Combat Bomb Wing, United States 8th Air Force. Dedicated 19th Sept 1981.'

The memorial is unusual in that it based on a B-17 tail shape, superimposed on a plan of the airfield.

HORSHAM ST FAITH
Station 123

County: Norfolk

UTM/grid: OS Map 133 – TG220138
Lat./Long.: N52°40.57 E001°17.0
Nearest town: Northern outskirts of Norwich

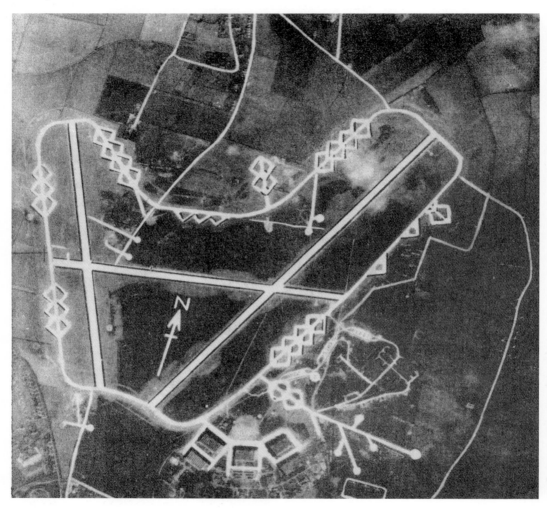

HISTORY

Now the site of Norwich International Airport, Horsham St Faith was one of the most interesting airfields in Norfolk and whilst it is best remembered by many as a very active Fighter Command base in the 1950s, this was only one of three main periods of use. This large flat area to the north of the city of Norwich had been selected in the mid-1930s for development as a standard bomber-airfield with full facilities, the five C-type hangars and

admin/technical site being built on the southern side of the airfield. During the construction period the airfield hosted its first aircraft when Blenheims of 21 Squadron dispersed here from Watton for a few days. Defiants of 264 Squadron deployed to Horsham the following May and were in place when the Station formally opened.

In May 1940 it was decreed that the opening-up party would assemble at Watton on 1 June 1940,

B-24 crew of the 753rd BS/458th BG; the Group flew 240 missions from Horsham St Faith. (US National Archives)

moving to Horsham three days later to have the Station ready to receive squadrons by 1 July although, as we have mentioned, the airfield was already in use. This timescale was subsequently accelerated so that the station was opened on 1 June under Group Captain F Wright and ready to receive the two squadrons of No.71 Wing by the middle of the month. These two units, 114 and 139 Squadrons, had suffered heavily as part of the forward-deployed elements of the RAF in France and the first task was to recuperate and to re-equip with the Blenheim; however, both were soon back in action as part of No.2 Group's day and night attacks on German-occupied Europe, Oulton being used as a satellite and the main base for 114 Squadron.

As the threat of invasion increased, the main target-area was focussed on ports and harbours. Offensive operations continued into 1941, with the Blenheim units flying cloud-cover and Circus operations, the Station having returned to two-squadron strength with the arrival in July 1941 of 18 Squadron. A number of significant attacks were made during 1941, such as the power station at Knapsack; however, it was an attack on another power station, this time at Gosnay, that is invariably noted in the records – not because of any particular dramatic effect of the attack but because during it a box was dropped for the Germans to collect; the box contained a set of artificial legs for one of their most famous (and no doubt difficult) prisoners – Douglas Bader. Of more significance in 1941 was the arrival in December of 105 Squadron and the introduction to operational service of the de Havilland Mosquito. By early 1942 they were the only operational unit in residence but, in June, 139 Squadron re-formed here with Mosquitoes and trained with No.1655 Mosquito Training Unit. What looked like a promising future

with the Mosquito ended in September, when the squadrons moved west to Marham.

Horsham was released for use by the Americans but an RAF Care and Maintenance party remained on site, as did No.1508 BATF, the latter continuing to fly from here until April 1943; official transfer of the airfield took place on 12 April. However, the first USAAF use took place in autumn 1942 with the B-26 Marauders of the 319th Bomb Group; this was one of the transient units of 12th Air Force and by the end of the year they had moved on. Some development work took place at Horsham, but the airfield was still grass and its next users were the P-47 Thunderbolts of the 56th Fighter Group, who arrived on 5 April from Kings Cliffe and flew their first mission a week later. 'Zemke's Wolfpack' only stayed until early July and then flew out to Halesworth to free Horsham for major development.

Three runways were laid down, with the main 2,000-yard strip oriented 230 degrees – towards the city. The other two strips were 1,400 yards and all were linked by a perimeter track from which sprouted loop-type dispersal areas, although six of the previous fighter dispersals were also kept. When the airfield re-opened at the end of 1943 it joined 2nd Air Division and, as such, received a B-24 unit. The 458th Bomb Group had been activated in July 1943 and deployed to the UK in January, taking up residence at Horsham – now Station 123 – towards the end of the month. Under the command of Colonel James H Isbell, and later Colonel Allen F Herzberg, the Group was to fly 240 missions from this, its sole, operational base. The first operation was flown on 24 February and by the time the last was flown on 25 April 1945 the Group had suffered forty-seven aircraft missing in action and had dropped over 13,000 tons of bombs on a wide range of targets. Other than its role in evaluating the Azon guided-bomb, the 458th was an 'ordinary' unit with no particular claims to fame, but for fifteen months almost 3,000 Americans lived and worked at this Norfolk airfield.

A number of tragic incidents occurred, some when bombers crashed into nearby built-up areas – always a risk with the main runway oriented towards the city – and at least one on-base explosion. The 458th departed Horsham St Faith in June–July 1945 and the airfield was handed back to the RAF; within weeks a number of squadrons had moved in and the airfield was busier than ever, with a diverse range of aircraft types, from Mosquitoes to Oxfords.

The airfield became a major Fighter Command base with the establishment of the Horsham Wing and, although units and aircraft types changed, this remained the case for nearly fifteen years. The resident squadrons had entered the jet age with the

AIRFIELD DATA DEC 1944

Command:	US 8th AF 2nd BD	Runway surface:	Concrete
Function:	Operational	Hangars:	5 × C
Runways:	230 deg 2,000 × 50yd	Dispersals:	50 × Loop (four-engine), 6 Fighter
	280 deg 1,400 × 50yd	Personnel:	Officers – 443
	350 deg 1,400 × 50yd		Other Ranks – 2,529

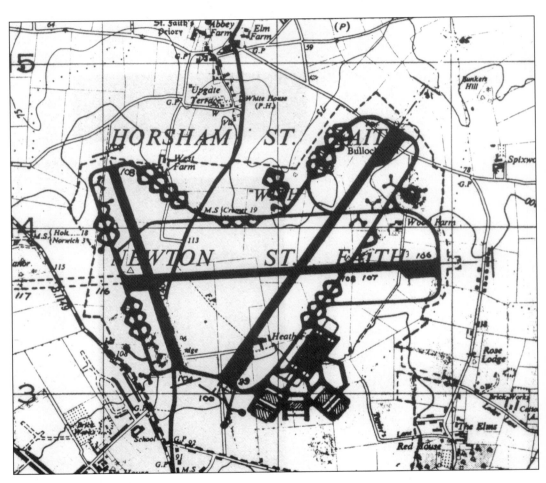

arrival of Meteors and, during its tenure at Horsham, 245 Squadron spent two prolonged detachments at Lubeck, six weeks in autumn 1946 and eight weeks the following summer, being joined on the latter occasion by the other Horsham Meteor units, 257 and 263 Squadrons. The only other significant and routine deployments that feature in the movements records were those to Acklington for APC, these usually lasting two weeks. No.695 squadron dis-

banded at Horsham in February 1949 but, as it instantly became 34 Squadron and remained at the airfield, nothing had, in effect, changed and the diverse collection of aircraft remained in use.

By the early 1950s the station had an establishment of two day- and one night-fighter units and the progression of classic RAF jets could be seen by visitors to the airfield – Meteors, Venoms, Hunters and Javelins. More unusual types were also present,

Meteor of 141 Squadron being worked on in one of Horsham's hangars.

such as the search and rescue Sycamore helicopters of 275 Squadron. Runway work took place in 1956 to switch the main circuit-pattern away from the suburbs of Hellesdon and over more open country and this helped reduce the number of noise complaints! Despite complaints, the station had established a good relationship with the local community and the annual Battle of Britain 'At Home' days were always well attended – and as Horsham's squadrons were famed for their aerobatics and formation flying, visitors were always sure of a good show.

However, all this had ended by 1960 with the departure of the final fighter squadron to Coltishall and Horsham's once hectic tarmac had no resident users. The airfield was maintained and the HQ of No.12 Group remained on site, becoming HQ.12 (East Anglia) Sector in 1963 – one of those strange and unpopular changes of nomenclature – and moving out in July. RAF Horsham St Faith was formally deactivated on 1 August 1963 and negotiations began as to its future. The airfield was subsequently sold to Norwich City and the County Borough Council for development as Norwich Airport, although parts were also used as an industrial estate. As well as a thriving airport, the former wartime base also boasts the excellent City of Norwich Aviation Museum.

DECOY SITES

| | Mousehold Aerodrome | TG250102 |
| Q/K | Crostwick | TG263155 |

The Crostwick site was located in a field at Church Farm and the majority of the dummy aircraft were Blenheim type.

UNITS

HQ units at Horsham

2nd BD	13 Sep 1943–10 Dec 1943
20th BW	14 Sep 1943–24 Sep 1943
93rd BW	1 Nov 1943–10 Jan 1944
96th BW	11 Jun 1944–1 Jun 1945
No 12 Group	14 Aug 1959–Jul 1963

1939–1945

18 Sqn	13 Jul 1941–5 Nov 1941,	Blenheim
	5 Dec 1941–4 Mar 1942	
19 Sqn	17 Apr 1940–16 May 1940	Spitfire
21 Sqn det	Nov 1939–Dec 1939	Blenheim
66 Sqn	16–29 May 1940	Spitfire
105 Sqn	9 Dec 1941–22 Sep 1942	Mosquito
110 Sqn det	Jun 1939–?	Blenheim
114 Sqn	10 Jun 1940–10 Aug 1940	Blenheim
139 Sqn	10 Jun 1940–13 Jul 1941,	Blenheim,
	23 Oct 1941–9 Dec 1941,	Mosquito
	8 Jun 1942–29 Sep 1942	

264 Sqn	May 1940–Jul 1940	Defiant
1508 Flt	4 Apr 1941–20 Dec 1941	Blenheim, Wellington
FTF	Dec 1941–21 Jan 1942	Hudson
1508 Flt	19 Jan 1942–4 Apr 1943	Oxford
1655 MTU	30 Aug 1942–28 Sep 1942	Mosquito, Blenheim
MCU	30 Aug 1942–29 Sep 1942	Mosquito
1444 Flt	Dates not known	Hudson
1689 Flt	15 Feb 1944–7 May 1945	Spitfire, Hurricane

245 Sqn	16 Aug 1946–27 Jun 1955	Meteor
257 Sqn	15 Apr 1947–27 Oct 1950	Meteor
263 Sqn	15 Apr 1947–23 Oct 1950	Meteor
275 Sqn det	Nov 1954 – Sep 1959	Sycamore, Whirlwind
307 Sqn	24 Aug 1945–29 Nov 1946	Mosquito
695 Sqn	11 Aug 1945–11 Feb 1949	various
102 GS	mid-1945–Jun 1953	Cadet
BBF	3 Nov 1961–1 Apr 1963	Lancaster, Spitfire, Hurricane

USAAF Units
319th BG

Squadrons:	437th BS, 438th BS, 439th BS, 440th BS
Aircraft:	B-26
Dates:	4 Oct 1942–11 Nov 1942

56th FG

Name:	Zemke's Wolfpack
Squadrons:	61st FS, 62nd FS, 63rd FS
Aircraft:	P-47
Dates:	6 Apr 1943–9 Jul 1943
First mission:	13 Apr 1943

458th BG (96th CBW)

Identifying letter:	K
Squadrons:	752nd BS (Hussar), 753rd BS (Fiction), 754th BS (Cotstring), 755th BS (Affab)
Aircraft:	B-24H, B-24J, B-24L, B-24M
Dates:	Jan 1944–14 Jun 1945
Missions:	240
First mission:	24 Feb 1944
Last mission:	25 Apr 1945

Post-1945

23 Sqn	14 Jan 1952–4 Jul 1952, 12 Oct 1956–28 May 1957, 7 Sep 1958–5 Jun 1959, 31 Mar 1960–11 Jul 1960	Mosquito, Venom, Javelin
34 Sqn	11 Feb 1949–20 Jul 1951	various
64 Sqn	15 Aug 1945–6 Aug 1946	Mustang, Hornet
65 Sqn	14 Mar 1946–11 Aug 1946	Mustang, Spitfire, Hornet
74 Sqn	14 Aug 1946–1 Jul 1947, 28 Aug 1947–8 Jun 1959	Meteor, Hunter
118 Sqn	8 Sep 1945–10 Mar 1946	Mustang
141 Sqn	14 Oct 1956–28 May 1957	Venom
228 Sqn	Nov 1959–Aug 1964?	Sycamore, Whirlwind

MEMORIALS

1. Inside airport terminal is a memorial display of the 458th BG plus plaque with inscription: 'Dedicated in memory of the 458th Bombardment Group (H) USAAF Horsham St Faith January 1944–June 1945.'

2. The City of Norwich Aviation Museum is located on the side of the airfield by the village of Horsham and is not accessed via the airport. The museum has a fine collection of aircraft and exhibits, part of which tell the story of the airfield.

IPSWICH

County: Suffolk

UTM/grid: OS Map 169 – TM190415
Lat./Long.: N52°01.43 E001°11.47
Nearest town: Located on SE outskirts of Ipswich

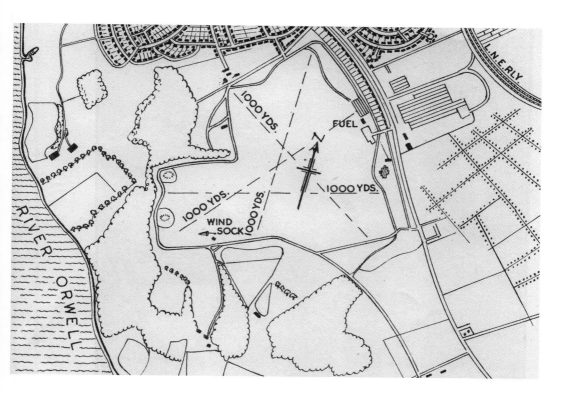

HISTORY

A pre-war civil field, Ipswich was opened on 26 June 1930 and was used by the Suffolk Aero Club. By July 1939, the grass airfield was being used by 45 E&RFTS for training VR pilots and it had also been in use with the Civil Air Guard. However, the approach of war brought this to an end and Ipswich was allocated as a dispersal satellite for Wattisham. Blenheim deployments appear to have taken place from summer 1939 but, unlike other dispersal airfields, no actual operational flying appears to have taken place. The airfield continued to be used for bomber dispersal but, from mid-1941, it also acted as a forward airfield for fighters, the first of which appears to have taken place on 12 August when three Spitfire squadrons – 19, 66 and 266 – used Ipswich to support an attack by No.2 Group Blenheims on Knapsack and Quadrath power stations near Cologne. Almost 20 per cent of the attackers failed to return and the Spitfires from Ipswich helped the survivors fend off fighter attack over the Channel.

Fighter deployments became a routine feature during 1942, as the airfield was transferred to No.12 Group and allocated to Martlesham Heath; for much of the summer of that year there was at last one Spitfire squadron in residence. Ipswich was also home to a diverse collection of Flights and other units, this element becoming increasingly evident from March 1943, when the airfield acquired full RAF Station status. The main users were various units engaged in providing target-towing for both aerial and ground-to-air gunnery use, as well as searchlight co-operation. One of the major customers was the naval – units based in and around Harwich. The Austers of 652 Squadron had arrived from Ayr in December 1943 and spent four months operating from Ipswich as part of their work-up for D-Day, co-operating with local army units. In addition to the likes of the Henleys and Martinets used by the target-towing units, Ipswich was also home to the Spitfires and

AIRFIELD DATA DEC 1944

Command:	RAF Fighter Command (ADGB)	Runway surface:	Grass
Function:	Parent Anti-Aircraft Co-operation Unit	Hangars:	one civil airport type (unserviceable)
		Dispersals:	nil
Runways:	NE/SW 1,250yd	Personnel:	Officers – 13
	NW/SE 1,250yd		Other Ranks – 292

Ipswich was used for short periods by various squadrons and aircraft; however, one of the longer resident types was the Auster, with 652 Squadron here from December 1943 to March 1944. (Note: Auster RT470 is not a 652 Squadron aircraft and this is not Ipswich.)

Hurricanes of No.1696 Bomber Defence Training Flight from March 1944 to April 1945. Gliders appeared at the airfield from October 1944 and, although the airfield was reduced to Care & Maintenance on 1 August 1945, the gliders continued to operate from here.

The airfield was handed back for civil use in 1946 and became a thriving private-flying field once more, with attempts to make it 'Ipswich Airport.' Sadly, it fell to local-government pressure in recent years and has now become a housing estate.

UNITS

1939–1945

86 Sqn det	Mar 1941–May 1941	Blenheim
107 Sqn det	May 1939–Mar 1941	Blenheim
110 Sqn det	Jun 1939–Mar 1942	Blenheim
129 Sqn	6–13 Jul 1942	Spitfire
131 Sqn	24–31 Aug 1942	Spitfire
154 Sqn	10–15 Aug 1942	Spitfire
268 Sqn	26–28 Apr 1941	Lysander
287 Sqn det	Nov 1941–	various
302 Sqn	21–29 Sep 1942	Spitfire
308 Sqn	15–21 Sep 1942	Spitfire
331 Sqn	7–14 Sep 1942	Spitfire
340 Sqn	20–26 Jul 1942	Spitfire
402 Sqn	29 Jun 1942–1 Jul 1942	Spitfire
577 Sqn det	Dec 1943–	various
611 Sqn	27 Jul 1942–1 Aug 1942	Spitfire
616 Sqn	1–7 Sep 1942	Spitfire
652 Sqn	7 Dec 1943–25 Mar 1944	Auster
679 Sqn	1 Dec 1943–26 Jun 1945	various
45 ERFTS	3 Jul 1939–3 Sep 1939	Magister, Hind
1508 Flt	15 Feb 1941–4 Apr 1941	Blenheim, Wellington
1517 Flt	4 Nov 1941–19 May 1946	Oxford
3 AAPC	Feb 1943–17 Jun 1943	
1616 Flt	13 Mar 1943–1 Dec 1943	Henley
1627 Flt	17 Jun 1943–1 Dec 1943	Lysander, Martinet
1499 Flt	19 Jun 1943–15 Feb 1944	Martinet
1696 Flt det	15 Feb 1944–29 Apr 1945	Spitfire, Hurricane
104 GS	Oct 1944–Apr 1948	Cadet, Sedbergh
88 Gp SU	7 Sep 1945–1 Dec 1945	

KNETTISHALL
Station 136

UTM/grid: OS Map 144 – TL970795
Lat./Long.: N52°22.6 E000°53.4
Nearest town: Thetford 6 miles to north-west

County: Suffolk

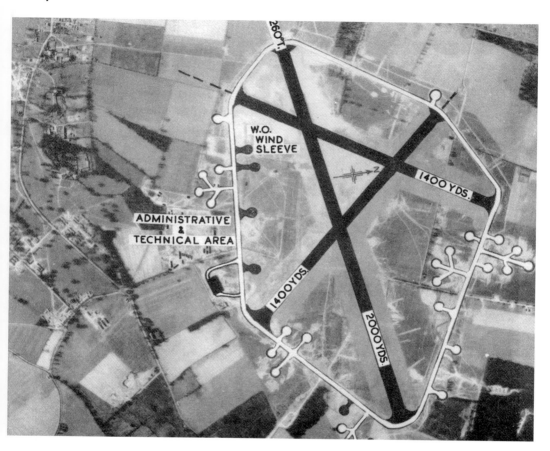

W.O.
WIND
SLEEVE

1400 YDS.

ADMINISTRATIVE
&
TECHNICAL AREA

1400 YDS.

2000 YDS.

260°T.

HISTORY

Yet another tract of East Anglian heathland that was determined suitable for the construction of a large bomber-airfield, Knettishall, named after the village on the northern edge of the airfield, was constructed in 1942 by W & C French to the standard pattern of runways, perimeter track and buildings. The airfield opened in January 1943, notionally as a No.3 Group satellite for Honington, but nothing happened at the site and by spring it had been allocated to the USAAF, becoming Station 136.

On 23 June the 388th Bomb Group, under the command of Colonel William B David, took up residence – this was to be their only operational station and they remained to the end of the war. The B-17s flew their first mission on 17 July, the target being an aircraft factory near Amsterdam; this proved to be the first of around 330 ops, which cost the Group 142 aircraft missing in action. The loss rate was average overall but the Group did suffer one disastrous mission, losing eleven B-17s during a 6 September 1943 attack on Stuttgart – the losses included all the aircraft from the 563rd Squadron. It is impossible to imagine the effect this would have had back at Knettishall as the remnants returned to a peaceful corner of Suffolk. The previous month the 388th – 'Johos' Jokers' – had received the first of two Distinguished Unit Citations, this one for the 17 August attack on Regensburg.

AIRFIELD DATA DEC 1944

Command:	US 8th AF 3rd BD	Runway surface:	Tar-covered concrete, partly wood-chipped
Function:	Operational	Hangars:	one × T.2
Runways:	220 deg 2,000 × 50yd	Dispersals:	50 × Loop
	270 deg 1,400 × 50yd	Personnel:	Officers – 421
	330 deg 1,400 × 50yd		Other Ranks – 2,473

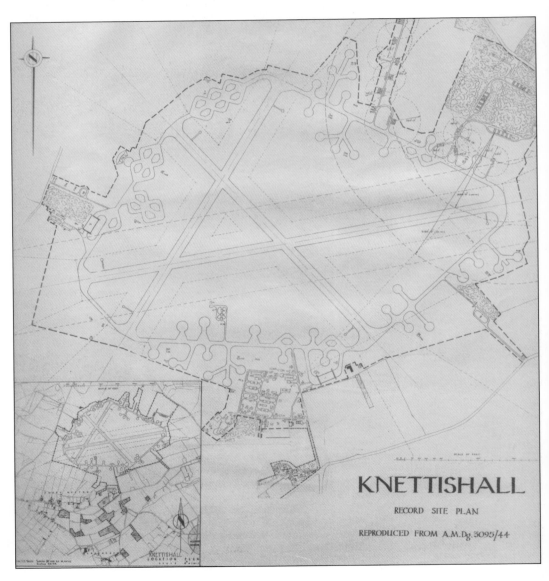

KNETTISHALL

RECORD SITE PLAN

REPRODUCED FROM A.M.Dg.3095/44

B-17 'Mary Ellen' and crew of the 388th BG, October 1943.

In addition to the usual routine of daylight bombing, the Group, or more particularly the 560th BS, was responsible for the trials with explosive-packed B-17 'flying bombs' under Project Aphrodite, although the satellite airfield at Fersfield was used for these operations. In common with most American Bomb Groups, the final mission over Germany was flown in late-April, by which time the thoughts of many American airmen were with the hoped-for quick return home. By August 1945 aircraft and personnel had gone and the airfield passed back to RAF control. It was held on RAF charge for another decade before being declared surplus to requirements and was finally sold off in the early 1960s. Agriculture has returned and fields dominate a landscape where once B-17s operated; there are very few traces of the airfield to be seen as you drive the Suffolk lanes, but in one wooded corner is a fine memorial stone.

UNITS

1939–1945
USAAF Units
388th BG (45th CBW)

Identifying letter:	H
Squadrons:	560th BS (Soapdish), 561st BS (Caprice), 562nd BS (Darklock), 563rd BS (Fairman)
Aircraft:	B-17F, B-17G
Dates:	Jun 1943–Aug 1945
Missions:	306
First mission:	17 Jul 1943
Last mission:	Apr 1945

MEMORIALS

Stone memorial with inscription: 'United States Army Air Forces, 388th Bomb Group (H), RAF Knettishall Station 136, 23 Jun 1943–5 August 1945. Fortress for freedom. 306 missions, 191 aircraft lost, 222 enemy aircraft destroyed, 8051 sorties, 542 killed, 801 prisoners. In fond memory of those men of the 388th Bomb Group (H) who flying from this field served with honour and died bravely in the cause of freedom. This memorial was dedicated on May 17, 1986 by survivors of the 388 Bombardment Group (H).'

The memorial records the statistics for the Group and incorporates the effective symbology of a B-17 breaking the chain of Nazi oppression.

LAKENHEATH

County: Suffolk

UTM/grid: OS Map 144 – TL740820
Lat./Long.: N52°24.18 E000°33.10
Nearest town: Brandon 4 miles to north-east

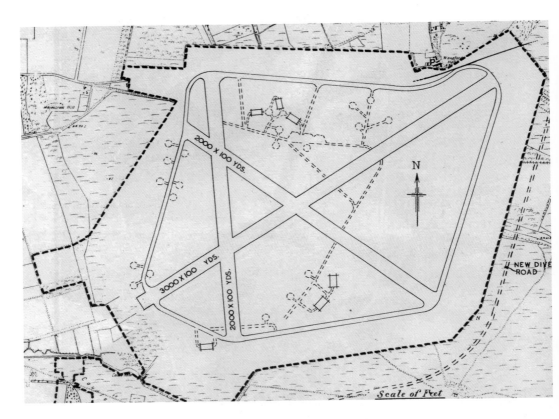

HISTORY

Lakenheath is the sole remaining USAAF airfield in the UK operating combat-types; the F-15s of the 48th Fighter Wing are all that is left of an American combat strength that once numbered thousands of aircraft, many of them based in East Anglia. The Americans have been in residence at Lakenheath for almost sixty years (since 1948), but the airfield had its origins as one of the wartime-build bomber stations so desperately needed in the early 1940s.

Authority was given in October 1940 to acquire land for a satellite for Mildenhall. Construction work on this large area of sandy heath took place in 1941 and, with limited facilities but three good runways, it opened late that year for No.3 Group of Bomber Command. Initial use was as a satellite for Mildenhall, just a few miles to the south-west, and the Stirlings of 149 Squadron began using the airfield

from November 1941, finally moving in as a resident unit the following April. The airfield was also used from early 1942 by the squadron's Conversion Flight before this was finally absorbed into the main unit later in the year. In November 1942 Lakenheath joined the ranks of Victoria Cross airfields when this highest gallantry award was made to Sergeant R Middleton of 149 Squadron for his actions on the Turin raid of 28–29.

As part of the reorganization of Bomber Command that took effect in spring 1943, Lakenheath became a sub-station for No.32 Base, its base stations being Mildenhall and Methwold, but remained part of No.3 Group, Bomber Command. This arrangement took effect on 24 March 1943 and a second squadron arrived in June to boost the operational strength. No.199 Squadron arrived with Wellingtons but

Stirlings of 149 Squadron operated from Lakenheath from November 1941 to May 1944, one of the longest-serving Stirling units.

The post 1945 period has seen almost unbroken use of Lakenheath by the USAF; these F-84s were on detachment in 1953. (US National Archives)

re-equipped with Stirlings to become part of the Group's contribution to Main Force although, by this time, the operational limitations of the Stirling were increasingly apparent. By January 1944 it had been decided to move the Stirlings to other tasks and 199 Squadron duly trained in special operations and moved to North Creake to join No.100 Group, whilst 149 Squadron went to Methwold. Lakenheath was reduced to care and maintenance in May 1944 for reconstruction, as the site had been allocated for redevelopment as a very-heavy-bomber station for the B-29. This work was still underway when the war ended but, unlike other airfields that had been designated for this use, Lakenheath did actually receive B-29s.

The Superfortresses of the 2nd Bomb Group arrived in July 1948 as part of the American response to the Berlin Crisis; this was the first of what became a routine of TDY (Temporary Duty) deployments by Strategic Air Command bombers to Lakenheath over the next eight or so years. During that time some thirty Bomb Groups/Wings rotated through the base, most staying for around ninety days. Not all of these movements are reflected in the unit table. Many of the deployments were supported by tankers, initially KB-29s and, later, KC-97s. Bomber types included B-47s and the massive B-36 Peacemaker. The bomber rotations ended in 1956 and the base was fairly quiet until the arrival of the 48th Fighter Wing and its F-100s, the first aircraft touching down from Chaumont on 15 January 1960. During more than forty years of this unit's tenure at Lakenheath it has operated the F-100, the F-4 (from January 1972), the

AIRFIELD DATA DEC 1944

Command:	RAF Bomber Command	Runway surface:	Concrete
Function:	Operational	Hangars:	3 × Glider, 2 × T.2, one × B.1
Runways:	186 deg 2,000 × 100yd	Dispersals:	36 × Heavy Bomber
	246 deg 3,000 × 100yd	Personnel:	Officers – 150 (6 WAAF)
	322 deg 2,000 × 100yd		Other Ranks – 1,800 (239 WAAF)

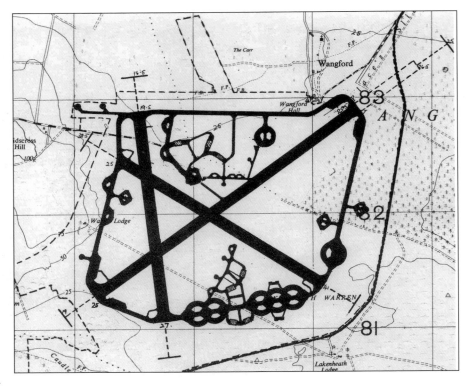

F-111 (from March 1977) – perhaps the type with which the 'Liberty Wing' is most associated – and latterly the F-15 (from February 1992) in both its 'C' and 'E' models, one squadron with the single-seat F-15C and two with the two-seat F-15E. The airfield itself has undergone many changes over the past thirty years, most notable being the construction of the Hardened Aircraft Shelters, although seldom a year goes by without some construction work at the airfield. The Group has taken part in numerous operational deployments in the past twenty years, from the strike on Libya to the various actions in Iraq and Bosnia.

Lakenheath also acts as parent station for Feltwell, home of Space Command's 5th Space Surveillance Squadron.

DECOY SITE

Q	Brandon

UNITS

1939–1945

149 Sqn	Nov 1941–15 May 1944	Stirling
199 Sqn	20 Jun 1943–1 May 1944	Wellington, Stirling
149 CF	13 Feb 1942–2 Oct 1942	Stirling

Post-1945
USAF Units

2nd BG	Jul 1948–	B-29
43rd BG	Aug 1949–	B-50, KB-29
48th FW	Jan 1960–date	F-100, F-4, F-111, F-15
93rd BG	Jan 1951–	B-50, KB-29

LANGHAM

County: Norfolk

UTM/grid: OS Map 132 – TF990420
Lat./Long.: N52°56.2 E000°57.47
Nearest town: Holt 5 miles to south-east

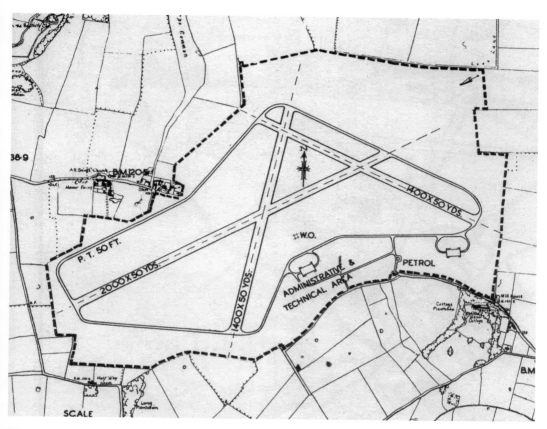

HISTORY

As home to one of Coastal Command's Strike Wings, Langham had a hectic 1944 and played its role in ensuring that German shipping was never safe from sudden air-attack; however, for most of its wartime history this Norfolk airfield was somewhat quieter. As little more than a clear stretch of land requisitioned by the Air Ministry, Langham opened in 1940 as an emergency landing-ground but before long it was officially a satellite for Bircham Newton and was being used by detachments from that increasingly busy airfield. Throughout its operational history the airfield was used by various units for detachments and deployments and, in typical Coastal Command fashion, the same squadron might be split between a number of nearby airfields for a specific operation or a

short-term deployment, thus making it difficult at times to list the units at a particular base. In the case of Bircham Newton, Docking and Langham there was always a close connection.

By summer 1940 the first of Langham's own identifiable units was in residence – 'M Flight' of No.1 Anti-Aircraft Co-operation Flight having moved across from Bircham to continue the role of target-towing in the Stiffkey coastal ranges. This primarily Henley-equipped unit was joined by 'K Flight' in December and both flew from Langham until they were re-designated in November 1942, becoming No.1611 and No.1612 Anti-Aircraft Co-operation Flights.

In July 1942 Langham was raised to the status of an independent station, this being signified by the

AIRFIELD DATA DEC 1944

Command:	RAF Coastal Command	Runway surface:	Tar on concrete
Function:	Operational	Hangars:	4 × Blister, 3 × T.2
Runways:	202 deg 1,400 × 50yd	Dispersals:	36 × Spectacle
	253 deg 2,000 × 50yd	Personnel:	Officers – 161 (14 WAAF)
	305 deg 1,400 × 50yd		Other Ranks – 2,254 (380 WAAF)

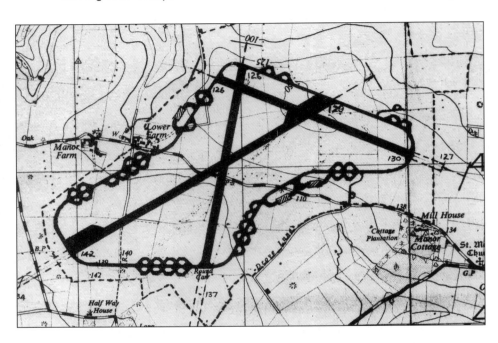

opening of a station headquarters on 16 July. First to arrive were the Swordfish biplanes of 819 Squadron, Fleet Air Arm, the intention being for them to fly night attacks on shipping; it appears that Langham had no torpedo storage at the time – or the RAF wouldn't give the Navy any – as the Swordfish had to go to Thorney Island to pick up weapons before returning to Langham to hold readiness. In August they departed, by which time the airfield was home to 280 Squadron with its Air Sea Rescue aircraft, although they, too, stayed only briefly. By the end of 1942 all the flying units had gone and Langham was under Care and Maintenance whilst building work took place. Other than runway and dispersal extensions, it is hard to determine what the rebuild involved; for example, was it at this time that one of the airfield's surviving (and now fairly rare) structures was built – the dome trainer (sometimes referred to as an astro dome and at other times as a gunnery dome).

When the airfield re-opened on 22 February 1944 it was for offensive purposes within No.16 Group and it now had three hard-runways of tar-on-concrete, thirty-six spectacle dispersal-points and seven hangars. It was the closest airfield to the north Norfolk coast, only two miles inland, and the sand spit at Blakeney Point was an excellent visual reference feature for the low-flying Beaufighters that now made their home at Langham.

In early April two experienced squadrons moved in from Leuchars, the Australian 455 Squadron and the New Zealand 489 Squadron, both flying the definitive anti-shipping Beaufighter X, capable of operating with torpedoes or rockets in addition to cannon and machine-gun. The Coastal Strike Wings are one of the most fascinating, and under-researched, aspects of RAF history and the role these Wings played in devastating German shipping in the last year of the war was crucial to the overall Allied strategy. Operations were flown either as opportunity sweeps (Rovers) with no planned target in mind or as strikes against a specific target spotted by air reconnaissance. In the latter instance the size and nature of the convoy and its defences would be assessed and the weapon mix – torpedo and RP, as well as flak suppression – would be decided, as would the need for any aerial escort, this latter often being provided by RAF Mustangs. Most German convoys were heavily defended by flak, and sometimes by fighter patrols, and some targets were set as traps for the attackers. Fortunately, the Beaufighter was able to take a tremendous amount of punishment and still keep flying – an aspect to which the hard-working ground crew at Langham could attest, as it was their task to patch up battle damage and keep the maximum number of aircraft serviceable. If the target was big enough or important enough, more than one Strike Wing would combine and Langham's Wing participated in a number of these big missions.

By late-1944 the number of suitable targets had reduced and the Strike Wing moved to new hunting-grounds, leaving Langham far quieter, although the ASR 280 Squadron returned for a few weeks. With German shipping increasingly seeking the cover of night Langham returned to ops, with the presence of two RAF squadrons with Wellingtons for night attack and a FAA squadron with Albacores. Although the Albacores only stayed to the end of the

year, Wellingtons, operated by a variety of squadrons, remained operational from Langham to the end of the war. However, whilst the operational flying was important, the airfield was also playing a vital role in a number of support functions, one of the most important being meteorological research. With its diverse collection of aircraft, from Gladiator to B-17 Fortress, 521 Squadron flew daily met-sorties, providing information vital to accurate forecasting.

This twin role of offence and support saw Langham through to the end of the war and, whilst it is not an airfield that people readily call to mind, it was, without doubt, one of Norfolk's most interesting wartime locations.

With the end of the war Langham became a centre of excellence for met flying and in addition to the well-established 521 Squadron a number of other units operated here, or even formed here for initial training before deploying elsewhere. A brief re-appearance by anti-shipping Beaufighters and Mosquitoes of 254 Squadron in November 1945 was not an indicator of the airfield's post-war future and they departed in early 1946. However, Langham was not destined for immediate closure, despite this cessation of flying. The airfield was used from July 1946 by a Royal Netherlands Air Force Technical Training School, part of the support

Wellington XIV of 524 Squadron, Langham 1945; the airfield was a major offensive base for Coastal Command – its most dramatic period being that of the Beaufighter-equipped Strike Wing in 1944.

Langham has one of the rare buildings surviving in this region – a dome trainer that at various times was used for anti-shipping and as an astro trainer for night navigation.

being given to that air force as it re-established itself. However, in September the following year the Station was reduced to Care and Maintenance, a position that for most airfields at this time was a death sentence. Langham managed a second lease of life during the RAF's re-expansion in the 1950s for the Korean War and the Cold War. Beaufighters and Mosquitoes returned, but in the guise of target-towers with No.2 Civil Anti-Aircraft Co-operation Unit, this unit also having a number of Vampire T.11s in its final months at Langham. Cessation of flying came again in November 1958 but the airfield was maintained for a few more years, partly because its runways had been refurbished in the early 1950s, and was used as an ELG (back to its original function) by Sculthorpe. Final disposal came in October 1961 but the fact that this was once an airfield is still evident to anyone driving along the road that runs across the centre of the site: to one side you can see the old control-tower along with a number of other buildings, as well as traces of runway and perimeter track and, of course, that rare dome-trainer.

DECOY SITES

| Q | Salthouse Heath | TG073422 |
| Q | Warham St Mary | TF938433 |

UNITS

1939–1945

254 Sqn	26 Nov 1945–6 May 1946	Beaufighter, Mosquito
280 Sqn	31 Jul–1 Nov 1942, 6 Sep–30 Oct 1944, 3–23 Nov 1945	Anson, Warwick
407 Sqn det	14 Apr–10 May 1945	Wellington

455 Sqn	13 Apr–24 Oct 1944	Beaufighter
489 Sqn	8 Apr–24 Oct 1944	Beaufighter
521 Sqn	30 Oct 1944–3 Nov 1945	Gladiator, Hudson, Hurricane, Spitfire
524 Sqn	1 Nov 1944–25 May 1945	Wellington
612 Sqn	17 Dec 1944–9 Jul 1945	Wellington
819 Sqn FAA	Jul 1942–Aug 1942	Swordfish
827 Sqn FAA	Nov 1944–Dec 1944	Barracuda
1 AACU det	Jul 1940–1 Nov 1942	Henley, Defiant
1611 Flt	1 Nov 1942–9 Nov 1942	Henley
1612 Flt	1 Nov 1942–8 Dec 1942	Henley
2 AAPC	16 Feb 1943–17 Jun 1943	Lysander
1626 Flt	17 Jun 1943–30 Nov 1943	Lysander

Post-1945

CC FATU	1 Sep 1945–6 Jan 1946	
1402 Flt	4 Dec 1945–10 May 1946	
1561 Flt	17 Dec 1945–11 Feb 1946	Spitfire
1562 Flt	17 Dec 1945–11 Feb 1946	Spitfire
2 CAACU	23 Mar 1953–1 Nov 1958	various

MEMORIALS

Set of kneelers in the church, dedicated 3 Sep 1989.

There is no memorial at the airfield but the church includes a fine set of embroidered kneelers.

LAVENHAM
Station 137

County: Suffolk

UTM/grid: OS Map 155 – TL895525
Lat./Long.: N52°08.04 E000°46.16
Nearest town: Lavenham 3 miles to south-east

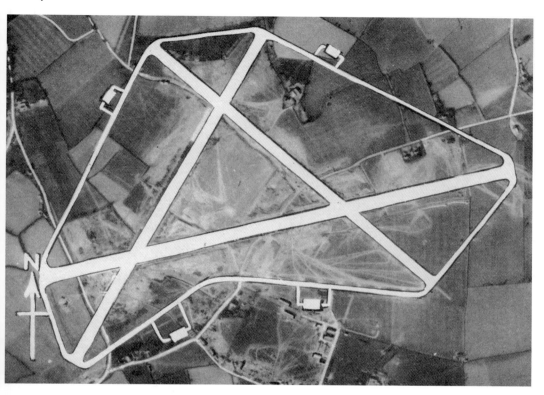

HISTORY

This was one of the final airfields built for the Eighth and construction at Lavenham took place in 1943, the majority of the work being carried out by John Laing & Son, working to the well-established Class A airfield pattern. It was designed from the outset for a USAAF Bomber Group and had the usual two T.2 hangars and fifty hardstands, in addition to one main runway of 2,000 yards and two secondary runways of 1,400 yards each. Other than that, the main airfield site was fairly bleak, with few buildings other than the control tower – the bulk of the temporary buildings being located in clutches around the airfield, in the case of Lavenham mainly to the south.

Under the command of Lieutenant Colonel Beirne Lay Jr, the B-24s of the 487th Bomb Group arrived at Lavenham in April 1944 and were to be the airfield's only operational residents. The Group quickly settled in and its first mission was flown on 7 May, the focus

of attacks being connected with the bombing strategy preparing the way for the forthcoming Allied invasion of France. Within days of commencing ops, the CO's aircraft failed to return from a mission, but it was soon discovered that Beirne Lay had evaded capture. The Group subsequently re-equipped with the B-17 (August 1944), in line with the rest of 3rd Bombardment Division, and by the end of the war had flown a total of 185 missions for the loss of forty-eight aircraft missing in action. Although the 487th were not awarded any distinctions, they were acknowledged for their bombing expertise, leading the bombing accuracy table from January 1945 to the end of the war.

With the end of the war in Europe the bombers and their personnel soon departed and by September there was little trace of the once massive American presence in this corner of Suffolk. The RAF took

AIRFIELD DATA DEC 1944

Command:	US 8th AF 3rd BD
Function:	Operational Station
Runways:	270 deg 2,000 × 50yd
	220 deg 1,400 × 50yd
	330 deg 1,400 × 50yd

Runway surface:	Concrete, 6in layer
Hangars:	2 × T.2
Dispersals:	50 concrete
Personnel:	Officers – 421
	Other Ranks – 2,473

The B-17s of the 487th BG operated from Lavenham from April 1944 to the end of the war, flying 185 missions.

control of the airfield and it appeared on the books of Transport Command; they, however, had no use of yet another airfield in this area and handed it to Maintenance Command on 31 July 1946. This transfer was brief and it moved on to Bomber Command on 20 August. As far as one can tell, no use was made of the site and it was declared surplus in 1948, finally being sold off in April 1958.

Thanks to the landowner, much of the site and certain of the technical/domestic areas still exist and, whilst it is not routinely open for viewing, visitors can go to the site. The control tower is a house but one group of Nissen huts houses an aviation museum.

Atmospheric shot of early 1944 (B-24 period for the Group) showing T.2 hangar and clutch of Nissen huts. (US National Archives)

UNITS

1939–1945
USAAF Units
487th BG (92nd CBW/4th CBW)

Identifying letter:	P
Squadrons:	836th BS (Winner), 837th BS (Rathmore), 838th BS (Entrap), 839th BS (Bluntish)
Aircraft:	B-24H, B-24J, B-17G
Dates:	4 Apr 1944–26 Aug 1945
Missions:	185
First mission:	7 May 1944
Last mission:	21 Apr 1945

MEMORIALS

1. Plaque (dedicated 2 Aug 1970) on wall in the village marketplace, inscribed: 'Dedicated to the men of the 487th Bomb Group (H) who sacrificed their lives in World War II that the ideals of democracy might live.'

2. Plaque (dedicated 10 May 1986) on the old control tower, inscribed: 'USAAF Station 137 Lavenham. 487th Bomb Group (H) were stationed here November 1943 to October 1945.

LEISTON
Station 373

UTM/grid: OS Map 156 – TM430645
Lat./Long.: N52°13.23 E001°33.38
Nearest town: Saxmundham 3 miles to west

County: Suffolk

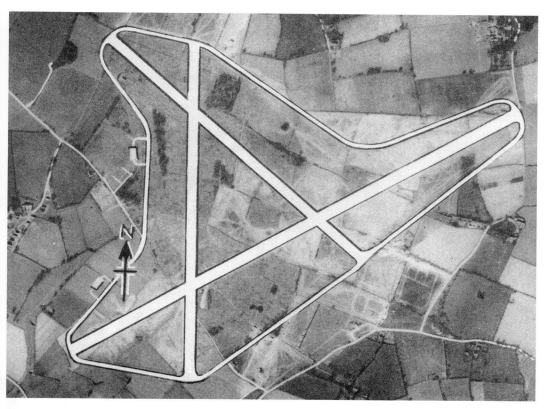

HISTORY

Located only three miles from the east coast and thus only a few minutes flying time from enemy territory, Leiston was an ideal location for a fighter airfield and it was as such that it was constructed for USAAF use in 1943. Although provided with the standard general layout of runways and dispersals, it is suggested that the latter were built to a lower specification, as they were only going to be used by fighters; furthermore, a number of the dispersals were provided with blast wall protection, perhaps an indication of a perceived threat from hit-and-run raiders across the sea. To say that the airfield was given standard facilities is not strictly true; the data sheet for late-1944 shows that, although the runways were hard-paved (perhaps a waste for a fighter field), the dispersal types were non-standard. These comprised thirty-eight frying-pan and twelve fighter-type, each capable of holding

two aircraft, and seventeen with PSP surfaces, giving a total of sixty-seven dispersals rather than the usual fifty. Likewise, Leiston had more hangar space, being provided with twelve Blister hangars in addition to the normal two T.2s. This might, perhaps, be explained by the fact that the airfield had a subsidiary function to provide lodger facilities for an RAF fighter-squadron – not that one was ever based at the airfield.

A number of aircraft landed at the airfield whilst it was still under construction – to a stricken bomber it was one of the first bits of friendly runway likely to come into view – but it was not until November 1943 that the first planned unit took up residence. The P-47s of the 358th Fighter Group moved in to Station 373 from Goxhill and on 20 December flew their first escort mission. In the period to the end of January

AIRFIELD DATA DEC 1944

Command:	US 8th AF	Runway surface:	Tarmac and concrete
Function:	Operational	Hangars:	12 × Blister, 2 × T.2
Runways:	060 deg 2,000 × 50yd	Dispersals:	38 × Frying Pan, 17 × PSP, 12 × Double Fighter Pens
	130 deg 1,400 × 50yd	Personnel:	Officers – 215
	180 deg 1,400 × 50yd		Other Ranks – 1,799

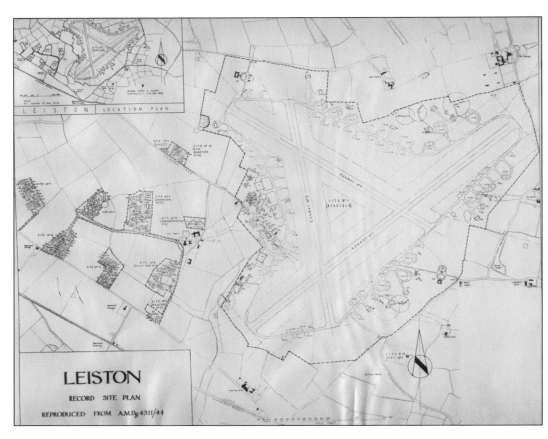

LEISTON

RECORD SITE PLAN

REPRODUCED FROM A.M.D₃ 4311/44

1944 they flew seventeen missions for the cost of four aircraft missing in action. Their stay at Leiston was curtailed by the decision to swap units between the 8th and 9th Air Force; in this case the 358th changed places with the 357th at Raydon. The Mustang-equipped 357th had been at Raydon since the end of November but had yet to commence ops; their transfer to Leiston was part of VIIIth Fighter Command's desire to operate the P-51 in the escort role. This was the first such Group to operate with the 8th and, from its operational debut on 11 February, it was involved in what became the full range of Mustang missions – from close escort and sweep, to ground attack. In its fifteen months of operations from Leiston it logged 313 missions for the loss of 128 aircraft missing in action; in exchange it claimed 609½ enemy aircraft in air-to-air combat and 106½ destroyed on the ground (giving it the second-highest score in the Command). The unit had a number of claims to fame, including the fastest rate of victories for 1945 amongst 8th Air Force fighter units and the highest claims on a single mission – on 14

Pilots of the 357th FG; the Group operated various marks of the P-51 from January 1944 to the end of the war. (Bob Dorr)

During its period of ops from Leiston the Group claimed over 600 enemy aircraft, for the loss of 128 of its own aircraft.

January 1945 the group claimed fifty-six enemy aircraft. During its operational period it was awarded two Distinguished Unit Citations, one of which was tied in with the record claim for victories.

Whilst for most USAAF bases the end of the war meant abandonment as resident units flew west for America, from Leiston the Mustangs flew east in July 1945, as the Group had been selected as one of the Allied Occupation Force units. The RAF took control of the airfield in October but it was never destined to continue as a flying station; instead it became No.18 Recruit Training Centre within Technical Training Command, a surprising choice considering the station's remote location. This lasted less than a year and, with the closure of the Centre, the airfield stood abandoned until sold off in the mid-1950s.

MEMORIALS

1. Stone to 357th FG.

2. Plaque (dedicated 8 May 1980) on wall of old Post Office in Leiston, inscribed: 'United States Air Force Eighth Fighter Command 357th Fighter Group. Dedicated to the brave men who made the supreme sacrifice in the fight for freedom 1944–1945.'

UNITS

1939–1945
USAAF Units
358th FG
Squadrons:	365th FS, 366th FS, 367th FS
Aircraft:	P-47
Dates:	29 Nov 1943–Jan 1944
First mission:	20 Dec 1943

357th FG (66th FW)
Squadrons:	362nd FS, 363rd FS, 364th FS
Aircraft:	P-51B, P-51C, P-51D, P-51K
Dates:	31 Jan 1944–8 Jul 1945
Missions:	313 (including from other bases)
First mission:	11 Feb 1944
Last mission:	25 Apr 1945

LITTLE SNORING

County: Norfolk

UTM/grid: OS Map 132 – TF960335
Lat./Long.: N52°51.38 E000°54.45
Nearest town: Fakenham 3.5 miles to south-west

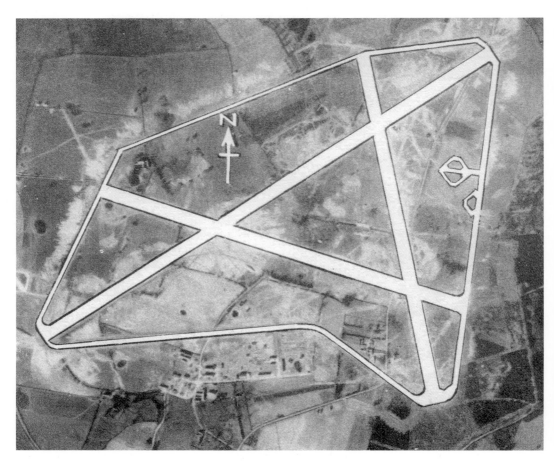

HISTORY

If Langham, five miles to the north, was famous for the exploits of its Coastal Command Strike Wing, then Little Snoring's wartime claim to fame is as a night-intruder base for Mosquitoes, although this was not the airfield's original purpose.

This area of Norfolk countryside was acquired in late-1942 and, over a period of months, a bomber station was created, complete with three runways, a perimeter track linking the runways, thirty-six loop-type hardstands and a limited range of buildings, including five hangars and a control tower. The new airfield was opened in July 1943 for use as a satellite airfield to Foulsham, but it was almost immediately

allocated to No.3 Group, Bomber Command and raised to independent station status. The following month, the Lancasters of 115 Squadron arrived from East Wretham, along with 1678 HCU, whose task it was to convert crews to the Lancaster, in this case the Hercules-engined Lancaster II; 115 Squadron was still in the process of converting to type having spent the first years of the war equipped with Wellingtons. However, it was only a matter of weeks before the Squadron moved out again, although by this time they had started bombing ops with their new aircraft. The HCU had already departed, in September, and the airfield was cleared ready for its new role with

Lancaster of 115 Squadron undergong engine servicing at Little Snoring; the Squadron spent four months here in 1943. (Andy Thomas)

No.100 Group, many of the airfields in this part of Norfolk having been handed to this new, specialist organization. The transfer took place on 7 December and 169 Squadron took up residence, being joined by No.1692 Flight with its Defiants and Mosquito IIs. The Squadron received Beaufighter IIs in January and crews were converted to night-fighter ops and the use of special equipment, such as Serrate, by the instructors of 1692 Bomber Support Training Flight. Operations commenced on 20 January, the first task being in the Berlin area, and the first success came a few nights later, on 30 January. It is worth noting that the scoreboards of Little Snoring's night-fighter units are preserved and displayed on a wall in the village church.

A second night-fighter unit, 515 Squadron, had also arrived in December and soon converted to Mosquitoes from Beaufighters, eventually opening its new operational phase in March. Night intruding was not the sole prerogative of the RAF and the Luftwaffe scored numerous successes against aircraft over the UK – they even attacked airfields from time to time and on the night of 19–20 April a German aircraft sowed bombs along Little Snoring's runway. The nightly cat-and-mouse tactics of the intruders brought a string of successes and some losses; the airfield was to remain operational in this role to the end of the war.

With the arrival of 23 Squadron in early June 1944, two units left – 619 Squadron and 1692 Flight both moving to Great Massingham. The 'new boys' were experienced intruders, but from the Mediterranean theatre of ops, and with 515 Squadron to add a touch of European experience and an intensive training-programme, including low-level night flying, the

Squadron was soon back in action – specializing in low-level attacks on airfields. For the remaining months of the war the two squadrons participated in a variety of sorties and continued to add to their scores; their final missions were flown on the night of 2–3 May 1945, bringing to an end an impressive record of operations in one of the most hazardous of roles.

Wartime achievements were no guarantee of survival in the post-war period and, with almost unceremonious haste, 515 Squadron was disbanded on 10 June 1945, to be followed in September by 23 Squadron, although as a low-numbered squadron the latter was subsequently re-born. A brief appearance by another night-fighter unit, 141 Squadron, led to yet another disbandment at Little Snoring, this unit giving up its aircraft in September (but reforming the following year at Wittering).

With so many Mosquitoes on the airfield from disbanded squadrons it was, perhaps, logical to use the Station for storage and disposal of the type and, in December, No.112 Sub Storage Unit took over this task. However, in 1947, the airfield was placed into Care and Maintenance and its fate looked to be sealed. There was a final burst of flying activity when No.2 Civilian Anti-Aircraft Co-operation Unit, operated by Marshalls of Cambridge, was based here from July 1951 to March 1953 operating Spitfires, whilst the Beaufighter element continued to operate from Cambridge. The departure of the CAACU brought the airfield's career to an end and it was disposed of in the late-1950s.

Parts of the airfield survived and, indeed, not all flying ceased, as the site was used as a General Aviation airfield for a while.

AIRFIELD DATA DEC 1944

Command:	RAF Bomber Command	Runway surface:	Concrete
Function:	Operational	Hangars:	2 × T.2, 2 × Glider, one × B.1
Runways:	130 deg 1,400 × 50yd	Dispersals:	36 × Loop
	190 deg 1,400 × 50yd	Personnel:	Officers – 165 (10 WAAF)
	250 deg 2,000 × 50yd		Other Ranks – 2,003 (352 WAAF)

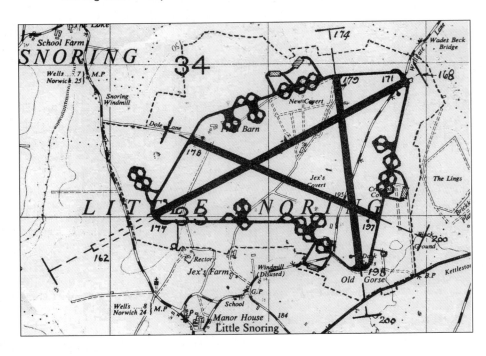

UNITS

1939–1945

23 Sqn	2 Jun 1944–25 Sep 1945	Mosquito
115 Sqn	6 Aug 1943–26 Nov 1943	Lancaster
141 Sqn	3 Jul 1945–7 Sep 1945	Beaufighter, Mosquito
169 Sqn	8 Dec 1943–4 Jun 1944	Mosquito
515 Sqn	12 Dec 1943–10 Jun 1945	Beaufighter, Mosquito
1678 HCU	6 Aug 1943–16 Sep 1943	Lancaster
1473 Flt	28 Nov 1943–12 Dec 1943	
1692 Flt	10 Dec 1943–21 May 1944	Mosquito, Anson

Post-1945

2 CAACU	20 Jul 1951–23 Mar 1953	Spitfire

MEMORIALS

Plaques in Little Snoring church, plus squadron score-boards; the village sign incorporates a Mosquito.

The night intruder role performed by the Station's Mosquitoes as part of No.100 Group was part of the tactic to reduce bomber losses; Mosquito RS566 of 515 Squadron. (Andy Thomas)

LUDHAM
(HMS *Flycatcher*)

County: Norfolk

UTM/grid: OS Map 133 – TG395195
Lat./Long.: N52°43.07 E001°33.12
Nearest town: Norwich 12 miles to south-west

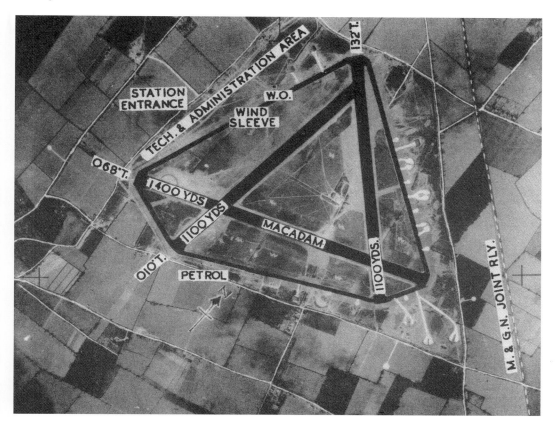

HISTORY

Located within a few miles of the coast of north-east Norfolk, Ludham was one of the few airfields in the county to be used purely as a fighter station by the RAF and, for most of its operational life, it was home to Spitfire units. The airfield was laid out during 1941 and it appears to have been used from autumn that year as a forward deployment airfield, before its official opening in December. The first resident flying unit was 19 Squadron, bringing their Spitfire IIAs in from Matlask as No.12 Group repositioned its remaining fighter squadrons for the new offensive role, whilst maintaining a defensive posture covering major cities – in this case Norwich. Ludham was officially a satellite for Coltishall and its location made it ideal for Spitfire ops; whilst this fighter was an undoubtedly superb machine for aerial combat, it was

very limited in range and, until the advent of long-range fuel tanks, the stationing of aircraft as far forward as possible was the only way of increasing the radius of action. For the Spitfires of 19 Squadron, tasks included convoy escort and patrol, and bomber escort – usually as part of a 'Circus' operation – in addition to defensive patrols and readiness. As a satellite station the airfield's facilities were limited, but this was not a problem for fighter ops and the squadron settled in over the winter, coping with the poor weather that is a feature of winter in this part of Norfolk.

In April 1942 the Squadron departed for Hutton Cranswick, but as one bunch of Spitfires left another arrived, the newcomers being Spitfire Vs of 610 Squadron, the two units simply exchanging airfields.

Ludham opened in late 1941 and although very few units spent long here it was an important base for fighter detachment; the first operational users were the Spitfires of 19 Squadron. (Note: this 19 Squadron aircraft is not at Ludham).

In terms of operations little changed and convoy work and offensive sweeps remained the main tasks, although with an increase in German night-bomber activity the Squadron was also tasked with night standby – the so-called 'Fighter Nights' – a role for which the Spitfire was supremely unsuited!

October brought another changeover of unit: 610 Squadron exchanging places at Castletown with 167 Squadron. With a high proportion of Dutch pilots in its ranks, the unit was glad to leave its quiet post in Scotland and move south for some real operational flying; Ludham was particularly apt, as it was only a short distance from Holland. Although convoy patrols were still on the agenda, the bulk of the Squadron's work involved cross-Channel offensive sweeps and bomber escorts. East Anglia was not, however, immune to attack and German fighter-bombers made a number of raids during 1943, the Fw190 having been adapted to this role. The Spitfire V was outclassed in performance terms by the latest German types, so the Typhoon-equipped 195 Squadron arrived at Ludham in May 1943, displacing the Spitfires. This was a short-lived venture and, whilst the Typhoons flew both offensive and defensive missions, primarily as 'on the job' training for the invasion role the Typhoon was destined to play in 1944, there was little advantage to them operating from this corner of Norfolk. In July they moved out, albeit only as far as Matlask and then Coltishall, before going to Fairlop in September. Spitfire IXs were more of a match for the Fw190 but the appearance of 611 Squadron with this type was only transitory – a mere four days, although the unit remained in East Anglia for some months.

The reason given for the departure of the flying unit was that Ludham was scheduled for re-development, the intention at this stage being to allocate it to the USAAF as a fighter base. Some development took place and Ludham eventually ended up with three concrete-and-tarmac runways and fifty new dispersals of 'PSP USAAF type'. For some reason the Americans did not move in and, although the airfield remained officially allocated to VIIIth Fighter Command, its next occupants were the Fleet Air Arm, with the airfield becoming HMS *Flycatcher* from August 1944. For the Fleet Air Arm this was an important unit, as it was to be home to the Mobile Naval Airfield Organization.

However, no operational units arrived and, on 16 February 1945, it returned to RAF control in exchange for Middle Wallop. A few days later two Spitfire XVI squadrons flew in and Ludham was back in the war again. The operational role had not really changed and Ludham's fighters were soon ranging over Europe looking for air and ground-targets, as well as pouncing on shipping, in the latter role often working with Coastal Command Beaufighters. Both squadrons left in April and the same month the final operational unit took up residence, 91 Squadron bringing its Spitfire XXIs from Manston for the final few days of the war. They were joined by the similarly equipped 1 Squadron in May and both remained in residence until July, ironing out some of the problems with this latest Spitfire variant.

AIRFIELD DATA DEC 1944

Command:	US VIIIth Fighter Command	Runway surface:	Concrete and tarmac
Function:	Operational for Fleet Air Arm	Hangars:	4 × Blister, one × T.2
Runways:	078 deg 1,400 × 50yd	Dispersals:	50 × PSP USAAF Type, 12 × Pens,
	198 deg 1,100 × 50yd		9 × Permanent hardstands
	322 deg 1,100 × 50yd	Personnel:	Officers – 190
			Other Ranks – 1,519

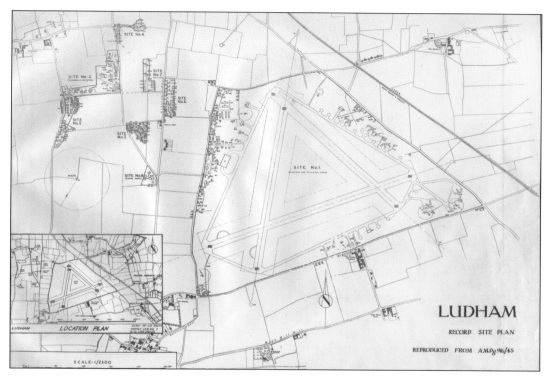

The end came quickly for Ludham; the squadrons departed and, after a brief allocation to No.60 Group in September, the airfield was effectively out of commission by the end of 1945.

A stretch of the old runway 07/25 is still in use as a private airfield and a number of buildings survive at the site. For those wanting to fly in to Ludham Aerodrome it is strictly PPR and you need to refer to one of the published Flight Guides.

DECOY SITE

Q   Somerton   TG485205
This site may also have been used as a Starfish decoy for Great Yarmouth.

UNITS

1939–1945

1 Sqn	14 May 1945–23 Jul 1945	Spitfire
19 Sqn	1 Dec 1941–4 Apr 1942	Spitfire
91 Sqn	8 Apr 1945–14 Jul 1945	Spitfire
167 Sqn	14 Oct 1942–1 Mar 1943,	Spitfire
	15 Mar–13 May 1943	
195 Sqn	13 May 1943–31 Jul 1943	Typhoon
602 Sqn	23 Feb 1945–5 Apr 1945	Spitfire
603 Sqn	24 Feb 1945–5 Apr 1945	Spitfire
610 Sqn	4 Apr 1942–15 Oct 1942	Spitfire
611 Sqn	31 Jul 1943–4 Aug 1943	Spitfire
1489 Flt det	Dec 1942–? 1943	Lysander, Martinet

MARHAM

County: Norfolk

HISTORY

As the RAF's major reconnaissance base, Marham continues to play a central role in the RAF's operational commitments and each of the current squadrons is involved with one or other of the ongoing United Nations or Coalition tasks. This operational involvement has been a feature of Marham throughout its history.

The airfield opened in September 1916 as the home for the HQ Flight and 'C Flight' of 51 Squadron (the other two flights being at Tydd St Mary and Mattishall), established as part of the Home Defence network. Equipped primarily with FE2bs and Avro 504s, although additional types such as BE12b and Martinsyde G100 were also used, the Squadron joined

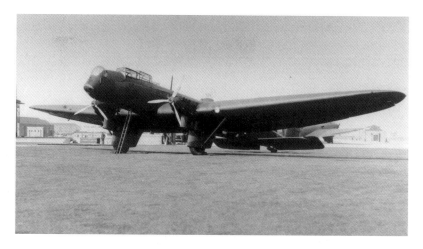

Fairey Hendon night bombers equipped 38 Squadron from 1937 and were not replaced, by Wellingtons, until 1940.

the RFC's routine of standing patrols and operational standbys. Marham had been chosen as the German airships often used the Wash as a pointer towards London but, despite this, the 51 Squadron crews saw little action. December 1917 saw the arrival of 191 (Night) Training Squadron under the command of Major Arthur T Harris, later to become famous as head of Bomber Command during World War Two.

The role for 51 Squadron remained primarily that of Home Defence, but it was also tasked with carrying out trials on potential night-fighter types and a variety of aircraft passed through the station, including at least one DH10. The end of the war was used as an excuse by crews to 'attack' the nearby training airfield at Narborough – the Marham aircraft dropped flour bombs but soon suffered retaliation when the Narborough units returned the favour using soot bombs!

Marham did not survive the post-war disbandment phase and the landing-ground site returned to agriculture. However, as part of the RAF's 1930s Expansion Programme, Marham was again chosen to become an operational airfield. On 1 April 1937, Marham opened as a standard two-squadron heavy-bomber station in No.3 Group, Bomber Command; shortly afterwards, the Heyfords of 38 Squadron arrived from Mildenhall to become the first operational unit. The second squadron, 115 Squadron, was formed by the then standard expedient of splitting the existing unit in two and building both up to full strength. By the summer both units had re-equipped, 38 Squadron with Hendons and 115 Squadron with Harrows. All RAF units were put on standby and a war footing was established with the 1938 Munich Crisis; fortunately, the crisis passed and the RAF had another year in which to accelerate re-equipment programmes. For the Marham units this saw the welcome arrival of Wellingtons, the first aircraft

(L4230) being delivered to 38 Squadron on 28 September 1938; bomber strength continued to increase and on 1 June 1939 the New Zealand bomber squadron (later to become 75 Squadron) was formed. The pace of events increased and Marham began to make use of a satellite field at Barton Bendish.

With the German invasion of Poland on 1 September 1939, the RAF came to full alert and, as part of the pre-planned dispersal operation, 38 Squadron moved its aircraft to Barton Bendish, whilst other Wellingtons were dispersed around the edges of Marham itself.

The first operational sortie was flown on 8 October, when six crews of 115 Squadron joined a similar number from 99 Squadron on a raid against German shipping. It was, like many of these early missions, un-productive. It was to be a similar story for the next six months: very few ops and most of those bringing no result.

Everything was to change in May 1940 and, from that point onwards, the 'real' war arrived for Marham and Bomber Command. During May the Marham units operated on fifteen nights against targets in Norway, Holland and Germany. The first bombs to be dropped on Marham 'arrived' on 10 July, when 'at 0600 an enemy aircraft dropped eighteen light bombs on both sides of the main road. A simultaneous attack was made on the dummy airfield leaving eighteen small craters.' November 1940 saw 38 Squadron depart for Malta, their place at Marham being taken by the Wellingtons of 218 Squadron from Oakington. It was the same pattern into 1941, with targets in Germany and the invasion ports – Marham units being involved on most occasions. The following year, 115 Squadron was chosen as a trials unit for the new GEE navigation-system and, in February,

Bombing-up a Wellington of 115 Squadron on the outskirts of the airfield, by Ladywood, 1940.

The Mosquito period for Marham was a fascinating one during which new tactics and techniques were developed by the Station's squadrons; 105 Squadron Mossies await the next mission.

undertook a number of trials that proved the validity of the system. At around the same time, 218 Squadron was commencing its conversion to the RAF's first four-engined bomber, the Stirling.

The Wellingtons and Stirlings continued to take part in Main Force raids throughout the summer and then, in September, came news that Marham was to change roles to become home to two Mosquito units. The 'heavies' moved out to Downham Market and Feltwell and, on 29 September 1942, the Mosquitoes of 105 and 139 Squadrons arrived. The station acquired an impressive reputation, expressed well by Flying Officer Hayes of 105 Squadron when he said, 'Why listen to the news, we made the news.'

The Mosquito crews ranged over most of northern Europe, attacking pinpoint targets or flying nuisance raids over cities. The first ops were flown from Marham on 1 October and over the next few weeks the squadron undertook met reconnaissance, high-level bombing, cloud-cover raids, low-level and shallow-dive attacks. December 6 brought the first of the 'classic' raids, with eight aircraft tasked to attack the Philips valve-and-radio works at Eindhoven, the mission being led by Wing Commander Hughie Edwards VC, OC 105 Squadron. The Marham effort was part of an overall attack force of ninety-three aircraft: six of the Marham crew bombed the target, the other two being chased off by Fw 190s (although both Mosquitoes returned safely). The two operational squadrons were kept busy, but Marham was

Marham introduced the B-29 Washington I into RAF service and in addition to the conversion role maintained a Wing of these 'bombers on loan'; formation of 115 Squadron Washingtons.

also home to 1655 MTU (Mosquito Training Unit), with responsibility for converting crews to the aircraft.

In 1944 the Mosquitoes acquired an additional role in support of the Main Force operation; loss rates to night fighters had reached such proportions that greater efforts were made to disrupt the enemy night-fighter airfields and the Marham units joined this campaign by attacking airfields such as Deelen, Leeuwarden, Venlo and Gilze-Rijen. The run-down began in March with the departure, on 7 March, of 1655 MTU to Warboys. Two weeks later 105 Squadron and its associated 9105 Servicing Echelon moved to Bourn, followed in early April by 109 (and 9109 SE) to Little Staughton. Marham passed to the custody of the Clerk of Works for major construction work to turn it into a very-heavy-bomber base. The intention was to create three runways, the main one being 3,000 yards by 100 yards and the other two 2,000 yards by 100 yards. It was a huge project, involving the laying of over one million square yards of concrete. The work force peaked at 1,100 and at one stage they were laying 1,850 cubic metres of concrete a day! Although work was not completed in time for Marham to see any further operational use during World War Two, the new construction did at least guarantee the base a post-war future.

In February 1946 the Central Bomber Establishment moved in to the west Norfolk base from Feltwell; Marham was now ready to play a crucial role in the development of bomber tactics for what was to become the Cold War era. It was a slow build-up for the unit, although trials work had commenced as soon as the first aircraft arrived, and much of Marham still resembled a building site. Meanwhile, CBE continued to acquire, usually on a short-term basis, a variety of aircraft types for specific trials. However, the majority of work was carried out by various marks of either Lancasters or Mosquitoes. Development Wing was the primary trials-organization but it is important to realize that Marham *was* the CBE; it was not simply a case of CBE being just another unit. Amongst the trials was that of Project Ruby, which also involved an operational American detachment.

The American connection was reinforced in July 1948 with the arrival, on detachment, of the B-29s of the 340th BS, in what was to become a regular series of visits by such USAF heavy-bomber units over the next three decades. The Berlin crisis the following year brought an even bigger influx of USAF bombers to the UK, Marham receiving the HQ of the 3rd Air Division, along with aircraft of the 370th and 371st Squadrons of the 307th BG from McDill Air Force Base. In November they were replaced by units of the 97th BG as the Cold War tensions continued.

The decision was taken to return Marham to operational status as the RAF's B-29 base; so the CBE moved to Lindholme by April 1949 to clear Marham once more for bomber ops. The aircraft were to be provided under the MDAP (Mutual Defence Assistance Program) and the first four arrived on 22 March 1950. Major construction work on the dispersal areas was required and it was during this period that Marham acquired the distinctive strip of concrete along the front of its hangars. As home of the Washington Conversion Unit, the station was tasked with crew (air and ground) conversion for all B-29 Washington (as the aircraft was called in RAF service) units. The first operational unit was 115 Squadron, appropriately enough after its distin-

AIRFIELD DATA DEC 1944

Command:	RAF Bomber Command	Runway surface:	Concrete
Function:	Operational	Hangars:	5 × C
Runways:	245 deg 3,000 × 100yd	Dispersals:	10 × Very Heavy Bomber
	293 deg 2,000 × 100yd	Personnel:	Officers – 149 (10 WAAF)
	335 deg 2,000 × 100yd		Other Ranks – 2,523 (334 WAAF)

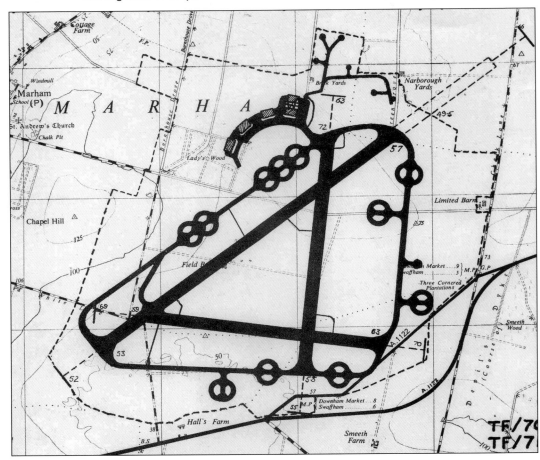

guished wartime record at Marham. By late-summer 1951 the bulk of the initial conversion work was completed and the operational squadrons – 35, 90, 115 and 207 – were busy getting to grips with their new aircraft and trying to achieve their monthly flying task of 315 hours.

The routine continued through the early 1950s but by 1953 the end of the RAF's B-29 period was in sight and the 'return to the USA' plot was promulgated as Operation Home Run, to 'return thirty-seven B-29s,

having become surplus to requirements, to the USA'. All but one were to be ferried to the storage base at Davis Monthan; the first series of flights took place in July with four aircraft going on each of three days during the month. By December, only seventeen B-29s were left at Marham – and in the same month the first of the English Electric Canberra B.2s arrived, this being the type with which the Marham squadrons were to re-equip. As one of Bomber Command's Canberra Wing bases, the Station was to receive four

Marham acquired two HAS sites for its Tornado squadrons; II (AC) Squadron eventually took over the site vacated by 617 when the latter moved to Lossiemouth.

squadrons for the 'night medium-bomber role'. Initially, 90, 115 and 207 re-equipped, each receiving an establishment of twelve aircraft; the final unit, 35 Squadron, followed in April 1954. It was to be a short-lived period, as the Canberras had been intended as a stop-gap and jet introduction pending delivery of the 'real' jet bombers, the 'V-bombers' – in Marham's case this was to mean the arrival of the Vickers Valiant. No.90 Squadron was first to go, reforming with Valiant B(PR)1s in June 1956. They were not, however, the first Valiant squadron at Marham, 214 Squadron having arrived in January.

The 1954 survey shows Marham with a main runway of 9,070ft × 300ft, with significant overruns at each end (750–1,000ft). Further extension would be difficult as 'to the NE it would involve filling in the valley running in from the NW; a large barn would also have to be demolished'. Neither of the other two runways could be extended because of the terrain. In addition to the twenty-two loop-hardstands of 100ft diameter, Marham now had an impressive 384,000sq ft apron area.

By summer 1956, 207 and 148 Squadrons had also taken on Valiants, whilst the run-down of Canberras continued. Although the new bombers had only been in service a matter of months, the Suez Crisis of late-1956 brought the base to operational readiness as aircraft were prepared for deployment to Malta. Three of the Valiant units sent aircraft and crews to Malta as part of Operation Albert in September, with the Marham Station Commander, Group Captain L Hodges, acting as Force Commander.

Calamity struck in mid-1964 with the discovery of major airframe-cracks in the Valiants and the demise of the fleet was inevitable. However, May 1965 saw the station acquire the aircraft and role that was to be its forte for the next twenty-eight years, when the Handley Page Victor B(K)1A arrived with 55 Squadron. By January Marham had two operational Victor tanker-squadrons, 57 Squadron having also

arrived. The final unit of the Tanker Wing units to acquire the Victor was 214, this unit changing its Valiant tankers for the 'new' type.

The Victor K.2 variant replaced the older variants in mid-1975; the following year, Marham entered its second phase of Canberra ops with the arrival of 100 Squadron from West Raynham in the target facilities role in January 1976 and, in February, the aircraft of 231 Operational Conversion Unit. Marham remained a hectic base, with a large number of aircraft and a worldwide commitment; with the requirement to keep a Victor on operational standby to support the QRA (Quick Reaction Alert) fighters, the base was very much still in the front line.

With the Argentine invasion of the Falkland Islands in April 1982, the British military was faced with a major logistical problem in mounting a recovery operation. Land-based air power relied on in-flight refuelling in order to fly missions from the nearest base at Ascension Island. Marham's Victors flew hundreds of support sorties for a wide range of aircraft and the Victor detachment was, without doubt, the lynch-pin of the RAF's operations.

The next major change came with the arrival of a Tornado strike-wing in 1983, two GR.1 squadrons taking up residence in the HAS sites that sprouted on the east side of the airfield. A sad event was the demise of the Victor in 1993 – after yet another significant contribution to an offensive campaign with the Gulf Conflict of 1990–91. Tornado strength was increased, as the reconnaissance GR.1As of II Squadron moved to Marham from Laarburch as part of the RAF's draw-down of strength in Germany. It was not long, however, before the resident strike-attack squadrons moved out – much to the delight of II Squadron, as they could take over one of the vacated HAS sites. The decision was taken to create a reconnaissance force at Marham and the second GR.1A unit, XIII Squadron, moved in from Honington. The final element was the Canberras of 39 (1 PRU) Squadron, thus giving Marham its third period with the Conberra.

All of Marham's units continued to be involved in operations on a worldwide basis and it was one of the busiest stations in the UK; however, with the final closure of RAF bases in Germany it became even busier, with the arrival of two more Tornado squadrons; all four units now fly GR.4 variants.

Marham is now the RAF's premier offensive station and home to one of the most capable reconnaissance Wings in NATO. One of the standing jokes in the RAF is that the final RAF flying squadron (probably a joint number of 1/617 Squadron) with its single Eurofighter Typhoon will operate from RAF Marham (otherwise known as 'Sandringham Airport').

Decoy Sites

Q	South Acre	TF796122
Q/K	South Pickenham	TF8504
Q/K	Swaffham	TF832038
Q	Wormegay	TF653125
Q/K	Barton Bendish	TF720045

Barton Bendish was also referred to as East Moor landing ground and was a dispersal satellite for Marham in 1939–1940, before taking up its role as a day-and-night decoy. The area covered some 340 acres and Wellingtons were dispersed here from December 1939. There was some subsequent use as a landing ground; for example, by Tomahawks of 26 and 268 Squadrons in the period June to September 1942 and perhaps by 218 Squadron's Conversion Flight in late-1942.

Units

Pre-1919

51 Sqn	7 Aug 1917–14 May 1919	FE2b, BE2e
191 NTS	6 Nov 1917–Jul 1918	FE2b, BE2c
192 NTS	10 Oct 1917–14 Nov 1917	FE2b, FE2d

1920–1938

38 Sqn	5 May 1937–12 Nov 1940	Hendon, Wellington
115 Sqn	15 Jun 1937–24 Sep 1942	Hendon

1939–1945

38 Sqn	5 May 1937–12 Nov 1940	Hendon, Wellington
115 Sqn	15 Jun 1937–24 Sep 1942; 13 Jun 1950–1 Jun 1957	Hendon, Harrow, Wellington
105 Sqn	22 Sep 1942–23 Mar 1944	Mosquito
109 Sqn	5 Jul 1943–2 Apr 1944	Mosquito
139 Sqn	29 Sep 1942–4 Jul 1943	Mosquito
NZ Flt	1 Jun 1939–27 Sep 1939	Wellington
3 Gp TTF	14 Feb 1940–18 Nov 1941	
218 CF	20 Jan 1942–2 Oct 1942	Stirling
1418 Flt	6 Jan 1942–1 Mar 1942	Wellington
ABTF	13 Jul 1942–15 Mar 1943	
1483 Flt	13 Jul 1942–29 Jun 1943	Lysander, Wellington
1427 Flt	5 Sep 1942–2 Oct 1942	Stirling, Halifax
1655 MTU	28 Sep 1942–1 May 1943; Jul 1943–7 Mar 1944	Mosquito

MCU	29 Sep 1942–18 Oct 1942	Mosquito

Post-1945

2 Sqn	1 Dec 1991–date	Tornado
9 Sqn	17 Jul 2001–date	Tornado
13 Sqn	1 Feb 1994–date	Tornado
15 Sqn	29 Nov 1950–4 Feb 1951	Lincoln
27 Sqn	1 May 1983–Dec 1993	Tornado
31 Sqn	Jul 2001–date	Tornado
35 Sqn	1 Sep 1951–16 Jul 1956	Washington, Canberra
39 Sqn	Dec 1993–date	Canberra
44 Sqn	7 Feb 1951–9 Apr 1951	Washington
49 Sqn	26 Jun 1961–1 May 1965	Valiant
55 Sqn	24 May 1965–15 Oct 1993	Victor
57 Sqn	1 Dec 1965–30 Jun 1986	Victor
90 Sqn	4 Oct 1950–1 May 1956	Washington, Canberra
100 Sqn	5 Jan 1976–5 Jan 1982	Canberra
115 Sqn	13 Jun 1950–1 Jun 1957	Canberra, Washington
148 Sqn	1 Jul 1956–1 May 1965	Valiant
149 Sqn	9 Aug 1950–17 Oct 1950	Washington
207 Sqn	4 Jun 1951–27 Mar 1956	Washington, Canberra
214 Sqn	21 Jan 1956–1 Mar 1965	Valiant
218 Sqn	25 Nov 1940–8 Jul 1942	Wellington, Stirling
242 Sqn	1 Oct 1959–30 Sep 1964	Bloodhound
617 Sqn	1 Jan 1983–Apr 1994	Tornado
CBE	25 Sep 1945–14 Apr 1949	
BC WTS	23 Feb 1950–1 Jul 1950	Washington
WCU	1 Jul 1950–1 Sep 1951, 16 Jun 1952–27 Mar 1953	Washington
BC JCF	16 Nov 1953–30 Sep 1954	
1 AEF	1 Apr 1963–?	Chipmunk
1 Gp SU	Feb 1968–Dec 1968	Victor
231 OCU	12 Feb 1976–31 Aug 1982	Canberra
232 OCU	6 Feb 1970–4 Apr 1986	Victor
611 VGS	Apr 1996–1 May 1996	

Memorials

1. Very impressive station history-room.

2. Plaques in operations block.

3. Gate Guard Victor.

MARTLESHAM HEATH
Station 369

County: Suffolk

UTM/grid: OS Map 169 – TM245455
Lat./Long.: N52°03.03 E001°16.24
Nearest town: Ipswich 3 miles to west

HISTORY

To many people, Martlesham Heath, or simply Martlesham as it is frequently called, is best known for its wartime role as an American fighter-base; however, this slice of Suffolk countryside just east of Ipswich had a far more complex and interesting history than most of the airfields in this region and, as home to various trials establishments, played an important role in RAF history.

The airfield was established in 1916 as a Home Defence station, part of the new defensive arrangement being made by the RFC to protect the east of England against German bombing, and the first occupants appear to have been 'A Flight' of 37 Squadron. This unit was not, however, primarily here

in an air-defence role, as in May it was absorbed by the Experimental Establishment. In January 1917, the Testing Squadron of the Central Flying School moved in from Upavon, absorbing the units already at Martlesham and firmly establishing the airfield's experimental and testing credentials. Such was the scale and importance of the work being carried out that, on 16 October, it was re-designated as the Aeroplane Experimental Station. From its collections of hangars and huts, the staff of the AES operated dozens of Allied and German types on all manner of tests and evaluations and it must have been a truly fascinating airfield in the latter months of the war.

P-47 of the 356th FG; the Group flew over 400 mission from Martlesham between October 1943 and the end of the war.

Martlesham survived the post-war disbandments and, although reduced in size, continued its work, which was extended to include civil types – often modified ex-military types. On 16 March 1922 the unit became the Aeroplane Experimental Establishment, a further change of title coming in March 1924 to the Aeroplane and Armament Experimental Establishment (usually abbreviated to A&AEE). Two squadrons were formed to conduct these elements; 15 Squadron taking on the armament work and 22 Squadron looking after the aeroplane aspect, the latter being designated as 'handling and performance'. There were further organizational and nomenclature changes over the next fifteen years but, in essence, the Establishment maintained its role as an RAF Centre of Excellence, whose pilots were responsible for evaluating – and where necessary criticizing – the offerings of the manufacturers.

Secrecy was very much the order of the day by the mid-1930s and the variety of aircraft types passing through Martlesham must have been impressive; a time-travelling aviation historian would certainly list this as one of the places he would like to sneak a look at! The trials reports issued by the Establishment are essential reading for anyone interested in a particular aircraft or weapon. The Experimental Co-operation Unit (ECU) was formed at Martlesham in September 1937 to undertake trials with the new Radio Direction Finding (RDF) equipment and, whilst records of the unit are scanty, it appears to have been active on the airfield to just before the war.

However, with the approach of war, it was obvious that the exposed location of this highly secret and vital installation was not ideal and it was inevitable that the A&AEE would have to move. This move took place in early September 1939 to Boscombe Down, the airfield with which A&AEE is more usually associated and which has led to a general ignorance of the part played by Martlesham. An east-coast location was, of course, well suited for fighter operations and, after a few months of tenure by No.4 Recruit Training Pool, the airfield was allocated to Fighter Command. As convoy escort and patrol was a major task for the Command this airfield was ideal for fighter detachments and this tended to be the routine for Martlesham for the next two years – rotational detachments of squadrons from other airfields rather than as a home base for any one unit. The airfield was also used as an advanced base for specific operations and most units stayed no more than a matter of weeks, or even days. The tabular list of units shows the impressive number of squadrons that spent time in this corner of Suffolk.

During the Battle of Britain, Martlesham was attacked on a number of occasions, with two raids in August 1940 causing a certain amount of damage and casualties. The fighters claimed successes throughout

Typhoon of 182 Squadron at Martlesham Heath November 1942. (Andy Thomas)

AIRFIELD DATA DEC 1944

Command:	US 8th AF	Runway surface:	Sand-mix hard runway
Function:	Operational Station	Hangars:	3 × Blister, one × A, one × G, one × GS
Runways:	040 deg 1,700yd	Dispersals:	20 temporary steel matting
	220 deg 1,650yd	Personnel:	Officers – 190
			Other Ranks – 1,519

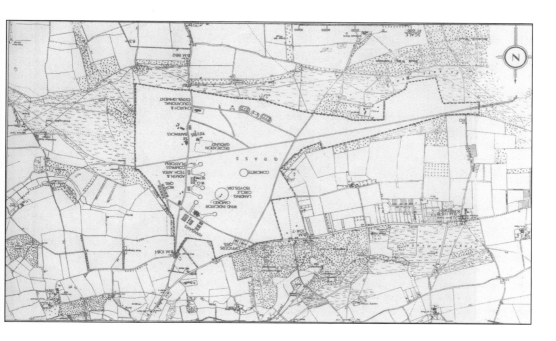

this period and, with the Luftwaffe turning to night bombing, Martlesham's rotation of units began to include night-fighter squadrons. In addition to its fighter role the airfield's easterly position made it suitable as a base for air-sea rescue operations and 277 Squadron operated a detachment from here from December 1941 to early 1944, flying a variety of types.

The heathland on which the original station was built was not ideal for large-scale development, in terms of what had become a standard airfield-pattern by the mid-war years but, nevertheless, an improvement programme was instituted to include new runways, perimeter track and dispersals. Two long runways were laid but, as the plan shows, this was very much an unusual overall layout. However, it proved more than adequate for its next users; on 15 October 1943 the P-47s of the 356th Fighter Group arrived from Goxhill under the command of Lieutenant Colonel Harold J Rau. The unit had been

at Goxhill since August, working up on its Thunderbolts, and so was soon in action, flying its first mission from Station 369 on 15 October. Mustangs were received in November and the Group went on to fly over 400 missions from Martlesham, but with a loss of 122 aircraft missing in action against claims of 276 (201 aerial victories) it had the poorest kill ratio of any 8th Air Force Fighter Group. The Group was awarded one Distinguished Unit Citation, for its work in supporting airborne operations in Holland during September 1944.

With the rapid departure of the Americans after the war, the RAF moved back in and Martlesham was returned to its trials role, the first significant residents being the Blind Landing Experimental Unit and the Bomb Ballistics Unit, both of which operated a variety of aircraft. To start with, it was only the scientific staff that were at Martlesham, the flying element of the BLEU remaining at Woodbridge, but they were all brought together in spring 1946, with the airfield operating as a satellite to Felixstowe. So it was back to 'business as usual', as the airfield was once more playing a key role in assessing both Allied and ex-German equipment. The two units were merged in November 1949 into real alphabet spaghetti as the BBBLEE (Bomb Ballistics and Blind Landing Experimental Establishment). The following May it became the much more manageable Armament and Instrument Experimental Establishment, this organization being under the functional control of the Ministry of Supply. One reason for the presence of this unit at Martlesham post-war was the fact that the range area at Orfordness was only ten miles away. The disbandment of the A&IEE in June 1957 brought Martlesham's trials role to an end but, when its pre-1939 and post-1945 career is taken into consideration, it is evident that the airfield and its resident units deserve far more historical credit than they usually receive.

The final few years of the airfield's RAF career brought brief occupation by a variety of units, flying and ground. After a period in Care and Maintenance to mid-April 1958, the next arrivals were the Communications Flight of No.11 Group, the latter equipped with Ansons and Meteors. On 2 June 1958, HQ Fighter Command moved in and for just over two years Martlesham was a significant location for Fighter Command; however, following a major reorganization of the Command in December 1960, all units disbanded and Martlesham was once more returned to Care and Maintenance. Only months before (March 1960) the Queen had approved the station badge with a Latin motto that translated as 'all deeds well done' – it would be a fitting summary of the station's history, for on 9 April 1963 RAF Martlesham closed and was put up for disposal.

The last flying unit to leave had been the Air Training Corps gliders of 612 VGS and it is also worth mentioning that, for a brief period, the RAF Battle of Britain Flight had been in residence.

Whilst the operating surfaces have gone, vanishing under buildings and roads, a significant number of the airfield's buildings survive, including the restored control tower that is now used as a museum.

DECOY SITES

| Q/K | Hollesley Heath | TM350462 |

UNITS

1920–1938

| 15 Sqn | 20 Mar 1924–31 May 1934 | DH9A, Horsley |
| 151 Sqn det | Dec 1938–17 May 1940 | Hurricane |

| ECU | Sep 1937–17 Feb 1941 | Anson, Harrow |

1939–1945

1 Sqn	15 Feb 1944–3 Apr 1944	Typhoon
3 Sqn	3 Apr 1941–23 Jun 1941	Hurricane
17 Sqn	16 Dec 1939–30 Apr 1940, 9 Oct 1940–26 Feb 1941	Hurricane
25 Sqn det	Oct 1939 – Sep 1940	Blenheim
26 Sqn	11–16 Jul 1943	Mustang
41 Sqn	15–30 Jun 1942	Spitfire
54 Sqn	4–24 Aug 1941	Spitfire
56 Sqn	6–15 Aug 1943, 4 Oct 1943–15 Feb 1944	Typhoon
64 Sqn	9–15 May 1941, 19–27 Jul 1942	Spitfire
65 Sqn	9–15 Jun 1942	Spitfire
71 Sqn	5 Apr 1941–23 Jun 1941, 14 Dec 1941–2 May 1942	Hurricane, Spitfire
72 Sqn	22–29 Jun 1942	Spitfire
111 Sqn	21–27 Sep 1942	Spitfire
122 Sqn	29 Jun 1942–6 Jul 1942, 29 Sep 1942–3 Oct 1942	Spitfire
124 Sqn	5–13 Jul 1942, 7–21 Dec 1942	Spitfire
132 Sqn	23 Sep 1942–28 Feb 1943	Spitfire
133 Sqn	22–31 Aug 1942	Spitfire
182 Sqn	25 Aug 1942–7 Dec 1942, 30 Jan 1943–1 Mar 1943	Hurricane, Typhoon
198 Sqn	5 Jun 1943–19 Aug 1943	Typhoon
222 Sqn	1–29 Apr 1943	Spitfire
236 Sqn	9 Dec 1939–29 Feb 1940	Blenheim
239 Sqn	27 Jun 1943–9 Jul 1943	Mustang
242 Sqn	16 Dec 1940–9 Apr 1941	Hurricane
257 Sqn	5 Sep 1940–8 Oct 1940, 7 Nov 1940–16 Dec 1940	Hurricane
258 Sqn	10 Jul 1941–3 Oct 1941	Hurricane
264 Sqn	7 Dec 1939–10 May 1940, Aug 1940–Oct 1940	Defiant
266 Sqn	1 Mar 1940–14 May 1940	Spitfire
277 Sqn det	Dec 1941–Oct 1944	various
278 Sqn	May 1944–15 Feb 1945	various
284 Sqn	17 May 1943–Jun 1943	no aircraft?
303 Sqn	26 Mar 1943–8 Apr 1943	Spitfire
310 Sqn	26 Jun 1941–20 Jul 1941	Hurricane
312 Sqn	20 Jul 1941–19 Aug 1941	Spitfire
317 Sqn	29 Apr 1943–1 Jun 1943	Spitfire
350 Sqn	7–16 Jul 1942; 7–15 Sep 1942	Spitfire
401 Sqn	28 Jul 1942–3 Aug 1942, 21–31 Jul 1943	Spitfire
402 Sqn	23 Jun 1941–10 Jul 1941, 3–9 Aug 1942	Hurricane, Spitfire
403 Sqn	3 Oct 1941–22 Dec 1941, 3–19 Jun 1942	Spitfire
412 Sqn	1 May 1942–4 Jun 1942	Spitfire
416 Sqn	16 Jul 1942–23 Sep 1942, 8–24 Nov 1942	Spitfire
421 Sqn	10–22 Apr 1943	Spitfire
453 Sqn	24 Nov 1942–7 Dec 1942	Spitfire

The control tower has been restored and is now used as a museum; the signals square with it MH code is also still in place by the tower.

485 Sqn	15–22 Feb 1943	Spitfire
501 Sqn	17 May 1943–5 Jun 1943	Spitfire
504 Sqn	24 Dec 1939–7 May 1940	Hurricane
605 Sqn	25 Feb 1941–31 Mar 1941	Hurricane
607 Sqn	20 Aug 1941–10 Oct 1941	Hurricane
611 Sqn	10–20 Jul 1942	Spitfire
Experimental Flt	1939–15 Sep 1939	Battle
ASRF	14 May 1941–22 Dec 1941	Lysander
1488 Flt	7 Jun 1942–17 Aug 1943	Lysander, Master
1616 Flt	1 Nov 1942–13 Mar 1943	Henley

USAAF Units
356th FG (67th FW)

Squadrons:	359th FS, 360th FS, 361st FS
Aircraft:	P-47D, P-51D/K
Dates:	5 Oct 1943–4 Nov 1945
Missions:	413
First mission:	15 Oct 1943
Last mission:	7 May 1945

Post-1945

22 Sqn det	Jun 1955–Jun 1956	Sycamore, Whirlwind
66 Sqn	6 May 1948–10 Jun 1948	Meteor
BLEU	Jul 1946–1 Nov 1949	various
BBU	Jul 1946– 1 Nov 1949	various
104 GS	Apr 1948–1 Sep 1955	Cadet, Sedbergh
BBBLEE	1 Nov 1949–1 May 1950	various
AIEU	1 May 1950–30 Jun 1957	various
612 VGS	1 Sep 1955–6 May 1963	
11 Gp CF	15 Apr 1958–31 Dec 1958	Anson, Meteor
BBMF	16 May 1958–3 Nov 1961	Lancaster, Spitfire, Hurricane

MEMORIALS

On former parade ground memorial (dedicated 13 Jun 1946), inscribed: 'In grateful memory of the members of the 356th FG USAAF from this station who gave their lives during the war 1939 to 1945. This plaque was erected by their British friends to commemorate the stay of the USAAF at Martlesham Heath.'

MATLASK

County: Norfolk

UTM/grid: OS Map 133 – TG158345
Lat./Long.: N52°51.40 E001°11.31
Nearest town: Holt 5 miles to north-west

HISTORY

As part of No.12 Group's fighter screen across north-east Norfolk, it was decided that the Sector Station at Coltishall needed two satellites; the second of these was constructed over an area of farmland at Matlaske (the RAF dropped the 'e' from Matlaske in most of its records). This unprepossessing area of fields was developed into a simple grass-airfield with very few facilities other than a perimeter track, dispersals and a number of hangars, along with a limited admin and technical area along the northern edge of the roughly square site. However, during its wartime career it was home to every RAF fighter-type, including the little-used Westland Whirlwind.

The site was requisitioned in early 1940 and the 'building' work was soon complete, the first unit, 72 Squadron, deploying its Spitfires from Coltishall for a few days in early November. It seems likely that other fighter units made use of the airfield on a temporary basis over the next few months but, as a satellite airfield, the records are poor. The next definite

occupants were the Spitfires of 222 Squadron in June 1941 and the Hurricanes of 601 Squadron in July, neither of which stayed for more than a few weeks. Matlask was well placed for aircraft operating over the sea and convoy patrols were a routine task, as they were from all the fighter bases in the region. The Spitfire IIs of 19 Squadron took up residence in August 1941 and stayed to the end of the year when they were replaced by the distinctive Whirlwinds of 137 Squadron. This unit operated from Matlask for some months, during which time it specialized in shipping protection and shipping attack, although it did have the odd tussle with German fighters. A few of the fighter pens still survive at Matlask and, with a bit of imagination, the visitor can envisage one of these sleek and aggressive-looking rarities sitting waiting for the call to action. The Squadron had mixed fortunes during its time here and in August 1942 moved to Snailwell to hunt shipping further south.

AIRFIELD DATA DEC 1944

Command:	RAF Fighter Command (ADGB)	Runway surface:	Grass
Function:	Operational	Hangars:	5 × Blister, one × D.2
Runways:	NW/SE 1,600yd	Dispersals:	21 concrete dispersals
	SW/NE 1,300yd	Personnel:	Officers – 110 (2 WAAF)
			Other Ranks – 2,567 (132 WAAF)

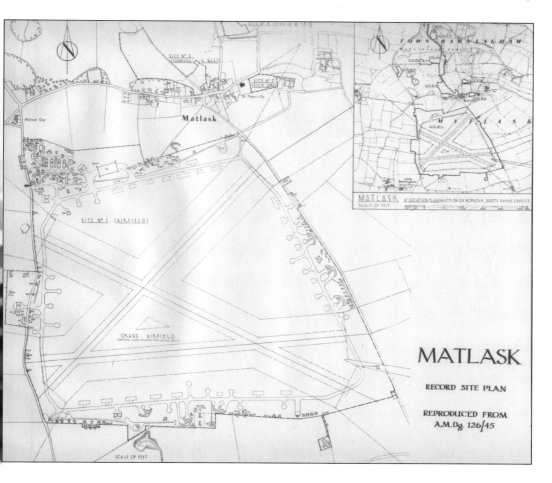

Meanwhile, the airfield had acquired additional flying units in the shape of air-sea rescue operators, 278 Squadron having moved in during October 1941 with a mixed bag of aircraft, including the Walrus and Lysander. A new type appeared at the airfield in mid-1942 with the arrival of the Typhoon-equipped 266 Squadron, although after only a few days here in August they were replaced by the similarly-equipped 56 Squadron. This unit remained at Matlask for almost a year, during which they honed their skills with the potent, but, in its early days, troublesome, Typhoon. The major emphasis was on offensive operations and the squadron flew a large number of 'Rhubarbs', attacking a variety of targets 'across the water'. Defensive scrambles, along with Sector patrols, were also a regular feature as, during 1943, the Luftwaffe increased its hit-and-run fighter operations against targets on the East coast.

The airfield was closed in August 1943 for improvement work, primarily involving consolida-

Typhoon of 56 Squadron at
Matlask in 1943; the airfield
was frequently used as a forward-deployment base by
fighter units.

tion of the grass flying-surface and reconstruction
work on the perimeter track and dispersals, in part
to fit the airfield for the new tactical concept of
operating aircraft in Wings of three squadrons.
During its closed period there was still some activity
and an American unit, the 3rd Engineer Aviation
Battalion, undertook training here during March
and April. The task of the EAB was rapid airfield-
construction and they were rehearsing for their role
in the invasion; it seems likely that they installed –
and perhaps then removed – the temporary
airfield surfaces, such as PSP and SMT, that would be
used for building airfields in the Normandy beach-
head.

A three-squadron Wing of Tempests operated
from Matlask for a week in September 1944, the first
operational flying from the airfield for almost a year;
as soon as they left they were replaced by three
squadrons of Mustangs. The latter stayed slightly
longer and flew a number of escort and offensive missions; with their departure in October, they were
replaced by Spitfire squadrons, some of which
remained into spring 1945. The last of the Spitfires
left in April but Matlask's final wartime months had
been busy ones. With the end of the war the airfield
had one final period of flying activity, as home to two
Auster squadrons for the latter part of 1945, but its
lack of facilities meant that there was little point in
keeping it on the books. The Austers departed at the
beginning of October and the airfield was rapidly
closed down.

UNITS

1939–1945

3 Sqn	21–28 Sep 1944	Tempest
19 Sqn	16 Aug 1941–1 Dec 1941; 4–20 Jun 1943; 28 Sep 1944–4 Oct 1944	Spitfire; Mustang
56 Sqn	24 Aug 1942–22 Jul 1943; 23–28 Sep 1944	Typhoon; Tempest
65 Sqn	29 Sep 1944–14 Oct 1944	Mustang
72 Sqn	30 Oct 1940–2 Nov 1940	Spitfire
122 Sqn	28 Sep 1944–14 Oct 1944	Mustang
137 Sqn	1 Dec 1941–24 Aug 1942	Whirlwind
195 Sqn	31 Jul 1943–21 Aug 1943	Typhoon
222 Sqn	6 Jun 1941–1 Jul 1941	Spitfire
229 Sqn	22 Oct 1944–20 Nov 1944	Spitfire
266 Sqn	2–11 Aug 1942	Typhoon
278 Sqn	1 Oct 1941–10 Apr 1942	Lysander, Walrus
451 Sqn	23 Feb 1945–6 Apr 1945	Spitfire
453 Sqn	18 Oct 1944–6 Apr 1945	Spitfire
486 Sqn	19–28 Sep 1944	Tempest
601 Sqn	2 Jul 1941–16 Aug 1941	Hurricane
602 Sqn	18 Oct 1944–20 Nov 1944	Spitfire
609 Sqn	22 Jul 1943–18 Aug 1943	Typhoon
611 Sqn	1–31 Jul 1943	Spitfire
658 Sqn	10 Jul 1945–2 Oct 1945	Auster
659 Sqn	10 Jul 1945–2 Oct 1945	Auster
ASR Flt	Jul 1941–1 Oct 1941	Walrus
12 Gp TTF	13 Apr 1942–8 Dec 1942	Lysander
1489 Flt	13 Apr 1943–2 Jun 1943	Lysander, Martinet

MENDLESHAM
Station 156

UTM/grid: OS Map 155/156 – TM130635
Lat./Long.: N52°13.53 E001°07.15
Nearest town: Stowmarket 5.5 miles to south-west

County: Suffolk

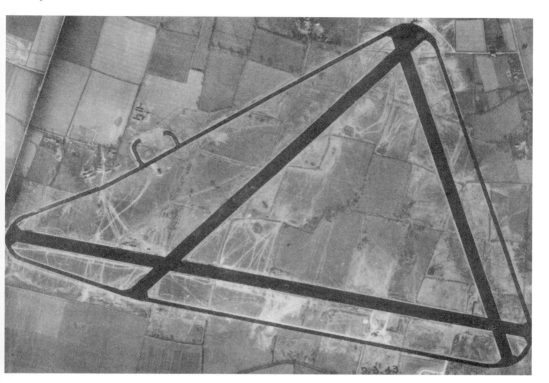

HISTORY

Mendlesham was one of the later airfields to open in East Anglia and, whilst the site was a fine, flat piece of land that required little more than hedge and ditch removal, it was sandwiched between the A140 – the major north–south road through Suffolk – and a B road. Anyone looking for the airfield in Mendlesham would be disappointed, as the village is on the wrong side of the A140, although the accommodation areas were clustered nearer to this village. The airfield was constructed during 1943 to the standard pattern of one main and two secondary runways and, with its hangar and hardstand allocation, it was destined for USAAF use. However, the first occupants when the airfield opened in spring 1944 were RAF Spitfires IXs of a Czech fighter-wing comprising 310, 312 and 313 squadrons. These units arrived towards the end of February 1944 and the last of them eventually left in early April.

The reason for the departure was the need to make

way for the American bomb-group that had been allocated to this Suffolk airfield, although the original reason for the appearance of the wing at this airfield is somewhat more difficult to discern. Having been activated in January 1941, the 34th Bombardment Group spent the first half of the war in the United States but, at the end of March 1944, it started its move to the UK. Under the command of Colonel Ernest J Wackwitz Jr, the Group arrived at Mendlesham on 18 April and, after five weeks of orientation and acclimatization, flew its first B-24 Liberator mission on 23 May. In just under a year of combat flying the Group notched up 170 missions for the loss of thirty-four aircraft missing in action. As part of the 3rd Bombardment Division, the Group converted to B-17s in mid-September 1944. Whilst it never received a Distinguished Unit Citation and is not one of the better-known Bomb Groups, it did have one claim to fame – that of not losing a single

AIRFIELD DATA DEC 1944

Command:	US 8th AF, 3rd BD	Runway surface:	Tarmac and concrete
Function:	Operational	Hangars:	2 × T.2
Runways:	010 deg 2,000 × 50yd	Dispersals:	48 Loop, 2 × Frying Pan
	160 deg 1,400 × 50yd	Personnel:	Officers – 443
	220 deg 1,400 × 50yd		Other Ranks – 2,529

Mendlesham had a brief period of RAF use and was then taken over by the 34th BG, firstly with B-24s, as here, and then with the B-17; the Group flew 170 missions from here.

aircraft to fighters over enemy territory, all the losses being to flak. Indeed, its only aerial losses were to a German intruder over the home airfield on 7 June – four aircraft being downed in a matter of minutes. After a long, hard mission of intense concentration it was inevitable that crews would relax when near their home airfields and many a bomber fell victim to fighters that over 'badlands' might well have been spotted and dealt with.

With the war in Europe over, the 34th BG was quick to depart, the majority of its personnel having gone by July. The RAF took over the site but, as with most of East Anglia's airfields, there was no real need for Mendlesham and, after a brief usage by No.94 Maintenance Unit for ammunition storage, the main task was that of disposal. By the mid-1950s this process was well underway and a variety of new owners, from agriculture to industry, moved in. It is worth noting that, whilst Mendlesham was one of the last airfields to enter service, it was one of the first to have a memorial to those who had operated from its runways; the impressive 34th BG memorial was erected in 1949 and is unusual in that it was designed by a well-known sculptor, Henry Berge, and was symbolic in that it depicted a pilot leaning out of a bomber cockpit.

B-24 'the Wrangler' sits in its dispersal at Mendlesham – note the bicycles, the universal mode of transport at airfields!

HQ units at Mendlesham

93rd BW   30 Mar 1944–11 Jul 1945

UNITS

1939–1945

310 Sqn	19–21 Feb 1944, 25 Feb–8 Mar 1944	Spitfire
312 Sqn	19–22 Feb 1944, 3 Mar–4 Apr 1944	Spitfire
313 Sqn	19 Feb–14 Mar 1944, 20 Mar–4 Apr 1944	Spitfire

The memorial shows a B-17 pilot reaching down out of his cockpit.

USAAF Units

34th BG (93rd CBW)

Identifying letter:	S
Squadrons:	4th BS (Daisy), 7th BS (Extol), 18th BS (Bawdry), 391st BS (Laurel)
Aircraft:	B-24H, B-24J, B-17G
Dates:	26 Apr 1944–25 Jul 1945
Missions:	170
First mission:	23 May 1944
Last mission:	20 Apr 1945

MEMORIALS

Memorial of pilot in B-17 cockpit, inscribed: 'To the American Airmen of the 34th who, in valour, gave their lives to the victory that made real the challenge for world peace and unity. The 34th Heavy Bombardment Group. A unit of the United States Eighth Air Force in World War II. April 1944 to June 1945. Mendlesham Aerodrome, Suffolk. Henry Berge 49.'

METFIELD
Station 366

County: Suffolk

UTM/grid: OS Map 156 – TM310790
Lat./Long.: N52°21.40 E001°23.45
Nearest town: Harleston 5 miles to north-west

Aerial view of Metfield in May 2002.

HISTORY

Metfield sits on top of an area of high land (by East Anglian standards) at 177ft AMSL in the centre of a rectangle formed by the airfields at Bungay, Halesworth, Horham and Thorpe Abbotts, each of which is only five miles away. The village after which it is named is less than a mile from the western boundary of the airfield and, in common with many airfields built during this period, a country road had to be closed to accommodate the space requirements of the three runways. When the airfield was constructed by John Laing & Son in 1943 it was to standard bomber-pattern and the runways were of concrete and wood-chippings. The ends of the runways were joined by straight stretches of perimeter track and dispersal points were distributed around the entire length of the perimeter, the initial build including fifty loop-type dispersals although, as the

plans shown here reveal, the airfield eventually acquired a mix of dispersal types. As was usual, the operating surfaces were completed first and this meant that even before the airfield was finished it was usable. Advantage was taken of this situation to move in a fighter group and 353rd FG arrived in August 1943, after completing its training at Goxhill. Under the command of Lieutenant Colonel Joseph A Morris, the unit flew the P-47 and went into action within days of arriving at Metfield; its first mission as a Group took place on 12 August but, three days previously, it had provided a number of aircraft for a mission flown by the 56th FG.

For the remainder of 1943 the Group flew the routine bomber-escorts that were the bread and butter of VIIIth Fighter Command's squadrons; however, by early 1944, some fighter units were adopting

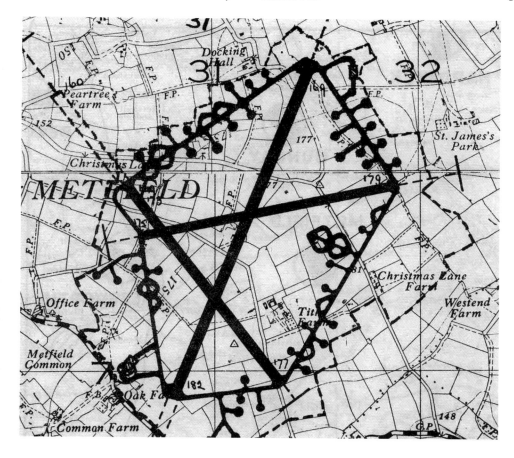

a more aggressive policy and, once cleared of an escort task, took to strafing German airfields and other positions. This was hazardous work and most losses of US fighters during this period were as a result of ground fire. Nevertheless, this aggressive policy was a good one and in due course it was decided to create a specialist group to devise, evaluate and then teach appropriate tactics. The 353rd was chosen for this task and, in early 1944, Colonel Glenn E Duncan, who had been in command since the previous November, was provided with volunteers from four fighter-groups to become the 353rd 'C' Fighter Group. The main requirement was to devise tactics and to that end Metfield became a dummy target, although it is not clear what changes, if any, were made to the airfield. Ultra low-level Thunderbolt flying was certainly part of the routine and the unit was referred to as 'Bill's Buzz Boys' (the Bill coming from William 'Bill' Kepner of VIIIth Fighter Command). However, in April 1944 the 353rd moved to Raydon to make way for a bomber

unit, the 'Ringmasters' of the 491st BG.

This Group had been activated in October 1943 but its ground echelon was transferred to B-29 units and so, when it arrived in the UK, it had few ground personnel; these were subsequently raised from existing bomber groups in the 8th Air Force. The unit, under Lieutenant Colonel Carl T Goldenburg, was in place at Metfield by late-April, but it took some while for all ground staff to arrive and it was 2 June before the first mission was flown. From that point on the Group played a full part in the bomber ops flown by 2nd Bombardment Division and went on to record the highest rate of B-24 operations of all B-24 groups.

As with so many airfields, Metfield had its day of tragedy: one of the most devastating accidents to befall the Eighth occurred here on 15 July 1944, when a bomb being unloaded from a truck at the bomb dump detonated, causing a huge explosion. At least five men were killed, a nearby farm was destroyed, numerous buildings and B-24s were damaged, while the explosion was heard over fifteen

AIRFIELD DATA DEC 1944

Command:	European Division Air Transport, USSTAF	Runway surface:	Concrete and wood-chippings
Function:	Operational	Hangars:	Two × T.2
Runways:	210 deg 2,000 × 50yd	Dispersals:	50 × Loop type
	270 deg 1,400 × 50yd	Personnel:	Officers – 421
	330 deg 1,400 × 50yd		Other Ranks – 2,473

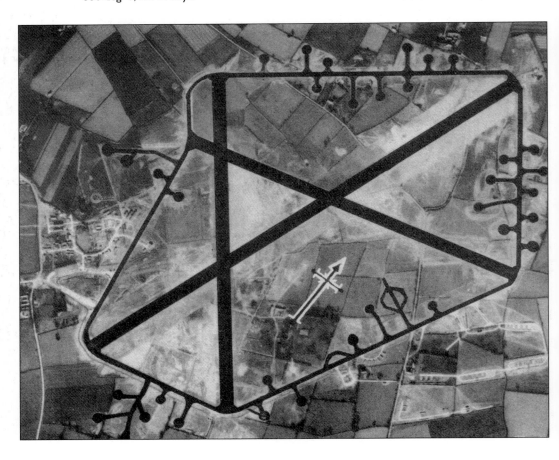

miles away. In the place of the bomb dump was a huge crater and this survived until it was filled in during the late-1960s, although at some times of the year it can still be seen from the air as a soil mark.

After only a short stay in Suffolk, the 491st were moved to North Pickenham on 15 August when the 9th Combat Wing was disbanded. This was not the end for the airfield and it was allocated to the European Division Air Transport of what, by then, was the combined Strategic Air Force (USSTAF). The exact nature of the operations that took place is

still uncertain but Metfield received regular visits from transport B-24s, C-47s and C-53s, some of which were operated by a secret unit tasked with ferrying people and supplies to Sweden and a number of other countries. This unit remained in place to the end of the war.

The RAF took control of the airfield in mid-1945, when the last of the American returned home, but it had no use for this remote and primitive location and the site soon became yet another abandoned wartime relic, although the land was not finally sold until the

The village church includes a brass plaque and Book of Remembrance.

mid-1960s. The B-road over the airfield is open again and the visitor can drive across the middle of the airfield, traces of the concrete surfaces can be seen on either side but, with the exception of one small group of buildings (now a garage), there is little else remaining.

UNITS

1939–1945
USAAF Units
353rd FG

Squadrons:	350th FS, 351st FS, 352nd FS
Aircraft:	P-47D
Dates:	3 Aug 1943–Apr 1944
Missions:	447 (including other bases)
First mission:	12 Aug 1943
Last mission:	25 Apr 1945 (from Raydon)

491st BG (95th CBW)

Identifying letter:	Z
Nickname:	The Ringmasters
Squadrons:	852nd BS (Ballot), 853rd BS (Farkum), 854th BS (Semen) 855th BS (Quadrant)
Aircraft:	B-24H, B-24J, B-24L, B-24M
Dates:	Apr 1944–Aug 1944
Missions:	187 (including North Pickenham)
First mission:	2 Jun 1944
Last mission:	25 Apr 1945 (from North Pickenham)

MEMORIALS

The church in Metfield village contains a small brass plaque and a Book of Remembrance; the inscription on the plaque states: 'In grateful remembrance of all ranks of the United States 8th Air Force who served at Metfield Airfield and of those who sacrificed their lives in the defence of freedom 1943–1945. 353rd Fighter Group, 491st Bomb Group and support units.' Below the plaque is a roll of honour.

METHWOLD

County: Suffolk

UTM/grid: OS Map 143 – TL735935
Lat./Long.: N52°30.46 E000°33.2
Nearest town: Brandon 5 miles to south-east

One of Methwold's T.2 hangars can be seen in the foreground of this September 2002 view, whilst the overall airfield plan is also clear.

HISTORY

Methwold spent its entire war as part of RAF Bomber Command and had the rare distinction of being the base for two Victoria Cross actions. Located on a stretch of flat land just south of the village, the area was requisitioned to become a satellite airfield for the bomber base at Feltwell, only two miles further south. As such it was given minimum facilities and was only a grass field; the airfield opened in 1939 as a satellite and Wellingtons of 214 Squadron were in residence at the outbreak of war as part of the Scatter Plan, to reduce the vulnerability of squadrons at main airfields. This squadron operated from Methwold for a number of months, moving to Stradishall in February 1940. Although the airfield did not receive a 'based' unit for nearly two years, it was used by the squadrons at Feltwell on an opportunity basis and Wellingtons were very much in evidence during 1941 and 1942.

However, in autumn 1942, the airfield was transferred to No.2 Group and received the Venturas of 21 Squadron, one of the Group's new American-types, the first mission being flown on 3 November to open what became a hectic operational period for Methwold. 'Circus' operations became the norm for the Squadron until it left the following April, at which point the airfield changed allegiance again, this time moving to No.3 Group. In August 1942 two new squadrons had formed at Feltwell, 464 Squadron RAAF and 487 Squadron RNZAF, both equipped with Venturas – it was these two units that made the short hop to Methwold on 3 April. Operations continued unabated and, for 487 Squadron, one of these was a black day indeed; on 3 May a formation of twelve Venturas took-off to attack the power station at Amsterdam: of the eleven that crossed the

AIRFIELD DATA DEC 1944

Command:	RAF Bomber Command	Runway surface:	Concrete
Function:	Operational	Hangars:	5 × T.2
Runways:	168 deg 1,400 × 50yd	Dispersals:	35 × Loop type, one × Pan
	237 deg 2,000 × 50yd	Personnel:	Officers – 166 (2 WAAF)
	294 deg 1,400 × 50yd		Other Ranks – 1,250 (64 WAAF)

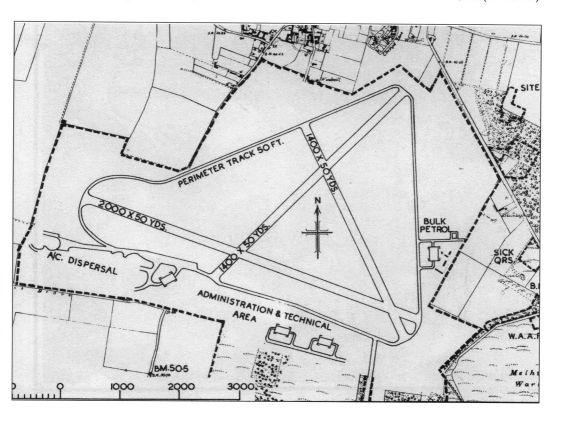

Channel only one returned. It was only after the war that the story of this mission was revealed; only one aircraft, flown by Squadron Leader Trent, reached and bombed the target. Trent was subsequently awarded the Victoria Cross, having spent the remainder of the war as a PoW.

In many ways this was just another example of how unsuited the Ventura was for the daylight-bomber role and it may have hastened the decision to replace the type. In August both squadrons received the Mosquito VI – but by then they were at Sculthorpe, having departed Methwold in July. The opportunity was taken for a major rebuild of the airfield and, despite the nearness of a major airfield at Feltwell,

Methwold was upgraded, with three hard-runways and additional facilities; by late-1944 it had five T.2 hangars and thirty-six dispersals. There were aircraft on the ground during the rebuild, as Methwold was being used for the open storage of Horsa gliders; pre-invasion production of these gliders led to a policy of storing thirty-two at each of a number of bomber airfields.

With its three new concrete-runways the airfield joined No.32 Base (Mildenhall) and Stirlings of 149 Squadron were first to arrive, followed by the similarly equipped 218 Squadron. Both converted to Lancasters soon after arrival and bomber ops continued from the airfield as the squadrons took part in a

Ventura of 21 Squadron at Methwold; the Squadron operated this less-than-satisfactory type from the airfield for five months.

variety of Main Force attacks. The departure of 218 Squadron to Chedburgh in December was partly off-set by increasing the size of 149 Squadron through the addition of a third Flight, this having become a fairly routine policy in Bomber Command in late-1944. Bomber operations continued from Methwold to the end of the war and the Lancasters remained in residence, the wartime unit having been joined in October by 207 Squadron, to April 1946 when they departed for Tuddenham.

Transferred to Flying Training Command the air-field was effectively in Care and Maintenance by late-1946 and for nearly ten years little happened, other than the routine of trying to keep the Station usable, although, as a satellite for Feltwell, it was used from time to time. During 1955 there was a brief flurry of activity, when the Central Signals Establishment arrived whilst Watton's runways were being worked on, and this may well have seen the first jet usage of Methwold. The airfield remained with Flying Training Command until June 1958,

when the decision was taken that the RAF had no further use for the site.

Much of the airfield still remains, although agriculture now dominates this once-busy Suffolk bomber station.

DECOY SITES

Goodestone Warren	TF790012
Methwold Severals	TL7393

UNITS

1939–1945

21 Sqn	30 Oct 1942–21 Mar 1943	Ventura
57 Sqn	5 Jan 1942–4 Sep 1942	Wellington
149 Sqn	15 May 1944–29 Apr 1946	Stirling, Lancaster
207 Sqn	30 Oct 1945–29 Apr 1946	Lancaster
214 Sqn	3 Sep 1939–12 Feb 1940	Wellington
218 Sqn	4 Aug 1944–5 Dec 1944	Stirling, Lancaster
320 Sqn	15 Mar 1943–30 Mar 1943	Mitchell
464 Sqn	3 Apr 1943–21 Jul 1943	Ventura
487 Sqn	3 Apr 1943–20 Jul 1943	Ventura

Lancaster NE971 of 149 Squadron basks in the sunshine; the unit operated Stirlings and then Lancasters from the Norfolk airfield.

MILDENHALL

County: Suffolk

UTM/grid: OS Map 143 – TL685768
Lat./Long.: N52°21.48 E000°28.48
Nearest town: Bury St Edmunds 12 miles to south-east

One of the main USAF bases in Europe, Mildenhall as seen in September 2002.

HISTORY

Now one of the USAF's most important bases in Europe, Mildenhall has had a long aviation history and been witness to a number of significant events. This Suffolk location was chosen in the early 1930s to be one of the RAF's expansion-period bomber airfields. This was a time when, after two decades in which Britain's military had been virtually stagnant, rapid expansion of the Royal Air Force led to the construction of a large number of well-equipped airfields from East Anglia to Yorkshire; this particular airfield was largely constructed by W & C French.

RAF Mildenhall (often referred to as Beck Row by locals – after the nearby village) opened on 16 October 1934 and the following month the cumbersome Handley Page Heyfords of 99 Squadron took up residence; the following year one Flight of this squadron became the nucleus of No 38 Squadron and

Mildenhall housed two Heyford bomber squadrons of RAF Bomber Command, although 38 Squadron soon received a few Fairey Hendon night-bombers. However, the most notable event in 1935 had been the presence on the airfield of over 350 RAF aircraft for the Silver Jubilee Review by King George V – an impressive spectacle that also served as a demonstration of RAF air power for the visiting German military mission, although one wonders how impressed they were by the serried ranks of antiquated-looking biplanes! A third squadron was formed in April 1937, No.149 Squadron being created by detaching a Flight of 99 Squadron. Finally, a fourth unit, 211 Squadron, formed in June, although this unit departed in September.

With the Munich Crisis of late 1938, the RAF came to a high state of readiness with aircraft bombed-up and ready for the call to action, these

AIRFIELD DATA DEC 1944

Command:	RAF Bomber Command	Runway surface:	Concrete
Function:	Operational	Hangars:	3 × C.2 × A.2 × T.2 (Glider)
Runways:	040 deg 1,400 × 50yd	Dispersals:	36 × Heavy Bomber
	113 deg 2,000 × 50yd	Personnel:	Officers – 204 (15 WAAF)
	159 deg 1,400 × 50yd		Other Ranks – 2,215 (338 WAAF)

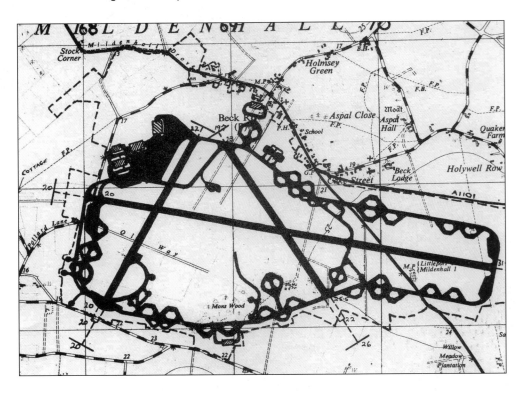

The dinosaur-like Heyfords of 99 Squadrons at Mildenhall in the mid 1930s.

aircraft still being the dinosaur-like Heyfords. The conflict with Germany was avoided for another year and, in that time, Bomber Command introduced a number of new and more advanced aircraft; for the Mildenhall units this was the Vickers-Armstrongs Wellington, the first of which arrived in October 1938 for 99 Squadron. The 'delayed' war broke out in September 1939 and the Wellingtons were soon in action, their targets being German naval units as, at this stage of the war, attacks on land targets were forbidden. Bomber Command's first winter of war was a fraught one; losses amongst the bombers on daylight missions were high and it was decided to switch to night operations. However, it was not until May 1940 that Prime Minister Winston Churchill authorized attacks on land targets and the RAF's bombing offensive against Germany truly began. Over the next two

Mildenhall went to war using the Wellington – and the early ops were not promising; aircraft of 149 Squadron.

Mildenhall was crammed with aircraft in July 1935 for the RAF Review, with serried ranks of biplanes.

years various Wellington-equipped units operated from Mildenhall as part of the Strategic Bombing Offensive against Germany. The Canadian-manned 419 Squadron formed here in December 1941 (and moved out in August 1942) and 75 (New Zealand) Squadron operated from here between August and November 1942, whilst 115 Squadron moved in from RAF Marham in September 1942.

In the latter part of 1941 the Wellingtons of 149 Squadron were replaced by four-engined Short Stirling bombers. The advent of heavier aircraft and the increased operational usage of the grass-covered airfield led to Mildenhall being closed in November 1942 for the construction of three hard-surface runways, in the standard triangular pattern for these mid-war bomber stations, this work taking some five

months to complete. The airfield re-opened in April 1942 as home to Stirlings of 15 Squadron, a Flight of this unit being used to form 622 Squadron in August. For the next eighteen months both units played a full part in the bombing offensive, an intensity of operations that continued when they re-equipped with Avro Lancasters in December 1943. According to RAF statistics, squadrons from Mildenhall flew over 8,000 bombing sorties during the war, dropping 23,000 tons of bombs – and losing 200 aircraft (each with six or seven aircrew).

As part of the reorganization of Bomber Command that took effect in spring 1943, Mildenhall became the base station for No.32 Base, its sub-stations being Lakenheath and Methwold, although this later changed to Methwold and Tuddenham, but remained part of No.3 Group, Bomber Command. This arrangement took effect on 24 March 1943 and remained in place until November 1945.

RAF Bomber Command retained control of Mildenhall in the late-1940s, with 44 Squadron undertaking operational trials on the Avro Lincoln and 15 Squadron using special Lancasters on heavy-bomb trials. These latter trials also involved a number of USAAF B-17s. In February 1949 the airfield housed four squadrons equipped with Lancaster B1(FE) bombers, but all four of these disbanded or left early the following year, by which time most of them had started to re-equip with Lincolns. After the hectic activity of a four-squadron bomber station Mildenhall fell quiet – but it was a temporary lull.

July 1950 brought the first American units, B-50Ds of the 329th Bomb Squadron of the 93rd Bomb Group, this move being brought about by the advent of the Cold War between NATO (North Atlantic Treaty Organization) and Russia but also by fears of a global conflict stemming from the Korean War. This was the start of a rotation of Bomb Groups over the next few years under control of Strategic Air Command (SAC), which formally took over Mildenhall in October 1951; this rotational activity was mirrored at nearby Lakenheath. Although bomber units continued to appear at the airfield from time to time, Mildenhall's primary role became that of a base for air-to-air refuelling and, subsequently, transport units. The first tanker aircraft to be based here were KC-97Es, which appeared in 1953, whilst the first major use by transports was by the 513th Troop Carrier Wing (TCW); from July 1958 the airfield was under the control of the 513th Tactical Airlift Wing.

Both roles have remained central to Mildenhall's operations over the past fifty years; a range of transport types (from C-118, C-124, C-130, C-141, C-5 and most recently C-17) opera-ting through the Suffolk base. The transport role was acquired in January 1959, when Burtonwood ceased to act as a transport centre; as a MATS (later Military Airlift Command) hub, the airfield was eventually handling some 100,000 passengers a year plus a considerable amount of freight.

The tanker type that came to dominate Mildenhall, and still does, was the KC-135 Stratotanker. As part of the European Tanker Task Force these aircraft were operated under the 306th Strategic Wing. However, there is one particular aircraft type that, to enthusiasts at least, came to symbolize Mildenhall – the SR.71 Blackbird. The high-flying, high-speed reconnaissance aircraft operated by the 9th Strategic Reconnaissance Wing (SRW) played a key role during the Cold War and the glimpse of one of these sleek spy-planes, or even better their appearance at one of the annual Mildenhall Air Fête was always popular.

These were not the only 'special' aircraft operated at or through this important airfield and various Command and Control types, such as the C-118s of the 7120th Airborne Control and Command Squadron (later replaced by the 10th ACCS), as well as detachments of even more specialized aircraft such as the RC-135, have been a regular feature of the base's operations. In the past two decades the tankers at Mildenhall have provided AAR for a wide range of operational deployments, whilst the strategic lift capability has proved essential as part of the air bridge between the United States and the European and Middle East theatres.

Since February 1992, Mildenhall has been home to the 100th Air Refuelling Wing and this remains the dominant organization at the base. The most recent unit to arrive was the 352nd Special Operations Group from Alconbury in 1995.

DECOY SITES

Q/K   Cavenham Heath   TL75069

The site opened in June 1940 and had two 'runways' cut out of the heath – and rabbit holes filled in. There were two gun-pits, a number of dummy Wellingtons and a real Tiger Moth, as well as a number of vehicles. The site was bombed a number of times. Cavenham closed in early 1942.

Q	Littleport	TL584852
	Tuddenham	TL745687

UNITS

HQ units at Mildenhall

No.3 Group	Jan 1937–Sep 1939
No.4 Group	1 Apr 1937–
No.5 Group	Jul 1937–
USAF 7th AD	
USAFE 3rd AD	1962–

1920–1938

38 Sqn	16 Feb 1935–5 May 1937	Heyford, Hendon
73 Sqn	15 Mar 1937–12 Jun 1937	Fury
99 Sqn	11 Nov 1934–9 Sep 1939	Heyford, Wellington
149 Sqn	12 Apr 1937–6 Apr 1942,	Heyford, Wellington, Lancaster, Lincoln
211 Sqn	24 Jun 1937–2 Sep 1937	Audax, Hind
5 Gp PF	Aug 1937– Jan 1938	Tutor

1939–1945

15 Sqn	14 Apr 1943–20 Aug 1946	Stirling, Lancaster

In recent years Mildenhall has been famous for two things: its superb annual air displays and, as shown on the hangar banner, the presence of an SR-71 detachment. In reality, however, its main importance is as a strategic transport and tanker base and hub.

75 Sqn	15 Aug 1940–1 Nov 1942	Wellington, Stirling
115 Sqn	24 Sep 1942–8 Nov 1942, 15 Feb 1949–1 Mar 1950	Wellington, Lancaster, Lincoln
218 Sqn	13 Jun 1940–18 Jul 1940	Battle, Blenheim
419 Sqn	12 Dec 1941–12 Aug 1942	Hampden
622 Sqn	10 Aug 1943–15 Aug 1945	Stirling, Lancaster
3 Gp TTF	Oct 1939– Jan 1940	Battle
1503 Flt	27 Jan 1941–5 Sep 1942	Wellington
1401 Flt	4 Feb 1941–25 Oct 1941	Gladiator
149 CF	20 Jan 1942–13 Feb 1942	Stirling
1505 Flt	5 Sep 1942–17 Dec 1942	Wellington
44 Sqn	25 Aug 1945–29 Aug 1946	Lancaster

Post-1945

35 Sqn	10 Feb 1949–23 Feb 1950	Lancaster, Lincoln
115 Sqn	15 Feb 1949–1 Mar 1950	Lancaster, Lincoln
149 Sqn	28 Feb 1949–1 Mar 1950	Lancaster, Lincoln

207 Sqn	28 Feb 1949–1 Mar 1950	Lancaster, Lincoln

USAF Units

93rd BG	Jul 1950–Feb 1951	B-50
509th BG	Feb 1951–May 1951	
2nd BG	May 1951–?	
22nd BG	??	
513th TCW	1966–31 Jan 1992*	
7120th ACCS	1965–	C-118, EC-135
10th ACCS	(replaced 7120th)	
9th SRW	Jan 1983–18 Jan 1990	SR-71, U-2
100th ARW	1 Feb 1992–date	KC-135
352nd SOG	1995–date	

*The 513th underwent a number of name changes, becoming the 513th TAW (1968) and 513th ACCW (Jun 1987).

MEMORIALS

Stained glass window in chapel on airfield plus plaque in church. There is also a commemorative plaque to mark the 1935 Royal Review.

NEWMARKET HEATH

County: Suffolk

UTM/grid: OS Map 154 – TL620630
Lat./Long.: N52°14.37 E000°22.30
Nearest town: Newmarket 3 miles to east

HISTORY

A perfect stretch of grass for a racecourse also makes a perfect landing strip and, since World War One, this area just to the west of the Suffolk town of Newmarket has performed this dual role. The first military occupants arrived in November 1917, the FE.2s of 192 Night Training Squadron taking up residence as a night training unit for bomber and fighter pilots. They were joined in March 1918 by 190 Squadron from Rochford, another NTS. This training role was important and the flare paths at Newmarket Heath witnessed the first tentative night-flying of many a pilot. With the end of the war

the run-down of squadrons began and 190 Squadron disbanded in October, their sister-unit surviving to the following April.

The landing strip has always been used on race days and between the wars the rich and famous would sometimes appear by air. However, it was simply a grass landing-area with no specific airfield-facilities. The RAF never forgets a good landing-area and so, with the outbreak of World War Two, Newmarket was once more pressed into service as an airfield.

Wellingtons of 99 Squadron dispersed here from

Mildenhall at the beginning of September and flew their first operations later in the year, including a disastrous attack on shipping on 14 December that saw the loss of six of their aircraft. The well-drained and large grass-area was ideal for bomber operations and although the buildings of the racecourse were not ideal, they did provide at least limited facilities – and were, marginally, better than tents. Some new buildings were erected, the most significant being the various hangars that, over a period of time, sprang up around the airfield. The Wellingtons remained operational from Newmarket until March 1941 and this stalwart twin-engined bomber was to re-appear at Newmarket Heath a few months later. From November 1940 the Glider Flight/Glider Training Squadron of the Central Landing Establishment (CLE) spent a few weeks in the area, at Side Hill, before moving on to Thame. This was the first of a number of 'other units', some small and some larger and more significant, that used Newmarket during the rest of the war; these are listed in the units table but not all are mentioned in the text.

Some records suggest that the Stirlings of 7 Squadron, whose home base was Oakington, operated briefly from Newmarket, although the first significant appearance of this massive four-engined bomber did not occur until November 1942, with 75 Squadron. This unit had arrived with Wellingtons on 1 November, but was in the process of converting to the new type. Grass airfields were not usually suitable for the large and heavy Stirling, but Newmarket had a good surface and exceptionally long runs, the longest being over 2,500 yards. Nevertheless, a heavily-laden Stirling was involved in one tragic incident. On the night of 16 December 1942, a Stirling failed to clear Devil's Dyke and, having clipped the top of the bank, span in and the large mines it was carrying exploded with a deafening roar. It is hard to imagine, as you look across today's peaceful scene, the effect this would have had on the RAF personnel at the airfield.

From March 1941 the airfield was in use by the secretive Lysanders of No.1419 Flight, their task being clandestine operations in occupied Europe. In August, the Flight was expanded to become 138 Squadron and, with a variety of aircraft types, this unit flew from Newmarket to the end of the year. Their departure to Stradishall in December did not mean the end of this type of mission from the heath and the airfield was used as a forward base and, from February 1942, a second unit, 161 Squadron, was formed at Newmarket.

The large grass area also proved suitable for a few unusual visitors, amongst which were the Hamilcar glider and the prototype jet-powered Gloster F9/40, although these were fleeting appearances and

The pilot of a 99 Squadron Wellington inspects the fin of his aircraft having safely returned from a mission with half the fin shot away.

Newmarket remained very much a Main Force Bomber Command base.

As part of the reorganization of Bomber Command that took effect in spring 1943, Newmarket became a sub-station for No.32 Base, its base station being Mildenhall, but remaining part of No.3 Group, Bomber Command. This arrangement took effect on 24 March 1943 and remained in place until Newmarket was transferred to Maintenance Command on 1 March 1945. The last operational unit, 75 Squadron, moved out in June 1943 and, for a short while, only the target-towing aircraft of No.1483 Flight were in permanent residence. However, from autumn 1943 to the end of the war, the airfield housed one of the Command's most interesting units, the Bombing Development Unit (BDU), whose remit was to evaluate new equipment and investigate problems highlighted by the operational units. The Unit was divided into two flights, Development Flight and Radar Training Flight, the work of the latter including trials and training with

AIRFIELD DATA DEC 1944

Command:	RAF Bomber Command	Runway surface:	Grass
Function:	Operational	Hangars:	3 × T.2, 3 × B.1, 2 × Blister, one × Double Blister
Runways:	E/W 2,500yd	Dispersals:	24 Clock type
	SE/NW 1,800yd	Personnel:	Officers—108 (3 WAAF)
	NE/SW 1,600yd		Other Ranks—1,183 (142 WAAF)

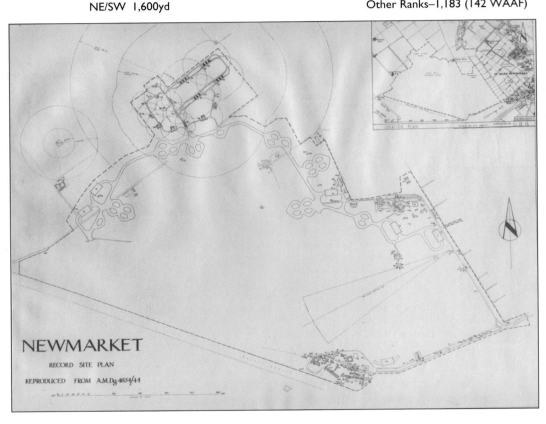

NEWMARKET

RECORD SITE PLAN

REPRODUCED FROM A.M.Dg 4854/44

H2S, one of the greatest technological innovations of the war.

The BDU was a busy unit and operated a wide range of aircraft, some on a routine basis and others as virtual one-offs for specific trials. This was one of the unsung units of World War Two but, like all of the Development Units, it is impossible to overstate the important part they played. Newmarket may not have been sending bombers to attack the enemy but it was certainly playing its part in the war. In March 1944, No.1483 Flight became No.1688 Bomber Defence Training Flight but with no real change in the nature of its task.

The hectic nature of flying at Newmarket continued into the New Year but then, in February, both resident units moved to Feltwell and almost overnight the acres of grass fell silent. By summer 1945 the RAF had completely abandoned the site and what had once been a key station was left to revert to its original role as a racetrack.

Flying still takes place during race days; four grass-runways, the longest being only 1,000 yards, are marked out at Rowley Mile, which incidentally is the other name that Newmarket Heath was sometimes called.

UNITS

Pre-1919

190 RS	14 Mar 1918–5 Oct 1918	
192 RS	14 Nov 1917–31 May 1919	FE2b, FE2d

1939–1945

75 Sqn	1 Nov 1942–28 Jun 1943	Wellington, Stirling
99 Sqn	1 Sep 1939–8 Mar 1941	Wellington
138 Sqn	25 Aug 1941–16 Dec 1941	Lysander, Whitley, Halifax
161 Sqn	15 Feb 1942–1 Mar 1942	Lysander, Hudson, Whitley
215 Sqn	9 Dec 1941–5 Jan 1942	Wellington
453 Sqn	6–14 Mar 1943	Spitfire
GF/GTS(CLE)	22 Nov 1940–1 Jan 1941	

1419 Flt	Mar 1941–Aug 1941	Lysander
3 Gp TF	21 May 1941–7 Feb 1942	Wellington
1483 Flt	18 Nov 1941–13 Jul 1942	Lysander, Wellington
ABTF	15 Jun 1942–13 Jul 1942	
1504 Flt	3 Nov 1942–21 Aug 1943	Oxford
1483 Flt	29 Jun 1943–11 Mar 1944	Wellington, Martinet
BDU	13 Sep 1943–25 Feb 1945	
1688 Flt	11 Mar 1944–25 Feb 1945	

MEMORIALS

On approach to the racecourse is a Wellington propeller from T2888, inscribed: 'In memory of officers and men of 99 Squadron Bomber Command Royal Air Force based here in the defence of freedom September 1939 to March 1941.'

NORTH CREAKE

County: Norfolk

UTM/grid: OS Map 132 – TF895385
Lat./Long.: N52°54.38 E000°49.15
Nearest town: Little Walsingham 2 miles to south-east

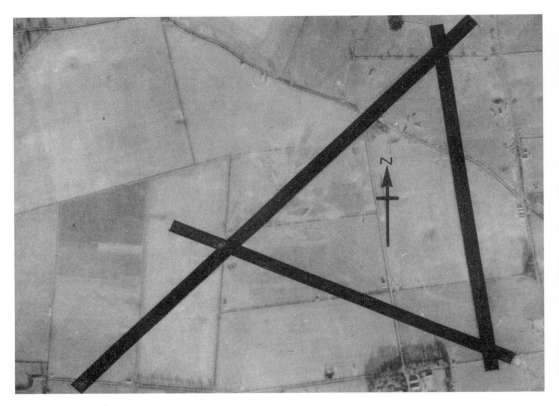

HISTORY

North Creake had a very brief but very interesting operational career, which lasted less than a year but involved two of the RAF's most secretive squadrons. On 21 September 1944, the Chester Herald (Mr Heaton-Armstrong), responsible for handling requests for RAF badges, acknowledged a letter from Wing Commander Renaut of 171 Squadron concerning 'your new squadron' and asking for more details of the type of motif the squadron would like. The squadron's commanding officer replied on 8 October: 'I am not at liberty to discuss the role of the Squadron, as it is engaged on work of a most secret nature. I would suggest, however, a shield of Hermes, with flashes of lightning, as the Squadron is engaged on work of a Signals nature.'

The site for this airfield had been in use as a decoy airfield, for Docking, since 1941 and it was fairly

unusual for such a site to be taken on for full-scale development but, with the pressing need for new airfields in East Anglia and no further need for decoy sites, these Norfolk fields were turned into a bomber base.

North Creake opened on 23 November 1943 for No.3 Group but within days had been re-allocated to No 100 Group, the decision having been taken to concentrate this new Group in Norfolk, partly for reasons of remoteness, as its activities were highly classified. However, it was immediately placed in Care and Maintenance whilst further development took place, with an intention to turn it into a super-heavy-bomber station with long concrete runways. This plan was changed in spring 1944, the development of Marham and Lakenheath into SHB bases having already commenced, and the airfield duly

AIRFIELD DATA DEC 1944

Command:	RAF Bomber Command	Runway surface:	Concrete
Function:	Operational	Hangars:	2 × T.2, one × B.1
Runways:	190 deg 1,400 × 50yd	Dispersals:	36 × Loop
	240 deg 2,000 × 50yd	Personnel:	Officers – 116 (8 WAAF)
	310 deg 1,400 × 50yd		Other Ranks – 1,568 (328)

Stirling of 199 Squadron; this was one of two RAF Radio Counter-Measures units to operate from this remote Norfolk airfield.

became operational when the Stirlings of 199 Squadron turned up in May. The primary role of this unit was radio countermeasures and for this it employed a jamming system called 'Mandrel', but also operated as part of the Special Window Force (SWF). The 'Mandrel' system was designed to operate against the enemy early-warning radars and 199 had been pioneers in the use of the equipment, a standard technique having been devised of flying accurate racetrack-patterns to blank out a particular area of interest.

In September, the third Flight of the Squadron was split off to become 171 Squadron, the latter promptly converting to Halifaxes. The RCM war continued for both units, although 199's Stirlings were eventually replaced by Halifaxes in March 1945, the last operational Stirling unit in Bomber Command. North Creake despatched its final wartime sorties on 2 May and, by July, both squadrons had disbanded. The airfield was placed in Care and Maintenance on

30 September but for two years was used as an aircraft storage site, primarily Mosquitoes, with No.274 Maintenance Unit – many an aircraft being scrapped.

This task over the airfield was abandoned by the RAF; if the decision to make North Creake a super-heavy-bomber base had been maintained, then it would almost certainly have survived the war and might even still be in use. Instead, there is little trace of this airfield, which once played such a key role in Main Force operations.

UNITS

1939–1945

171 Sqn	8 Sep 1944–27 Jul 1945	Stirling, Halifax
199 Sqn	1 May 1944–19 Jul 1945	Stirling, Halifax

MEMORIALS

A memorial was unveiled on 24 April 2004.

NORTH PICKENHAM
Station 143

County: Norfolk

UTM/grid: OS Map 144 – TF850070
Lat./Long.: N52°37.30 E000°44.00
Nearest town: Swaffham 2.5 miles to north-west

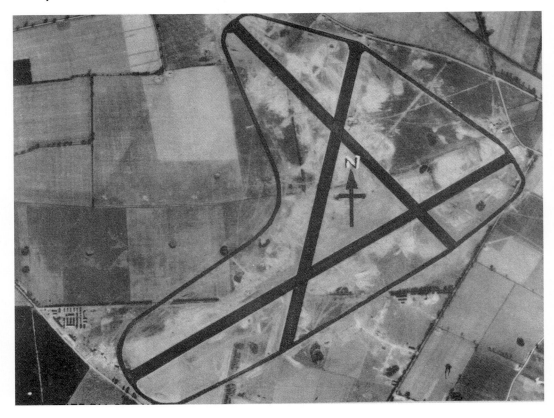

HISTORY

Although built to the standard Class A specification for heavy bombers, North Pickenham was somewhat unusual, because the local topography restricted its main-runway length to 1,900 yards instead of the normal 2,000 and most of the hardstands were laid to one side (north-east) of the airfield.

Two B-24 Liberator units used the station, the first being the 492nd BG, which arrived in April 1944. The unit had been activated in October 1943 and its air echelon was subsequently joined by a ground echelon formed from existing 8th Air Force bomber Groups. Under Colonel Eugene H Snavely, the Group flew its first mission on 11 May but in an operational period of only three months it suffered heavily, becoming known in some quarters as the 'hard luck Group'. This B-24 unit was only operational between May and August but, during its sixty-four missions, it lost fifty-one aircraft to enemy action – the highest loss rate for any 8th Air Force Bomb Group. The decision was taken to disband the unit and move its personnel to other Groups; this was not a reflection on the crews but jinxes were taken very seriously and the overall morale effect had to be considered – better, therefore, to 'start again'.

The unit's title transferred to a special operations unit at Harrington, while its place at North Pickenham was taken by the 491st BG, which moved in from Metfield. The 'Ringmasters' of the 491st had flown their first operational mission on 2 June and the move to North Pick didn't affect the pace of operations; indeed, the Group had the distinction of setting the highest rate of operations of all the 8th's

AIRFIELD DATA DEC 1944

Command:	US 8th AF, 2nd BD	Runway surface:	Tarmac and concrete
Function:	Operational	Hangars:	2 × T.2
Runways:	190 deg 1,400 × 50yd	Dispersals:	50 concrete hardstands
	240 deg 1,900 × 50yd	Personnel:	Officers – 421
	320 deg 1,400 × 50yd		Other Ranks – 2,473

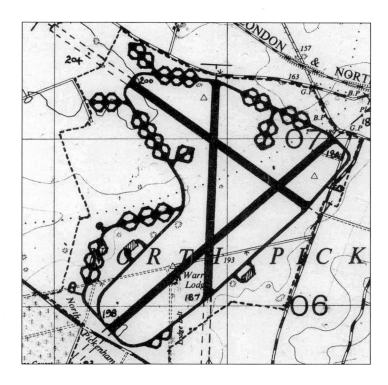

B-24 groups. The Group earned a Distinguished Unit Citation for the Misburg mission of 26 November.

With the war over, the Americans bade farewell to this corner of west Norfolk, the Liberators flying out in early June, and North Pickenham was transferred to the RAF. The next few years saw it pass from one Command to another and it was used for various purposes – it even went back to USAF control, briefly, in 1954. Its first, brief, use was as sub-site for No.258 MU at Shipdham, part of Maintenance Command; for a short while from October 1948 it was transferred to Bomber Command but, having proved unsuitable for further development, it was handed back to Maintenance Command. The Americans were next in line and North Pick was back with them in August 1954, before it was selected as a Thor missile site and allocated to Bomber Command on 1 December 1958.

Three massive concrete launch-pads were constructed on the east side of the airfield, along with support buildings and an impressive security fence, and in July 1959 the site was occupied by 220 Squadron. As part of the RAF's new missile force, North Pickenham was one of the key installations of the early part of the Cold War. The three white missiles, with their RAF roundels, were one of the main elements of the strategic nuclear deterrent. However, with the cancellation of the follow-on Blue Streak missile, the RAF's venture into the ballistic-missile world was short-lived and, in 1963, the Thor complexes were abandoned. For North Pickenham there was one final flurry of activity when, between October 1964 and November 1965, the Hawker Siddeley P.1127 Kestrel (the prototype Harrier jump jet) underwent trials at the airfield.

Examining a B-24 that force-landed at North Pickenham. The airfield was first used by the 491st BG but after a disastrous operational start they were replaced by the 492nd BG.

The site was sold in 1967 but parts of the runway layout and perimeter track survive, as do a small number of huts on what is now farmland.

UNITS

1939–1945
USAAF Units
491st BG (14th CBW)

Identifying letter:	Z
Nickname:	The Ringmasters
Squadrons:	852nd BS (Ballot), 853rd BS (Farkum), 854th BS (Semen), 855th BS (Quadrant)
Aircraft:	B-24H, B-24J, B-24L, B-24M
Dates:	15 Aug 1944–4 Jul 1945
Missions:	187 (including ops from Metfield)
First mission:	2 Jun 1944 (from Metfield)
Last mission:	25 Apr 1945

492nd BG (14th CBW)

Identifying letter	U
Squadrons	856th BS, 857th BS, 858th BS, 859th BS
Aircraft	B-24H, B-24J
Dates	18 Apr 1944–5 Aug 1944
Missions	64
First mission	11 May 1944
Last mission	7 Aug 1944

Post-1945

220 Sqn	22 Jul 1959–10 Jul 1963	Thor

MEMORIALS

Stone in North Pickenham village, inscribed: 'In memory to the men of the USAAF who flew from North Pickenham 1944–1945. 492 BG April 1944–August 1944. 491 BG August 1944–May 1945.'

The memorial to the 'men of the USAAF' is situated in a quiet corner of the village near the airfield boundary.

OLD BUCKENHAM
Station 144

County: Norfolk

UTM/grid: OS Map 144 – TM085940
Lat./Long.: N52°30.04 E001°03.40
Nearest town: Old Buckenham 1.5 miles to south-west

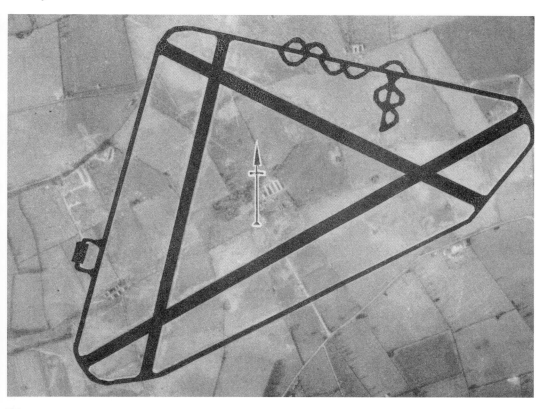

HISTORY

Old Buckenham was constructed to standard bomber-pattern in 1942–43 by Taylor-Woodrow Ltd, its main runway pointing towards the nearby village. Within the geographic territory of the USAAF 2nd Bombardment Division this was to be a B-24 Liberator base for the duration of its active career and its sole operational unit, the 453rd Bomb Group, arrived late-December 1943. The Group was activated in the USA in June 1943 and, under Colonel Joseph A Miller, it spent the first few weeks in Norfolk familiarizing itself with the area and operational procedures before flying its first mission on 5 February. This proved to be the first of 259 missions, with a cost to the Group of fifty-eight aircraft missing in action. Whilst it did not receive any Distinguished Unit Citations, one of its component units, the 733rd Bomb Squadron, notched up a record of eighty-two consecutive missions without loss. Its other 'claim to fame' was

the presence of film star James Stewart as the Group's EXO (Executive Officer) from March 1944.

The Group flew its last mission in early April, as it was earmarked for return to the United States, to re-equip with B-29s for the war against Japan. By early May, the American presence had reduced to those whose task it was to make the final ceremony of lowering the Stars and Stripes and to hand the airfield to the RAF. These occasions are rarely recorded but they must have been poignant affairs, especially where a Group, such as the 453rd and Old Buck, had only operated from the one airfield, with all the associated highs and lows of comradeship and combat flying.

The Air Ministry had little use for yet another airfield in this area and, other than some utilization as a sub-site for maintenance units, the airfield remained deserted. Final disposal came on 20 June 1960 and

One of the brightly-coloured assembly ships; the 453rd BG was the sole operational user of Old Buckenham and flew 250 missions from here.

The airfield is now an active General Aviation site and the presence of vintage types such as this Tiger Moth helps the atmosphere.

much of the area returned to farmland. However, the airfield is now alive once more, as a very active General Aviation airfield with a 650-yard stretch of one of the wartime runways back in use. A number of other buildings are in use by the Touchdown Aero Centre and the ops-room/restaurant includes mementoes of the 453rd BG. Other wartime buildings survive around the airfield perimeter. Old Buckenham is now an active GA airfield, enhanced by the presence of a few vintage types.

UNITS

1939–1945
USAAF Units
453rd BG (2nd CBW)

Identifying letter:	J
Squadrons:	732nd BS (Lightman), 733rd BS (Tripup), 734th BS (Dizzy), 735th BS (Bowfinch)
Aircraft:	B-24H, B-24J, B-24L, B-24M
Dates:	23 Dec 1943–9 May 1945
Missions:	259

First mission:	5 Feb 1944
Last mission:	12 Apr 1945

MEMORIALS

1. Memorial stone near flying club, inscribed: 'United States Army Air Forces Station 144 Old Buckenham. The 453rd Bombardment Group (H), 2nd Combat Wing, 2nd Air Division, Eighth Air

Memorial slab in the shape of a B-24 fin; the clubhouse in the background houses a collection of 453rd BG memorabilia.

AIRFIELD DATA DEC 1944

Command:	US 8th AF 2nd BD	Runway surface:	Concrete with partial wood-chippings
Function:	Operational Station	Hangars:	2 × T.2
Runways:	075 deg 2,000 × 50yd	Dispersals:	50 concrete
	027 deg 1,400 × 50yd	Personnel:	Officers – 421
	130 deg 1,400 × 50yd		Other Ranks – 2,473

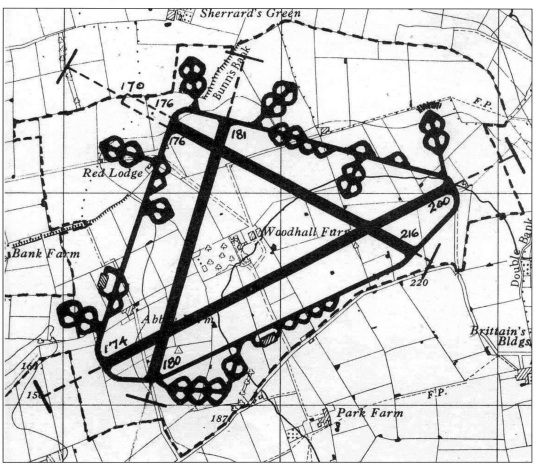

Force, served here December 1943–May 1945. From this airfield B-24 Liberators of 732, 733, 734 and 735 Bombardment Squadrons (H) flew 259 missions, dropped 15,084 tons of bombs, lost 58 aircraft missing in action. 366 air crew lost their lives. To these brave Americans and to all who served here during World War II this memorial is dedicated. 29th July 1990.'

2. Memorial stone adjacent to road, inscribed: 'In memoriam Flt Lt Eric William Harper, born 14th Dec 1916, died 6th Nov 1995, former officer commanding No 94 MSU RAF Old Buckenham 1953–1956 (RAF service 1933–1964). RIP. Commemorating all RAF personnel who served here 1945–1956 (especially those under his command). This site marks the former unit gatehouse/guardroom.'

OULTON

County: Norfolk

UTM/grid: OS Map 133 – TG 145275
Lat./Long.: N52°48.01 E001°11.03
Nearest town: Aylsham 3 miles to east

HISTORY

Oulton was opened as a satellite for Horsham St Faith on 31 July 1940 and maintained this function to September 1942; during that period it was used by a number of units, the first being the Blenheim-equipped 114 Squadron. This squadron had moved into Horsham to recover after its experiences in France as part of the RAF forces forward-deployed to try and stem the German advance. Essentially re-formed and with new aircraft, it moved across to Oulton on 10 August and returned to the fray with daylight low-level attacks on shipping and land targets. The Squadron was heavily tasked and, despite increasing loss rates in the Blenheim units, there was little option for Bomber Command. With the departure of 114 Squadron to Thornaby in March 1941, their place was taken by another Blenheim unit – 18

Squadron with its Blenheim IVs. Tasking remained the same, with anti-shipping work still a high priority. The Squadron moved to Horsham St Faith in August, but continued to use Oulton from time to time; for example, the ground crew taking up residence whilst the aircraft were deployed to Malta.

At the end of 1941 a new type appeared at Oulton – the rotund shape of the Hudson, along with No.1428 Flight, whose task it was to provide Hudson conversion. Their first customers were 139 Squadron; this unit had been flying Blenheims from Oulton since July 1941 but later in the year it was earmarked to deploy to the Far East with Hudsons – hence the arrival of the Hudson Conversion Flight. After a quick conversion, the squadron departed with its Hudson IIIs in January and were promptly disbanded.

Airfield Data Dec 1944

Command:	RAF Bomber Command	Runway surface:	Concrete
Function:	Operational	Hangars:	4 × T.2
Runways:	070 deg 1,400 × 50yd	Dispersals:	30 × Spectacle
	120 deg 2,000 × 50yd	Personnel:	Officers – 110 (6 WAAF)
	170 deg 1,400 × 50yd		Other Ranks – 1,375 (205 WAAF)

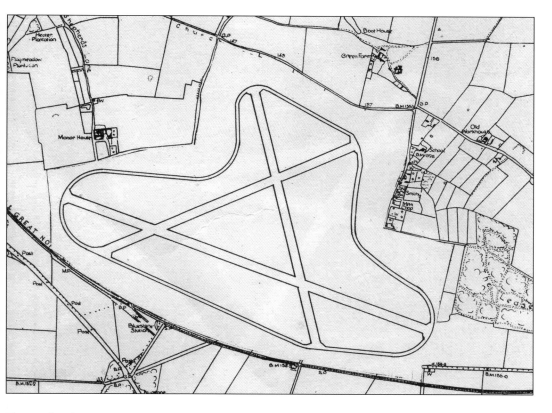

The numberplate was resurrected in June at Horsham and, in the same month, 139 Blenheim Squadron was once more at Oulton, albeit only for a matter of days. Virtually every RAF station took over one or more nearby stately homes to provide HQ or accommodation and, for Oulton, this was Blickling Hall, an imposing Tudor mansion.

Two other units operated from the airfield in 1941: Beaufighters of 236 Squadron between July and September and Bostons of 88 Squadron. The former were operating with Coastal Command on anti-shipping work and the latter as part of No.2 Group, Oulton now acting as a satellite for Swanton Morley. The Bostons opened the next hectic phase of bomber ops and were here for six months. Although this squadron left in early 1943, it was replaced by 21 Squadron, which brought another new type, the Ventura. Mitchells began to replace the Venturas during the summer but, before conversion was complete, the unit moved to Sculthorpe.

On 10 September Oulton was then transferred to No.3 Group, as a satellite for Foulsham, and the opportunity was taken to rebuild parts of the airfield; it was this phase that created the airfield detailed in the December 1944 data. The overall plan had changed, the airfield was transferred to the No.100 Group and it was with this specialist organization that Oulton was to end its war. The RAF's first experience with the B-17, in the early part of the war with 90 Squadron, had not been a happy one but the

Liberator of 223 Squadron at Oulton in 1944; the Squadron spent almost a year at this Norfolk airfield as part of the RCM force.

Fortress was subsequently used by coastal and specialist units; it was in the latter guise that it arrived in Norfolk. No.214 Squadron's Fortresses moved to Oulton from Sculthorpe in May and were joined by the Radio Counter Measures B-17s and B-24s of the 803rd BS, one of very few USAAF RCM units. The Americans left in August but the Liberator-equipped 223 Squadron formed later the same month, to maintain the station's strength of two RCM units. No.1699 Flight was a training unit tasked with providing Fortress conversion, although this role was subsequently changed to Bomber Support Conversion. Both RAF squadrons remained busy to the end of the war, providing screening to the Main Force bombers as well as undertaking a number of special operations.

Post-war, one of the squadrons disbanded and one, 214 Squadron, moved overseas, leaving this once important station with little future. The airfield transferred to Maintenance Command in October and became yet another sub-site for No.274 Maintenance Unit at Swannington. The main role was Mosquito storage and disposal, but this role came to an end in November 1947 and the airfield went out of use. It was probably sold as part of the 1950s disposal.

UNITS

1939–1945

18 Sqn	3 Apr 1941–13 Jul 1941,	Blenheim
	Nov 1941–Dec 1941	
21 Sqn	1 Apr 1943–27 Sep 1943	Ventura
88 Sqn	29 Sep 1942–30 Mar 1943	Boston
114 Sqn	10 Aug 1940–2 Mar 1941	Blenheim
139 Sqn	13 Jul 1941–23 Oct 1941,	Blenheim,
	Dec 1941; 15–20 Jun 1942	Hudson
214 Sqn	16 May 1944–27 Jul 1945	Fortress
223 Sqn	23 Aug 1944–29 Jul 1945	Liberator,
		Fortress
236 Sqn	3 Jul 1942–19 Sep 1942	Beaufighter

1428 Flt	29 Dec 1941–6 Jun 1942	Hudson
1699 Flt	16 May 1944–24 Oct 1944	Fortress,
		Liberator
1699(BS)CU	24 Oct 1944–29 Jun 1945	Fortress

USAAF Units

803rd BS	May–Aug 1943	B-17, B-24

MEMORIALS

1. Memorial stone in village – note that the memorial is at Oulton Street not Oulton! Inscription: 'RAF Oulton. In memory of and in honour of the men and women of the British, Commonwealth and American Air Forces who served at RAF Oulton 1940–1945. Those who died for our freedom will live forever in our hearts. Royal Air Force 18, 21, 88, 114, 139, 214, 223, 236 Sqns, 1428 and 1699 Conversion Flights. 8th USAAF 803rd Bombardment Sqn.'

2. Excellent history room at Blickling Hall.

RACKHEATH
Station 145

County: Norfolk

UTM/grid: OS Map 133 – TG285145
Lat./Long.: N52°40.30 E001°23.00
Nearest town: Norwich 5 miles to south-west

HISTORY

One of a clutch of airfields around the city of Norwich – indeed, it is now in the industrial suburbs of the city – the land for this airfield was requisitioned in early 1943. The name of the airfield was not based on a village but rather a patch of heathland – Rackheath – that gave its name to various places, such as Rackheath Park. The bulk of the construction was carried out by John Laing & Sons, a firm that built many of the wartime airfields in this region, and the airfield with its three runways and bomber-airfield infrastructure was ready for occupation by the end of 1943. Its allocation had already been decided, as this was firmly US bomber territory for 2nd Bombardment Division.

The 'Rackheath Aggies' – the 467th Bomb Group, under the command of Colonel Albert J Shower – arrived with their B-24s in early March 1944 and Rackheath was to be their only wartime base. The first mission was flown on 10 April and, by the end of the war, the Group had completed 212 ops for the loss of twenty-nine aircraft missing in action, one of lowest loss rates in the 8th Air Force. One of the Group's aircraft, B-24 'Witchcraft', flew 130 mis-

sions, a record for a B-24 in the Eighth. Although the Group was not awarded a Distinguished Unit Citation, it established a fine reputation for bombing accuracy, at one time leading the statistics for the 8th Air Force. As has been mentioned in many of these brief histories, most airfields had at least one tragic event in their record; for Rackheath this occurred on 29 December 1944, when aircraft attempted to take-off in poor visibility: two crashed on the edge of the airfield, killing fifteen crewmen and two others were damaged and subsequently crashed. This particular type of loss is not included in the statistics of 'lost to enemy action' but the tragedy of such incidents was, in many respects, more immediate, as it happened 'at home'.

The Group flew its final mission on 25 April and, after a few weeks of celebrating the end of the war and preparing to go home, the 467th bade farewell to Rackheath in June and July 1945. The RAF had no use for this airfield and it was one of the first to be put up for disposal, part of the site returning to farmland and part being used for industrial purposes; indeed, the present Rackheath Industrial Estate still contains

B-24 of the 467th BG; the four squadrons of the Group flew over 200 missions from Rackheath.

AIRFIELD DATA DEC 1944

Command:	US 8th AF, 2nd BD	Runway surface:	Concrete
Function:	Operational	Hangars:	2 × T.2
Runways:	210 deg 2,000 × 50yd	Dispersals:	50 × Concrete eyeglass
	260 deg 1,400 × 50yd	Personnel:	Officers – 421
	320 deg 1,400 × 50yd		Other Ranks – 2,473

'Witchcraft' was a record-breaking Liberator, clocking-up 130 combat missions.

a number of the original temporary wartime buildings and is also the site of the memorial stone.

UNITS

1939–1945
USAAF Units
467th BG (96th CW)

Identifying letter:	P
Nickname:	The Rackheath Aggies
Squadrons:	788th BS (Shirtmaker), 789th BS (Acford), 790th BS (Hamos), 791st BS (Baron)
Aircraft:	B-24H, B-24J, B-24L, B-24M
Dates:	11 Mar 1944–12 Jun 1945
Missions:	212
First mission:	10 Apr 1944
Last mission:	25 Apr 1945

MEMORIALS

1. Stone memorial on the industrial site, inscribed: '467th Bombardment Group Heavy, 2nd Air Division 8th Air Force, United States Army Air Force, under the command of Colonel Albert J Shower, flew 212 combat missions, 5538 aircraft sorties with losses of 235 airmen,

The airfield has vanished under an industrial park and housing but a memorial stone marks the existence of this once busy airfield.

46 aircraft, in B-24 Liberator bombers from this airfield from March 11th 1944 to July 5th 1945. Over 5000 American airmen stationed here made a major contribution to the defeat of Nazi Germany in World War II. Dedicated July 29th 1990. The Four Hundred and Sixty Seventh Bombardment Group Heavy Association Ltd.'

2. At Holy Trinity Church are two benches with plaque inscribed: 'Dedicated 8 October 1983 to the memory of our comrades who died in training and in 212 combat missions flown in B-24 Liberator bombers from Station 145, Rackheath, Norfolk, England from 10 April 1944 to 25 April 1945 and to all assigned or attached to the 467th Bombardment Group (Heavy).'

RATTLESDEN
Station 126

County: Suffolk

UTM/grid: OS Map 155 – TL965555
Lat./Long.: N52°10.02 E000°52.13
Nearest town: Rattlesden 3 miles to north

HISTORY

Construction work began on this remote site in Suffolk in 1942, with the intention that the airfield would be used to house medium-bombers and act as a satellite for nearby Rougham (Bury St Edmunds). The bulk of the construction work was carried out by Wimpey and a standard layout of three intersecting concrete runways was squeezed in amongst the roads and lanes, although a few local routes had to be shut or diverted. The airfield, actually nearer the village of Felsham, was handed to the Americans on 1 October and a few weeks later the ground personnel of the 322nd Bomb Group, a B-26 Marauder unit, arrived at the base. The Group was not complete, but a number of Marauders arrived for work-up and evaluation purposes as part of the 3rd Bomb Wing. However, in April 1943, the Group moved to Rougham and it was from there that they eventually became operational.

With a policy decision to change the concentration of aircraft types and Groups, Rattlesden was allocated to the 8th Air Force's heavy-bomber element of the 4th Combat Bomb Wing as a B-17 base. The changeover was not instant and for a few months the airfield was without a resident flying unit. In November, the 447th Bomb Group, led by Colonel Hunter Harris Jr and equipped with B-17Gs, arrived at Rattlesden; this unit was to undertake its entire wartime career from this airfield. After a few weeks to settle in, the Group flew its first mission on 24 December, the start of a 257-mission total that incurred ninety-seven aircraft missing in action.

Rattlesden's home-based 'bad day' came on 21 April 1944, when several of the Group's personnel were killed and three B-17s destroyed in a bombing-up incident. Considering the very large numbers of

AIRFIELD DATA DEC 1944

Command:	US 8th AF 3rd BD	Runway surface:	Tarmac and concrete
Function:	Operational Station	Hangars:	2 × T.2
Runways:	243 deg 2,000 × 50yd	Dispersals:	50 × Loop
	177 deg 1,400 × 50yd	Personnel:	Officers – 421
	310 deg 1,400 × 50yd		Other Ranks – 2,473

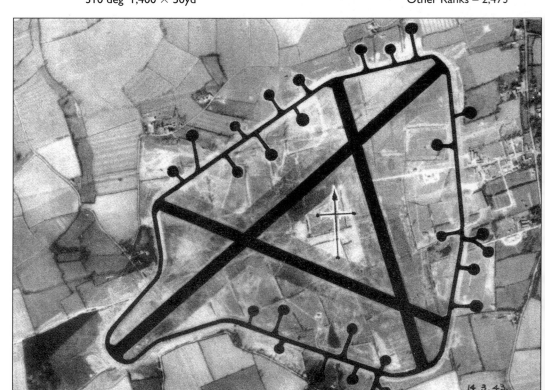

bombs handled at airfields such as this, and the often primitive conditions, this kind of incident was remarkably infrequent – but nonetheless tragic.

Amongst the Group's claims to fame was an aircraft with a record total of missions within the 3rd Air Division – 'Milk Wagon' clocking up 129 missions – and a Medal of Honour recipient. The latter was a posthumous award made to Second Lieutenant Robert E Femoyer, a navigator with the 711th Bomb Squadron, for a mission on 2 November 1944.

Rattlesden witnessed its share of badly damaged bombers returning with dead or injured crew and it always seems trite to use phrases such as 'the Group continued to operate as part of the daylight offensive, undertaking a variety of missions', as this does little to convey the nature of day-to-day existence at an air

base with over 2,000 people. However, in simple terms such a phrase does summarize what happened at this and many other similar airfields. The 447th remained operational to the end of the war, flying its last mission on 21 April.

The airfield was soon empty as the Americans departed for home; the RAF took control of Rattlesden on 10 October but the only immediate post-war use was as a storage site by the Ministry of Food, this task lasting less than a year. Following this the airfield fell quiet, but was retained and, in December 1959, part of the site was once more active, as 266 Squadron established a Bloodhound surface-to-air missile-site here as part of the air defence structure of East Anglia. This unit and its missile launchers remained in residence to June 1964, after which the site was put up for disposal.

Rattlesden's Flying Fortresses flew 257 missions between November 1943 and the end of the war.

In more recent years, flying returned when the Rattlesden Gliding Club was established in 1976; the Club makes use of one of the original runways and uses the wartime control tower as its clubhouse.

UNITS

1939–1945
USAAF Units
447th BG (4th CBW)
Identifying letter: K
Squadrons: 708th BS (Munru), 709th BS (Kirkland), 710th BS (Inlay), 711th BS (Curlhair)
Aircraft: B-17G
Dates: 29 Nov 1943–1 Aug 1945
Missions: 257
First mission: 24 Dec 1943
Last mission: 21 Apr 1945

Post-1945
266 Sqn   1 Dec 1959–30 Jun 1964   Bloodhound

MEMORIALS

1. Memorial stone (dedicated 3 Jun 1984), inscribed:

'Dedicated to the members of the 447th Bomb Group and their supporting units in remembrance and gratitude of their fight in the cause of freedom from Rattlesden Airfield (Station 126) 1943–1945.'

2. The control tower is now the base for a gliding club and contains some memorabilia.

The memorial is hard to find – so look out for the twin flagpoles (always a good indication of a wartime memorial at an ex USAAF site).

ROUGHAM (Bury St Edmunds) Station 468

UTM/grid: OS Map 155 – TL880645
Lat./Long.: N52°14.5 E000°46.0
Nearest town: Bury St Edmunds 2 miles to west

County: Suffolk

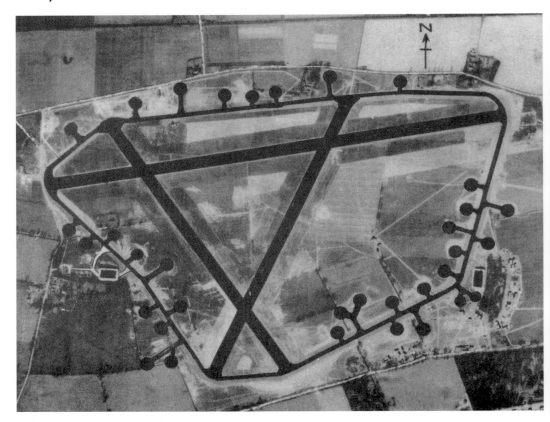

HISTORY

The airfield at Rougham was constructed in late-1941/early 1942 by Costain Ltd on a stretch of farm-land to the east of Bury St Edmunds; with the hedges removed and ditches filled, this stretch of Suffolk countryside was laid out as a bomber base with three runways, one of which pointed straight at Bury, and the usual perimeter-track with its fifty dispersal points. This was one of a small number of airfields that had two official names, starting as Rougham and ending up, at least in RAF records, as Bury St Edmunds. Assigned for use by the USAAF, it received its first aircraft in September 1942 when the A-20 Havocs of the 47th Bomb Group moved in. However, they quickly departed for Horham and, despite the fact that construction work at Rougham was still underway, another unit, the 322nd BG,

arrived in December. The majority of the 'off-airfield' sites were clustered to the east and south-east, towards Rougham Hall, with the large bomb-dump connected to the airfield by a concrete road.

The incomplete nature of the airfield was not an immediate problem for this B-26 Group as, for the first few months, only the ground personnel were present and it was not until March that the Marauders flew in. The Group, under the command of Lieutenant Colonel Robert M Stillman undertook an intensive training programme as part of the 3rd Bombardment Wing; their first mission was flown on 14 May 1943 and three days later the CO's aircraft was lost on operations – he became a PoW. These two missions had been low-level attacks on targets in Holland and had revealed flaws in both tactics and

Heavy damage but a safe return for this B-17 of the 94th BG. (US National Archives)

September 1943 over England; the 94th BG had arrived at Rougham in June and remained operational from the Suffolk base to the end of the war.

aircraft. As part of a move-round of units, which saw the B-26 Groups concentrating at airfields in Essex, the 322nd flew out to Andrews Field in June.

This made way for the 94th BG and its B-17s, a unit that had already spent brief periods at Bassingbourn and Earls Colne, flying their first mission from the latter airfield. Arriving at Rougham, usually known as Bury St Edmunds by this time, in mid-June, the Group continued to fly a range of daylight missions. The unit went on to fly 324 missions

at the cost of 153 aircraft missing in action, although the gunners put in claims for 342 enemy aircraft, plus a further 92 probables and 154 damaged. The Group was awarded two Distinguished Unit Citations; the first for the 17 August 1943 Regensburg mission and the second for Brunswick on 11 January 1944.

The end of the war saw the Group's B-17s remain on active service, originally intended as one of the air units for the occupation force in Germany, and they flew leaflet-dropping missions over Europe. This task was, however, soon over and the occupation plan changed, so that the 94th lost aircraft and personnel to other units or en route for home. By mid-December the last Americans had left and, on 20 December, the RAF formally took control of the airfield. The following year it was with Bomber Command, but this was a paperwork exercise and, as no-one wanted the airfield, it was offered up to the War Office. Final disposal took place in the 1950s. The technical site was subsequently developed as an industrial estate, with a large number of buildings still in place, although some are in poor condition.

The old control tower has survived and is now the centre of attention for the Rougham Tower Association; this organization was formed in 1993 and has done a great job on restoring the tower and preserving the hisotry of the airfield – in recent years it has also acquired a number of Nissen huts.

AIRFIELD DATA DEC 1944

Command:	US 8th AF 3rd BD	Runway surface:	Concrete, partially tarred and wood-chipped
Function:	Operational Station	Hangars:	2 × T.2
Runways:	275 deg 2,000 × 50yd	Dispersals:	50 × Concrete loop
	160 deg 1,400 × 50yd	Personnel:	Officers – 443
	220 deg 1,400 × 50yd		Other Ranks – 2,529

DECOY SITE

Q   Ixworth/Stowlangtoft   TL948714

UNITS

HQ units at Rougham

4th BW	13 Sep 1943–18 Jun 1945
14th BW	13 Sep 1943–26 Aug 1945
92nd BW	18 Nov 1944–12 Feb 1945

1939–1945
USAAF Units

47th BG	Sep 1942–Oct 1942	A-20

322nd BG

Squadrons:	449th BS, 450th BS, 451st BS, 452nd BS
Aircraft:	B-26
Dates:	1 Dec 1942–Jan 1943
First mission:	14 May 1943

94th BG (4th CBW)

Identifying letter:	A
Squadrons:	331st BS (Agmer), 332nd BS (Rotate), 333rd BS (Cedar), 410th BS (Total)
Aircraft:	B-17F/G
Dates:	Jun 1943–Dec 1945
Missions:	324 (including missions flown from other bases)
First mission:	13 May 1943 (from Earls Colne)
Last mission:	21 Apr 1945

MEMORIALS

There is no memorial at the airfield site but a pub, the Flying Fortress, is located on the edge of the former airfield. The main memorial is located in the Abbey Gardens in Bury St Edmunds and comprises a memorial rose-garden along with a stone

The Group's memorial is located in the Abbey Gardens, Bury-St-Edmunds.

monument; inscription: 'Presented to the people of Bury St Edmunds. A memorial honouring those men of the 94th Bombardment Group who gave their lives during World War II. 4th Combat Bombardment Wing, 8th Air Force. Rougham airfield Bury St Edmunds 1943–1945. 94th Bombardment Group. Squadrons 331st, 332nd, 333rd, 410th and supporting units US Army Air Force. 15 October 1977.'

SCULTHORPE

County: Norfolk

UTM/grid: OS Map 132 – TF860315
Lat./Long.: N52°50.94 E000°45.6
Nearest town: Fakenham 4 miles to east

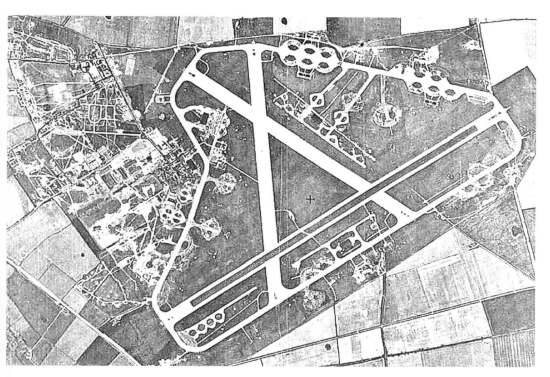

HISTORY

One of the 1942-built stations for the light-bomber force of No.2 Group, then stationed in East Anglia, Sculthorpe opened in January 1943 as a satellite for West Raynham, this major airfield being located just four miles to the south; indeed, Sculthorpe was 'surrounded' by other airfields, with eventually six other airfields within a 5-mile radius. The airfield was constructed with a three-runway pattern and extensive dispersal-areas, with most of its 'off airfield' sites grouped just to the west.

The first flying machines to appear were Horsa gliders, brought here, as with many airfields in the region, for storage; it was 1943 before the first based-unit arrived, the Bostons of 342 Squadron flying in from West Raynham on 15 May. The French-manned 'Lorraine' Squadron had only formed in April and its main occupation at Sculthorpe was crew training, although it did commence ops from here in June; it was short-stay and, in July, the squadron

moved to Great Massingham. However, two Ventura squadrons arrived from Methwold, although the main desire of 464 Squadron and 487 Squadron was to get rid of the Venturas and acquire a more suitable air-craft!

The Australians and New Zealanders were delighted with their new Mosquito FB.VIs and an intensive training-programme was soon underway, including new tactics, as the Group's philosophy had turned increasingly to aggressive intruder operations by day and night. A third Mosquito unit, 21 Squadron, arrived in September, to create a very effective and powerful three-squadron Wing – as 140 Airfield. This was part of the major re-organization of tactical air-power, including the creation of the 2nd Tactical Air Force, in preparation for the planned invasion of Europe in 1944. The three squadrons became operational in October and were soon ranging far and wide over Europe, attacking a variety of

AIRFIELD DATA DEC 1944

Command:	RAF Bomber Command	Runway surface:	Concrete
Function:	Operational	Hangars:	4 × T.2, one × B.1
Runways:	131 deg 2,000 × 100yd	Dispersals:	36 × Heavy Bomber
	182 deg 2,000 × 100yd	Personnel:	Officers – 148 (9 WAAF)
	243 deg 3,000 × 100yd		Other Ranks – 2,034 (400 WAAF)

Note: Completion to this standard due Aug 1945.

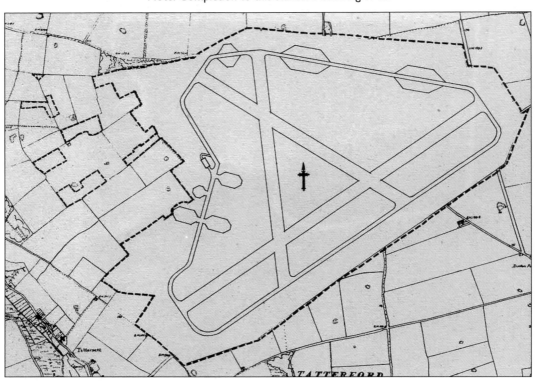

targets. Hardly had the Mossies got into their stride when they were moved to Hunsdon; in part, this was to place them nearer one particular target area but it was also because a new organization had need of Sculthorpe's concrete runways.

The formation of No.100 Group, in late-1943, was of great importance to Bomber Command, as the specialist Radio Counter Measures (RCM) role performed by the Group would play a large part in reducing the unacceptable loss-rates being suffered by Main Force. Sculthorpe was one of the Norfolk airfields chosen to host units of this new Group and, in January 1944, the Stirlings of 214 Squadron duly arrived; later in the month they were joined by the 803rd Bomb Squadron of the 8th Air Force with specially-equipped B-17s. The RAF unit acquired a

number of B-17s, operated as the Fortress II, and intensive training began. Operations did not commence until early April and it was only a matter of weeks before the squadrons left for Oulton.

It had been decided that Sculthorpe would close and be developed into a very-heavy-bomber station with one very long and strengthened runway for B-29 operations. These decisions were usually based on the ease of extending the main runway and the overall suitability of expanding an airfield's facilities but, in the case of Sculthorpe, the December 1944 analysis suggested 'no extension possible' and, at that date, the airfield was still listed as operational with Bomber Command. Nevertheless, construction work went ahead, not so much on lengthening the runways but on strengthening them and providing increased

Sculthorpe was an important Cold War airfield and in the 1950s and 1960s housed a number of American units, including short-term rotations. The B-45, including the RB-45 variant, was a frequent site in the early 1950s, with the recce marks flying secret surveillance missions over Europe and the Soviet Union.

support facilities, including extra fuel- and bomb-storage. At the end of the war the airfield was still not operational; indeed, it did not re-open until December 1948.

Anyone with an interest in the Cold War would have found Sculthorpe a veritable treasure trove in the 1950s and early 1960s, as this airfield became one of the main American installations in the UK, performing a variety of roles and with a truly impressive array of aircraft using its concrete over a period of fifteen years. The airfield had re-opened as an RAF station, but its primary use during the first two years was as a deployment base for Strategic Air Command units on their ninety-day rotations to Europe. The first B-29 detachment, from the 92nd BG, arrived in February 1949 and they were followed by B-29s and B-50s from a number of SAC units. In January 1951 the base was formally handed to the Americans and, in May, the first permanent unit arrived – and also opened a new operational era for Sculthorpe in the world of 'intelligence gathering'. The aircraft were RB-45s and the unit was the 91st Strategic Reconnaissance Group; this unit was tasked with long-range flights, including penetration of Russian-controlled airspace, and a number of their aircraft subsequently wore RAF markings. It is only in recent years that details of the Group's operations and the RAF's participation are becoming known.

The ground and air defence of an airfield is usually not mentioned in airfield histories so, perhaps, mention of the 39th AAA Brigade, which arrived in February 1951 to take over Sculthorpe's defence, is

appropriate; this was a vital base and so its defence against air – and ground – attack was essential. Other US Army units included the 50th RCAT (Radio Controlled Airplane Target) Detachment and the 172nd Smoke Generating Company; the Army left in 1957.

The specially equipped air-sea-rescue aircraft, SB-29s and HU-16s, of the 9th Air Rescue Squadron also operated from Sculthorpe in the early 1950s, as did transport aircraft of the 60th Tactical Cargo Wing, but it is as a bomber and reconnaissance base that the airfield played its major role. Two squadrons of the 47th BG, equipped with the B-45 Tornado, arrived to boost the overall strength at Sculthorpe and, with the departure of the reconnaissance units, the airfield was very much a bomber base, the B-45 Tornado subsequently giving way to B-66 Destroyer.

A major increase in capability came in 1956, with the arrival of tankers; the 420th Air Refuelling Squadron setting up at Sculthorpe with KB-29s, although these were replaced the following year by KB-50s. The squadron was tasked with providing aerial refuelling for USAFE and NATO units throughout Europe and this role was maintained from Sculthorpe to 1964, by which time Mildenhall had been designated as the main tanker-base. The airfield had become a major NATO installation but, by the early 1960s, a restructuring programme was underway and, despite the excellent facilities at Sculthorpe, the Americans abandoned the airfield in 1964. Sculthorpe was reduced to Care and Maintenance under RAF control, although the USAFE regained control in April 1967, and over the next twenty years was maintained in operational condition as a standby airfield; during that time it witnessed numerous detachments (for example, the author flew Canberras with 231 OCU out of Sculthorpe when Marham's runway was out of action). The airfield was also used as a storage and disposal site for fighter types provided to various NATO air forces and, at one stage in the late-1970s, housed numerous F-100s, F104s and other 'Century' fighters, many of which found their way into aviation museums.

The main period of standby activity was over by 1985 and the airfield languished, awaiting any future requirement; however, it was officially closed in 1992.

Decoy Site

Q/K	Coxford Heath	TF828307

Units

1939–1945

Unit	Dates	Aircraft
21 Sqn	27 Sep 1943–31 Dec 1943	Mosquito
214 Sqn	16 Jan 1944–16 May 1944	Stirling, Fortress
342 Sqn	15 May 1943–19 Jul 1943	Boston
464 Sqn	21 Jul 1943–31 Dec 1943	Ventura, Mosquito
487 Sqn	20 Jul 1943–31 Dec 1943	Ventura, Mosquito
MCF	22 Aug 1943–?	Mosquito
1699 Flt	24 Apr 1944–16 May 1944	Fortress

USAAF Units

Unit	Dates	Aircraft
803rd BS	19 Jan 1944–16 May 1944	B-17F, B-17G

Post-1945
USAF Units

Unit	Dates	Aircraft
91st SRG	May 1951–Mar 1955	RB-45C
9th/67th ARS	Aug 1951–Oct 1953	SB-29, SA-16A
60th TCW	May 1952–Dec 1954	C-119
47th BG	May 1952–Jun 1962	B-45, B-66
19th TRS	Jun 1952–Feb 1959	RB-45C, B-66
7554th TTF	Jul 1952–Jun 1962	TB-26, L-5
49th ADCF	Apr 1954–Jun 1956	L-20A, T-33A
47th OS	Dec 1954–Feb 1958	various
420th ARS	Jan 1956–Mar 1964	KB-29, KB-50
78th FBS	Apr 1957–Sep 1957	F-84F
28th WRS	Aug 1962–Dec 1962	WB-50D

The RAF had used the airfield in the latter part of World War Two, Mosquito units such as 464 Squadron spending a few weeks or months operating from here.

SEETHING
Station 146

County: Norfolk

UTM/grid: OS Map 134 – TM320955
Lat./Long.: N52°30.30 E001°24.45
Nearest town: Norwich 9.5 miles to north-west

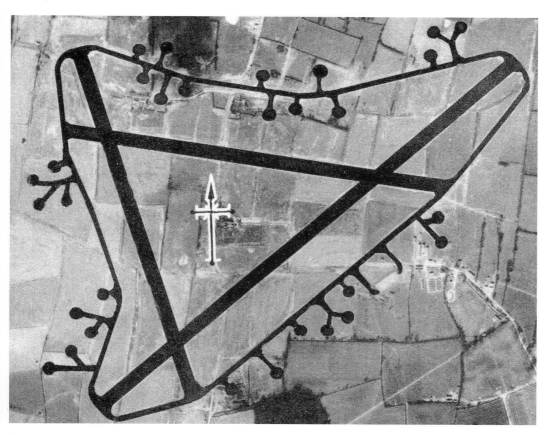

HISTORY

This Class A, heavy-bomber airfield was constructed in 1942–1943 to the south of Norwich, covering an extensive area of farmland centred on Upgate Farm. As usual, a number of minor roads had to be closed to make room for the three runways and the majority of the 'off airfield' support sites were constructed to the south in the Hedenham Wood area. Most of the construction work was undertaken by John Laing & Son and the airfield was complete by late-summer 1943, ready for its USAAF bomber group.

The sole occupants of Seething, the 448th Bomb Group, arrived in November 1943 under the command of Colonel James M Thompson; this Group was to remain operational out of Seething for the rest of the war. The first mission was flown on 22 December

and, over the next eighteen months, the 448th flew 262 missions with their B-24s for the loss of 101 aircraft missing in action. From the operational perspective there was nothing remarkable about the Group's operations, it was an average performer and suffered average losses – which by no means denigrates the courage and resilience of its air and ground personnel. The airfield, and the Group, suffered one particular tragic incident, when four aircraft were shot down over the airfield by a German intruder on 22 April 1944, a fifth aircraft crashing into a wreck on landing. This must have been a devastating night for all those based at Seething and when you stand on the present runway at Seething it is hard to picture a peaceful spring evening turning into such a holocaust.

AIRFIELD DATA DEC 1944

Command:	US 8th AF, 2nd BD	Runway surface:	Concrete
Function:	Operational	Hangars:	2 × T.2
Runways:	010 deg 1,400 × 50yd	Dispersals:	51 × Communal and Pan
	070 deg 2,000 × 50yd	Personnel:	Officers – 421
	300 deg 1,400 × 50yd		Other Ranks – 2,473

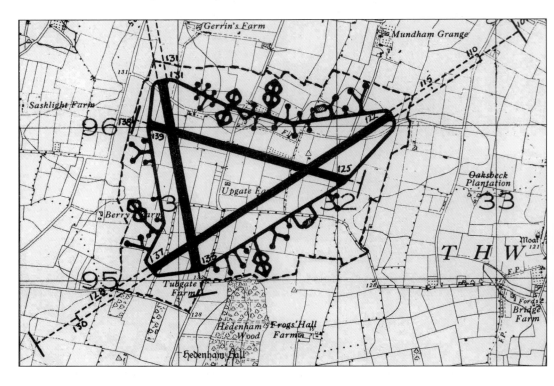

Having flown its last mission on 25 April, to Salzburg, the Group began to wind down and, in common with most USAAF bomber-groups, it redeployed to the US in June–July 1945. There was no further military use for the airfield and it was eventually sold off in the mid-1950s, the majority of the area returning to farmland. However, in 1950, part of the airfield was acquired by the Waveney Flying Club; although much of the infrastructure and runways have gone, runway 06/24 remains in use and parts of another runway and the perimeter track are still evident or in use. The wartime control-tower has also survived and is now home to a small museum commemorating the wartime exploits of the 448th BG.

UNITS

1939–1945
USAAF Units
448th BG (20th CW)

Identifying letter:	I
Squadrons:	712th BS, 713th BS, 714th BS, 715th BS
Aircraft:	B-24H, B-24J, B-24L, B-24M
Dates:	Nov 1943 – Jul 1945
Missions:	262
First mission:	22 Dec 1943
Last mission:	25 Apr 1945

The 448th BG were the sole users of this late-build airfield but managed to clock-up 262 missions – for the loss of 146 Liberators.

Seething has two memorial stones, one by the clubhouse and one adjacent to the restored control tower, which also acts as a museum.

MEMORIALS

1. The control tower has been restored and is a museum to the 448th BG. Memorial stone by tower with a layout of the airfield and a list of the flying and support units.

2. Stone by clubhouse, inscribed: '448th Bombardment Group (Heavy) 712, 713, 714 and 715 Squadrons, 20th Combat Wing, 2nd Air Division, 8th United States Air Force. From this airfield in WWII the 448th BG launched 262 missions, flew 7343 sorties and dropped 15296 tons of bombs. Losses were 146 B-24 Liberators and 350 crewmen killed and 47 enemy aircraft destroyed. To the memory of those brave young men who were lost in our struggle for freedom this marker is humbly dedicated by the survivors of the 448th June 6th 1984 the 40th Anniversary of D-Day.'

3. Memorial in Seething churchyard, inscribed: '448th Bomb Group. In memory of the men of the 448th Bomb Group 8th United States Air Force who served at Seething airfield December 1943 to April 1945 fighting for freedom. 350 men killed in action. Dedicated 6th June 1984.'

SHEPHERD'S GROVE

County: Suffolk

UTM/grid: OS Map 155 – TL990730
Lat./Long.: N52°19.00 E000°55.15
Nearest town: Bury St Edmunds 9 miles to south-west

Shepherd's Grove from the air August 1998.

HISTORY

Although intended for the USAAF and constructed during 1943, Shepherd's Grove was not brought into use until April 1944, for No.3 Group of Bomber Command as a satellite for Stradishall. The airfield took its name from a nearby wood, the nearest village being Walsham le Willows, and it was somewhat squeezed-in between a number of other airfields to the north and east of Bury St Edmunds. It was constructed to the, by then, standard airfield pattern with three concrete runways, the longest of which was oriented almost north/south, unusual for East Anglia. The perimeter track linking the runways was dotted with spectacle-type dispersals but the number of buildings was limited and, when it was assigned to the USAAF, it only had two T.2 hangars.

In May, the Stirlings of No.1657 Heavy Conversion Unit arrived and it was with this aircraft type that Shepherd's Grove was to be most involved. The HCU was responsible for converting crews for the Stirling squadrons of No.3 Group and the new airfield was well suited to the task, except for the busy nature of the airspace around the area. Like all the HCUs, this one had a number of additional training-types and 'hacks' and the runways would have witnessed such diverse types as Spitfires and Oxfords. The training task ended in October, when the HCU moved to Stradishall. The Station was transferred to No.38 Group and, in January, two operational Stirling IV units arrived from Wethersfield; these units flew supply-dropping missions often engaged in dropping supplies to SOE and the resistance organizations. In addition to supply dropping, the Stirlings were also equipped for glider towing and performed this task during Operation 'Varsity', the crossing of the Rhine. The Martinets and Oxfords of No.1677 Target Towing Flight were also in residence from January to April 1945, working with a number of units in the area.

AIRFIELD DATA DEC 1944

Command:	RAF Bomber Command	Runway surface:	Concrete
Function:	not specified	Hangars:	2 × T.2
Runways:	010 deg 2,000 × 50yd	Dispersals:	49 × Spectacle, one Pan
	080 deg 1,400 × 50yd	Personnel:	Officers – 184 (12 WAAF)
	140 deg 1,400 × 50yd		Other Ranks – 2,2576 (532 WAAF)

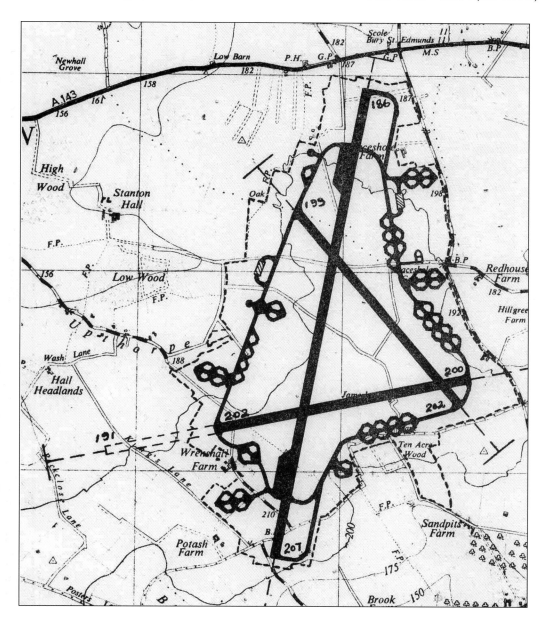

F-86 Sabres at Shepherd's Grove August 1951; the 81st FIW arrived in 1951 and remained to 1958.

In the immediate post-war period the two Stirling squadrons remained active, as there was a massive transport-task to move men and material worldwide; however, by early 1946, this role had reduced and both units were disbanded. Shepherd's Grove was transferred to No.60 Group in May 1946 and became a satellite for the Radio Warfare Establishment (Central Signals Establishment from September 1946) at Watton. This unit was equipped with a variety of aircraft and was very busy in the post-war period, evaluating a wide range of Allied and German equipment. However, the airfield went out of use in February 1950 and was placed under Care and Maintenance. At some point, Operational Readiness Platforms had been placed at each end of the main runway (01/19) and this runway had subsequently been extended at both ends.

The station was re-activated in 1951 to become a base for USAF fighter detachments, part of a NATO reaction to the Korean War and in the belief that the conflict might spread to a more general war with communism. First arrivals were the F-86 Sabres of the 116th Fighter Interceptor Squadron of the 81st Fighter Interception Wing. A second squadron, the 92nd FIS from this Wing, arrived soon afterwards and, for the next seven years, Shepherd's Grove was a USAF fighter base, although in April 1954 the 78th Fighter Squadron (created by renumbering the 116th) received F-84F Thunderstreaks and became a

fighter-bomber unit. The Americans moved out to Woodbridge in December 1958 and construction work began on one small area of the airfield to create a Thor missile-base. The three missiles were operated by 82 Squadron, which formed here in July 1959, and for four years Shepherd's Grove was part of the RAF's ballistic-missile force.

With the disbandment of the Thor force the airfield was finally abandoned and, within a short space of time, had been put up for disposal. Part of the site is now occupied by an industrial park and a number of buildings survive around the airfield.

UNITS

1939–1945

196 Sqn	26 Jan 1945–16 Mar 1946	Stirling
299 Sqn	25 Jan 1945–15 Feb 1946	Stirling
1657 HCU	14 May 1944–5 Oct 1944	Stirling
30 GS	May 1944–Jan 1946	Cadet
1677 Flt	28 Jan 1945–18 Apr 1945	Martinet, Oxford

Post-1945

| 82 Sqn | 22 Jul 1959–10 Jul 1963 | Thor |

USAF Units

| 81st FIW | Aug 1951–Dec 1958 | F-86, F-84 |

SHIPDHAM
Station 115

County: Norfolk

UTM/grid: OS Map 144 – TF985075
Lat./Long.: N52°37.38 E000°56.00
Nearest town: East Dereham 3.5 miles to north

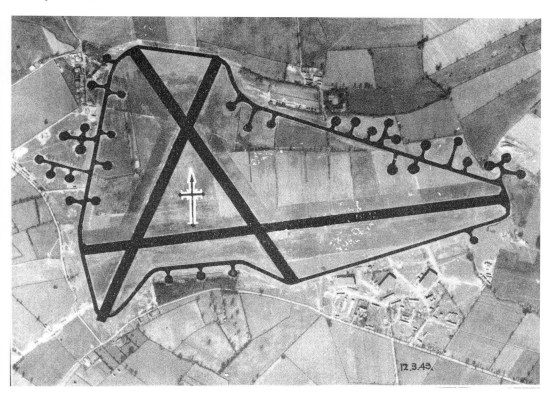

12.3.43.

HISTORY

Shipdham had the distinction of being the first USAAF heavy-bomber base in Norfolk and was constructed during early 1942, just east of the village that gave it its name. The overall airfield-pattern was to RAF bomber specification, with three runways and a perimeter track dotted with concrete dispersals. The southern edge of the airfield mirrors a road and the perimeter track on the northern side bends to accommodate Park Farm but, other than that, the land was highly suitable, having few other obstacles requiring removal.

The original intention was for the RAF to take on the airfield but, by early 1942, the search for bases for the expected influx of American units was underway and it was decided to allocate the new airfield to this use. Shipdham opened in September 1942 and was allocated to the medium bombers, B-26 Marauders, of the 319th Bomb Group. However, whilst the ground echelon moved in that month, the aircraft were still en route –

and, by the time they arrived in the UK, the Group had transferred to Horsham St Faith. This Marauder presence in the UK was always intended as short term, the units being designated for service in the North African campaign, and of more significance was the build-up of an American strategic-bomber force in eastern England – the 8th United States Army Air Force. It was to this formation that the airfield was now allocated.

In October the 'Flying Eightballs', two squadrons of the 44th Bomb Group, arrived with B-24D Liberators, after originally going to Cheddington in September; this unit remained at Shipdham for the rest of the war. The unit was the first to receive the B-24 and, as such, it pioneered Liberator operations with the USAAF. With barely any time to settle in, the Group flew its first mission on 7 November and the early experiences were not promising, as loss rates started to mount; indeed, the Group was to suffer the highest missing in

AIRFIELD DATA DEC 1944

Command:	US 8th AF 2nd BD	Runway surface:	Macadam
Function:	Operational	Hangars:	3 × T.2
Runways:	030 deg 1,400 × 50yd	Dispersals:	50 × concrete
	090 deg 2,000 × 50yd	Personnel:	Officers – 443
	210 deg 1,400 × 50yd		Other Ranks – 2,529

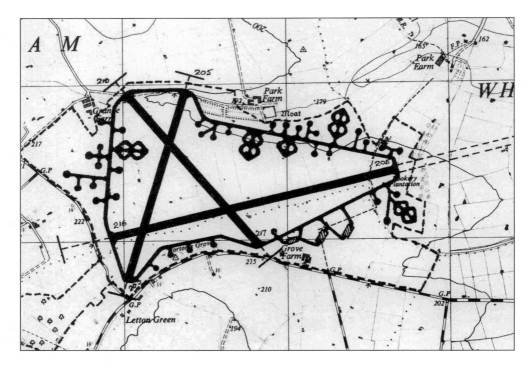

action total (153 aircraft) of any of the 8th Air Force Liberator units, although it must be remembered that it was also the longest-serving such unit.

The summer of 1943 saw the 44th BG move temporarily to North Africa and from there it took part in the Ploesti raid, for which it received a Distinguished Unit citation and for which the Group CO, Colonel Leon W Johnson received the Medal of Honour. Another detachment to North Africa followed in August–September 1943, before the unit concentrated on European operations. During its operational period the 44th flew 343 missions and clocked up various achievements: it was the first to fly the B-24, claimed more enemy-fighter kills than any other 8th Air Force Liberator Group (330-74-69) and flew operations from the UK for the longest period.

The Liberators left in June 1945, bringing to an end one of the longest associations of an American

bomber Group and a single airfield; a period when American servicemen were regular visitors to the nearby villages and pubs – and, perhaps, the fact that there are no less than three memorials to this association is a reflection of the relationship. In the immediate post-war period the site was used as a transit airfield for flights taking German PoWs home to Germany from Florida, although this task was over by 1947 and the airfield, once so alive with dozens of Liberators, fell silent. By the early 1960s the airfield had been sold off for agricultural use; however, the runways, or at least a part of one of them, were in use with Arrow Air Services from 1970. Today, Shipdham Aero Club operates the field, making use of a single hard-runway (02/20), and a number of general aviation fly-ins are held by the club each year. Various buildings survive around the site, one or two of which include original wall murals.

Towing tractor being used to manoeuvre a B-24 into one of Shipdham's T.2 hangars.

UNITS

1939–1945
USAAF Units
319th BG

Squadrons	437th BS, 438th BS, 439th BS, 440th BS
Aircraft	B-26
Dates	12 Sep 1942–4 Oct 1944

44th BG (14th CW)

Identifying letter:	A
Nickname:	The Flying Eightballs
Squadrons:	66th BS, 67th BS, 68th BS, 506th BS
Aircraft:	B-24D, B-24H, B-24J, B-24L, B-24M, B-17G
Dates:	Oct 1942–15 Jun 1945
Missions:	343 (includes 18 from North Africa)
First mission:	7 Nov 1942
Last mission:	25 Apr 1945

MEMORIALS

1. Inscription on village war memorial: 'To the fallen of the 8th Bomber Command USAAF.'

2. Stone (dedicated 3 Sep 1983) in village churchyard, inscribed: 'Shipdham 44 BG. To those brave Americans who served and died in defense of their country and allies. In memory 44th Bomb Group (H) 1942–1945. United States Army Air Force.'

3. Stone on airfield near clubhouse, inscribed: '8th

Memorial plaque outside the clubhouse at Shipdham airfield; other memorials are located in the churchyard.

Air Force B-24 Liberators. First mission 7 Nov 1942. Last mission 25 April 1945. Shipdham AAF Station 115. "Flying Eyeball Group." "Aggressor Beware." 344 combat missions, 153 aircraft lost in action, 330 enemy planes destroyed. Awarded the Distinguished Unit Citation for Kiel Germany 14 May 1943, Ploesti Rumania 1 Aug 1943. Ready then – ready now – ready tomorrow. 44th Bomb Group (H), Bomb Wing (VH), Strategic Missile Wing (SAC). Dedicated by the 44th Heritage Memorial Group 24 Sep 1988.'

4. The clubhouse includes displays relating to the 44th BG.

SNETTERTON HEATH
Station 138

County: Norfolk

UTM/grid: OS Map 144 – TM005895
Lat./Long.: N52°28.01 E000°57.03
Nearest town: Thetford 8 miles to south-west

HISTORY

The site of this airfield, a patch of Norfolk heathland, was chosen in 1941 and construction took place the following year, the prime contractor being Taylor-Woodrow Ltd, of an airfield originally intended for RAF bomber use. It was laid out with the, by then, standard three intersecting-runways and given thirty-six frying-pan hardstands; however, dispersal provision was increased to fifty when it was decided to allocate the airfield to the USAAF. In some respects it was a strange choice of site, as the area was constrained by a railway and a major road

and also involved the closing of a number of minor roads. One effect of this was to constrain support facilities, and most of the dispersals, to the south and east of the site. Despite these restrictions, work was also undertaken on an extension at Eccles, just across the main road, for an Air Depot, and a number of additional T.2 hangars were erected before this plan was cancelled.

The need for airfields was such that, not unusually for this period, aircraft arrived before the site was complete, although this was intended as a temporary

AIRFIELD DATA DEC 1944

Command:	US 8th AF 3rd BD	Runway surface:	Concrete, wood-chipped
Function:	Operational Station	Hangars:	2 × T.2
Runways:	230 deg 2,000 × 50yd	Dispersals:	50 × Loop
	180 deg 1,400 × 50yd	Personnel:	Officers – 443
	270 deg 1,400 × 50yd		Other Ranks – 2,529

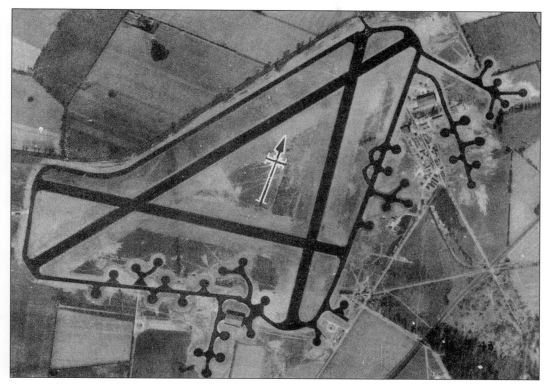

measure, as the B-26 Marauders of the 386th BG were simply here for a period of work-up training, having arrived in the UK during the first week of June 1943.

The Marauders stayed one week and then flew out to Boxted, from where they flew their first ops at the end of July. However, Snetterton was not empty for long as, on 12 June, the B-17s of the 96th Bomb Group moved in from Andrews Field, Essex. This Fortress-equipped Group had arrived in the UK in April, under the command of Colonel Archie J Old Jr, and the air echelon had initially moved into Grafton Underwood, from where they had flown their first mission. The Group became part of 3rd Air Division, whose HQ was not far away at Elveden Hall, and for much of the remainder of the war the airfield was also home to the HQ of the 45th Combat

Bomb Wing, to which the Group belonged. The 96th remained operational from Snetterton to the end of the war, clocking up a total of 321 missions for the loss of 189 aircraft missing in action. During its operational career the Group received two Distinguished Unit Citations; for Regensburg on 17 August 1943 and for Poznan on 9 April 1944; it was also the first double-strength Bomb Group in the 8th Air Force and amongst the many raids it led was the first shuttle-mission. The latter took place on 17 August 1943 and earned the first DUC, with the bombers flying-on to North Africa after attacking the target. Sadly, the 96th also had the highest total of 'missing in action' aircraft in the 3rd Division. However, its gunners fought back hard and claimed 354½-100-222. Little development took place at the airfield during its

Unusual shot recording an aspect all too often ignored – airfield defence; B Battery of the 455th Anti-Aircraft Battalion.

two-year period of operations, although a number of buildings were doubtless modified – or at least decorated with murals or other types of personalization – but this type of alteration is seldom recorded.

With the end of the war in Europe, the Group was scheduled to join the Allied occupation force in Germany and it began flying transport and support missions over Europe; like all these immediate post-war sorties – known as 'Cook's Tours' by the RAF – crews were amazed at the level of destruction caused to German cities. The plan changed and the 96th was slated instead to return to the United States. Aircraft departed in November, followed by the ground personnel in December, and this once hectic base fell out of use, being handed back to the RAF, who placed it into Care and Maintenance. It was allocated to No.262 Maintenance Unit and a number of the hangars were used for a short period; however, there was no long term future for Snetterton and the site was sold-off in 1952. The airfield surfaces were still in good condition and the site was acquired with a view to establishing a racing circuit – the first meeting taking place the following year. Since then the Snetterton Circuit has become world famous and it would be interesting to discover how many of its race-goers are familiar with the site's previous history. Racing circuits appear to be one of the commonest uses of old airfields, although poultry farms are still in the lead in terms of usage!

Whilst few buildings survive on the airfield, there are a number of survivors just across the present A11 road. A visitor is rewarded by the sight of one of the most impressive of all airfield memorials, clearly visible on a patch of ground adjacent to the pay booths of the racing circuit.

DECOY SITE

Q　　　　　　Breckles　　　　　　TL952950

UNITS

HQ units at Snetterton Heath

45th BW	13 Sep 1943–18 Jun 1945
20th BW	13 Jun 1945–6 Aug 1945

1939–1945
USAAF Units
386th BG

Squadrons:	552nd BS, 553rd BS, 554th BS, 555th BS
Aircraft:	B-26
Dates:	3 Jun 1943–10 Jun 1943

96th BG (45th CBW)

Identifying letter:	C
Squadrons:	337th BS (Paintbrush), 338th BS (Grating), 339th BS (Bookie), 413th BS (Cabbage)
Aircraft:	B-17F, B-17G
Dates:	12 Jun 1943–12 Dec 1945
Missions:	321 (including missions flown from other bases)
First mission:	14 May 1943 (from Grafton Underwood)
Last mission:	21 Apr 1945

MEMORIALS

1. Impressive metal monument with plinth, dedicated 8 Sep 2001, inscribed: 'Dedicated to all personnel of the 96th Bombardment Group (H), 8th USAAF, who served on this airfield 1943–1945.'

2. Memorial to the 96th BG in Quidenham Church; this comprises a stained-glass window and a plaque with the inscription: 'Memorial Chapel. In memory of comrades who gave their lives in the cause of freedom 1943–1945. 96th Bombardment Group (H). United States Army Air Forces.'

Snetterton has one of the East Anglia's most dramatic memorials.

STIFFKEY

County: Norfolk

UTM/grid: OS Map – TF965440
Lat./Long.: N52°57.4 E000°55.4
Nearest town: Wells-next-the-Sea 3 miles to west

HISTORY

The anti-aircraft training range at Stiffkey, near Wanborough Hill, was very busy throughout the war and a number of Norfolk's airfields supported activities here. However, as with Weybourne, the decision was taken to erect on-site a catapult launch system for pilotless aircraft, although an unusual circular 'launch runway' was also built at Stiffkey. The site went out of use in the immediate post-war period and its work was taken on by Weybourne.

STRADISHALL

County: Suffolk

UTM/grid: OS Map 154 – TL720515
Lat./Long.: N52°07.54 E000°30.42
Nearest town: Haverhill 7 miles to south-west

Aircrew and ground-crew of 214 Squadron Wellington T2709 at Stradishall in 1940.

HISTORY

When RAF flying ceased at Stradishall in 1970, it brought to an end over thirty years of active life for one of Suffolk's most interesting stations. The dominant feature at Stradishall today is the prison (HMP Highpoint) and the once impressive stretches of runways and dispersals have all but vanished, although a significant number of airfield buildings survive.

The site was acquired in the mid-1930s as part of the RAF's expansion plan for bomber airfields in East Anglia and work commenced in 1937, the airfield being opened by Group Captain J Herring on 3 February 1938. With the standard arc of four C-type hangars and an assortment of brick-built buildings, Strad was a typical bomber-airfield of the late-1930s, the flying surface being a large grass-area that would allow aircraft to take-off in virtually any direction. The first two flying units, 9 Squadron and 148 Squadron, the latter created from a Flight of the former, arrived from Scampton on 10 March 1938 and their Heyfords and Wellesleys commenced intensive training as the situation in Europe deteriorated – with the RAF going onto a war footing in September (the Munich Crisis) and Bomber Command's squadrons being made ready for action. The crisis passed and, at Stradishall, re-development work commenced, including the laying of runways.

As war looked increasingly inevitable, the RAF underwent a number of organizational changes and movement of units; the two bomber squadrons at Stradishall left in July and September 1939, although this may in part have been to do with runway work, and the airfield was placed into Care and Maintenance. The airfield did not re-open as a No.3 Group bomber station until the following February but, in the meantime, it hosted a deployment by two Blenheim fighter squadrons, both of which – 254 Squadron and 236 Squadron – formed at the airfield at the very end of October. They remained in place until early December

for work-up training and then departed.

Bombers returned as the Wellingtons of 214 Squadron moved in from Methwold; this unit was to be Strad's main operational unit for the next two years, during which time its Wellington Is took part in a great many Bomber Command operations. As can be seen from the 'units list', numerous squadrons made brief appearances at the airfield, some on operational deployment, whilst others were here for re-equipment or re-organization. The crews of 214 Squadron continued to carry the operational burden, but the airfield was also home to a number of specialist flights and units; of these perhaps the most interesting was No.1419 Flight. This unit was involved in clandestine operations and arrived at Stradishall in early October 1940, acquiring a small number of Whitleys to add to its Lysanders. Designation was changed in March 1941 to No.1419 (Special Duties) Flight and, in August, it was raised to squadron status as 138 Squadron although, by then, it was primarily operating from Newmarket, not returning to Stradishall until December for a final few months.

The next major development was the arrival in

Stradishall in 1954.

AIRFIELD DATA DEC 1944

Command:	RAF Bomber Command	Runway surface:	Concrete
Function:	Operational	Hangars:	5 × C, 3 × T.2
Runways:	250 deg 2,000 × 50yd	Dispersals:	36 × Heavy Bomber
	320 deg 1,400 × 50yd	Personnel:	Officers – 194
	040 deg 1,400 × 50yd		Other Ranks – 2,026 (524 WAAF)

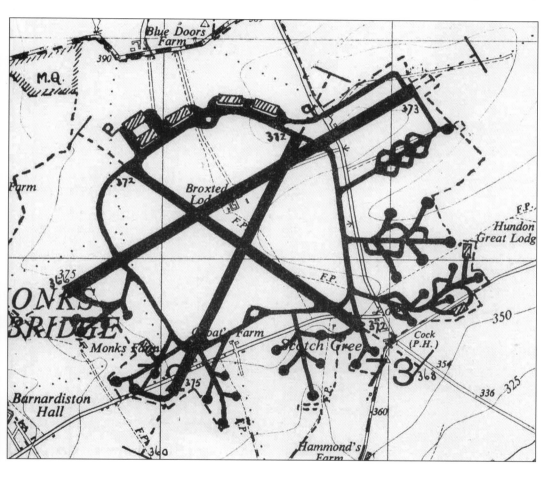

April 1942 of Stirlings to replace the ageing Wellingtons of 214 Squadron. This was part of a general re-equipment of No.3 Group with the type but, in the meantime, the airfield continued to host a variety of other units and the Wellington remained a common site over this part of Suffolk. One of the units using Wimpeys was 109 Squadron; this unit arrived in April 1942 and was involved in evaluation of new tactics and equipment, including 'window', and in July they received a number of Mosquitoes,

although the following month they moved out, followed in October by the long-serving 214 Squadron.

This freed Stradishall for a new role with the Shorts bomber, a role that it retained for the next two years – training. A number of Stirling conversion flights had been attached to squadrons, for example, 218 Squadron Conversion Flight to convert that squadron to the Stirling, but the decision had been taken in mid-1942 to combine such flights into formal conversion units. As part of this plan, No.1657

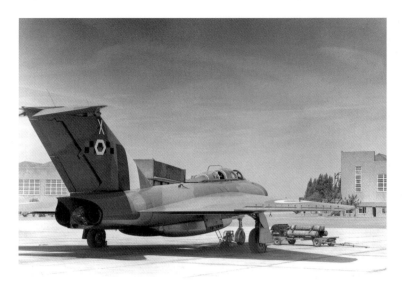

Javelin of 85 Squadron; the airfield was home to most of the RAF's post-war fighter types.

Heavy Conversion Unit formed at Stradishall in the first week of October 1942 by merging the conversion flights of 7, 101, 149 and 218 squadrons, along with No.1427 Flight, with an establishment of thirty-two Stirlings although, as with all HCUs, other types were also held on strength. It is worth noting that, although merged with the HCU, 1427 Flight retained its own identity until it disbanded the following year.

As part of the reorganization of Bomber Command that took effect in spring 1943, Stradishall became the base station for No.31 Base, its two sub-stations being Chedburgh and Wratting Common, all remaining part of No.3 Group, Bomber Command. This arrangement took effect on 26 April 1943 and was unusual in that the two sub-stations housed operational units. However, this situation changed in December, when the latter were replaced by HCUs to bring No.31 Base into line with the other such training formations.

The training task continued to December 1944 and, whilst the Stirling was no longer operational within Main Force Bomber Command, it played a vital role in the training of bomber crews, as well as performing operational roles with RCM and airborne forces.

Stradishall had a final period as an operational station with 186 Squadron, flying Lancasters. Having formed in 1943 as a fighter-bomber unit, 186 Squadron had disbanded in April 1944 only to re-form, this time as a Lancaster heavy-bomber unit, at Tuddenham in October. It arrived at Stradishall on 17 December and flew a number of ops to April 1945, following which it, like many Bomber Command squadrons, undertook troop and transport work in the immediate post-war period. The squadron disbanded at Strad on 17 July 1945; the

station moved from Bomber Command to Transport Command as part of No.47 Group and, in August, two Stirling units arrived for transport duties. Both these squadrons had gone by the following summer, although 51 Squadron had re-equipped with Yorks in the meantime. The airfield reverted to Bomber Command and, by late-autumn 1946, the airfield was home to four Lancaster bomber squadrons, all of which remained until early 1949 and, whilst aircraft establishments were lower than for the wartime period, this still made Stradishall a very busy airfield.

Then, on 18 February 1949, the airfield went into its second period of Care and Maintenance – and again it was short-lived. RAF Stradishall re-opened on 6 July as home to No.203 Advanced Flying School. This unit had formed at Keevil from No.61 OTU in July 1947 and operated a mix of aircraft types for fighter-pilot training, the main equipment being various marks of Spitfire. Within weeks of arriving, the designation was changed to No.226 Operational Conversion Unit. At Strad it acquired jets, in the shape of Meteors and Vampires, and jet training became its main pre-occupation; for the next five years (it left in mid-1955) this unit was kept busy and, in addition to its core types, operated a number of other aircraft, such as the Beaufighter, Mosquito and Martinet, for support roles such as target-towing.

As part of the Cold War re-assessment of assets it was decided to make Stradishall an operational fighter-base and, with the closure of the OCU, the Station was allocated to No.12 Group. The first of the operational units had actually formed whilst the OCU was still in residence, 125 Squadron reforming on 31 March with Meteor NF.11s for the night-fighter role. Stradishall specialized in night fighters for the next few years and a number of units formed and left or passed through, operating Meteors, Venoms or Javelins. There was a similar burst of activity in the late-1950s/early 1960s, this time focused on the Hunter, but the last unit, 1 Squadron, had gone by November 1961. This had been a frenetic few years that saw a large number of squadrons come and go and all of the classic 1950s fighter-types in residence at one time or another.

For its final period of RAF usage the airfield reverted to the more sedate training role and was transferred on 1 December 1961 to Training Command for use by No.1 Air Navigation School. This unit moved its collection of Marathons, Meteors and Varsities, and various support aircraft, from Topcliffe and continued the training of RAF navigators. A number of building works took place to provide appropriate teaching facilities but, as usual, there is no real detail in the records. New aircraft types joined the ANS in the mid-1960s, the main one being the Dominie. The routine of training sorties continued to late-August 1970, when the school was disbanded and its resources absorbed by No.6 Flying Training School at Finningley.

After a long and interesting history Stradishall soon passed into little more than a memory.

DECOY SITES

Q	Ashfield Green	TL772561
Q	Lidgate	TL712584
Q	Poslingford	TL787496

UNITS

1920–1938

148 Sqn	10 Mar 1938–6 Sep 1939, 30 Apr 1940–23 Jun 1940	Wellesley, Heyford, Wellington

1939–1945

9 Sqn	10 Mar 1938–15 Jul 1939	Heyford
51 Sqn	21 Aug 1945–20 Aug 1946	Stirling, York
75 Sqn	13 Jul 1939–4 Sep 1939	Anson, Wellington
101 Sqn	11 Aug 1942–29 Sep 1942	Wellington
109 Sqn	6 Apr 1942–6 Aug 1942	Wellington, Mosquito
138 Sqn	16 Dec 1941–11 Mar 1942	Whitley, Lysander, Halifax
150 Sqn	19 Jun 1940–3 Jul 1940	Battle
158 Sqn	17 Aug 1945–31 Dec 1945	Stirling
186 Sqn	17 Dec 1944–17 Jul 1945	Lancaster

214 Sqn	12 Feb 1940–1 Oct 1942	Wellington, Stirling
215 Sqn	5 Jan 1942–12 Feb 1942	no aircraft
236 Sqn	31 Oct 1939–9 Dec 1939	Blenheim
254 Sqn	30 Oct 1939–9 Dec 1939	Blenheim
NZ Flt	15 Jan 1940–12 Feb 1940	
1419 Flt	9 Oct 1940–25 Aug 1941	Lysander, Whitley
3 Gp TF	1 Feb 1941–21 May 1941	
1521 Flt	Oct 1941–15 Mar 1943	Oxford
214 CF	1 May 1942–9 Aug 1942	Stirling
1474 Flt	4–10 Jul 1942	Wellington
7 CF	4 Oct 1942–7 Oct 1942	Stirling
218 CF	2 Oct 1942–7 Oct 1942	Stirling
1657 HCU	2 Oct 1942– 14 May 1944, 5 Oct 1944–15 Dec 1944	Stirling
1427 Flt	2 Oct 1942–1 Apr 1943	Stirling, Halifax
1556 Flt	15 Sep 1945–Dec 1945	Oxford

Post-1945

1 Sqn	1 Jul 1958–7 Nov 1961	Hunter
35 Sqn	18 Sep 1946–10 Feb 1949	Lancaster
54 Sqn	13 Jul 1959–20 Nov 1961	Hunter
85 Sqn	30 Nov 1958–5 Jun 1959	Javelin
89 Sqn	15 Dec 1955–30 Nov 1958	Venom, Javelin
115 Sqn	9 Sep 1946–15 Feb 1949	Lancaster
125 Sqn	31 Mar 1955–10 May 1957	Meteor, Venom
149 Sqn	4 Nov 1946–28 Feb 1949	Lancaster
152 Sqn	11 Jun 1950–16 Jan 1957, 30 Aug 1957–31 Jul 1958	Meteor
207 Sqn	7 Nov 1946–1 Feb 1949	Lancaster
208 Sqn	29 Mar 1960–3 Jun 1960	Venom
245 Sqn	21 Jun 1955–30 Jun 1957	Meteor, Hunter
263 Sqn	30 Aug 1957–1 Jul 1958	Hunter
203AFS	19 Jul 1949–1 Sep 1949	Spitfire, Meteor
226 OCU	1 Sep 1949–3 Jun 1955	Vampire, Meteor
1 ANS	1 Dec 1961–26 Aug 1970	Valetta, Meteor, Varsity

MEMORIALS

1. Large brick memorial (unveiled 29 May 1994) by car park in front of old Officers' Mess showing a plan of the airfield and giving a list of all flying units, by Command, plus selected 'attached units.'

2. Village sign includes a Heyford.

SUDBURY
Station 174

UTM/grid: OS Map 155 – TL895435
Lat./Long.: N52°03.26 E000°45.45
Nearest town: Sudbury 2 miles to south-west

County: Suffolk

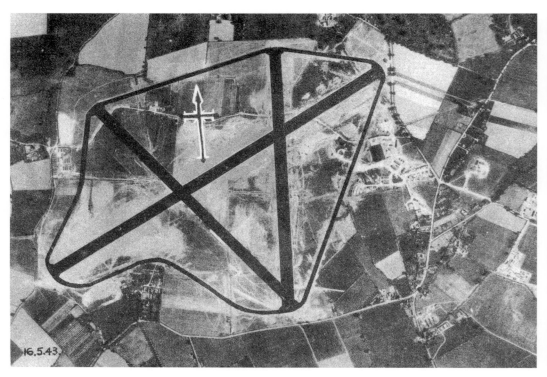

16.5.43

HISTORY

Sudbury was one of the late-build airfields and its site was a compromise between geographic location – the need to keep the airfields of a Group within a certain proximity – and the suitability of the area selected for development. The airfield was constructed to standard USAAF requirements in 1943 and it was only just possible to provide the three runways to standard lengths between the road system and groups of buildings; fortunately, USAAF bases required little in the way of on-airfield support facilities. The bulk of the admin, technical and domestic facilities were in sites to the east and south.

The four squadrons of the 486th Bomb Group departed the United States in March 1944 and Sudbury was to be their only operational base in the UK. The Group took up residence from early April and its B-24s flew their first mission on 7 May 1944. Under the command of Colonel William B Kieffer, the Group went on to fly 188 missions for the loss of thirty-three aircraft missing in action, flying the final op on 21 April 1945. At a time when loss rates were still high amongst 8th Air Force bombers, the Group's 834th Bomb Squadron flew its first seventy-eight missions for no loss of aircraft or personnel – an enviable record.

The Liberators were replaced by B-17s from summer 1944, to bring the Group in line with the rest of the Division, but, other than a minor change in Command structure – the 92nd Bombardment Wing HQ closing down at Sudbury – there was no change in the general pattern of operations. The 486th played its part in the daylight offensive to the end of the war and Sudbury's runways witnessed heavily laden bombers depart for Germany and damaged bombers return; although it sounds trite, this was an 'average' base with a daily routine that was witnessed at airfields throughout East Anglia. There were highs and lows, crews completing tours, colleagues and friends failing to return, dances and socializing, and no doubt the end of the war brought the same sense of relief at Sudbury as elsewhere.

This B-17 of the 486th BG crashed near the airfield on 31 December 1944; the Group was Sudbury's sole operational user.

The White Horse pub was one of the favoured watering holes for the 486th.

As at most 8th Air Force airfields, the run-down was rapid and the bulk of the Group's aircraft had flown out by early July; to be followed by the remainder of the Americans as Sudbury returned to its pre-war 'status' as a quiet Suffolk town. The airfield saw little use after the war, although the hangars were used for government storage until the site was sold in the early 1960s. There is not much left of the airfield, as the runways have been reclaimed, but parts of the perimeter track and some hardstands can still be seen and the practised eye can discern much of what once transpired at the once busy Station 174.

UNITS

HQ units at Sudbury
92nd BW   2 Mar 1944–18 Nov 1944

1939–1945
USAAF Units
486th BG (92nd CBW/4th CBW)
Identifying letter:	W
Squadrons:	832nd BS (Trappist), 833rd BS (Pebbly), 834th BS (Deepseat), 835th BS (Nightdress)
Aircraft:	B-24H, B-24J, B-17G
Dates:	Mar 1944–Aug 1945
Missions:	188
First mission:	7 May 1944
Last mission:	21 Apr 1945

AIRFIELD DATA DEC 1944

Command:	US 8th AF 3rd BD	Runway surface:	Tarmac and concrete
Function:	Operational Station	Hangars:	2 × T.2
Runways:	250 deg 2,000 × 50yd	Dispersals:	50 × Spectacle
	190 deg 1,400 × 50yd	Personnel:	Officers – 443
	150 deg 1,400 × 50yd		Other Ranks – 2,529

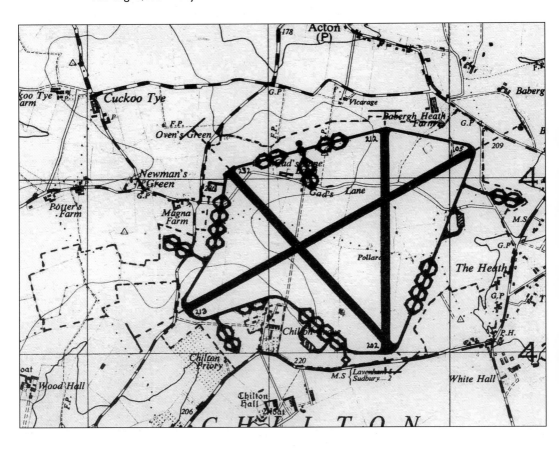

MEMORIALS

1. Town hall plaque, inscribed: 'To the citizens of Sudbury for their fellowship, understanding and hospitality, from the officers and men of the 486th Bombardment Group (H), 418 Air Services Group USAAF 1944–5.'

2. Memorial at St Gregory's church, inscribed: '485th Bombardment Group (H). The 486th flew 191 combat missions over Nazi held Europe from May 1944 to July 1945. This memorial was dedicated by survivors of the 486th and the town of Sudbury in honour of the 400 airmen who died in the cause of freedom. Dedicated 4th July 1987.'

3. At airfield a stone plaque, inscribed: 'In recognition of the USAAF 486th Bombardment Group (Heavy) operating from this airfield between March 1944 and August 1945.'

SWANNINGTON

County: Norfolk

UTM/grid: OS Map 133 – TG141205
Lat./Long.: N52°44.3 E001°10.1
Nearest town: Norwich 8 miles to south-east

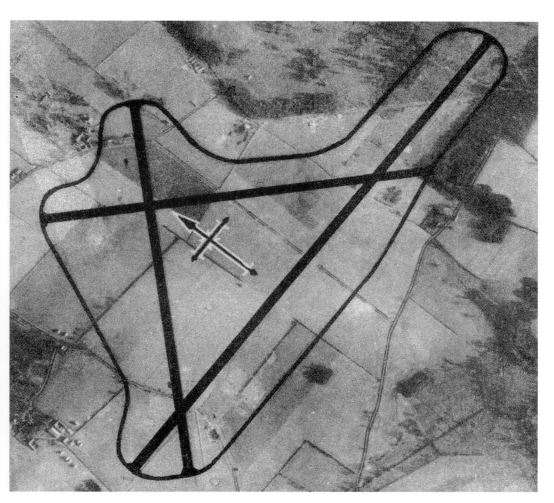

HISTORY

Work started here in late-1942, the main contractor being Kent & Sussex Construction Co. and a standard Class A airfield was laid, which involved having to close a number of minor roads. Three runways and thirty-six hardstands were laid and three hangars erected, along with a limited range of other buildings. Accommodation was primarily huts, but the nearby Haverinland Hall was taken over as the Officers' Mess. However, it was not until April 1944 that Swannington was opened as a base for No.100

Group, at which point it became home to Mosquito intruder units. The reason for this long gestation period is not clear, as there appears to have been little problem with the actual construction work on this standard-pattern airfield.

Both squadrons were experienced in the night-fighter game and, as part of the bomber-support operations of their new Group, their main task was offensive operations over enemy territory, harassing the German night-fighter force. The two squadrons

Airfield Data Dec 1944

Command:	RAF Bomber Command	Runway surface:	Concete
Function:	Operational	Hangars:	2 × T.2, one × B.1
Runways:	277 deg 2,000 × 50yd	Dispersals:	36 Spectacle
	320 deg 1,400 × 50yd	Personnel:	Officers – 154 (10 WAAF)
	230 deg 1,400 × 50yd		Other Ranks – 1,226 (260 WAAF)

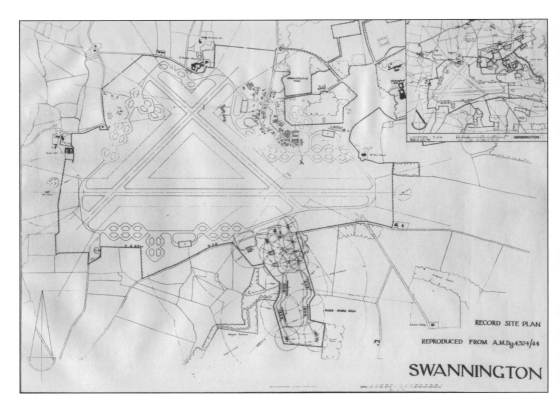

RECORD SITE PLAN

REPRODUCED FROM A.M.D₃4324/44

SWANNINGTON

arrived in May, 85 Squadron from West Malling and 157 Squadron from Valley, and were in action the following month, the first 'kill' being claimed on the night of 12–13 June. In common with the other intruder Mosquitoes of the Group, the squadrons flew nightly patrols over German airfields, as well as operating in and around the bomber stream; by the time the last sorties were flown on 2–3 May 1945, the Mosquitoes had claimed seveny-one enemy aircraft, forty-three of these falling to 85 Squadron. For a few weeks in late-July–August 1944, the majority of the aircraft had been detached to West Malling to provide night defence against V-1s.

With the end of the war there was little further need for Swannington and both squadrons left by September; however, the airfield then passed to No.274 Maintenance Unit for aircraft storage (mainly Mosquitoes), a role it retained to June 1947. There was some debate on keeping the airfield and developing it as a fighter station but, despite its suitable location, there were simply too many airfields with better facilities. Swannington then became part of the late-1950s general disposal of former wartime airfields, the site being sold in 1957, following which it has essentially returned to agriculture. However, a number of buildings survive on the site, including the control tower (in a poor state) and those around the factory that now houses the squadron scoreboards. Some of the buildings are in excellent condition – not bad for structures erected sixty years ago for temporary use!

MOSQUITO N.F. MK 30
MERLIN
MAY 1945

Night-fighter Mossies were the main residents with the squadrons of No.100 Group. (Note: Mosquito RK953 is not pictured at Swannington).

UNITS

1939–1945

85 Sqn	1 May 1944–27 Jun 1945	Mosquito
157 Sqn	7 May 1944–16 Aug 1945	Mosquito
229 Sqn	20 Nov 1944–2 Dec 1944	Spitfire
451 Sqn	24 Feb 1945–22 Mar 1945	Spitfire

MEMORIALS

The scoreboards of 85 and 157 Squadrons are on display in the reception of the factory on site; the author did not confirm this.

SWANTON MORLEY

County: Norfolk

UTM/grid: OS map 133 – TG010185
Lat./Long.: N52°43.33 E005°7.53
Nearest town: Dereham 4 miles to South

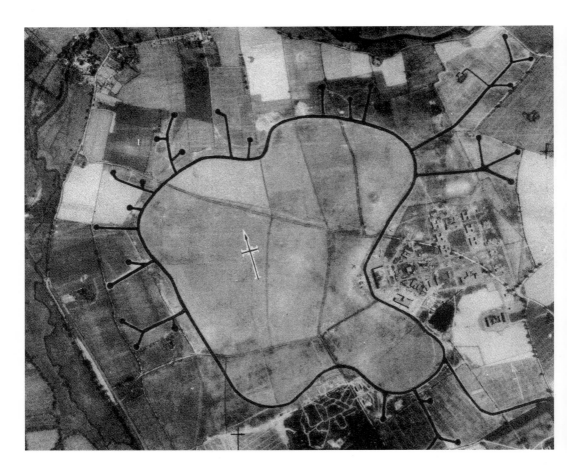

HISTORY

One of Norfolk's most famous airfields, and one that housed a wide variety of operational and non-operational flying units, Swanton Morley was built as a bomber station in the months leading up to the war, the prime contractor being Richard Costain & Co. Located on a ridge of well-drained soil the airfield was laid out to give a large grass operating surface and although this was not completely level it did provide an excellent surface with long runs in a number of directions. The original hangar provision was one large K-type, along with a group of technical, admin and support buildings. The airfield opened in September 1940 for No.2 Group's light bombers and

it was not long before the Blenheims of 105 Squadron arrived. For some months this was the only unit based here but with the crews taking a full and active part in attacks on shipping and coastal targets, as well night bombing as part of Bomber Command's strategic campaign, Swanton was very much in the war, especially as losses amongst the Blenheim units were high. July 1941 brought the first of a number of famous raids mounted by aircraft from Swanton Morley – and also saw the raid's leader, Wg Cdr Hughie Edwards, receive a VC for his outstanding leadership of that difficult mission.

The pace of activity increased in summer 1941

what either side thought of the other. As with most major airfields, Swanton was also parent to non-operational flying units, the Oxfords of No.1515 BATF being in residence from September 1941 to November 1943, after which a number of other specialist units used the airfield. Bostons of 88 Squadron re-appeared in March 1943 and for nearly six months they took part in the increasingly intensive daylight campaign over North-West Europe, finally moving out in August for Hartford Bridge to become part of a new Wing establishment.

A new aircraft shape appeared in mid 1943 when 226 Squadron received its first Mitchells as yet another upgrading of No.2 Group's offensive potential. The Poles of 305 Squadron appeared for a short time in summer to equip with the Mitchell and the same type made up part of the establishment of No.1482 Bombing and Gunnery Flight when they arrived in December (this unit subsequently became the No.2 Group Support Unit tasked with maintaining currency for aircrew as a holding pool of replacements for operational squadrons). That same month also saw Swanton Morley hosting its rarest operational incumbent when 3 Squadron brought in their Typhoons from Manston. This detachment lasted to mid February and its main aim was for the Tiffies to take part in the increased anti-shipping campaign as part of the long lead-in to the invasion. A variety of other units came and went in 1944, including another brief appearance by Mosquitoes.

With the re-organisation of Allied air power for the invasion, No.2 Group had become a Tactical Air Force and concentrated further South, leaving Swanton Morley available for No.100 Group, whose specialist units were concentrating in Norfolk. The Group's Bomber Support Development Unit moved in during December 1944 and remained to July 1945 operating a variety of aircraft types on the development and evaluation of equipment and tactics. Whilst no operational units were stationed at Swanton in these latter months of the war the role of the BSDU cannot be over-stressed – its work was vital to the missions flown by the Group. A number of other units, such as the Group Comms Flight, also used the airfield as did the Mosquito Servicing Squadron. A final flurry of testing captured German equipment at the end of the war and then Swanton bade farewell to its operational role.

The airfield was not however abandoned and following transfer to Training Command it received No.10 Air Navigation School, thus opening the final decade of activity for Swanton during which it played host to a number of training units, most staying only a few years. The Navigation School was followed in January 1947 by No.4 School of Signalling, which changed its name in 1951 to No.4 Radio School.

A Fortress of the Radar Warfare Establishment at Swanton in 1945; this unit was formed in July by re-designating the BSDU.

with the arrival of new units; for example, the Spitfire IIs of 152 Squadron arrived at the end August to provide fighter escort for the Group's attacks and stayed to the end of the year. A second Blenheim unit, 88 Squadron, turned up in August and took part in a number of missions whilst also converting to the Boston, and disappearing again in August; both the Boston and 88 Squadron would later have a second association with this airfield. When 105 Squadron bade farewell to Swanton in December, having commenced re-equipment with Mosquitoes, its place was taken by the Boston-equipped 226 Squadron from Wattisham; these American bombers had only been received a few weeks before but the Squadron was soon engaged on operational flying, with 'Circus' missions becoming the routine fayre, interspersed with the occasional special task. Throughout 1942 the Squadron maintained a hectic pace of operations and that summer they were joined by a detachment of the 15th Bombardment Squadron of the USAAF; this Boston unit was attached to 226 Squadron to 'learn the ropes' and on 29th June a Boston crewed by Americans flew out of Swanton Morley to undertake that country's first bombing raid over Europe. The 15th BS soon moved on (to Molesworth) leaving the RAF crews alone once more; there is little record of

AIRFIELD DATA DEC 1944

Command:	RAF Bomber Command	Runway surface:	Grass
Function:	Operational	Hangars:	4 × T.2, 4 × Blister, one × J
Runways:	NE–SW 1,650yd	Dispersals:	31 × Frying Pan
	NNW–SSE 1,600yd	Personnel:	Officers – 161
	NW–SE 1,350yd		Other Ranks – 1,811 (386 WAAF)

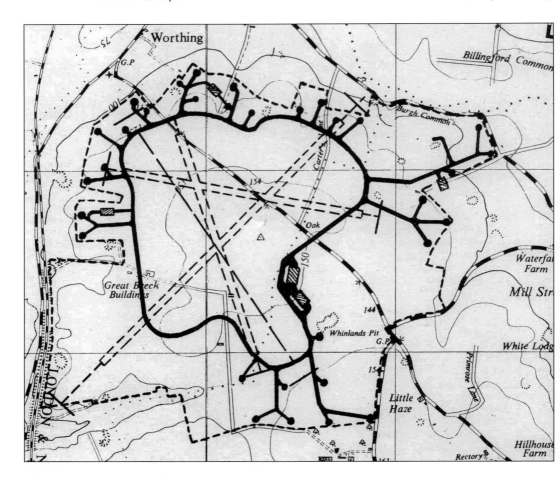

Training types such as the Anson were used by students to practise the techniques learnt in the classroom and with a continuing need for Air Signallers the unit underwent another name change within months, becoming No.1 Air Signallers School. In June 1955 a further change of name was introduced to reflect the changing nature of the role the students would perform on their squadrons and it was as No.1 Air Electronics School that this unit finally left Swanton in December 1957 for Hullavington.

The 1954 survey stated that 'the airfield does not lend itself to extension other than to the South-West on account of its convexity. It is said to be well drained.' Three main strips were listed, the longest being 5,100ft oriented 159–339 degrees. The airfield had a 50ft wide concrete taxiway and parking areas included 25 round hardstands (100ft diameter) and three aprons totalling 13,080sq ft.

Of the other units to have used the airfield post war the most interesting was the Central Signals

A Blenheim of 105 Sqn approaching the grass runway; the Squadron in 1945; this unit was formed in July by re-designating the BSDU

Development Establishment, which spent January to June 1958 in residence with Varsities evaluating electronic equipment. With the departure of this unit the only based flying to take place from Swanton was by Air Training Corps gliders and, from time to time, Air Experience Flight Chipmunks. The main unit at Swanton Morley for the remainder of its RAF ownership was the Central Servicing Development Establishment and whilst they held a variety of aircraft types on charge they were for use as ground instructional airframes. The unit performed the essential task of developing servicing schedules for a range of aircraft from Javelin to Harrier and it spent almost 40 years at Swanton, eventually leaving in mid 1995. The RAF closed the Station in December but Swanton is such a delightful location that the Army decided to take it on, as Robertson Barracks, and the hangars that once saw such a diverse collection of aircraft are now home to a diverse collection of combat vehicles.

If you mention Swanton Morley airfield in some circles you will hear about Stearman restoration and operation; until recently a lovely grass airfield, with two runways, was in operation on just to the East of the old RAF airfield – it was in fact part of the original field at one stage.

DECOY SITES

Q/K	North Tuddenham	TG034134

Pundit – SM

UNITS

3 Sqn	28 Dec 1943–14 Feb 1944	Typhoon
88 Sqn	8 Jul 1941–1 Aug 1941; 30 Mar 1943–19 Aug 1943	Blenheim; Boston
98 Sqn	Mar 1944–10 Apr 1944	Mitchell
105 Sqn	31 Oct 1940–8 Dec 1941	Blenheim
152 Sqn	31 Aug 1941–1 Dec 1941	Spitfire
180 Sqn	12-26 Apr 1944	Mitchell
226 Sqn	9 Dec 1941–13 Feb 1944	Boston, Mitchell
305 Sqn	5 Sep 1943–18 Nov 1943	Wellington, Mitchell
464 Sqn	25 Mar 1944–8 Apr 1944	Mosquito
487 Sqn	25-30 Apr 1944	Mosquito
613 Sqn	11-24 Apr 1944	Mosquito
1515 Flt	22 Sep 1941–1 Nov 1943	Oxford
1482 Flt	1 Dec 1943–1 Apr 1944	Mitchell, Martinet
1508 Flt	29 Aug 1943–24 Jun 1944	Oxford
2 Gp SU	1 Apr 1944–1 Aug 1945	Boston, Anson, Martinet
BSDU	Dec 1944–Jul 1945	various
100 Gp CF	Dec 1944–Jun 1945	
10 ANS	1 Dec 1945–30 Sep 1946	
4 SoS/RS	Jan 1947–May 1951	
1 ASS	1 May 1951–1 Apr 1957	Anson, Prentice
102 GS	Jun 1953–1 Sep 1955	Cadet
611 VGS	1 Sep 1955–1 Jun 1995	
1 AES	1 Apr 1957–23 Dec 1957	Anson
CSDU/E	1 Jan 1958–1995	no aircraft
1 GC	8 Dec 1961–9 Aug 1971	various
5 AEF	Sep 1966–Sep 1967	Chipmunk
15th BS	Jun 1942–Jul 1942	Boston

MEMORIALS

Stained glass window in parish church; grave plot in cemetery.

THORPE ABBOTS
Station 139

County: Suffolk

UTM/grid: OS Map 156 – TM185810
Lat./Long.: N52°23.0 E001°12.5
Nearest town: Diss 4 miles to west

HISTORY

Originally intended as a satellite airfield for Horham, Thorpe Abbots was built in 1942, the prime contractor being John Laing & Son, and was completed as a Class A heavy-bomber field, the original plan for thirty-six dispersal (RAF bomber standard) being raised to fifty (USAAF bomber standard). As was normal with this type of airfield, there were only two T.2 hangars and most buildings were in 'sites' dotted around the nearby countryside. The airfield opened in early 1943 and its one and only operational unit, the 100th Bomb Group, arrived from Podington in early June. The unit had been activated in June 1942 but it did not receive its B-17s until November; after initial training it left the United States in May 1943 and spent only a few days at Podington before moving to its war base. The Group flew its first mission on 25 June and, in the following two years, flew over 300 missions for the loss of 177 aircraft missing in action. Perhaps the best-known epithet for this Group is the 'Bloody Hundredth' and, whilst it is true that on a number of ops they suffered particularly high losses, the effect of which must have been devastating on a tight-knit community such as Thorpe, their overall loss rate for the war was not significantly higher than many other Groups. Nevertheless, the name stuck and it is as the 'Bloody Hundredth' that they have gone down in history, the name having becoming something of a badge of honour.

The unit was awarded two Distinguished Unit Citations, for Regensburg (17 August 1943) and Berlin (4–8 March 1944). Fortress gunners claimed 261-101-139 enemy aircraft and the Group dropped over 19,000 tons of bombs. All of this activity came to a halt with the end of the war and, although the 100th was slated to be one of the USAAF occupation units, this plan was changed (as it was for virtually all of the American units given this assignment) and the bombers left for the US from October; by December this 'Little America' had vanished and the airfield was transferred back to the RAF in 1946. With a surfeit of airfields of similar quality in East Anglia, the RAF put Thorpe Abbots into Care and Maintenance and it sat unused and pretty much unloved until sold-off in 1956. Whilst the bulk of the land area is now back under agriculture, significant parts of the airfield surfaces remain intact, as do a number of buildings. The control tower had become

Thorpe Abbots in the snow; an artistic framing of a 100th BG B-17 at dispersal.

'BossLady', B-17 of the 'Bloody Hundredth'; the Group flew 306 missions from this airfield between June 1943 and the end of the war.

derelict but has been restored and is now an aviation museum.

UNITS

1939–1945
USAAF Units
100th BG (13th CW)

Identifying letter:	D
Nickname:	The Bloody Hundredth
Squadrons:	349th BS (Kidmeat), 350th BS (Poohbah), 351st BS (Mafking),

AIRFIELD DATA DEC 1944

Command:	US 8th AF 3rd BD	Runway surface:	Concrete, wood-chippings
Function:	Operational	Hangars:	2 × T.2
Runways:	099 deg 2,100 × 50yd	Dispersals:	50 × Special concrete loop
	350 deg 1,400 × 50yd	Personnel:	Officers – 421
	043 deg 1,400 × 50yd		Other Ranks – 2,473

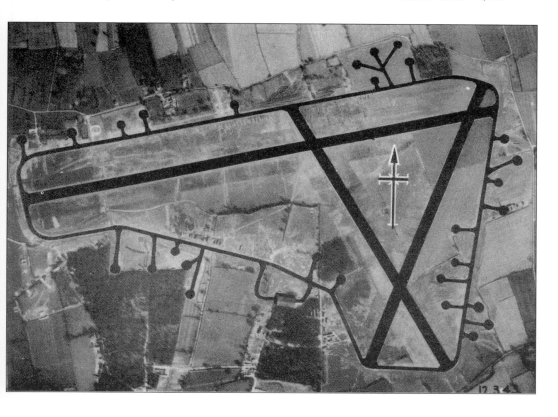

	418th BS (Rubber)
Aircraft:	B-17F, B-17G
Dates:	9 Jun 1943–20 Dec 1945
Missions:	306
First mission:	25 Jun 1943
Last mission:	20 Apr 1945

MEMORIALS

Control tower has been restored and is now 100th Bomb Group museum; other buildings have been added to the site and the volunteers are doing a tremendous job of preserving the memory of the airfield.

TIBENHAM
Station 124

County: Norfolk

UTM/grid: OS Map 156 – TM145885
Lat./Long.: N52°27.16 E001°09.14
Nearest town: Diss 5.5 miles to south

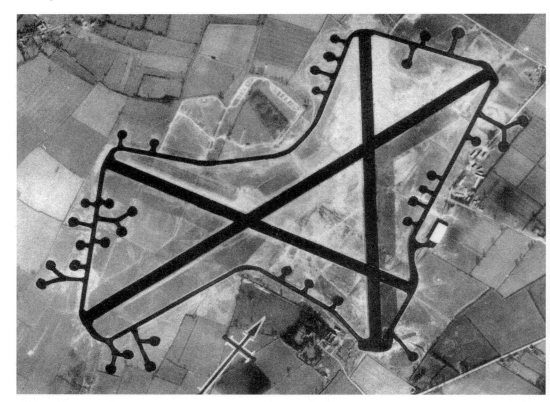

HISTORY

This patch of Norfolk was first used for military aviation in World War One but, as with many such landing grounds, details are sketchy. The records of the existence of the landing ground do not appear to have been lost and when the Air Ministry was on the hunt for airfield sites in the early 1940s the name Tibenham cropped up and a survey of the site's suitability was carried out. Other than the standard routine of having to close minor roads, destroy one or two buildings, rip out hedges and fill-in ditches, the site was highly suitable and work commenced in 1941, prime contractors being W & C French Ltd. By the time construction was underway the airfield had been designated for bomber use, which in 1942 meant USAAF use, and, as such, the new site was given three runways, frying-pan hardstands and two T.2 hangars, as well as an aviation-fuel store and

bomb dump. The pristine airfield welcomed its one and only operational unit, the 445th Bomb Group, in November 1943. It is worth noting that the 320th Bomb Group's ground echelon had passed through for a few days in November 1942 when the airfield was not complete, although its B-26 Marauders had flown direct to their North African theatre of operations. As a 2nd Bombardment Division airfield, Tibenham had also been used on an incidental basis, for training, prior to the arrival of its main unit.

The Liberator-equipped 445th BG had been activated in April and, under Colonel Robert H Terrill, flew its first mission on 13 December. This proved to be the first of 282 missions, during which the Group lost 108 aircraft missing in action. One of Station 124's most famous residents was Hollywood actor James Stewart, who was CO of the 703rd Bomb

AIRFIELD DATA DEC 1944

Command:	US 8th AF 2nd BD	Runway surface:	Tarmac and concrete
Function:	Operational	Hangars:	2 × T.2
Runways:	211 deg 2,000 × 50yd	Dispersals:	50 × Loop
	268 deg 1,400 × 50yd	Personnel:	Officers – 421
	332 deg 1,400 × 50yd		Other Ranks – 2,473

Waiting for the return of the bombers was always a difficult time – counting the aircraft as they appeared over the airfield. (445th BG)

Squadron from November 1943 to March 1944; he subsequently became Executive Officer with the 453rd BG at Old Buckenham.

The Group was awarded one Distinguished Unit Citation, for its actions on the Gotha mission of 24 February 1944; however, on the down side, it recorded a high loss of aircraft when only thirty of the thirty-seven Liberators it sent out to Kassel on 27 September 1944 made it back to Tibenham; in human terms over 230 aircrew didn't make it back. It could have been worse; with twenty-five Libs shot down in quick succession, the survivors were only saved by the intervention of the 361st Fighter Group. It is impossible to imagine the scene at the airfield that day, as officers and airmen scanned the sky looking for returning bombers. Despite this incident, the Group continued to make its contribution to the daylight offensive and, for the final few months of the war, recorded the best bombing accuracy in 2nd Bombardment Division.

With the European war over, the first B-24 departed for home on 17 May and, by the end of the month, most of the Group had gone. In July, Tibenham reverted to the RAF and it saw immediate post-war use as a Maintenance Unit satellite, as well

as a repatriation centre for soldiers returning from Greece and Italy. The airfield was 'kept on the books' and well maintained and the main runway was even lengthened in 1955 – to act as an emergency runway for the increasing number of jets operating around East Anglia. However, it was finally closed in March 1959 and sold-off in the mid-1960s. Flying still takes place from this old 8th Air Force site and has done for many years, although it is not the throb of four-engined bombers but rather the more sedate activities of the Norfolk Gliding Club. If you look in a current flight-guide you will note a second Tibenham airfield, also known as Priory Farm, but this is a private grass-strip one mile to the west.

UNITS

1939–1945
USAAF Units
445th BG (2nd CW)

Identifying letter:	F
Squadrons:	700th BS (Displease), 701st BS (Wallet), 702nd BS (Markum), 703rd BS (Baffle)

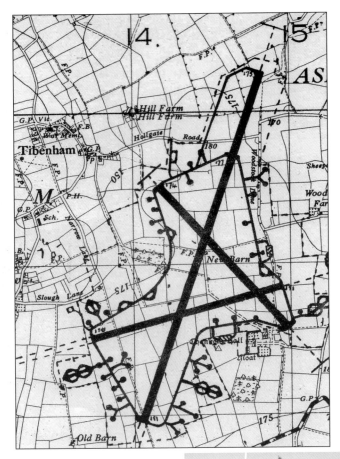

Aircraft: B-24H, B-24J, B-24L, B-24M
Dates: 4 Nov 1943–28 May 1945
Missions: 282
First mission: 13 Dec 1943
Last mission: 25 Apr 1945

MEMORIALS

1. Black marble slab on the airfield, inscribed: '445th Bombardment Group (H), 2nd Combat Wing, 2nd Air Division, 8th United States Air Force, 4th November 1943 to 28th May 1945. From this airfield the 445th Bombardment Group launched 280 missions and flew 6323 sorties. This memorial is humbly dedicated to those airmen who gave their lives and those who served fighting for the liberation of Europe during World War II. 700th BS. 701st BS. 702nd BS. 703rd BS. Dedicated 25th May 1987.'

2. Memorial plaque in church, dedicated 1990.

The memorial is located close to the clubhouse.

TUDDENHAM

County: Suffolk

UTM/grid: OS Map 155 – TL760715
Lat./Long.: N52°18.44 E000°34.24
Nearest town: Mildenhall 3 miles to north-west

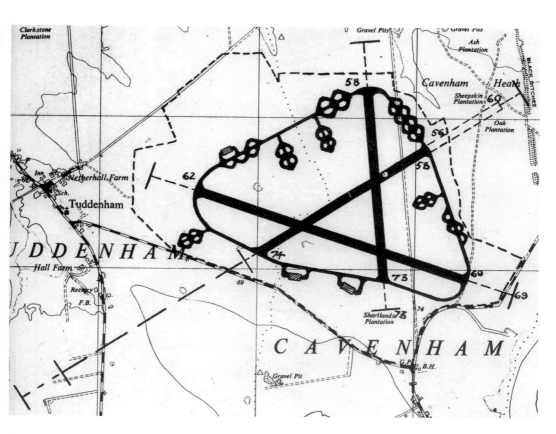

HISTORY

Tuddenham was a late-build airfield and was constructed by M J Gleeson Ltd in 1942, to the standard bomber pattern of three surfaced-runways, linked by a perimeter track interspersed with dispersal points and with two T.2 hangars in loops off the southern perimeter track. The airfield was allocated to Bomber Command's No.3 Group and, even before it opened, was part of a reorganization of the Command that took effect in spring 1943; Tuddenham became a sub-station for No.32 Base, its base station being Mildenhall, but remaining part of No.3 Group, Bomber Command. This arrangement had taken effect in March 1943 and Tuddenham became the third sub-station. This was a Stirling Group and so 90 Squadron moved in from Wratting Common on 13 October – and was to stay for over three years. The

first operation from Tuddenham took place four days later and, between that event and the end of the war, the Squadron was fully engaged as part of Main Force, converting to Lancasters in May 1944. With its wartime record from this airfield it is appropriate that 90 Squadron is recorded on the memorial stone in the village and that a Lancaster appears on the village sign. Tuddenham was one of the select number of airfields to be equipped with the FIDO system, installation work being carried out in early 1944 for runway 12/30.

In October a second operational unit, 186 Squadron, was created, using 'C Flight' from 90 Squadron as a core of experience. However, this new squadron moved out in December and Tuddenham remained a one-squadron station until the arrival of 138 Squadron in March 1945.

AIRFIELD DATA DEC 1944

Command:	RAF Bomber Command	Runway surface:	Concrete
Function:	Operational	Hangars:	2 × T.1, one × B.1
Runways:	300 deg 2,000 × 50yd	Dispersals:	38 × Loop
	067 deg 1,400 × 50yd	Personnel:	Officers – 124
	186 deg 1,400 × 50yd		Other Ranks – 1,190 (276 WAAF)

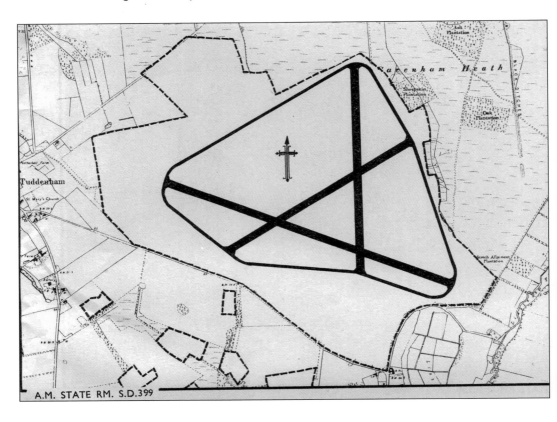

A.M. STATE RM. S.D.399

Post-war the airfield remained with Bomber Command as a Lancaster base and its paper strength was boosted with the arrival of two more squadrons although, as was common during this period, none of the units was at full strength. In November 1946, all four units departed, two to Wyton and two to Stradishall and with the departure of the flying units Tuddenham was reduced to Care and Maintenance.

However, in the uncertain post-war Europe, the airfield was retained for possible future use and, indeed, was allocated to the Americans at the end of 1954 as a sub-station for North Pickenham. There was no significant usage but, a few years later, construction work was underway in one corner of the airfield, as three massive concrete structures were built. Tuddenham had been chosen as a Thor missile-base and the standard three launch-pads were put in place ready for the arrival of 107 Squadron in July 1959, this unit having re-formed from 77 Squadron. With its high-security fencing and military police patrols Tuddenham was in the front line of the Cold War, but it was all very short-lived and the RAF's ballistic-missile era came to an end in 1963.

With the departure of the missileers the base finally closed and the land was disposed of. Little now remains of Tuddenham, although traces of the airfield's surfaces can be seen.

Lancaster crew of 90 Squadron, Tuddenham's main operational unit during World War Two.

The airfield was used as a Thor missile site in the early 1960s by 107 Squadron.

UNITS

1939–1945

90 Sqn	13 Oct 1943–11 Nov 1946	Stirling, Lancaster
138 Sqn	3 Mar 1945–12 Nov 1946	Lancaster
186 Sqn	5 Oct 1944–17 Dec 1944	Lancaster

Post-1945

107 Sqn	22 Jul 1959–10 Jul 1963	Thor
149 Sqn	29 Apr 1946–4 Nov 1946	Lancaster
207 Sqn	29 Apr 1946–8 Nov 1946	Lancaster

MEMORIALS

Memorial stone to 90 Squadron on village green, inscribed: 'For all those who served their country as members of XC Squadron RAF.' Plus Lancaster image on village sign.

WATTISHAM
Station 377

County: Suffolk

UTM/grid: OS Map 155 – TM025510
Lat./Long.: N52°07.27 E000°57.40
Nearest town: Stowmarket 5 miles to north

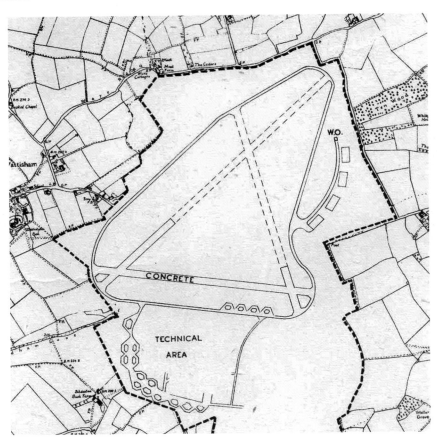

HISTORY

The Suffolk airfield of Wattisham has been associated with fighters for most of its career, but this generalization ignores the original operational purpose of the base when it was home to Blenheims of No.2 Group and saw an intensive period of offensive operations. The site at Wattisham was part of the 1938 RAF expansion programme, built by a firm that was responsible for a number of airfields in East Anglia, John Laing & Son, and, whilst it started life as a grass area, it was provided with the usual range of brick buildings and four C-type hangars. The main camp area was situated on the east side of the field and the road from Great Bircett was diverted to make room

for the airfield. The small village of Wattisham was situated just to the west of the airfield boundary.

RAF Wattisham opened in March 1939 for Bomber Command's No.2 Group and the first units arrived in May: Blenheim Is of 107 Squadron from Harwell and 110 Squadron from Waddington. The airfield was in the war from 'day one', a formation of Blenheims hunting shipping at Wilhelmshaven; it was not an auspicious start and five of the ten aircraft failed to return, four of the five being from 107 Squadron. High loss-rates were to be a feature of Blenheim ops by No.2 Group but, in the absence of other aircraft, there was no option but to keep going and for over two years the Group's squadrons took

Blenheims were the main operational type during the RAF's wartime use of the airfield.

the war to the enemy. The two squadrons operated side by side from Wattisham, as well as deploying to other airfields from time to time for specific missions and when 107 Squadron moved to Great Massingham, in May 1941, their place was taken by 226 Squadron and Blenheim operations retained their intensity; indeed, a number of other Blenheim squadrons used Wattisham for short periods during 1940–41. The station was also home to a number of training Flights during the early 1940s.

Early 1942 brought a new twin-engine type to the base, with a five-month detachment of Beaufighters from 236 Squadron for anti-shipping duties, although a number of special ops were also flown. This intensive period was about to end, as the decision had been taken to hand the airfield to the Americans; in preparation for this, the RAF units moved out by summer 1942 and the airfield was closed while the runways were laid and facilities upgraded for the expected bomber group. The building work also included facilities for an Air Depot, involving a major extension to the south with an area of dispersals and hangars (four T.2s) around Park Wood.

The plan was changed in mid-build and, whilst the Air Depot role would go ahead, the bomber element would be replaced by a fighter element; the net result of this was to halt runway construction, leaving Wattisham with an unusual pattern of runways, perimeter track and dispersals. One long runway was almost complete and this was continued in steel matting, whilst a cross runway was consolidated and ended up as a mix of grass, concrete and matting. The airfield duly became the 4th Strategic Air Depot, specializing in fighter repairs and, whilst this was very much part of Wattisham, the USAAF gave it the name of Hitcham (as Station 470), whereas the main airfield became Station 377. The 4th SAD handled a wide variety of types, including bombers in its early months, and a great many aircraft were returned to service from its workshops. This role continued to

the end of the war and deserves more credit than it usually receives.

In terms of operational types, the first American users were the P-39Ds of the 6th Observation Group, who used the airfield from October to December 1942. It was not until May 1944 that Wattisham's main fighter unit turned up; the last Fighter Group to join the 8th Air Force, the 479th FG 'Riddle's Raiders', arrived with P-38s on 15 May, under the command of Lieutenant Colonel Kyle L Riddle. The Group flew the first of its 351 missions on 26 May and was engaged on bomber escort, although increasingly, like all the Fighter Groups, it undertook ground-attack missions. Indeed, the 479th became expert at the hazardous role of attacking enemy airfields and this earned them a Distinguished Unit Citation in autumn 1944. The last mission was flown on 25 April 1945 and, during this, Lieutenant Hilton Thompson shot down an enemy aircraft, the last aerial claim by the 8th Air Force. Having re-equipped with P-51Ds in September 1944, the Group's total wartime record comprised 155 air and 279 ground victories, for the loss of sixty-nine aircraft missing in action.

Wattisham had recorded a fine wartime history with its RAF Blenheims and USAAF fighter operations but, with the departure of the Americans in late-1945, the fate of this somewhat unusual airfield was uncertain. It was handed back to the RAF and for a year little happened; however, it had been decided that it was easier to develop the runways and take advantage of the permanent buildings, rather than construct the latter at one of the many airfields that had runways but little else. Meteors of 266 Squadron arrived from Boxted in October 1946, but this was a short detachment of only a few months, as was that by 56 Squadron. It had, however, put down a 'marker' for Fighter Command and for the next forty-plus years Wattisham was to be a front-line fighter base.

It was essential that at least one long runway be constructed; this work was undertaken in the late-1940s and, along with other building work, established the airfield's basic infrastructure for future

Blenheim crash-landing in a field near the airfield.

AIRFIELD DATA DEC 1944

Command:	US 8th Air Force	Runway surface:	Concrete and tarmac
Function:	Operational	Hangars:	4 × T.2, 4 × L
Runways:	060 deg 2,000 × 50yd	Dispersals:	52 × Spectacle, 19 × Frying pan
	110 deg 1,400 × 50yd	Personnel:	Officers – 190
	350 deg 1,400 × 50yd		Other Ranks – 1,519

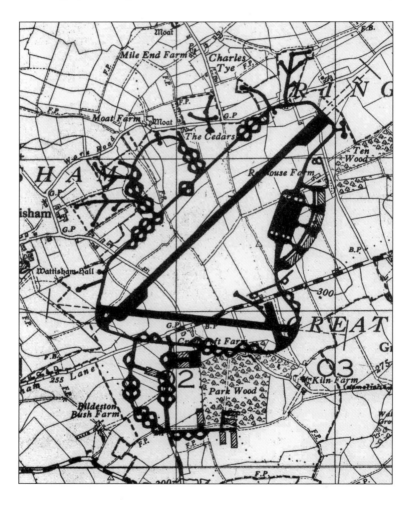

operations. Permanent flying occupation re-commenced in autumn 1950, with the arrival of three jet-fighter squadrons, all operating Meteor F.4s but soon converting to the more definitive Meteor F.8. Night-fighter Meatboxes also appeared when 152 Squadron re-formed here with Meteor NF.12s and, throughout the 1950s, this was a very active and interesting airfield. In November 1954, the base was in the headlines, as one of its units, 257 Squadron, was the first in the RAF to equip with Hunter F.2s; for the next few years the Hunter became the main type in service at Wattisham, although Javelins also made a brief appearance. Further runway work was undertaken in the late-1950s, in preparation for the next new aircraft – the Lightning. Two of the RAF's great fighter-squadrons, 56 and 111, operated this most British of aircraft from Wattisham and, to many, this aircraft will always be associated with Wattisham. A third Lightning operator, 29 Squadron, replaced 56 when the latter moved to Cyprus in January 1971 but the cycle of air-defence exercise and Southern Q continued. To the dismay of many, the Lightnings were eventually replaced, but in their place came another classic fighter – the F-4 Phantom – and the RAF saw out its tenure of this Suffolk airfield operating this potent aircraft.

Squadrons changed around but the air-defence role remained the focus of the station's activities, until the run-down of RAF strength as part of a series of defence cuts prompted by the end of the Cold War. The RAF finally departed Wattisham on 31 Oct 1992. However, the British Army are never slow to spot a good thing and, with a requirement for airfields in the UK for Army Air Corps units returning from Germany, Wattisham was an ideal location (close to major army training-areas such as the STANTA near Thetford) and so changed colour from 'blue' to 'brown'. The army took control of the airfield in March 1993 and that summer the first flying units arrived: 3 Regiment Army Air Corps, comprising 653, 662 and 663 squadrons, equipped with the Gazelle and the Lynx. They were joined by the similarly equipped 4 Regiment (659, 669 and 654 squadrons) in 1995. These two units have kept the airfield very busy and, with the AH-64 Apache now entering service with the AAC, Wattisham's military potential remains strong.

Two other units operate helicopters from the airfield: the RAF has a detachment of 22 Squadron Sea Kings for SAR duties and, since September 2000, the Suffolk Police have based their EC135 here.

Decoy Sites

Q/K	Boxford	TL955385

Built Dec 1939 and provided with twelve dummy Wellingtons.

Q	Gislingham	TM064731
Q	Nedging	TM007476
	Whatfield	TM0246

Units

HQ units at Wattisham

XIIth FC	12 Sep 1942–17 Sep 1942
HQ 12th AF	12 Sep 1942–22 Sep 1942

1939–1945

18 Sqn	9 Dec 1941–10 Jan 1942	Blenheim
86 Sqn	3 Mar 1941–12 May 1941	Blenheim
107 Sqn	11 May 1939–3 May 1941	Blenheim
110 Sqn	11 May 1939–Mar 1942	Blenheim
114 Sqn	31 May 1940–10 Jun 1940	Blenheim
226 Sqn	27 May 1941–9 Dec 1941	Blenheim, Boston
236 Sqn	9 Feb 1942–3 Jul 1942	Beaufighter

Lightnings of 111 Squadron on the apron; the Squadron spent 16 years at Wattisham operating Hunters and then Lightnings.

1517 Flt	Oct 1941–4 Nov 1941,	Oxford
1508 Flt	19 May 1942–14 Nov 1942	
	18 Jan 1941–15 Feb 1941	Blenheim,
		Wellington

USAAF Units:

| 68th OG | Oct 1942–Dec 1942 | P-39D |

479th FG (65th FW)

Nickname:	Riddle's Raiders
Squadrons:	434th FS, 435th FS, 436th FS
Aircraft:	P-38J, P-38L, P-51D, P-51K
Dates:	15 May 1944–23 Nov 1945
Missions:	351
First mission:	26 May 1944
Last mission:	25 Apr 1945

Post-1945

22 Sqn det	?–date	Sea King
23 Sqn	1 Nov 1975–30 Mar 1983	Phantom
29 Sqn	10 May 1967–31 Dec 1974	Javelin,
		Lightning
41 Sqn	3 Jul 1958–6 Dec 1963	Javelin
56 Sqn	5 Nov 1946–17 Apr 1947,	Meteor,
	10 Jul 1959–6 Aug 1959,	Hunter,
	15 Oct 1959–11 Apr 1967,	Lightning,
	21 Jan 1975–Jul 1992	Phantom

74 Sqn	19 Oct 1984–1 Oct 1992	Phantom
111 Sqn	18 Jun 1958–30 Sep 1974	Hunter,
		Lightning
152 Sqn	1 Jun 1954–11 Jun 1956,	Meteor
	16 Jan 1957–30 Aug 1957	
257 Sqn	27 Oct 1950–10 Jun 1956,	Meteor,
	15 Jan 1957–31 Mar 1957	Hunter
263 Sqn	27 Oct 1950–28 May 1956,	Meteor,
	16 Jan 1957–30 Aug 1957	Hunter
266 Sqn	4 Nov 1946–5 Dec 1946,	Meteor
	4 Jan 1947–16 Apr 1947	
AMSDU	Mar 1947–Apr 1950	
3 Regt AAC	1993–date	Lynx,
		Gazelle
4 Regt AAC	1995–date	Lynx,
		Gazelle

MEMORIALS

1. Memorial plaque to 479th FG in station briefing room, dedicated Oct 1988.

2. The Wattisham Airfield Museum opened in the old Station Chapel in November 1991 to preserve the history of the airfield and its operators.

F-4 Phantom of 56 Squadron; Phantom squadrons at Wattisham formed part of the UK's air defence network for over 20 years.

WATTON
Station 376

County: Norfolk

UTM/grid: OS Map 144 – TL945000
Lat./Long.: N52°33.53 E000°51.45
Nearest town: Watton one mile to west

HISTORY

Watton is an airfield with three distinctive histories; first as a light-bomber base with No.2 Group, followed by service as an American Air Depot and, post-war, as a centre for Signals Command and a variety of flying units (but dominated by the Canberra). Construction of the airfield took place in 1938/early 1939, the prime contractor being John Laing & Son, and the usual selection of buildings, including four C-type hangars, was built on the northern side of the site, the flying surface being a large oval oriented east/west.

The airfield opened in early 1939 for No.2 Group, Bomber Command and in March received its complement of two Blenheim squadrons, 21 Squadron from Eastchurch and 34 Squadron from Upper Heyford. Both units were fairly new to the Blenheim and intensive training was the order of the day, especially as war looked increasingly imminent. With the departure in August of 34 Squadron, strength was maintained by the arrival of 82 Squadron and Watton's Wing of Blenheim IVs was ready for action on the outbreak of war. Over the next two years the station's squadrons were involved in a variety of tasks and, like all the Blenheim units of No.2 Group, they suffered heavy losses; for example, twice in 1940 the aircrew of 82 Squadron were all but annihilated – on the second such mission, only one of the twelve attackers returned. The satellite airfield at Bodney, just to the west, was in use from spring 1940 and the Blenheims operated from both locations, as well as deploying to other airfields for specific operations. Throughout this period to early 1942 the airfield played temporary host to a number of other squadrons; most of these were equipped with Blenheims, but Watton also witnessed the RAF's first use of the B-17 Fortress, when 90 Squadron re-formed here in May 1941. Little Fortress flying appears to have taken place from Watton and the aircraft used Bodney and other airfields in East Anglia before the squadron moved to West Raynham in mid-May.

AIRFIELD DATA DEC 1944

Command:	US 8th AF 325th PRW	Hangars:	4 × C.4, 3 × T.2, 3 × Blister, 2 × B.1
Function:	Photo Reconnaissance	Dispersals:	41 × Eye Glass, 12 × Concrete frying pan
Runways:	110 deg 2,000 × 50yd	Personnel:	Officers – 190
Runway surface:	Concrete		Other Ranks – 1,519

The departure of the Blenheim units brought Watton's operational career to a temporary halt, as the next occupants were the training types of No.17 Pilot Advanced Flying Unit, who were based here from January 1942 to May 1943. This unit formed at Watton on 29 January for No.21 Group and had an establishment of 174 (yes, 174) Masters, although a number of support types were used in small numbers. Bodney continued to be used as a satellite and intensive flying-training – with this number of aircraft the circuit must have been interesting – took place every day. This was a long way east for such a training unit but, fortunately, the airfield was not attacked! The PAFU moved to Calveley in May 1943 and Watton was freed up for use by the 8th Air Force.

Allocated to a newly forming Air Depot, the airfield required construction work to create a hard-surface east/west runway and a comprehensive network of perimeter track and dispersals; this work also included a major extension to the south, to create an area of hangars, dispersals and other buildings for the depot. This site was known as Neaton (despite being located adjacent to the village of Griston) and designated Station 505, whereas Watton itself became Station 376. The primary task of the 3rd Strategic Air Depot was maintenance and refurbishment of the B-24 Liberators of 2nd Air Division and this task kept the technical staff of the SAD busy, as it was essential to return as many battle-damaged aircraft as possible to the operational units. Standard policy was to base an operational unit at such airfields and, in April 1944, the 803rd Reconnaissance Group took up residence. This Group operated a mix of Mosquitoes, B-17s and B-24s and was primarily tasked with weather reconnaissance. A name change in August to 25th BG (R) brought no change in the basic task and this unit remained at Watton to the end of the war.

Most airfields in this region had ground-based air defence and, whilst for many this was little more than a few post-mounted machine-guns, Watton was home to the HQ and two batteries (C and D) of the 445th Anti-Aircraft Artillery; indeed, it was the first American airfield in this region to receive such a dedicated AA unit. The only recorded downing of a German aircraft over the airfield had actually taken place on 18 February 1941, when a lone He111

Blenheim Is of 21 Squadron at Watton 1939.

Armourers of 21 Squadron take a break from loading the Squadron's Blenheims; the unit was one of a number of Blenheim operators to use Watton.

attempted a cloud-cover attack and was engaged by the airfield's Parachute and Cable (PAC) system. In a rare success for this 'aerial minefield', the Heinkel was brought down and its crew were taken prisoner.

On 27 September 1945 the airfield was returned to RAF control and, almost immediately, became home to the Radio Warfare Establishment. The RWE had formed out of No.100 Group's Bomber Support Development Unit in July and moved into Watton on 27 September, to open a fascinating period in the Station's history. This unit operated a very mixed bag of aircraft, many of which sprouted aerials connected with a diverse test-and-evaluation programme on all manner of electronic equipment. The RWE became the Central Signals Establishment the following September and for twenty years it operated all

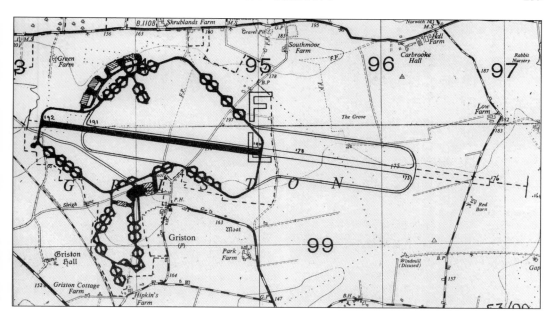

manner of aircraft, although the flying elements became squadrons in the early 1950s, the first of which was 192 Squadron. Various changes of squadron numberplate took place over the next decade or so (*see* Unit list) but this did not detract from the importance of CSE and its work.

The 1954 survey listed Watton as part of Signals Command; the airfield had a single asphalt-runway (100/280 degrees) of 6,000ft × 150ft, plus two grass strips each of 4,200ft (155/335 degrees and 041/221 degrees). It was stated that the airfield had been 'provisionally accepted for extension to Class I, but that the proposal is in abeyance'. The survey also investigated further extension to 11,000ft, but concluded that this would be difficult. Hangar facilities were listed as four C-type plus three T.2, whilst dispersals comprised thirty-seven loop (160sq ft) and eleven round (110ft diameter), plus eight aprons totalling 150,000sq ft and one large apron of 229,500sq ft.

Of all the aircraft connected with CSE and Watton during this period to the unit's disbandment in July 1965, the main one was the Canberra, the English Electric twin-jet proving highly adaptable to trials installations. The closure of CSE meant an end to regular flying at Watton but not an end to RAF utilization.

As part of the UK radar-structure, Eastern Radar was based at Watton from 1965 to 1988, providing radar service to a large part of south-east England.

Restructuring of the radar network in the late-1980s meant that Eastern Radar became Border Radar and, as such, it continued to operate at Watton until 1992. The closure of this unit pretty much brought RAF involvement to an end, although the gliders of 611 Volunteer Gliding School (for the Air Training Corps) moved in from an increasingly busy Marham in 1995. The army has made use of the airfield, including helicopter operations, as Watton is very close to the major training range of STANTA, but, in 1995, part of the site was sold off for housing development. The military ceased maintenance of most of the buildings and it did not take long for the site to take on a deserted and unwanted appearance – a sad situation for an airfield with such a history. Further sell-offs took place in 1998 and some buildings have been demolished from mid-2000 although, if you fly over the airfield, the main area (runway and hangars) still appear in fine condition. HMP Griston now occupies part of the airfield – to the south where the BAD once operated.

DECOY SITES

	Bodney	TL8398
	East Bradenham	TF937074
	North Tudenham	TG034134
Q	Breckles	TL952950
K	Hillborough	TF8200?
Q	West Bradenham	TF912070

UNITS

1939–1945

18 Sqn	20–26 May 1940	Blenheim
21 Sqn	2 Mar 1939–24 Jun 1940, 14 Jun 1941–26 Dec 1941	Blenheim
34 Sqn	2 Mar 1939–12 Aug 1939	Blenheim
82 Sqn	25 Aug 1939–21 Mar 1942	Blenheim
90 Sqn	7 May 1941–15 May 1941	Fortress
105 Sqn	10 Jul 1940–31 Oct 1940	Blenheim
1508 Flt	20 Dec 1941–19 Jan 1941	Oxford
17 (P)AFU	29 Jan 1942–1 May 1943	Master
RWE/CSE	Sep 1945–1 Jul 1965	various

USAAF Units

803rd RG	22 Apr 1944–9 Aug 1944 (became 25th BG (R))	B-17, B-24, Mosquito

25th BG (R)

Squadrons:	652nd BS, 653rd BS, 654th BS
Aircraft:	B-17, B-24, B-26, P-38, L-5
Dates:	9 Aug 1944 – 23 Jul 1945
First mission:	22 Apr 1944 (as 803rd RG)

Post-1945

51 Sqn	21 Aug 1958–31 Mar 1963	Canberra
97 Sqn	25 May 1963–2 Jan 1967	Canberra, Hastings, Varsity
98 Sqn	1 Oct 1963–17 Apr 1969	Canberra
115 Sqn	21–25 Aug 1958	Varsity, Valetta
116 Sqn	1 Aug 1952–21 Aug 1958	Anson, Lincoln, Hastings, Varsity
151 Sqn	1 Jan 1962–25 May 1963	Canberra, Lincoln, Hastings, Varsity
192 Sqn	15 Jul 1951–21 Aug 1958	various
199 Sqn	16 Jul 1951–17 Apr 1952	Lincoln, Mosquito
245 Sqn	21–25 Aug 1958	Canberra
263 Sqn	1 Jun 1959–30 Jun 1963	Bloodhound
360 Sqn	1 Apr 1966–21 Apr 1969	Canberra
527 Sqn	1 Aug 1952–21 Aug 1958	various
GCAOS	Sep 1946–10 Mar 1952	Lancaster, Tiger Moth
GCAS	Sep 1946–10 Mar 1952	
611 VGS	1 Jun 1995–Jan 1996; 1 May 1996–	Vigilant, Viking

MEMORIALS

1. Near the side of the demolished officers' mess is a memorial area containing a twisted Blenheim propeller plus two plaques, inscribed: 'To the memory of those of the Royal Air Force and Commonwealth Air Forces who lost their lives while serving at RAF Watton and Bodney.' and 'This propeller was recovered from Blenheim R3800 which was shot down over Aalborg, Denmark, on 13th August 1940 whilst operating out of Watton.' A third plaque, with memorial stone, commemorates the 8th Air Force, inscribed: 'Seasoned airmen gathered here among allies to continue the great first cause. Dedicated in memory of those who served. 25th Bomb Group (RCN SP). Time to remember 1944–1945.'

2. In the grounds of Griston village church, a stone commemorates the 3rd Strategic Air Depot, inscribed: 'A tribute to the American airmen who served their country and its Allies from this base by maintaining the B-24 Liberator bombers of the Eighth Air Force', followed by a list of units.

Watton's post-1945 career was with Signals Command and the Canberras of 98 Squadron were one of the main flying units.

The memorial area at Watton is located close to the site of the Officers Mess and commemorates the RAF and USAAF units.

WENDLING
Station 118

UTM/grid: OS Map 132 – TF925150
Lat./Long.: N52°41.48 E000°50.49
Nearest town: Dereham 5 miles to east

County: Norfolk

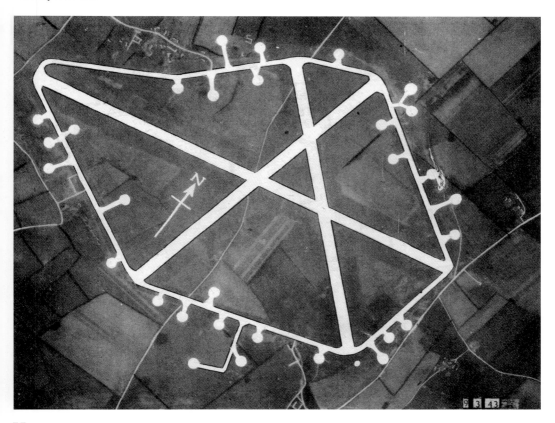

HISTORY

For anyone trying to track airfields by village sign-posts, Wendling would be impossible to find, as it is located on the opposite side of the A47 to the village and is nearer the village of Beeston, although partly within the parish of Beeston-with-Bittering and partly within the parish of Wendling. It is just one of many examples of strange logic in the naming of wartime airfields.

The site was requisitioned in 1941 for the construction of a bomber station and the main build-phase, by Taylor Woodrow, took place in 1942, with the laying out of three runways linked by a perimeter track from which sprouted thirty or so RAF-preferred frying-pan dispersals. With the decision to allocate the airfield to the Americans, the major change was the addition of more dispersals of the USAAF-preferred loop variety. Wendling was provided with the standard two T.2 hangars, a control tower and an assortment of other buildings and huts, plus a bomb store in Honeypot Wood on the south-east edge of the airfield.

Requisitioning of land was often tricky and in the case of Wendling the owner of Cannister Farm flatly refused to move out; when you look at the plan of the airfield you can see that the north-west perimeter track bends-in to avoid the farm. The Americans, who subsequently occupied the site, reckoned this was not a bad thing, as it meant a ready source of milk and eggs. This part of the airfield became home to the 576th Bomb Squadron of the 392nd Bomb Group; each of the four squadrons being allocated a sector of the airfield.

AIRFIELD DATA DEC 1944

Command:	US 8th AF 2nd BD	Runway surface:	Wood-chips with
		protective covering	
Function:	Operational	Hangars:	2 × T.2
Runways:	010 deg 2,000 × 50yd	Dispersals:	50 concrete
	260 deg 1,400 × 50yd	Personnel:	Officers – 421
	130 deg 1,400 × 50yd		Other Ranks – 2,473

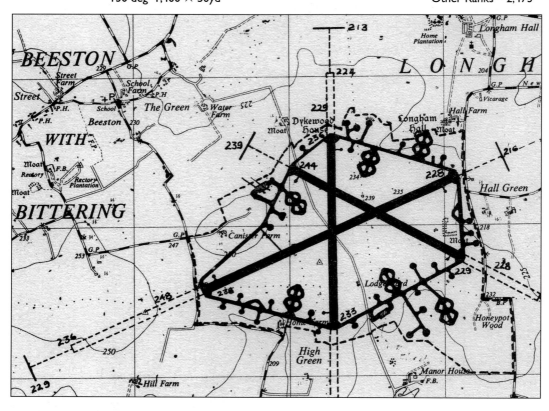

Wendling opened in early 1943 and the Liberators of the 392nd arrived in August, under the command of Colonel Irvine A Rendle. The Group flew 285 missions from Wendling, the first of these taking place on 9 September 1943 and, during its operational career, lost 127 aircraft missing in action; it was awarded one Distinguished Unit Citation (for Gotha on 24 February 1944) and put in claims for 144-45-49 enemy aircraft. During its time at Wendling, it flew four versions of the B-24 and was the first 8th Air Force Group with the H-model. Only just over a month after flying its last combat mission, the Group was sending aircraft back to the States; by mid-June virtually everyone had gone and Wendling was taken over by the RAF for use by Maintenance Command. There appears to have been little activity at what was now a satellite airfield and the site was eventually closed in November 1961 and put up for disposal two years later.

In what became a typical scenario for ex-military airfields, the concrete runways were taken over by poultry farmers and sprouted low wooden-sheds; at Wendling a number of other buildings survive around the area but the most abiding feature is the memorial garden, dedicated in 1945 and one of the most atmospheric of any in the UK.

The 392nd BG arrived at Wendling in July 1943, flying the first of its 285 missions in September.

B-24 'Ford's Folly' receiving a mixed load for a mission in June 1944. (US National Archives)

Stripes) located in village of Beeston and dedicated 2 Sep 1945, inscribed: 'Dedicated to the men of US Army Air Forces Station 118 who through their efforts, devotion and duty, aided in bringing victory to the Allies in World War No 2. 392nd Bombardment Group (H) Headquarters, 576th Bombardment Squadron (H), 577th Bombardment Squadron (H), 578th Bombardment Squadron (H), 579th Bombardment Squadron (H) of the United States Eighth Air Force. 465th Sub-Depot (Class I), 10th Station Complement Squadron, 1217th QM Service Group (RS), 1825th Ordnance S&M Co (Avn), 1287th Military Police Det. "A" 806th Chemical Co. (AO) Det A, 586th Army Postal Unit, 208th Finance Detachment, 2101st Eng-Fire-Fighting Platoon of the United States Eighth Air Force.' and '392nd Bomb Group, 8th Air Force, US Army Air Forces, Station 118 Wendling. In honour of 747 airmen who gave their lives and all who served with them at this base. July 1943–June 1945.'

UNITS

1939–1945
USAAF Units
392nd BG (14th CW)

Identifying letter:	D
Nickname:	The Crusaders
Squadrons:	576th BS (Vitos), 577th BS (Caldron), 578th BS (Hazard), 579th BS (Faceup)
Aircraft:	B-24H, B-24J, B-24L, B-24M
Dates:	Jul 1943–15 Jun 1945
Missions:	285
First mission:	9 Sep 1943
Last mission:	25 Apr 1945

MEMORIALS

Impressive and well maintained memorial park, complete with car park, obelisk and two flagpoles (usually flying the Union Jack and the Stars and

The memorial garden, complete with obelisk, is a good place to reflect on the human cost of Allied bomber operations.

WESTLEY

County: Suffolk

UTM/grid: OS Map 155 – TL834645
Lat./Long.: N52°14.53 E000°41.12
Nearest town: Bury St Edmunds

The site of Westley is hard to discern on this 1947 aerial shot; comparison with the plan on the following age makes it possible to pick out the airfield. (Ken Wallis)

HISTORY

A small airfield was laid out at Westley in 1938 for the West Suffolk Aero Club, although this was little more than a stretch of grass with two small hangars and a club house. The club used two Taylorcraft Plus Cs (a type that later re-appeared at Westley with 652 Squadron) but on the outbreak of war the airfield was closed. There was, however, a need for army co-operation aircraft to work with the troops in the Bury area, such as Gibraltar Barracks and Blenheim Camp,

and the RAF took over the field, forming 268 Squadron here on 30 September 1940. The squadron was primarily constituted from 'A Flight' of 2 Squadron and 'B Flight' of 26 Squadron and was equipped with Lysanders. In some records the airfield is recorded as Bury St Edmunds rather than Westley, which causes some confusion to historians as the late bomber airfield was also known as Bury St Edmunds, although this, too, had an alternative name – Rougham.

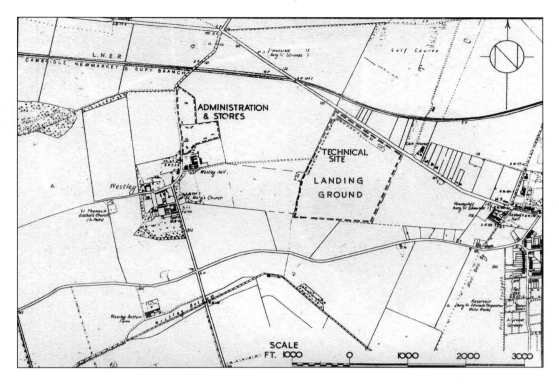

Although army co-operation exercises were the main part of the unit's work, including trials with gas canisters, the Lysanders also flew coastal patrols during this 'invasion scare' period. With the departure of 268 Squadron to Snailwell in April 1941, their place was taken by another Lysander unit, 241 Squadron, although they only stayed until July. Proximity to Bury with its army presence meant that the airfield was still used on an opportunity basis by liaison and communication aircraft, but it was not until August 1942 that another resident unit arrived, when 652 Squadron moved in from Bottisham. This was one of the new series of army-support units formed as part of the tactical lessons of other campaigns and designed to improve air-ground co-operation for the invasion of France. The squadron was equipped with a variety of aircraft but it was the Auster that became the definitive type for them and other similar squadrons. Although this squadron moved out of Westley in January 1943, other Auster units used the airfield on an infrequent basis, at least until mid-1944. With the army and its supporting aircraft now operating in France, there was no further need of Westley and it fell into disuse.

The site of the airfield has now vanished under the urban sprawl of Bury St Edmunds.

Lysander of 268 Squadron at Westley. (Ken Wallis)

UNITS

1939–1945

241 Sqn	11 Apr 1941–1 Jul 1941	Lysander
268 Sqn	30 Sep 1940–1 Apr 1941	Lysander
652 Sqn	11 Aug 1942–1 Jan 1943	Tiger Moth, Taylorcraft, Auster
103 GS	Oct 1943–Apr 1944, Jun 1944–20 May 1946	Cadet

WEST RAYNHAM

County: Norfolk

UTM/grid: OS Map 132 – TF850245
Lat./Long.: N52°47.09 E000°44.32
Nearest town: Fakenham 5 miles to north-east

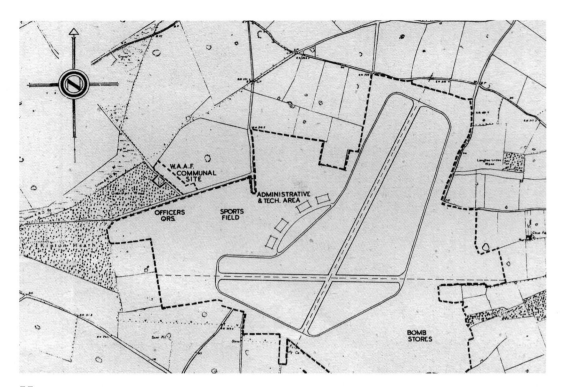

HISTORY

The land for West Raynham airfield was requisitioned in late-1935 and work commenced the following year, although progress was initially slow, as one of the main contractors, F R Hipperson & Son, was also engaged on other airfield work in Norfolk. A standard expansion-period airfield was laid out, with the arc of four C-type hangars and an extensive collection of brick buildings to one side of the large, grass landing-area. The Station opened on 5 April 1939, under the command of Group Captain A S Maskell, for use by Bomber Command and the following month the Blenheims of 101 Squadron arrived from Bicester, being joined a few days later by those of 90 Squadron. The prime role of the two units was as Group Pool squadrons to train Blenheim crews and, as the name suggests, to provide a pool of trained crews that the operational squadrons of No.2 Group could call on; the Group also based its target-towing flight here from October 1939. However, despite this training role, the

Station's squadrons also flew a number of operational sorties. A number of other squadrons passed through during early 1940, some on work-up and some on forward deployment, but Raynham remained primarily a training base until late-1940 – by which time the Luftwaffe had made a number of attacks on the airfield, although these were invariably a lone bomber dropping a number of low-calibre bombs. To counter such attacks the airfield mounted a number of machine-guns on posts, but also had three Bofors guns, manned by the army, as well as a PAC (Parachute and Cable – or officially, Pyrotechnic Aerial Curtain) system. Ground defences, again army manned, included sixteen pill-boxes, more than usual for an airfield, some of which survive.

By mid-1940, Bomber Command had adopted a new training system, with dedicated Operational Training Units, and squadrons that had performed this role now became operational; thus, West Raynham

AIRFIELD DATA DEC 1944

Command:	RAF Bomber Command	Runway surface:	Concrete and tarmac
Function:	Operational	Hangars:	4 × C
Runways:	040 deg 2,000 × 50yd	Dispersals:	36 × Heavy Bomber
	100 deg 1,400 × 50yd	Personnel:	Officers – 168
			Other Ranks – 1,508 (348 WAAF)

took on an offensive role within No.2 Group and the Blenheims of 101 Squadron became part of the daylight attacks on enemy shipping and continental targets. The squadron re-equipped with Wellingtons in April 1941 and flew a number of sorties from Raynham with the new aircraft before moving to Oakington to become part of Main Force. However, the station retained an operational role with Blenheim squadrons into 1942, the resident unit being 114 Squadron, although training units were also present during this period. As the Group began to phase out the Blenheim, new types, such as the Boston and Mitchell, arrived at Raynham but, in December 1943, the station was transferred to No.100 Group.

During the early summer the airfield had been temporarily closed whilst George Wimpey's contractors were constructing two concrete-runways; the main runway was oriented north-east/south-west and was 2,000 yards, whilst the secondary runway ran east/west. The target-towers of No.1482 Flight, mainly Martinets, moved back even before work was complete but, by September, the airfield was ready for full use. For the remainder of the war the airfield was home to two Mosquito-intruder squadrons, 141 and 239, both of which operated at night over Germany, hunting enemy night-fighters in the air and on the ground. The squadrons proved highly effective in both roles as part of No.100 Group's support of bomber operations; these missions continued to late/early May 1945, the final operational sortie from Raynham being flown on 2 May.

Hunters and Javelins frame the apron used for this June 1961 parade.

In the latter part of 1944, the airfield was one of four chosen in this part of East Anglia for development as a very-heavy-bomber station but, unlike its near-neighbour Marham, the plan was changed and Raynham remained undeveloped, except for a new control tower. By mid-July 1945 both Mossie squadrons had gone – 141 Squadron to Little Snoring and 239 suffering the fate of many wartime units and disbanding. In the same month the airfield was transferred to No.12 Group and became part of Fighter Command. However, rather than becoming a normal fighter-station, Raynham became one of the most important airfields in Fighter Command when the Central Fighter Establishment arrived from Tangmere. This was a diverse and fascinating organization whose component units included a veritable alphabet-spaghetti of abbreviations (see Unit list) and included the Day Fighter Development Wing, incorporating the Air Fighting Development Squadron, the Day Fighter Leaders School and, logically enough, the Night Fighter Development Wing, as well as the Fighter Interception Development Squadron and Naval Air Fighting Development Unit. The acronyms changed a number of times, as the specific tasks of CFE changed to reflect new aircraft and new tactical thoughts.

Mosquito NT362 of 239 Squadron at Raynham; the Squadron was here from December 1943 to July 1945.

All manner of fighter types, prop and jet, passed

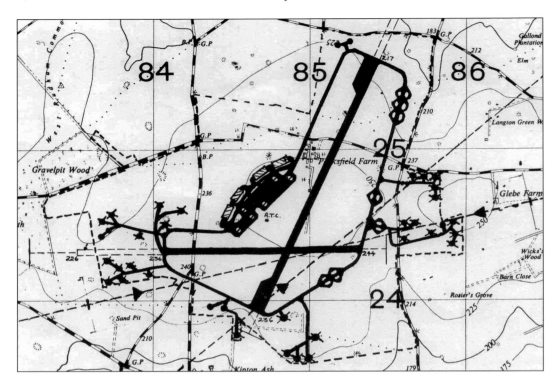

though the books of CFE's units over the next twenty years and it must have been a truly amazing location for any aircraft spotter. While the scale of the Establishment's activities reduced from the late-1950s, the activity level at Raynham was maintained by the arrival, in autumn 1960, of 85 Squadron with its Javelins. The Establishment finally moved out in October 1962 and Raynham entered what was to be its last decade as a fighter station, during which time it specialized in Hunters, whilst also flirting for a few years with Canberras, when 85 Squadron re-equipped with the type for facilities work. Four Hunter squadrons used West Raynham between 1963 and 1972 and it was from this base that the 'famous' flight was made that resulted in the loss of a number of Hunters when fog formed over the whole of East Anglia and the aircraft had nowhere to land – leaving pilots to abandon their aircraft as they ran out of fuel.

There were various developments at Raynham during the 1960s, one of the most interesting being the formation in October 1964 of the Kestrel Evaluation Squadron; this forerunner of the Harrier was tested by a joint-evaluation team for just over a year. The airfield had also been chosen as a Bloodhound Surface-to-Air Missile site and 41 Squadron became active in this role on 1 September

1965; the missiles stayed five years and were then withdrawn. Meanwhile, Raynham's flying career was very much with the Canberra and the facilities role, with 85 Squadron and 100 Squadron flying a variety of marks in a variety of roles. In December 1975, all the Canberras were taken over by 100 Squadron, making this one of the RAF's largest squadrons, and 85 re-formed with Bloodhound missiles, as West Raynham was once more designated as a SAM site, as well as being the parent unit for the other Bloodhound sites in the UK. The latter role meant that the station housed a number of support units, such as the Bloodhound School and the Missile System Maintenance School. The RAF's Bloodhound network contracted in the late-1980s so, before long, only Rayham was left and, in addition to its active launchers, it was storing redundant missiles on the old runways. It is worth noting that the RAF's other SAM system, Rapier, had also been active at Raynham with the RAF Regiment, the first such unit, 66 Squadron RAF Regiment, having formed here in 1983. This Rapier unit continued to use the airfield as its home base, although frequently deployed away, until all activity at this Norfolk airfield came to an end in 1994.

RAF West Raynham finally closed on 1 September 1994, but remains under MoD control. The airfield

West Rayham's Canberras were used for target facilities work in the 1960s and 1970s.

342 Sqn	7 Apr 1943–15 May 1943	Boston
2 Gp Pool	14–19 Sep 1939	
2 Gp TTF	Oct 1939–Mar 1941, 30 Sep 1941–Nov 1941	Battle, Lysander
1420 Flt	19 Jul 1941–15 Nov 1941	Blenheim
1482 Flt	Nov 1941–29 May 1943	Lysander, Blenheim, Defiant
1482 Flt	17 Sep 1943–1 Dec 1943	Mitchell, Martinet
1694 Flt	24 Jan 1944–21 May 1944	Martinet
CFE	1 Oct 1945–5 Oct 1962	various
NFDW	1 Oct 1945 –?	Mosquito, Beaufighter
NFLS	1 Oct 1945–Jul 1950	

has been used for a number of exercises, as well as storage, but its domestic site has been left to deteriorate; for example, broken windows and grazing sheep are the picture one sees in the married-quarters area.

DECOY SITES

Q/K	Fulmodestone	TG009306

Located east of Brown's Covert, this site was bombed at least once; most dummy aircraft were of Blenheim type.

Q	Gateley	TF952245

UNITS

1939–1945

18 Sqn	8 Sep 1940–3 Apr 1941	Blenheim
76 Sqn	30 Apr 1940–20 May 1940	Hampden
90 Sqn	10 May 1939–7 Sep 1939, 14 May 1941–28 Jun 1941	Blenheim
98 Sqn	12 Sep 1942–15 Oct 1942	Mitchell
101 Sqn	6 May 1939–1 Jul 1941	Blenheim, Wellington
114 Sqn	19 Jul 1941–15 Nov 1942	Blenheim
139 Sqn	30 May 1940–10 Jun 1940	Blenheim
141 Sqn	4 Dec 1943–3 Jul 1945	Beaufighter, Mosquito
180 Sqn	13 Sep 1942–19 Oct 1942	Mitchell
239 Sqn	9 Dec 1943–1 Jul 1945	Mosquito
268 Sqn	20–21 Jun 1941	Tomahawk

Post-1945

1 Sqn	13 Aug 1963–18 Jul 1969	Hunter
4 Sqn det	1 Sep 1969–13 Mar 1970	Hunter
41 Sqn	1 Sep 1965–18 Sep 1970	Bloodhound
45 Sqn	1 Aug 1972–29 Sep 1972	Hunter
54 Sqn	14 Aug 1963–1 Sep 1969	Hunter
85 Sqn	8 Sep 1960–25 Apr 1963, 28 Jan 1972–?	Javelin, Canberra, Meteor; Bloodhound
100 Sqn	1 Feb 1972–5 Jan 1976	Canberra
FCITF/S	20 Feb 1950–Feb 1956	
AWFLS	Jul 1950–15 Mar 1958	Meteor, Javelin
AWW	3 Jul 1950–Feb 1956	Javelin
FSDU	29 Jan 1951–?	Spitfire
AWDS	Feb 1956–Aug 1959	Javelin, Meteor
FCIRF/S	Feb 1956–1 Jun 1963	Vampire, Hunter
AWFCS	15 Mar 1958–1 Jul 1962	Javelin
DFCS	15 Mar 1958–13 Nov 1962	Hunter
KES	15 Oct 1964–30 Nov 1965	Kestrel
FCTU	1 Feb 1966–30 Jun 1967	Lightning

MEMORIALS

No real memorial, but the lamps in the Station church commemorate AVM David Atcherley.

WEYBOURNE

County: Norfolk

UTM/grid: OS Map – TG103436
Lat./Long.: N52°56.9 E001°07.7
Nearest town: Sheringham 3.5 miles to east

HISTORY

Located on the coast of north Norfolk, the site at Weybourne was in use from the mid-1930s by the army for anti-aircraft gunnery summer-camps, the target-towing aircraft being provided by Bircham Newton, but a field adjacent to the guns being used as a landing ground. In 1939 a catapult was built on the cliff top for launching Queen Bee drones, these being provided by 'X Flight' of the AACU, which arrived on 16 May. By early 1941, a hangar and a number of huts had been erected for the AACU, who also used Carvel Farmhouse as an office. The site was attacked on the night of 24-25 May by a He111, but no significant damage was caused. The flying element of this AA site had closed by July 1942.

In the post-war period, pilotless aircraft re-appeared for No.1 Anti-Aircraft Practice Camp, aircraft being launched by catapult and recovered (if they survived) by parachute. With other AA gunnery sites closing, Weybourne became increasingly busy and was also used by the Americans. The site eventually closed in 1958.

UNITS

1939–1945

AACU	16 May 1939–	Queen Bee

WOODBRIDGE

County: Suffolk

UTM/grid: OS Map 169 – TM330487
Lat./Long.: N52°05.19 E001°24.30
Nearest town: Ipswich 8 miles to west

HISTORY

Woodbridge was one of three emergency airfields constructed along the east coast as safe havens for aircraft that were damaged, lost, short of fuel, or in any other sort of difficulty. The need for such airfields had become pressing by early 1942, with an ever-increasing number of forced landings, aircraft bale-outs or crashes at operational stations. The site at Woodbridge was acquired from the Forestry Commission and, after the felling of around one million small trees, the contractors moved in to lay a massive runway that ran for 3,000 yards roughly east/west and was 250 yards wide; when you remember that a standard runway was only 50 yards wide and that the longest at the time were 2,000 yards, you can appreciate the scale of the Woodbridge runway. The size did cause a number of problems for pilots, in that the perspective they were used to seeing on approach to a runway 50 yards wide was very different and flaring for landing was hard to assess on this unusual runway. However, it was intended for emergency use and so, in effect, pilots drove the aircraft onto the runway and, in some cases, needed the entire length in which to stop, some even requiring the 500 yard over-run provided at each end. All the dispersal points were to the south, as was the clutch of hangars and support buildings. The runway was provided with a series of lateral markings (and lights), which essentially divided it into three runways, and it was also

given the fog-dispersing FIDO system, although one of the reasons for selecting this site had been its good-weather factor and clear approaches.

Work commenced in July 1942 and a year later, before construction was complete, a B-17 that was short of fuel opened Woodbridge's career as an emergency airfield. The airfield officially opened in November 1943 and by the end of the month it had recorded thirty-six landings. As the day and night bombing-offensives increased, so too did the number of aircraft making use of Woodbridge and by spring 1944 the monthly average was 100-plus aircraft. Accidents were not infrequent, as damaged aircraft slid across the runway, undercarriages collapsed, aircraft crashed into other aircraft – and a variety of other problems. Crash and medical services were well equipped and saved many lives, as did the fact that pilots could land aircraft at Woodbridge that might otherwise be totally lost.

One unusual – but welcome – visitor was a Ju88G night fighter, whose crew had become lost and, when short of fuel, landed at the first airfield they saw, thinking they were in Holland. This Ju88 carried the latest equipment and was of great benefit to the RAF in the night war, as it enabled the experts to study its equipment and devise counter-measures.

By August 1944 the airfield had recorded its 1,000th landing and by the end of the year this figure had risen to over 2,700. This hectic pace continued into 1945 and, by the end of the war, Woodbridge's statistics showed that over 4,000 aircraft had taken advantage of its singe welcoming runway – how many of those would have been lost, and how many aircrew killed, if Woodbridge had not been built?

The airfield continued to perform its emergency service post-war, but it was also used by various detachments on experimental work, including dropping Tallboy and Grand Slam bombs on the nearby range at Orfordness; the Bomb Ballistics Unit had actually formed here in May 1944. For the next

few years the RAF used the airfield, but on a small scale, and on 15 March 1948 it was reduced to Care and Maintenance. This was not, however, to be the end of Woodbridge as, on 2 June 1952, the USAF took control and for the next forty years it was to be an important American base. During this time it housed a variety of units and underwent major construction work, such as aircraft shelters. First allocation was to the 79th FBS of the 20th FBW and the F-84G; the F-100 arrived as a replacement in 1957 and, as part of a general re-organization the following year, the controlling unit became the 81st Tactical

Repairing a Lancaster of 514 Squadron at Woodbridge in 1944; this emergency airfield had received over 4,000 'visitors' by the end of the war.

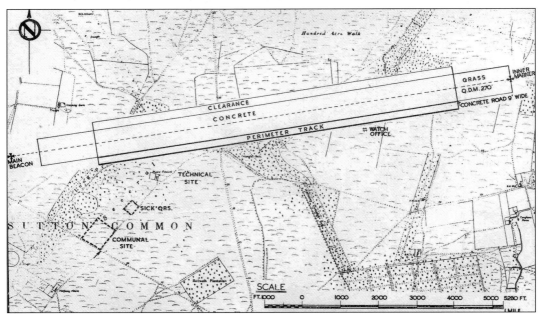

AIRFIELD DATA DEC 1944

Command:	RAF Bomber Command	Runway surface:	Sand-mix with Bitumen
Function:	Emergency runway	Hangars:	1 × B.1, 1 × Blister (planned not built)
Runways:	270 deg 3,000 × 250yd, with 500 yd grass extension each end	Dispersals:	8 × Loop each for 15 heavy aircraft
		Personnel:	Officers – 18 Other Ranks – 567

A-10s of the 81st TFW were based at Woodbridge and Bentwaters; the USAF was in residence from 1952 to 1993.

Fighter Wing, who continued to 'own' Woodbridge to the end of its USAF period, operating a 'twin base' scenario with nearby Bentwaters. However, for part of this period, the airfield was used by the 67th Aerospace Rescue & Recovery Squadron, whose HH-3E 'Jolly Giant' helicopters moved in from Moron in Spain during autumn 1969.

As part of the general draw-down of NATO forces in the early 1990s, the USAF abandoned the twin bases and the once-thriving airfields lost their aircraft. The withdrawal of the Americans in 1993 did not bring an immediate end to the airfields, as there was much debate as to the future use of what were very well appointed and maintained air bases. However, the RAF finally decided that they could not make use of either airfield and so disposal proceedings began. The Bentwaters Aviation Society was formed in May 2003 and plans for a museum are well underway; this will commemorate the Cold War activities of the twin bases.

UNITS

1939–1945

298 Sqn	21–24 Mar 1945	Halifax
BBU	22 May 1944–Jul 1946	Halifax
BLEU	1 Oct 1945–Jul 1946	

Post-1945
USAF Units

20th FBW	1952–Jun 1958	F-84, F-100
81st FG	Jul 1958–1 Jul 1993	F-101, F-4, A-10, F-16

MEMORIALS

None. (See Bentwaters.)

World War One Airfields and Landing Grounds

ALDEBURGH

County: Suffolk
UTM/grid: OS Map 156 – TM442593
Lat./Long.: N52°10.7 E001°34.2
Nearest town: Aldeburgh 2 miles to east

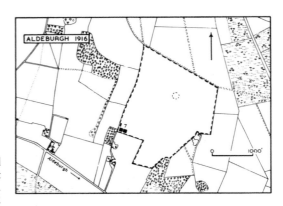

HISTORY

This 105-acre site was established as a landing ground in October 1915 as a satellite for RNAS Great Yarmouth and was also known locally as Hazelwood. The LG saw some use by aircraft, primarily BE2 variants, on short deployments but this was on an as-required basis. In August 1918 the School for Anti-Submarine Inshore Patrol Observers formed at Aldeburgh, equipped with a variety of aircraft. This unit became the Marine Observers School in October and disbanded in September 1919. The airfield closed the following year.

UNITS

SoASIPO	Aug 1918–Oct 1918	BE2s, DH6, Kangaroo, DH9
MOS	Oct 1918–Sep 1919	

BACTON

County: Norfolk
UTM/grid: OS Map 133 – TG343325
Lat./Long.: N52°50 E001°28.7
Nearest town: North Walsham 4 miles to south-west

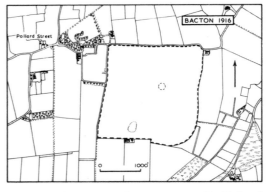

HISTORY

Situated just to the south of the abbey ruins, near Bacton Grange, this field was used as a night landing-ground from 1915 to early 1919 by aircraft operating from the Naval Air Station at Great Yarmouth. It has one claim to fame in that a BE2e operating from here and flown by Flight Sub-Lieutenant Pulling shot down airship L21 on 28 November 1916; in fact, he appears to have been the last pilot of a number who claim to have engaged the airship over East Anglia. The landing ground covered an area of around 125 acres and had few facilities other than a clear landing-area, tented accommodation and a searchlight to aid night operations, although two 'sheds' provided by Norwich-based Boulton and Paul were also erected. In November 1919, No.470 (Fighter) Flight detached three Camels here and this unit remained in at least notional occupation of the field until sometime in 1919. By summer that year the RAF presence had ended and the field was once more simply a field.

UNITS

219 Sqn det	Jul 1918 –?	various
470 Flt det	11 Nov 1918–1919	Camel

BURGH CASTLE

County: Norfolk
UTM/grid: OS Map 134 – TG484048
Lat./Long.: N52°35 E001°40
Nearest town: Great Yarmouth 2 miles to east

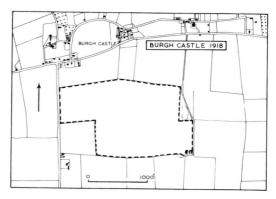

HISTORY

Burgh Castle was one of a series of night landing-grounds used during World War One in Norfolk as part of the Air Home Defence network and was probably active from mid-1915 for the units operating from Great Yarmouth. The Naval period is not well recorded but with the formation of the RAF the site came under the control of No.4 Group and some development took place. In June 1918 three hangars were erected and the grass areas improved, although tents were still the order of the day for accommodation. As a night landing-ground, some lighting, including a searchlight, was probably provided. With the formation of the RAF, many of the old, numbered Flights were amalgamated to become squadrons; in the case of Burgh Castle the resident unit became a detachment of 273 Squadron, which had been formed by amalgamating No.485 and No.534 Flights. The new unit operated a variety of types, most of which may have appeared at the Burgh site. However, in July 1919, the squadron disbanded and the site was abandoned.

UNITS

273 Sqn	Aug 1918– 5 Jul 1919	DH4, Camel

BUTLEY

County: Suffolk
UTM/grid: OS Map – TM342506
Lat./Long.: N52°06.15 E001°25.3
Nearest town: Melton 3.5 miles to west

HISTORY

The 54-acre site at Butley, adjacent to the B1084, was probably used from 1916 as an experimental station by the RFC and was associated with the experimental establishments at Orfordness and Martlesham. Aircraft operated from Butley in conjunction with various trials but details are lacking. In 1918, the airfield received a based unit with the Camels of No.487 Coastal Patrol Flight, this eventually becoming part of 273 Squadron. The site was sold in July 1919.

The Camel was operated from Butley by 487 Coastal Patrol Flight. (Note: this photo is not taken at Butley)

UNITS

487 CPF	1918–1919	Camel

COVEHITHE

County: Suffolk
UTM/grid: OS Map – TM519810
Lat./Long.: N52°22.08 E001°41.6
Nearest town: Wrentham 1.7 miles to north-west

HISTORY

Opened in September 1915 as a night landing-ground for Great Yarmouth, the 82-acre site at Covehithe was assigned to No.73 Wing for use on anti-Zeppelin patrols. As with most of these sites,

aircraft deployed on an as-required basis and much of its value was in providing somewhere for aircraft to land during those early days of night flying – a searchlight and a few dim paraffin-lights would mean a safe haven to a pilot. On 1 April 1918 the airfield was transferred to No.4 Group and in August it became home to a detachment from 273 Squadron; in effect it was known as No.534 Flight.

The Station closed in autumn 1919 and the buildings were auctioned in January 1920.

UNITS

273 Sqn   Aug 1918–5 Jul 1919   DH4, DH9, Camel

A variety of types were operated by 273 Squadron in the year they spent at Covehithe. (Note: this is not a 273 Squadron machine).

EARSHAM

County: Norfolk
UTM/grid: OS Map – TM310884
Lat./Long.: N52°26.4 E001°23.5
Nearest town: Bungay 2 miles

HISTORY

Located at Earsham Park Farm, this 54-acre landing ground was in use from 1916 to 1918 for Home Defence duties. It was little more than a partly-cleared

field with a few tents and a small number of aircraft – these at first being supplied by 75 Squadron and later by 51 Squadron. Although aircraft did not re-appear during World War Two, the site was brought back into military use when it became part of the largest USAAF bomb-dump in England. It was even provided with its own railway siding from the Waveney Line. In the immediate post-war period it was used by No.280 Maintenance Unit for storage, but this role had ended by the mid-1950s and the site was abandoned.

UNITS

51 Sqn
75 Sqn

FREETHORPE

County: Norfolk
UTM/grid: OS Map – TG413056
Lat./Long.: N52°35.4 E001°33.2
Nearest town: Reedham 2 miles to south

HISTORY

Located two miles from the railway station at Reedham, the landing ground at Freethorpe was forty-three acres and had virtually no facilities. It was allocated to 51 Squadron but formed part of the overall network of RFC Home Defence fields from 1916 to 1918.

UNITS

51 Sqn

FRETTENHAM

County: Norfolk
UTM/grid: OS Map – TG246190
Lat./Long.: N52°443.2 E001°19.3
Nearest town: Coltishall 1 mile to east

HISTORY

This 55-acre landing ground was part of the RFC Home Defence network from 1916 and was used by detachments of 51 Squadron, although it was never one of their designated Flight bases.

UNITS

51 Sqn

GOODERSTONE

County: Norfolk
UTM/grid: OS Map – TF787013
Lat./Long.: N52°34.5 E000°38.1
Nearest town: Swaffham 6 miles

HISTORY

Located close to the 'Zeppelin route' from the Wash towards London, Gooderstone Warren was used by the RFC's Home Defence aircraft from 1916–1918. This 65-acre site was typical of most of those in Norfolk, being nothing more than a field from which it was relatively safe to operate aeroplanes! It was used by 51 Squadron on an as-required basis and was out of commission by late-1918. In common with other World War One landing grounds it was brought back into use twenty years later – this time as a decoy site for Marham. It was definitely a K site, provided with dummy Wellingtons, and was possibly also used as a Q site. In the latter part of the war it was used as a bombing range.

UNITS

51 Sqn

GREAT YARMOUTH

County: Norfolk
UTM/grid: OS Map 134 – TG533044
Lat./Long.: N52°35 E001°44
Nearest town: In Great Yarmouth

HISTORY

Where a caravan park now resides was once the most important Naval Air Station in East Anglia and one that played a leading role in developing naval aviation. The site of RNAS Great Yarmouth occupied some eighty-five acres and was bounded by the River Yare to the west and the harbour mouth to the south, with the sea on the east. The airfield was commissioned on 15 April 1913, making it one of the earliest military airfields in East Anglia, and received its first aircraft in late-May. By July 1913, a diverse collection of aircraft had taken up residence and the airfield had started its task of developing naval aviation, working closely with fleet units. RNAS Great Yarmouth operated both land and sea types, including float planes and flying boats – hence the reason for its location – and its work involved trials and, from August 1914, operational flying. The first war patrol was flown on 8 August and the airfield took on a dual operational-role with shipping patrol and air defence, the Home Defence of the UK residing at this stage with the Admiralty.

The 'fighter' types proved completely inadequate when the German airships began bombing operations over England and this was eventually to lead, in 1916, to the RFC taking over responsibility for Home Defence. However, in the meantime, the station developed an extensive network of night landing-grounds from which its aircraft could operate as required. The shipping role involved patrol work covering Allied ships as well as long-range reconnaissance, for which the flying boats such as the H-12 and F.2a were particularly useful. However, offensive operations were also undertaken against enemy ships, land targets and patrol aircraft. Attempts to find and destroy German U-boats occupied a good deal of effort but with little result.

With the decision to create an independent air force, all naval air assets were absorbed by the newly formed RAF and so, on 1 April 1918, Great Yarmouth became part of No.73 Wing within No.4 Group and for the remaining two years of its existence was an RAF station and home to a number of squadrons that had formed from various Flights.

The squadrons that had formed in August 1918 had all departed by spring the following year and the Station was quickly run down – as plans to develop a civil airport came to nothing this once important airfield and seaplane base fell into disuse. One wonders how many of the caravanners who sit and stare out over the sea realize the importance of the site. The site was abandoned in the early 1920s.

UNITS

212 Sqn	20 Aug 1918–7 Mar 1919	DH4, DH9, DH9a
228 Sqn	20 Aug 1918–30 Apr 1919	F.2a, H.12, H.16
229 Sqn	20 Aug 1918–3 Mar 1919	various
273 Sqn	Jun 1919–5 Jul 1919	cadre only

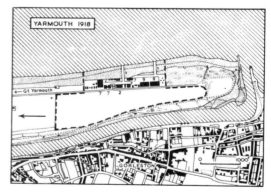

HADLEIGH

County: Suffolk
UTM/grid: OS Map – TM064424
Lat./Long.: N52°02.3 E001°00.3
Nearest town: Hadleigh 2 miles to west

HISTORY

Hadleigh was in use for the RFC's Home Defence aircraft from 1916 and comprised a 30-acre field with few facilities. The site was upgraded to Class I status in 1917 and was used by detachments from 51 Squadron to May 1918 and by 44 Squadron's Camels for a short period in 1918. The field was abandoned post-war but a private flying-club was established on the site in the 1920s.

UNITS

44 Sqn	1918	Camel
51 Sqn	1916–May 1918	various

HARLING ROAD

County: Norfolk
UTM/grid: OS Map – TL983878
Lat./Long.: N532°7 E000°54
Nearest town: East Harling 1.5 miles to south-east

HISTORY

Situated close to Harling Road railway station, this site opened as an RFC landing ground in early 1916 and was provided with a number of semi-permanent buildings. It was raised to aerodrome status later in the year and the first resident unit was 'A Flight' of 51 Squadron, equipped with various BE types for night defence against German airships. When the Flight moved to Narborough the following August, its place was taken by 75 Squadron. However, the aerodrome was also used by a number of other squadrons for work-up prior to deployment to France and Harling was a reasonably busy station.

No.10 Training Depot Station formed here on 15 April 1918 within 39th Wing and operated a diverse collection of aircraft for its training task; the unit became No.10 Training School with effect from March 1919 and remained at Harling until it disbanded in March 1920. All flying ceased with the departure of the school but some of Harling's buildings were used by the army for storage for a

number of years before the site finally fell out of military use.

UNITS

51 Sqn det	Sep 1916–Aug 1917	BE2c, BE12
75 Sqn det	Sep 1917–May 1919	BE2c, BE2e, BE12
88 Sqn	2 Aug 1917–2 Apr 1918	F2b
89 Sqn	7 Aug 1917–17 Jul 1918	various
94 Sqn	2 Aug 1917–27 Jul 1918	various
10 TDS	15 Apr 1918–Mar 1919	various
10 TS	Mar 1919–Mar 1920	various
10 RS	14 Mar 1919–Nov 1919	

HICKLING BROAD

County: Norfolk
UTM/grid: OS Map – TG409226
Lat./Long.:
Nearest town:

HISTORY

The site at Hickling Broad was developed as a seaplane satellite for RNAS Great Yarmouth and was probably in use from 1914 to around 1920. It was a small site, comprising no more than 4–5 acres, including slipways.

HINGHAM

County: Norfolk
UTM/grid: OS Map – TG025022
Lat./Long.: N52°34.8 E000°59.2
Nearest town: Hingham

HISTORY

A landing ground was in use at Hingham from summer 1916 to the end of World War One but, as for many of these landing grounds, details are sketchy. The site was one of a number used by Norfolk's main night-fighter unit, 51 Squadron, who based its 'B Flight' here from August 1916, operating a mixture of types on air-defence duties; indeed, for a while it also acted as the HQ unit for the squadron. The following February the RFC's first dedicated night-bomber unit formed here – No.100 Squadron being created from a nucleus of 51 Squadron and undertaking initial training using the BE2c. It is not certain if the FE2b, with which the squadron was destined to operate, appeared at Hingham or if they were not acquired until 100 moved to Farnborough. The following year, however, a second night-bomber unit formed at Hingham and it certainly made use of

The BE2c was the commonest type to use Hingham. (Note: this is not a Hingham shot).

the FE2b as it moved with its operational type to France at the end of september 1917. By autumn the field was without a resident unit and from then on appears only to have been used on an infrequent basis. It was retained in service to the end of the war but disposed of in November 1918, leaving no trace.

UNITS

51 Sqn	23 Sep 1916–7 Aug 1917	various
100 Sqn	11–23 Feb 1917	BE2c
102 Sqn	9 Aug 1917–27 Sep 1917	FE2b

HOLT (Bayfield)

County: Norfolk
UTM/grid: OS Map 133 – TG084415
Lat./Long.: N52°56 E001°06
Nearest town: Holt 3 miles to south

HISTORY

This landing ground was laid out in a large field to the north of the market town of the same name, opposite Swans Lodge Farm, and eventually covered around ninety acres, including part of the site of the previous racecourse. Holt was used as a landing ground by Home Defence aircraft on an 'as required' basis from 1915 to 1918 and was allocated primarily to RNAS Great Yarmouth, although its position meant that the RFC's units in central and west Norfolk might also have used it from time to time. Records for this landing ground are sketchy but it was certainly out of use immediately after the war. The site was used by joy-riding aeroplanes in the 1920s but had been ploughed up by the end of that decade.

KINGS LYNN

County: Norfolk
UTM/grid: OS Map – TF612217
Lat./Long.: N52°46.1 E000°23.1
Nearest town: Kings Lynn

HISTORY

This eighty-acre piece of farmland at North Lynn Farm was acquired for test-flying aircraft built at the St Nicholas Iron Works in Kings Lynn. By the end of the war over 300 aircraft of various types had been built, ranging from DH1s to Avro 504s. The landing ground was too small for some of the larger types and these were taken by road to Narborough and flown from there. It seems likely that RFC Home Defence aircraft would also have used the Kings Lynn landing ground from time to time.

MARSHAM

County: Norfolk
UTM/grid: OS Map – TG197237
Lat./Long.: N52°45.9 E00°115.3
Nearest town: Norwich 8 miles to south

HISTORY

A small site located alongside the A140, close to Marsham church, the landing ground was reportedly in use by the RFC from late-1915 or early 1916. There are virtually no details of usage and the site may have been very short-lived.

MOUSEHOLD HEATH

County: Norfolk
UTM/grid: OS Map 134 – TG250102
Lat./Long.: N52°39 E001°20
Nearest town: In Norwich

HISTORY

Mousehold Heath, or simply Mousehold as it was more commonly known, is one of those forgotten airfields that were more important than this ignorance implies. As a World War One landing-ground it played a part in air defence, training and experimental work, and was also an Aircraft Depot. Post-war, its main claim to fame was with Boulton and Paul, as well as being a commercial airport. The site's first 'military' use occurred in 1549, when up to 10,000 soldiers camped here during Kett's Rebellion.

The site was a cavalry training-ground, taken over by the RFC in October 1914. The first confirmed unit to use the 263-acre field was No.9 Training Squadron, although its actual location is given as Norwich, where it formed in July 1915; it had a complement of FE2b and Henry Farman types, notionally nine of each. This unit remained at Norwich/Mousehold until moving to Sedgeford in January 1918.

Having formed at Northolt in May 1915, 18 Squadron moved to Mousehold in August, to complete its training, before deploying to France (St Omer) in November. Some records show a brief appearance in April 1916 by 37 Squadron, this unit forming at Mousehold for trials work but moving out to Orfordness within days; other records suggest it actually formed at the latter location.

Two other RFC units spent short periods at the Norwich field; 85 Squadron undertaking a few weeks of training before moving to France and 117 Squadron being brought together as a unit but not given their own aircraft until they went to Wyton in October 1918.

However, from May 1916, Norwich was home to HQ No.7 Wing of the RFC, which had responsibility for units at Narborough, Norwich, Orfordness, Sedgeford, Thetford and Wyton. A year later, a major repair-and-overhaul depot was established and this was soon extended to function as No.3 Acceptance Park for aircraft and components from companies in Norwich that had become involved in manufacture for the war effort – such as Boulton and Paul, Mann Egerton and Ransomes. The first Boulton and Paul aircraft, an FE2b from the Rose Lane works, flew in October 1915 and, by the end of the war, the firm had built over 2,500 aircraft of various types.

With the end of the war, some of the hangars and other buildings were taken over by Boulton and Paul, as this company had decided to continue in the

Mousehold Heath in June 1919. (Narborough History Society)

design and manufacture of aircraft. A number of interesting, but not necessarily classic, types, such as the Sidestrand and the Overstrand, emerged from the Mousehold facility but, in mid-1930 the decision was taken to transfer work to the Wolverhampton factory.

From early 1927 the airfield had also been home to the Norfolk and Norwich Aero Club and from 1933 to 1939 it was also Norwich Municipal Airport. The military were back from March 1937, No.24 Group operating a Motor Transport Storage unit to March 1939, by which time No.40 E&RFTS had formed here to train pilots. This unit, with its assortment of types from Audax to Magister, had departed by the outbreak of war. Mousehold Heath was subsequently designated as a decoy airfield for Horsham St Faith – an interesting choice bearing in mind its location close to Norwich – and it also subsequently served as Prisoner of War Camp No.253.

Nothing now remains of this once fascinating site; it has long since been swallowed by Norwich and a school and housing development now cover the area.

UNITS

HQ units at Mousehold

No.7 Wing RFC	1 May 1916–Jan 1918	

Pre-1919

18 Sqn	16 Aug 1915–18 Nov 1915	FB5, DH2
37 Sqn	Apr 1916	various
85 Sqn	10 Aug 1917–27 Nov 1917	various
117 Sqn	15 Jul 1918–Oct 1918	no aircraft
9 RS	27 Jul 1915–10 Jan 1918	
49 RS	23 Sep 1916–16 Oct 1916	

1939–1945

40 ERFTS	15 Aug 1939–3 Sep 1939	

NARBOROUGH

County: Norfolk
UTM/grid: OS Map 143 – TF750105
Lat./Long.: N52°40 E000°35
Nearest town: King's Lynn 8 miles to west

HISTORY

With an area of over 900 acres, Narborough was the largest military aerodrome in the UK during World War One, which makes it even sadder that nothing remains, as the last building was demolished not long ago. The airfield had its origins in 1915, when chosen by the Admiralty as one of the night landing-grounds for its Home Defence task. The airfield was taken over by the RFC the following year, when responsibility for air defence passed from the Admiralty.

However, its main use by the new 'owners' was as a training field for squadrons preparing for deployment to France. The first definite unit in residence was 35 Squadron, which moved its diverse fleet over from Thetford in June 1916. By the end of the year, two squadrons had formed at Narborough, 50 and 59 Squadrons, and the aerodrome's facilities continue to expand and included at least six large hangars.

Early the following year, two of the squadrons departed for France but were replaced by 53 Squadron from Sedgeford and 64 Squadron from Dover. However, at the end of the year, all three left, as the RFC re-organized its training system by amalgamating squadrons to form Training Depot Stations. Two new squadrons, 26 and 69, arrived for training and they were joined for a short period by 83 Squadron from Wyton, this latter squadron completing its work-up with FE2bs before going to France in March 1918. The Americans arrived in January, when members of the 24th Aero Squadron were attached to 121 Squadron, which had formed with DH9s that month.

The airfield underwent further changes in 1918, with at least one new hangar and other building work taking place, although the reason for this is confusing, as the airfield was designated as an 'Independent Force Station' but does not appear to have housed units for this strategic-bombing force, although HP V/1500s did make an appearance. As the war neared its end the squadrons departed and No.55 TDS arrived from Manston, being joined in November by the Aeroplane Repair Section of the 3rd Training Group.

After the Armistice – and the 'exchange of bombs' referred to in the Marham entry – Narborough was used as a disbandment centre for squadrons, or at least the cadres of squadrons, as they returned from active service. Amongst the units to disband here were 56, 60 and 64 squadrons – as well as the TDS itself.

The aerodrome was finally closed in December 1919 and before long the acres that once housed one of the RFC's busiest aerodromes returned to agriculture.

(*Thanks to Narborough History Society for this entry.*)

Units

35 Sqn	16 Jun 1916–26 Jan 1917	FE2b, FB5, FK8
59 Sqn	21 Jun 1916–13 Feb 1917	RE8
64 Sqn	1917, 14 Feb 1919–31 Dec 1919	no aircraft
83 Sqn	12 Dec 1917–6 Mar 1918	FE2b
121 Sqn	Jan 1918–10 Aug 1918	various
1 RS	1–10 Oct 1917	
26 RS	3 Feb 1918–1 Aug 1918	various
48 RS	2–13 Nov 1916	
50 RS	14 Dec 1916–30 Nov 1917	various
53 RS	14 Feb 1917–6 Dec 1917	RE8, Avro 504, DH6
55 TDS	12 Sep 1918–14 Mar 1919	various
64 RS	14 Apr 1917–12 Dec 1917	
69 RS	9 Dec 1917–1 Aug 1918	DH4, DH6, DH9

September 1916 and the not infrequent sight of a crashed aircraft!

Oblique aerial view of the large training aerodrome of Narborough. (Narborough History Society)

Narborough 1916.

NORTH ELMHAM

County: Norfolk
UTM/grid: OS Map – TF985205
Lat./Long.: N52°44.7 E000°56.4
Nearest town: East Dereham 4 miles to south

HISTORY

This RFC Class 3 landing ground was in use from late-1916, but there is little recorded use; like most of these primitive landing-grounds it was essentially little more than a field from which night flying could take place as part of the air defence against German airships.

NORWICH (Cromer Road)

County: Norfolk
UTM/grid: OS Map – TG215120
Lat./Long.: N52/39.4 E001/16.3
Nearest town: In Norwich

HISTORY

Although Boulton and Paul was the best-known aircraft manufacturer in Norwich, they were not alone and, during World War One, the Mann Egerton factory built several hundred aircraft, starting with the Short 184. The factory operated a sixty-acre airfield for test flying and various types were built under licence, but nothing came of any 'home grown' design. The final contract was completed in 1920, the airfield closed and Mann Egerton turned to other business.

SAXTHORPE

County: Suffolk
UTM/grid: OS Map – TG122310
Lat./long.: N52°50.0 E001°08.6
Nearest town: Aylsham 5 miles to north-west

HISTORY

This 37-acre, Class 2, RFC landing-ground was in use from some time in 1916 but there are no details of usage, other than the fact that it was one of many LGs allocated for use by 51 Squadron – Norfolk's main air-defence unit! The site probably closed in early 1918.

UNITS

51 Sqn

SPORLE

County: Norfolk
UTM/grid: OS Map – TF868118
Lat./Long.: N52°40.3 E000°45.7
Nearest town: Swaffham 4 miles to west

HISTORY

Another of 51 Squadron's night landing-grounds, Sporle's 43-acre site was in use from late-1916 to 1918.

UNITS

51 Sqn

PULHAM

County: Norfolk
UTM/grid: Map 156 – TM193837
Lat./Long.: N52°24.44 E001°13.3
Nearest town: Diss 5 miles to south-west

HISTORY

Pulham is one of Norfolk's more unusual sites and, in some respects, does not qualify under our heading of airfield, as it was an airship station – one of the largest in the UK. Situated about one mile south of Pulham St Mary, this 1,000-acre site was opened in February 1916 for use by airships of the Royal Naval Air Service and it retained its association with lighter-than-air activities into the late-1930s.

The airships based at Pulham were primarily tasked with coastal patrol work and most were of the 'blimp' variety, although various other airships also made use of the facilities at the station. Airship sheds and additional facilities were added during 1917 and 1918 and Pulham remained operational to the end of the war; unusual visitors in autumn 1918 included two surrendering German airships, L64 and L71. In early 1919, the site became the Airship Experimental Station and, as such, it was at the 'cutting edge' of developments in lighter-than-air technology, which many saw as having a great military and civil future; for example, the new experimental mooring-mast was first used by the R-23 in February 1921. Of more lasting military significance was the presence of the Experimental Balloon Establishment from 1926 to the late-1930s and much work was carried out on balloon barrages. However, with the outbreak of World War Two there was no operational use of the Station and it was used as an ammunition storage area, a role it retained to 1958.

One of the most famous landmarks near Bedford is the airship sheds at Cardington – one of those sheds

Airship R33 docked on Pulham's mast. This was an important airship station from 1916.

used to be situated at Pulham and was moved in the late-1920s. Other than that remote piece of Pulham, almost nothing remains of this once important Norfolk base, although a few buildings are in use for agriculture.

SEDGEFORD

County: Norfolk
UTM/grid: OS Map 132 TF730365
Lat./Long.: N52/54.5 E000/35
Nearest town: Hunstanton 5 miles to north-west

HISTORY

The first use of a landing ground at Sedgeford, near King's Lynn, was by naval aircraft charged with Home Defence duties, the parent unit being Great Yarmouth. However, with the decision in 1916 to hand Home Defence responsibility to the RFC, Sedgeford, along with a number of other landing grounds, had new 'owners'. It appears, however, that the main roles of units posted to Sedgeford were training or work-up for deployment to France and there is little mention of any air-defence duties. The first RFC unit to move in was 45 Squadron, arriving from Thetford in May 1916, and it was responsible for training pilots and observers for posting to operational squadrons, for which it operated a diverse fleet of aircraft. In August 1916, a second unit, 64 Squadron, formed from a nucleus of the existing squadron to help with the increasing training burden. However, this unit subsequently re-equipped with operational types and, after a period of operational work-up, moved to France in October 1917. The latter part of that year saw 87 Squadron pass through Sedgeford, whilst it acquired and trained with Dolphins, before it too went to the Western Front. Two further units went through a similar routine, although one departed for Mesopotamia and one went to South Kenley.

Post-war the most important resident was No.3 School of Aerial Fighting, this training and operational evaluation unit having moved in during November 1918. Finally, 13 Squadron moved to

Sedgeford from St Omer in March 1919 but, like many post-war units, it was only a cadre and was destined to disband at the end of the year. It seems likely that the airfield was abandoned by late-1919 or early 1920; it did re-appear on the RAF books in World War Two but, this time, as a decoy airfield for Bircham Newton, with dummy aircraft being positioned on the airfield, operating as both a K and Q site.

UNITS

13 Sqn	27 Mar 1919–31 Dec 1919	RE8
45 Sqn	21 May 1916–12 Oct 1916	HF H.20,
		1½ Strutter
64 Sqn	1 Aug 1916–14 Oct 1917	various
72 Sqn	1 Nov 1917–25 Dec 1917	Avro 504, Pup
87 Sqn	15 Sep 1917–19 Dec 1917	various
110 Sqn	26 Nov 1917–15 Jun 1918	various
122 Sqn	1 Jan 1918–17 Aug 1918	various
53 RS	1–14 Feb 1917	
65 RS	10 May 1917–25 Nov 1917	
3 SoAF	Nov 1918–Aug 1919	various
3 FS	Nov 1918–14 Mar 1919	
9 RS	10 Jan 1918–Aug 1918	
7 RS	14 Mar 1919–Oct 1919	

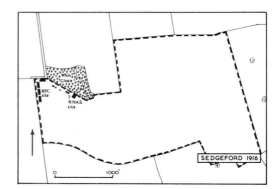

THETFORD (Snarehill)

County: Norfolk
UTM/grid: OS Map 144 – TL895805
Lat./Long.: N52°23.5 E000°45.0
Nearest town: Thetford 2 miles to north-west

HISTORY

This landing ground was more commonly known as Snareshill and was located close to Thetford. Some records suggest that it may have been in use as early as 1911 in connection with experimental use of aeroplanes on army manoeuvres and, as the Thetford area has always been an important military training area, this is possible. It appears that a landing ground was definitely laid out for the 1912 manoeuvres.

However, the airfield officially opened in November 1915 within No.7 Wing RFC and the following month its first resident unit, 25 Squadron, arrived. This unit underwent a few weeks training and then moved to France, to be replaced at Thetford by 35 Squadron, which formed at the Norfolk airfield and commenced training on a range of aircraft before moving to Narborough to complete its training. Over the next three years Thetford was home to a number of training units, the numbering of which causes confusion, with Reserve Aeroplane Squadrons becoming Training (Ex-Reserve) Squadrons, which in turn become Reserve Squadrons; amongst those to appear at Thetford were 12, 15, 25 and 73 Reserve Squadrons.

June 1916 brought the BEs of 51 Squadron: this unit being created to carry out night air-defence of

East Anglia in the face of increased attacks by German airships. This squadron, too, did not stay long and, in September, moved to Hingham, leaving Thetford without a resident unit. Various units either formed or trained here, none staying more than a few weeks or perhaps a few months. Typical of this activity was 128 Squadron, forming in February 1918 and being nominated to become operational with the DH9 but, in the meantime, training with a variety of aircraft; however, the situation by mid-1918 was such that the plan was changed and the Squadron disbanded. No.35 TDS formed here in mid-July 1918, but moved to Duxford in August. The final users of

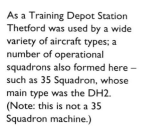

As a Training Depot Station Thetford was used by a wide variety of aircraft types; a number of operational squadrons also formed here – such as 35 Squadron, whose main type was the DH2. (Note: this is not a 35 Squadron machine.)

Thetford were No.4 School of (Aerial) Navigation and Bombing, which formed here as part of Midland Area in September 1918 and remained to the following April. The airfield was also home to a repair facility from mid-1917 to late-1918 but this, too, vanished with the end of the war.

The site was, however, retained and, during the 1930s, was used for bombing practice. By 1939 it had become a K decoy airfield for Honington, 'runways' being cut in the bracken and twelve dummy-Wellingtons being dispersed around the airfield; the presence of World War One vintage hangars helped the deception – to the extent that three RAF aircraft landed here and it was bombed at least once. It was also used as a Q site but, by the mid-years of the war, this function was not required and the site was used as a bombing range.

UNITS

Pre-1919

25 Sqn	31 Dec 1915–19 Feb 1916	various
35 Sqn	1 Feb 1916–16 Jun 1916	various
51 Sqn	1 Jun 1916–23 Sep 1916	BE2c, BE12
128 Sqn	1 Feb 1918–4 Jul 1918	various
12 RS	16 Nov 1915–15 Jul 1918	
15 RS	15 Dec 1915–1 Jan 1916	
25 RS	22 May 1916–15 Jul 1918	
73 RS	7–17 Jul 1917	
35 TDS	15 Jul 1918–21 Aug 1918	
4 SoNB	Sep 1918–26 Apr 1918	

TOTTENHILL

County: Norfolk
UTM/grid: OS Map – TF633116
Lat./Long.: N52/40.7 E000/24.9
Nearest town: King's Lynn 5 miles to north

HISTORY

This 43-acre, Class 3 landing ground was probably in use from 1916 to the end of the war and was yet another field allocated to 51 Squadron for Home Defence.

UNITS

51 Sqn

WEST RUDHAM

County: Norfolk
UTM/grid: OS Map – TF814255
Lat./Long.: N52°47.8 E000°41.4
Nearest town: Fakenham 7 miles to north-east

HISTORY

Located two miles from the railway station – always an important consideration when siting landing grounds and airfields – West Rudham was a 62-acre site to Class 2 standard and was in use between 1916 and 1918. The only unit to have been allocated to the site was 51 Squadron and even they only used the landing ground on an opportunity basis.

UNITS

51 Sqn	1916–1918

Abbreviations

All aspects of military aviation are crammed with abbreviations, especially when it comes to the designations of units. The following abbreviations have been used in this series, especially in the unit tables. This list is by no means exhaustive – at a rough estimate a complete list would run to 20,000+ abbreviations! However, it does include the abbreviations most relevant to this series. There is an element of logic the reader can apply where an abbreviation is not listed; for example, 'CU' is most commonly used for Conversion Unit, hence a WCU could be a Wellington Conversion Unit. The down-side of this logic is that it could also be Washington or Wessex, and so context – i.e. which is most likely – must also be taken into account.

AAC	Army Air Corps	ARD/S	Aircraft Repair Depot/Station
AACU	Anti-Aircraft Co-operation Unit	ARW	Air Refuelling Wing
A&AEE	Aeroplane and Armament	ASF	Aircraft Servicing Flight
	Experimental Establishment	ASP	Air Stores Park
AAF	Auxiliary Air Force	ASR(F)	Air Sea Rescue (Flight)
AAP	Aircraft Acceptance Park, Air	ASRTU	ASR Training Unit
	Ammunition Park	ASS	Air Signallers School
AAS	Air Armament School	ASU	Aircraft Storage Unit
ABTF	Air Bomber Training Flight	ASW	Anti-Submarine Warfare
ACCS	Airborne Control and Command	ATA	Air Transport Auxiliary
	Squadron	ATC	Armament Training Camp, Air
ACHU	Air Crew Holding Unit		Traffic Control, Air Training Corps
ACS/W	Airfield Construction	ATDU	Air Torpedo/Transport Development
	Squadron/Wing		Unit
ACU	Aircrew Holding Unit	ATF	Autogiro Training Flight
AD	Air Division	ATP	Advanced Training Pool
ADF/U	Aircraft Delivery Flight/Unit	ATW	Airship Training Wing
ADGB	Air Defence of Great Britain	AW	All-Weather
AEF	Air Experience Flight	AWDS	All-Weather Development Squadron
AF	Air Force	AWFCS	All-Weather Fighter
AFDS/U	Air Fighting Development		Combat/Conversion Squadron
	Squadron/Unit		
AFEE	Airborne Forces Experimental	BAD	Base Air Depot
	Establishment	BANS	Basic ANS
AFS/U	Advanced Flying School/Unit	BAS	Beam Approach School
AGS	Air Gunnery School	BATF	Beam/Blind Approach Training
AIEU	Armament and Instrument		Flight
	Experimental Establishment	BBBLEE	Bomb Ballistics and Blind Landing
AIS	Air Interception School		Experimental Establishment
ALS	Air Landing School	BB(M)F	Battle of Britain (Memorial) Flight
AMC	Air Mobility Command	BBU	Bomb Ballistics Unit
AMSDU	Air Ministry Servicing Development	BC	Bomber Command
	Unit	BCBRU	BC Bombing Research Unit
AMU	Aircraft Modification Unit	BCDU	BC Development Unit
ANS	Air Navigation School	BCFU	BC Film Unit
AONS	Air Observer and Navigator School	BCIS	BC Instructors School
AOP	Air Observation Post	BCMS	BC Missile School
AOS	Air Observers School	BDE	Balloon Development Establishment
APC/S	Armament Practice Camp/Station	BDU	Bombing Development Unit

BFTS	Basic Flying Training School
BG	Bombardment Group, Bomb Group
BGF/S	Bombing and Gunnery Flight/School
BLEU	Blind Landing Experimental Establishment
BS	Bombardment Squadron, Bomb Squadron
(BS)	Bomber Support
BSDU	Bomber Support Development Unit
BW	Bombardment Wing, Bomb Wing
CAACU	Civilian AACU
CAEU	Casualty Air Evacuation Unit
CBE	Central Bomber Establishment
CBW	Combat Bomb Wing
CC	Coastal Command
CF/U	Conversion Flight/Unit; Communications Flight/Squadron
CFE	Central Fighter Establishment
CFS	Central Flying School
CGS	Central Gunnery School
CLE/S	Central Landing Establishment/School
CNS	Central Navigation School
CPF	Coast(al) Patrol Flight
CRO	Civilian Repair Organization
CSF	Central Servicing Flight
CSE	Central Signals Establishment
CSDE	Central Servicing Development Establishment
CTTO	Central Trials and Tactics Organization
deg	degrees
det	detachment
DF	Development Flight
DFCS	Day Fighter Combat School
DFLS	Day Fighter Leaders School
DUC	Distinguished Unit Citation
DWI	Directional Wireless Installation
EAB	Engineer Aviation Battalion
EAC	Enemy Aircraft Circus
ECU	Experimental Co-operation Unit
EGS	Elementary Gliding School
E(R)FTS	Elementary (and Refresher) Flying Training School
FAA	Fleet Air Arm
FB	Fighter-Bomber, Flying Boat
FBDF	Flying Boat Development Flight
FBS/W	Fighter-Bomber Squadron/Wing
FC	Fighter Command; Ferry Command
FCPU	Ferry Command Preparation Unit
FEE	Fighter Experimental Establishment
FFU	Film Flight Unit

FG	Fighter Group
FIDO	Fog Investigation Dispersal Operation
FIS	Flying Instructors School
FIS/W	Fighter Interception Squadron/Wing
FIU	Fighter Interception Unit
FLS	Fighter Leaders School
Flt	Flight
F(P)P/U	Ferry (Pilots) Pool/Unit
FRS	Flying Refresher School
FSS	Flying Selection Squadron
FTF/U	Ferry Training Flight/Unit
FTS	Flying Training School
FW	Fighter Wing
FWS	Fighter Weapons School
FWTS	Fixed Wing Test Squadron
GC/S	Gliding Centre/School
GCF	Gunnery Co-operation Flight
GIF/S	Glider Instructors Flight/School
GOTU	Glider OUT
GPR	Glider Pilot Regiment
GR&ANS	General Reconnaissance and Air Navigation School
GRF/U	Gunnery Research Flight/Unit
GSEU	Glider Storage and Erection Unit
GTF	Gunnery Training Flight
GTS	Glider Training School/Squadron
GWDS	Guided Weapon Development Squadron
HAS	Hardened Aircraft Shelter
HC	Home Command
HCU	Heavy Conversion Unit
HD	Home Defence
HG	Heavy Glider
HGCU	Heavy Glider Conversion Unit
HQ	Headquarters
HSF	High-Speed Flight
HSL	High Speed Launch
HT	Heavy Transport
HTF	Heavy Transport Flight
IE	Initial/Immediate Establishment/Equipment
IRF/S	Instrument Rating Flight/Squadron
IRMB	Intermediate Range Ballistic Missile
ITF/S	Instrument Training Flight/Squadron
ITW	Initial Training Wing
JASS	Joint Anti-Submarine School
JATE	Joint Air Transport Establishment
JCF/U	Jet Conversion Flight/Unit
JEFTS	Joint EFTS
JEHU	Joint Experimental Helicopter Unit

KES	Kestrel Evaluation Squadron
KF	King's Flight
LAIS	Low Attack Instructors School
LAS	Light Aircraft School
LCF/S	Lightning Conversion Flight/Squadron
LFS	Lancaster Finishing School
LG	Landing Ground
LRDU	Long Range Development Unit
MA	Midland Area
MAC	Military Airlift Command
MAEE/U	Marine Aircraft Experimental Establishment/Unit
MC	Maintenance Command
MCS	Metropolitan Communications Squadron
MCU	Mosquito Conversion Unit
METS	Multi-Engine Training Squadron
MOS	Marine Observers School
MTU	Mosquito Training Unit; Mobile Training Unit
MU	Maintenance Unit
NA	Northern Area
NATO	North Atlantic Treaty Organization
NCS	Northern Communications Squadron
NF	Night Fighter
NFDW	Night Fighter Development Wing
NFLS	Night Fighter Leaders School
NTU	Navigation/Night Training Unit
NZ	New Zealand
OAF/PU	Overseas Aircraft Ferry/Preparation Unit
OATS	Officers Advanced Training School
OCF/U	Operational Conversion Flight/Unit
OEU	Operational Evaluation Unit
OG	Observation Group
ORTU	Operational Refresher Training Unit
OS	Ordnance Survey
OTU	Operational Training Unit
(P)AFU	Pilot Advanced Flying Unit
PAS/U	Pilotless Aircraft Section/Unit
PDC	Personnel Despatch Centre
PFF	Pathfinder Force
PFU	Practice Flying Unit
PoW	Prisoner of War
PRDE/U	Photographic Reconnaissance Development Establishment/Unit
PRF/U	Pilot Refresher Flight/Unit
PRU	Photographic Reconnaissance Unit
PRG	Photographic Reconnaissance Group

PSP	Pierced Steel Planking/Plating
PTS	Parachute Training School
QF	Queen's Flight
QRA	Quick Reaction Alert
RAAF	Royal Australian Air Force
RAuxAF	Royal Auxiliary Air Force
RAE	Royal Aircraft Establishment
RAFC	Royal Air Force College
RAFO	Reserve of Air Force Officers
RAFVR	Royal Air Force Volunteer Reserve
RASC	Royal Army Service Corps
RC	Reserve Command
RCAF	Royal Canadian Air Force
RCM	Radio Counter Measures
RE	Royal Engineers
RFC	Royal Flying Corps
RFTS	Refresher Flying Training School
RFU	Refresher Flying Unit
RLG	Relief Landing Ground
RNAS	Royal Naval Air Service
RNZAF	Royal New Zealand Air Force
ROC	Royal Observer Corps
RRE	Radar Research Establishment
RSU	Repair and Salvage Unit
RS	Radio School
RWE	Radio/Radar Warfare Establishment
RWTS	Rotary Wing Test Squadron
SAC	Strategic Air Command
SAD	Strategic Air Depot
SA(O)EU	Strike Attack (Operational) Evaluation Unit
SC	Support Command; Strike Command
SCBS	Strike Command Bombing School
SD (F)	Special Duties (Flight)
SDU	Signals Development Unit
SF	Station Flight
SFTS	Service Flying Training School
SFU	Signals Flying Unit
SHORAD	Short Range Air Defence
SHQ	Station Headquarters
SLAIS	Specialist LAIS
SLG	Satellite Landing Ground
SMT	Square-Meshed Track
SOG	Special Operations Group
SOM	Secret Organizational Memoranda
Sqn	Squadron
SRW	Strategic Reconnaissance Wing
STC	Strike Command
STS	Seaplane Training Squadron
SU	Support Unit
Schools	N.B. the 'o' is often omitted or used in full 'of'

SoAC	School of Army Co-Operation; Airfield Construction
SoAG	School of Air Gunnery
SoAN	School of Air Navigation
SoAP	School of Air Pilotage
SoAS	School of Air Support
SoASR	School of Air Sea Rescue
SoAT	School of Air Transport
SoFC	School of Fighter Control; Flying Control
SoGR&AN	School of General Reconnaissance & Air Navigation
SoL(A)W	School of Land (Air) Warfare
SoMR	School of Maritime Reconnaissance
SoNC	School of Naval Co-operation
SoP	School of Photography
SoRF/T	School of Refresher/Flying Training
SoSF	School of Special Flying
SoTT	School of Technical Training
T	Training
TAF	Tactical Air Force
T/VASF	Transit/Visiting Aircraft Servicing Flight
TAW	Tactical Airlift Wing
TC	Transport Command
TCG/S/W	Troop Carrier Group/Squadron/Wing
TDS	Training Depot Squadron/Station
TDY	Temporary Duty

TEU	Tactical Exercise/Evaluation Unit
TFS/U	Target Facilities Flight/Unit
TFU	Telecommunications Flying Unit
TRE	Telecommunications Research Establishment
TRS/W	Tactical Reconnaissance Squadron/Wing
TTF	Target Towing Flight
TTTE	Tri-national Tornado Training Establishment
TU	Training Unit
TW(C)U	Tornado/Tactical Weapons (Conversion) Unit
UAS	University Air Squadron
UN	United Nations
US(A)AF	United States (Army) Air Force
VC	Victoria Cross
VE	Victory in Europe
VGS	Volunteer Gliding School
VR	Volunteer Reserve
WA	Western Area
WAAF	Women's Auxiliary Air Force
WEE	Wireless/Winterization Experimental Establishment
WRS	Weather Research Squadron
WTS	Washington Training Squadron